# GCSE/KEY STAGE 4

# PHYSICS

Keith Palfreyman and Colin Maunder

Longman

**LONGMAN STUDY GUIDES**

SERIES EDITORS:
Geoff Black and Stuart Wall

TITLES AVAILABLE:
Biology
Business Studies
Chemistry
Economics
English
English Literature
French
Geography
German
Information Technology
Mathematics
Mathematics: Higher Level
Music
Physics
Psychology
Religious Studies
Science
Sociology
Spanish
Technology
World History

**Addison Wesley Longman Limited,**
*Edinburgh Gate, Harlow*
*Essex CM20 2JE, England*
*and Associated Companies throughout the world.*

© Longman Group Limited 1994
This edition © Addison Wesley Longman Limited 1997

First published 1994
Updated edition 1997
Second impression 1998

ISBN 0 582 31540 9

**British Library Cataloguing-in-Publication Data**

A catalogue record for this book is
available from the British Library

Set by 19QQ in 10/12pt Century Old Style
Produced by Addison Wesley Longman Singapore  Pte Ltd
Printed in Singapore

# CONTENTS

# EDITORS' PREFACE

Longman Study Guides are written by experienced examiners and teachers, and aim to give you the best possible faundation for success in examinations and other modes of assessment. Much has been said in recent years about declining standards and disappointing examination results. While this may be somewhat exaggerated, examiners are well aware that the performance of many candidates falls well short of their potential. The books encourage thorough study and a full understanding of the concepts involved and should be seen as course companions and study guides to be used throughout the year. Examiners are in no doubt that a structured approach in preparing for examinations and in presenting coursework can, together with hard work and diligent application, substantially improve performance.

The largely self-contained nature of each chapter gives the book a useful degree of flexibility. After starting with Chapters 1 and 2, all other chapters can be read selectively, in any order appropriate to the stage you have reached in your course. We believe that this book, and the series as a whole, will help you establish a solid platform of basic knowledge and examination technique on which to build.

*Geoff Black and Stuart Wall*

# ACKNOWLEDGEMENTS

We are grateful to the following Examination Boards for their assistance in the preparation of this book:

Midland Examining Group (MEG)
Northern Examinations and Assessment Board (NEAB)
Northern Ireland Council for Curriculum, Esaminations and Assessment (CCEA)
Southern Examining Group (SEG)
Edexcel Foundation (London) (ULEAC)
Welsh Joint Education Committee (WJEC)

Where particular permission to reproduce questions has been granted, further acknowledgement is given in the text. We accept full responsibility for any indication of answers to such questions, and answers or indications of mark schemes have not been approved by any Examination Board.

We are grateful to Stuart Wall and Geoff Black for their help in the publication and in dealing with our problems and enquiries and to our colleagues and students for their help.

*Keith Palfreyman and Colin Maunder*

I am indebted to Sally Ginns, Elaine Sanderson and Eleanor Wall for their help in typing my part of the manuscript; to Graham Baldry, Geoff Black, and especially to Stuart Wall for their help in the publication, and to Peter Norwood and Liz Hatten for their support and encouragement.

Finally to pupils of Impington Village College for their co-operation with the "Students' Answers".

*Colin Maunder*

I would like to express my thanks to my two sons for their help, especially Paul for his proof reading and constructive comments on my parts of the text and my wife Angela for yet more of her patience and coffee. I am also grateful to the pupils of Pope Pius X School for their help in preparing answers and review sheets and to its staff for their expertise when help was needed.

*Keith Palfreyman*

# GETTING STARTED

This book is designed to act as a guide to the whole of your GCSE Physics course, whether as a separate subject (Science: Physics) or as part of GCSE Science. It can be used alongside a conventional textbook throughout your course as well as for help with pre-examination revision. The study of physics requires you to understand ideas and be able to apply them in both familiar and new situations. *Understanding* takes time and effort and it is best to work steadily throughout your course rather than to leave everything to the last minute.

Each chapter refers to a **particular topic** or **area of study**, and contains the **essential principles** of that topic which are, in effect, the 'core' materials in the Physics part of the Science National Curriculum.

After covering the essential principles of a topic area, there is a discussion of **extension materials** in each chapter. These are the *additional* aspects you need to know on each topic area to gain a separate GCSE in Physics, i.e. Science: Physics.

**Examples** from GCSE examination papers are provided for practice, together with **outline answers**. One question is usually selected for **more thorough treatment** to give you an idea of what a *full* answer should include.

Finally each chapter contains a **Review Sheet** to give you the opportunity to check your understanding of the ideas encountered in that chapter.

# SCIENCE: PHYSICS AND KEY STAGE 4

**THE NATIONAL CURRICULUM**

**PROGRAMME OF STUDY**

**STATEMENTS OF ATTAINMENT AND LEVELS**

**THE SYLLABUSES**

**TIERS OF ASSESSMENT**

**SPELLING, PUNCTUATION AND GRAMMAR**

**GRADE DESCRIPTIONS**

**SCHEMES OF ASSESSMENT**

**EXAM GROUP ADDRESSES**

# ESSENTIAL PRINCIPLES

This book will be relevant both to those taking Physics as a separate GCSE subject (i.e. Science: Physics) and to those requiring extra help on the Physics part of their Science GCSE. Science is a compulsory subject for all pupils in state schools that must follow the National Curriculum and is, together with Mathematics and English, one of the "core" subjects. This first chapter will try to make the various rules and regulations of the different Examination Groups more clear. If you still need further information their addresses are at the end of the chapter.

Whatever your reason for reading this book remember that regular reading and revision will always lead to a clearer understanding – NEVER leave your revision to the last minute. Always try to plan your work so that you can cope with the demands that it will make on your time. If you have to hand in coursework assignments, find out when they are due and make sure that they are handed in on time. Being behind with work in one subject can mean that you lose time that should be spent on others and all your work suffers – planning avoids the problem and ensures some free time for enjoyment!

## 1 ▷ THE NATIONAL CURRICULUM

*Separate examination papers in the individual science subjects*

*You need to cover core and extension materials for a separate GCSE in Physics*

*Attainment Targets for Science*

*Science: Physics*

All pupils in years 10 and 11 (Key Stage 4) of the English state school system have to take either single science (about 12% of total timetable time) or double science (about 20% of total timetable time). An increasing number of pupils are choosing to take this last option by adding to the National Curriculum Science programme of study and taking *separate examination papers* in Science: Physics, Science: Chemistry and Science: Biology. The Examination Boards have provided this option by splitting the Science programme of study between the three subject areas and then adding extra material from the appropriate subject. In the near future this means that all pupils taking this option have to do all three "separate" subjects in order to meet the requirements of the law about National Curriculum but this might of course change. The additional material will of course mean a corresponding increase in the study time required.

It is best to think of the examination syllabus for each separate subject in two parts – the *"core"* that is part of the National Curriculum programme of study and the *extension* material needed to get a separate GCSE in that subject. The *core* materials are set out in the first part of each topic-based chapter; the *extension* materials are separately presented at the end of each topic-based chapter.

The National Curriculum programme of study for Science has four **Attainment Targets**:

- Attainment Target Sc1: Experimental and Investigative Science.
- Attainment Target Sc2: Life Processes and Living Things.
- Attainment Target Sc3: Materials and their Properties.
- Attainment Target Sc4: Physical processes.

Science: Physics usually covers some of Attainment Target Sc3 and all of Attainment Target Sc4 with suitable extensions. It will also include investigations that allow you to be assessed in Attainment Target Sc1. There is no coverage of any of Attainment Target Sc2 which is mainly biological in content.

### Attainment Target Sc1: Experimental and Investigative Science

The National Curriculum divides Attainment Target Sc1 into four strands as follows: Pupils should be taught to:

(i)  plan experimental procedures
(ii)  obtain evidence
(iii) analyse evidence and draw conclusions
(iv) evaluate the evidence that has been obtained

### Attainment Target Sc3: Materials and their Properties

The National Curriculum divides Attainment Target Sc3 into three strands as follows:
Pupils should be taught:

(i) classifying materials;
(ii) changing materials;
(iii) patterns of behaviour.

The physics syllabus is limited to parts of i) and ii) which deal with atomic structure, the atmosphere and geology.

The National Curriculum divides Attainment Target Sc4 into six strands as follows:

### Attainment Target Sc4: Physical Processes

Pupils should be taught:

(i) electricity and magnetism;
(ii) forces and motion;
(iii) waves;
(iv) the Earth and beyond;
(v) energy resources and energy transfer;
(vi) radioactivity.

The physics syllabus would usually include all of this target.

The National Curriculum sets out the ground to be covered for each of the Attainment Targets in more detail. The Examination Boards provide similar statements for their extension materials in Physics. There is more detail about this in section 8 which is about the assessment for individual examination schemes.

The National Curriculum no longer sets out levels for attainment at key stage 4. Your attainment will be reported as an examination level graded from G to A* and each Examination Board publishes a set of statements to show what you have to be able to do to reach some of the levels. A grade U is awarded to those who do not reach the lowest mark needed for the lowest grade in the tier for which they are entered. (See section 5.)

There are lots of possible ways of teaching and examining the same sort of material. The same examination scheme may be taught in different orders by teachers in different schools. Each of the Examination Boards states in a **syllabus** exactly what must be taught for its examination and also the length and style of its examination papers. Candidates would be wise to obtain a copy of their syllabus from their own school or college, or by writing directly to their Examination Group, checking their syllabus against the content of each chapter. The main chapter headings and their application to the Examination Groups are given in Fig. 1.1

In the tables the MEG syllabuses are noted as follows:

MEG 1 is Science : Physics (Salters)
MEG 2 is Science : Physics (Nuffield)
MEG 3 is Science : Physics Syllabus A

| Chapter and Topic | CCEA | MEG1 | MEG2 | MEG3 | NEAB | SEG | ULEAC | WJEC |
|---|---|---|---|---|---|---|---|---|
| 3 Forces and Structure | ✓ | ✓ | ✓ | ✓ | ✓ | ✓ | ✓ | ✓ |
| 4 Energy, Work and Power | ✓ | ✓ | ✓ | ✓ | ✓ | ✓ | ✓ | ✓ |
| 5 Forces and Motion | ✓ | ✓ | ✓ | ✓ | ✓ | ✓ | ✓ | ✓ |
| 6 Oscillations and Waves | ✓ | ✓ | ✓ | ✓ | ✓ | ✓ | ✓ | ✓ |
| 7 Circuits and Direct Current | ✓ | ✓ | ✓ | ✓ | ✓ | ✓ | ✓ | ✓ |
| 8 Electronics – Components | | ✓ | ✓ | ✓ | ✓ | ✓ | ✓ | |
| 9 Light and Optics | ✓ | ✓ | ✓ | ✓ | ✓ | ✓ | ✓ | ✓ |
| 10 Structure of Matter and Kinetic Theory | ✓ | ✓ | ✓ | ✓ | ✓ | ✓ | ✓ | ✓ |
| 11 Pressure and Hydraulics | ✓ | ✓ | ✓ | ✓ | ✓ | ✓ | ✓ | ✓ |
| 12 Heat Energy | ✓ | ✓ | ✓ | ✓ | ✓ | ✓ | ✓ | ✓ |
| 13 Magnetism and Electromagnetism | ✓ | ✓ | ✓ | ✓ | ✓ | ✓ | ✓ | ✓ |
| 14 Induced EMF and AC | ✓ | ✓ | ✓ | ✓ | ✓ | ✓ | ✓ | ✓ |
| 15 Atomic Structure and Radioactivity | ✓ | ✓ | ✓ | ✓ | ✓ | ✓ | ✓ | ✓ |
| 16 Electronics – Systems | | ✓ | ✓ | ✓ | ✓ | ✓ | | ✓ |
| 17 Earth, Space and Weather | ✓ | ✓ | | ✓ | ✓ | ✓ | ✓ | ✓ |

Fig. 1.1    Syllabus coverage chart

The following Fig 1.2 gives you an indication of which parts of the extension materials in each chapter are most relevant to the various Examination Groups.

| | CCEA | MEG1 | MEG2 | MEG3 | NEAB | SEG | ULEAC | WJEC |
|---|---|---|---|---|---|---|---|---|
| Chapter 3 | 11, 12, 14 | 11, 12, 14 | 11, 12, 14 | 11, 12, 14 | 11, 12, 14 | 11, 12, 14 | 11, 12, 14 | 14 |
| Chapter 4 | 12, 14 | 12, 14 | 12 | 12, 14 | 14 | 14 | 14 | 14 |
| Chapter 5 | 12, 13, 14, 15, 17 | 12, 14, 15 | 12, 13, 14 | 12, 13, 14 | 12, 15 | 14, 15 | 12, 15 | 12, 13 |
| Chapter 6 | | 10 | | 10 | | | | |
| Chapter 7 | 14, 15, 17, 18 | 15, 17, 18 | 15, 17 | 15, 17 | 15 | 15, 17 | 15, 17 | 14, 15, 17, 18 |
| Chapter 8 | | 10, 11, 12, 13, 14, 15 | 14 | 13, 14 | 13, 14 | 10, 11, 12, 13, 14 | | |
| Chapter 9 | 1, 2, 3, 4, 5, 10 | 3, 4 | | 1, 4, 6, 7 | 1, 2, 3, 4, 5, 10 | | 7 | 7 |
| Chapter 10 | 1 | | 1 | | | 2, 3 | 1 | 1 |
| Chapter 11 | | 1 | | | | 4 | | 3 |
| Chapter 12 | 4, 5 | 1, 4, 6 | 1, 4 | 1 | 4 | 2, 3, 4 | 4, 6 | 1, 4, 5, 7 |
| Chapter 13 | 1, 2, 3 | 1, 2, 3 | 1, 2, 3 | 1, 2 | 1, 2 | 1, 2 | 1, 2, 3 | 1 |
| Chapter 14 | 1, 2 | 1, 2, 3 | 1, 2 | 1, 2 | 1, 3 | 1, 2, 3 | 1, 2 | 1, 2 |
| Chapter 15 | 2, 3, 4 | 2, 3, 4 | 2, 4 | 2, 3 | 2, 3, 4 | 2, 3 | 2, 3, 4 | 2, 3 |
| Chapter 16 | | 1, 2 | | 1 | 1 | 1, 2 | | |
| Chapter 17 | 4, 7 | 1, 7 | 1, 4, 7 | 1, 6, 7 | 1, 4 | 1, 4 | 1 | 1 |

Fig. 1.2 Extension materials relevant to the various examination group syllabuses

Section 8 of this chapter will give you more detail of the ways in which you will be assessed for Science; Physics by each of the Examination Groups. You can always write to the Examination Group addresses given in Section 9 of this chapter to get an up-to-date copy of your syllabus.

## AIMS

The AIMS are a description of the purpose of the syllabus. They may be long term goals that cannot be assessed in the final examination but they should give you good reasons why you should follow this particular course. The **aims** for Science: Physics will follow those for the National Curriculum and are broadly the same for all of the Examination Boards. They usually include giving students an opportunity to:

 Aims of the syllabuses

- acquire a systematic body of scientific knowledge and develop an understanding of physics including its power and limitations;
- develop experimental and investigative abilities;
- develop an understanding of the nature of scientific ideas and activity and the basis for scientific claims;
- develop their understanding of the technological and environmental applications of science and of the economic, ethical and social implications of these.

## ASSESSMENT OBJECTIVES

These are a list of the abilities and skills which you will develop and on which you will be assessed. The attainment targets can be divided into two main groups of objectives; one group involves *investigations* under Attainment Target Sc1 (assessed by coursework) and the other group involves *knowledge and understanding* of physics (assessed in the examination). Again they are broadly the same for each of the Examination Boards:

1.  Objectives related to Sc1 : Scientific Investigation. (25% by coursework)

    Candidates should be able to:

    - carry out experimental and investigative work in which they plan procedures, use precise and systematic ways of making measurements and observations, analyse and evaluate evidence, and relate this to scientific knowledge and understanding.

 Two broad groups of assessment objectives

2.  Objectives related to Knowledge and Understanding of Physics: (75% by examination)

    Candidates should be able to:

    - recall, understand, use and apply the scientific knowledge set out in the syllabus;
    - communicate scientific observations, ideas and arguments using a range of scientific and technical vocabulary and appropriate scientific and mathematical conventions;
    - evaluate relevant scientific information, and make informed judgements from it.

 **TIERS OF ASSESSMENT**

You can enter for the examination in **one** of two "tiers". The tiers ask questions of different difficulty and lead to the grades in the following table. You should be entered for a tier that lets you answer as much as possible so that you can get your best possible grade. There is no point in entering for a level that is beyond your ability so that you get a lower grade than you would on the other level.

The grades that are available are as follows:

| *Tier* | *Grades* |
|---|---|
| Foundation | G, F, E, D, C. |
| Higher | D, C, B, A, A*. |

The advice for entry of candidates is as follows:

*You need to be entered for the correct tier*

| Expected Grade | Recommended Tier |
|---|---|
| G | Foundation |
| F | Foundation |
| E | Foundation |
| D | Foundation |
| C | Foundation/Higher |
| B | Higher |
| A | Higher |
| A* | Higher |

The usual rule is that a candidate entered for the foundation tier **cannot** get higher than grade C. A candidate entered for the higher tier who gets insufficient marks for grade D will be **ungraded (U)**.

## 6 SPAG

Spelling, Punctuation **and** Grammar must all carry marks towards your final grade. In coursework such as your practical investigations for Sc1 the assessment will be carried out by your teacher and then moderated by the Examination Board. To help teachers and examiners the following levels have been agreed by the Examination Boards:

**Threshold performance.** Candidates spell, punctuate and use the rules of grammar with reasonable accuracy; they use a limited range of specialist terms appropriately. (1 mark)

**Intermediate performance.** Candidates spell, punctuate and use the rules of grammar with considerable accuracy; they use a good range of specialist terms with facility. (2 marks)

**High performance.** Candidates spell, punctuate and use the rules of grammar with almost faultless accuracy, deploying a range of grammatical constructions; they use a wide range of specialist terms adeptly and with precision. ( 3 marks)

The marks will be scaled with your other coursework marks as a part of the 25% allocated.

## 7 GRADE DESCRIPTIONS

Grade descriptions are provided by the Examination Groups to give a general indication of the standards of achievement likely to have been shown by candidates awarded particular grades. They are only provided for grades F, C, and A. The grade awarded will depend in practice upon the extent to which the candidate has met the assessment objectives overall. Shortcomings in one aspect of the examination may be balanced by a better performance in another.

### GRADE F

Candidates devise fair tests in contexts which involve only a few factors; record observations and measurements in tables and graphs; offer simple explanations consistent with the evidence obtained.

Candidates use simple apparatus to make measurements appropriate to the task.

Candidates recall a limited range of information, for example, they suggest ways in which insulation is used in domestic contexts.

Candidates use and apply knowledge and understanding in some specific everyday contexts, for example, they explain that fuels are energy resources and that energy is sometimes 'wasted'.

Candidates obtain information from simple tables, charts and graphs and identify simple patterns in information and observations.

Candidates link cause and effect in simple contexts; make some us of scientific and technical vocabulary and make simple generalisations from information.

## GRADE C

Candidates use scientific knowledge and understanding to identify key factors to vary and control and where appropriate to make predictions; present data systematically, in graphs where appropriate, and use lines of best fit, draw conclusions consistent with their evidence and explain these using scientific knowledge and understanding.

Candidates use a range of apparatus to make careful and precise measurements and systematic observations and recognise when it is necessary to repeat measurements and observations.

Candidates recall a range of scientific information from all areas of the syllabus, for example, they recall correct units for quantities.

Candidates use and apply scientific knowledge and understanding in some general contexts, for example, they use quantitative relationships between physical quantities to perform calculations.

Candidates use scientific knowledge and understanding to make inferences and identify and explain patterns within data; make predictions from patterns in data.

Candidates describe links between related phenomena in different contexts; use diagrams, charts and graphs to support arguments, use appropriate scientific and technical vocabulary in a range of contexts.

## GRADE A

*An outline of what you must attain to achieve the grades in GCSE in Physics as a single subject*

Candidates use scientific knowledge and understanding to select an appropriate strategy for a task, identifying the factors to be considered and making predictions as appropriate; they select a method of presenting data appropriate to the task; they use information from a range of sources where it is appropriate to do so; they identify and explain anomalous observations and measurements and the salient features of graphs; use scientific knowledge and understanding to draw conclusions from their evidence; identify shortcomings in the evidence.

Candidates decide the level of precision needed in measurements and use a range of apparatus with precision and skill; make appropriately precise measurements; make systematic observations in qualitative work; decide which observations are relevant to the task in hand.

Candidates recall a wide range of knowledge from all areas of the syllabus.

Candidates use detailed scientific knowledge and understanding in a range of applications relating to scientific systems or phenomena, for example, they use a wide range of relationships between physical quantities to carry out calculations effectively.

Candidates use scientific knowledge and understanding to identify patterns and draw conclusions by combining data of more than one kind or from more than one source.

Candidates draw together and communicate knowledge from more than one area; use routinely scientific or mathematical conventions in support of arguments and use a wide range of scientific and technical vocabulary throughout their work.

## 8 > SCHEMES OF ASSESSMENTS

 How the Examination Groups will examine Physics as a single subject in the GCSE

The following are the schemes of assessment for the various examining groups for examination in 1998 and following years. Check with your teacher so that you are sure which scheme and which tier you are entered for.

**None of the question papers from any of the Examination Groups have a choice of questions.**

### MEG SCIENCE: PHYSICS SYLLABUS D (NUFFIELD)

*Terminal examination 75%* (Recall and understanding 60%, Communication and evaluation 15%)

Two papers per tier as follows:

Foundation Paper 1 – 1 hr 30 min – core (50%)
Foundation Paper 2 – 45 min – extension (25 %)
Higher paper 1 – 1hr 45 min – core – (50%)
Higher Paper 2 – 1hr – extension – (25%)

*Coursework 25%* assessed internally by the school and moderated by the Examination Group for Sc1.

No more than two thirds of the marks available in each written paper will be allocated to objective or short answer questions.

### MEG SCIENCE: PHYSICS SYLLABUS A

*Terminal examination 75%* (Recall and understanding 60%, Communication and evaluation 15%)

Two papers per tier as follows:

Foundation Paper 1 – 1 hr 30 min – core (50%)
Foundation Paper 2 – 45 min – extension (25%)
Higher Paper 1 – 1 hr 45 min – core – (50%)
Higher Paper 2 – 1 hr – extension – (25%)

*Coursework 25%* assessed internally by the school and moderated by the Examination Group for Sc1.

No more than two thirds of the marks available in each written paper will be allocated to objective or short answer questions. The two paper 1 will have some common questions as will the two paper 2. The common questions will target the overlapping grades C and D.

### MEG SCIENCE: PHYSICS SYLLABUS C (SALTERS)

*Terminal examination 75%* (Recall and understanding 45%, Application and interpretation 15%, Communication and evaluation 15%)

One paper per tier as follows:

Foundation – 2 hr
Higher – 2 hr 15 min.

*Coursework 25%* assessed internally by the school and moderated by the Examination Group for Sc1.

Papers will both contain core and extension work. The extension will be about 1/3 of each paper. No more than two thirds of the marks available in each written paper will be allocated to objective or short answer questions. The scheme considers realistic contexts to be important and candidates will be expected to be able to apply their knowledge to unfamiliar contexts. Both core and extension may be examined within the same questions in so far as they relate to the context.

## ULEAC SCIENCE: PHYSICS

*Terminal examination 75%* (Knowledge, understanding, application 60%, Communication and evaluation 15%).

Two papers per tier as follows:

Foundation Papers 1 – 1 hr 30 min – core (50%)
Foundation Paper 2 – 1 hr – extension (25%)
Higher paper 1 – 1 hr 30 min – core (50%)
Higher paper 2 – 1 hr – extension (25%)

*Coursework 25%* assessed internally by the school and moderated by the Examination Group for Sc1.

A variety of question types on each paper. Short answer questions will not account for more than two thirds of the total marks.

## WJEC SCIENCE: PHYSICS

*Terminal examination 75%* (Physical processes 50%, Subject extension 25%)

One paper per tier as follows:

Foundation – 2 hr
Higher – 2 hr 30 min.

*Coursework 25%* assessed internally by the school and moderated by the Examination Group for Sc1.

Short answer and objective questions will not account for more than two thirds of the credit on either paper. Each paper will have two sections A and B with section B of the Foundation paper being the same as section A of the Higher paper.

## NEAB SCIENCE: PHYSICS

*Terminal examination 75%* (Recall and understanding 60%, Communication and evaluation 15%)

One paper per tier as follows:

Foundation – 2 hr
Higher – 2 hr 15 min.

*Coursework 25%* assessed internally by the school and moderated by the Examination Group for Sc1.

Papers will contain question concerning the applications of science and candidates will be expected to be able to apply their knowledge to unfamiliar contexts.

## SEG SCIENCE: PHYSICS

*Terminal examination 75%* (Knowledge and understanding 60%, Communication and evaluation 15%)

Two papers per tier as follows:

Foundation Paper 1 – 1 hr 30 min – core (50%)
Foundation Paper 2 – 1 hr – additional content (25%)
Higher Paper 1 – 1 hr 30 min – core (50%)
Higher Paper 2 – 1 hr – additional content (25%)

*Coursework 25%* assessed internally by the school and moderated by the Examination Group for Sc1.

The papers will contain a range of different types of question.

### CCEA SCIENCE: PHYSICS

*Terminal examination 75%* (Recall and understanding 60%, Communication and evaluation 15%)

Two papers per tier as follows:

Foundation Paper 1 – 1 hr
Foundation Paper 2 – 1 hr 30 min
Higher Paper 1 – 1 hr 45 min
Higher Paper 2 – 1 hr 45 min

*Coursework 25%* assessed internally by the school and moderated by the Examination Group for Sc1.

The paper structure will be as follows:

Foundation Paper 1 – 20 objective questions, 20 short answer questions.
Foundation Paper 2 – 6 structured questions.
Higher Paper 1 – 5 structured questions.
Higher Paper 2 – 4 structured questions, 1 free response question.

Approximately 50% of the material tested at the Higher tier of entry will be drawn from the foundation material.

**9 > EXAMINATION GROUP ADDRESSES**

**CCEA**  Northern Ireland Council for Curriculum, Examinations and Assessment
29 Clarendon Road
Belfast
BT1 3BG
Tel. 01232261200          Fax. 01232261234

**MEG**  Midland Examining Group
Syndicate Buildings
1 Hills Road
Cambridge
CB1 2EU
Tel. 01223 553311          Fax. 01223460278

**NEAB**  Northern Examination and Assessment Board
Devas St.
Manchester
M15 6EX
Tel. 0161 9531180          Fax. 0161 2737572

**SEG**  Southern Examining Group
Stag Hill House
Guildford
Surrey
GU2 5XJ
Tel. 01483 506506          Fax. 01483 300152

**ULEAC**  Edexcel Foundation (London)
Stewart House
32 Russell Square
London
WC1B 5DN
Tel. 0171 331 4000          Fax 0171 331 4044

**WJEC**  Welsh Joint Education Committee
245 Western Avenue
Cardiff
CF5 2YX
Tel. 01222 265000          Fax 01222 575994

# EXAMINATION AND ASSESSMENT TECHNIQUES

## GETTING STARTED

As the exam approaches, you will *already* have contributed to your final mark by your coursework assessments over the past months and years. The exam itself will still, however, represent a considerable hurdle, and you should realise that just as assessments were conducted over a period of time, so too should your revision be a continuous process. No matter how good your memory is, physics cannot be 'learned' in a short time, and questions in GCSE are likely to test both your understanding and your ability to analyse and apply data, rather than to simply test your recall of facts.

This book can help as you *approach your exam*. It can also help *throughout your course* if you use it to revise a whole topic area shortly after you have covered it in your class. The past examination questions and answers should give you confidence in using and applying your knowledge. You should try all the questions on each syllabus topic – they have been selected from several Examination Boards and are representative of the standard which is common to *all* the Boards.

Having completed a question, check your answer with the one supplied. Look carefully to see whether you have missed any important points in developing your answer. Check that numerical work is clearly laid out, and that answers are given with the appropriate unit.

You will also find student answers with examiner comments at the end of each chapter. These will help you to see what the examiner is looking for. Each chapter concludes with a Review Sheet which you can use to check your understanding of what you have read in that chapter.

## MULTIPLE CHOICE QUESTIONS

## STRUCTURED QUESTIONS

## FREE-RESPONSE QUESTIONS

## INSTRUCTION WORDS IN EXAMS

## DIAGRAMS

## GRAPHS

## EQUATIONS

## NUMERICAL TECHNIQUES

## WRITING UP INVESTIGATIONS

## EXAMPLE INVESTIGATION AND MARKING SCHEME

## FINAL GRADES

# EXAMINATION QUESTIONS

**1 > MULTIPLE CHOICE QUESTIONS**

These are designed to test knowledge and understanding across the *whole* syllabus.

Look carefully at *all* the possible responses and in making your selection try to ensure that you are clear in your mind *why* you rejected all the other possible responses. Even if you are not quite sure of the *single* correct response, you can usually eliminate some of the other responses as clearly wrong. At the end, go through the whole paper and check each answer.

**2 > STRUCTURED QUESTIONS**

These are intended to test *more detailed* understanding of *particular areas* of the syllabus. Such questions usually have several parts or sections, each part following on from the previous part, i.e. there is a clear *structure* to the question. Most Examination Boards give an indication of the maximum mark to be awarded for each part of such a question – or imply the required length of answer by providing a number of lines below each question. The important thing to bear in mind is that where a mark is stated, e.g. (3), then it broadly reflects the number of significant points the examiners regard as relevant in answering that question. You must think carefully to ensure that your answer contains *sufficient* points to satisfy the examiner's idea of a 'good' answer. A six-mark question will obviously require a more detailed answer than a three-mark question. The answers to structured questions in this book give an indication of the likely requirements in this part of your examination.

**3 > FREE-RESPONSE QUESTIONS**

Examination papers will provide students with an opportunity to show what they know by using extended prose. This means that you have to organise your answer to that part of the question without the usual structure being provided. These questions often ask you to *suggest* solutions or explanations. Your answers will be marked according to the scientific knowledge that you use – they are not an opportunity for you to give an opinion without any supporting facts!

## ESSAY QUESTIONS

Essay questions need *planning*. Spend time in thinking about what you wish to say, and in making sure that you are responding to the statements *in the question*. You can draw up a *list* of points that you wish to make in your answer; perhaps each major point can have its own paragraph. Try to arrange the points so that they have a *logical* order, i.e. one point follows on 'naturally' from the previous point. An essay should have a brief *introduction* telling the examiner the points you are about to make. It should also have a brief *conclusion* where you comment on the major findings of your analysis.

## DATA ANALYSIS

Data analysis should show *how* an answer is arrived at. Do not rely on your calculator to provide the answer, but show on your exam paper how you get to your answer. Where a graph has to be analysed, draw appropriate lines to show how you arrived at values, intercepts or gradients. The main point here is to try to make your *method of working* clear to the examiner.

**4 > INSTRUCTION WORDS IN EXAMS**

Some words have quite exact meanings in examinations and you need to make sure that you understand what the examiner will want you to do.

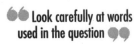
**Look carefully at words used in the question**

- **Calculate** Work out the value of something. **Do** show the working unless you are told that it is not needed. e.g. calculate the density of the metal.
- **Compare** Are the things in the question alike or similar? What are the similarities and differences? e.g. Compare the iris of an eye with the diaphragm of a camera.
- **Complete** Fill in the spaces in a sentence or a table. e.g. Complete the following table showing the names of the planets.

- **Define** Give the *exact* meaning of something. e.g. Define *half-life*
- **Describe** Write in detail about something. e.g. Describe what happens when you close the switch in the circuit.
- **Draw a diagram** Draw a clear *labelled* diagram. Use a pencil and ruler, this is *not* asking for a rough sketch. e.g. Draw a diagram of a simple thermometer.
- **Explain** Make it clear what is meant by something. e.g. Explain how air exerts a pressure.
- **Explain why** Give scientific reasons why something happens. Don't just describe what it is that happens – you are often told that in this sort of question anyway! e.g. Explain why the air rises in the syringe.
- **Name** Write down the name of something. You don't need to write about it at all, just write down the name. e.g. Name a gas that could be used to fill the balloon.
- **Plot** Put the exact points on a graph.
- **Predict** Use the information in the question to say what you think will happen.
- **State** Write down briefly the exact facts about something. It can mean the same as 'define' when it says 'state what is meant by'. e.g. State what is meant by *density*.
- **Suggest** Use your *scientific knowledge* to make *reasonable* suggestions. e.g. Suggest a use for the circuit shown.
- **What happens to** This usually just wants a short statement, a fact. e.g. What happens to the armature when the electromagnet is switched on? will just want you to state that the armature is attracted to the electromagnet.
- **Check the marks available** The number should be at the side of the question and will usually be the same as the number of facts that you are expected to give. This and the space allowed tells you the detail that you are expected to produce.

## 5 ⟩ DIAGRAMS

- Always draw a clear labelled diagram that fills the space that you are allowed on the examination paper. If you are writing on 'loose' A4 paper most diagrams will be about a third to a half of a page in size.
- Read the question carefully and make sure that you include the detail that is specially asked for.
- Always label your diagram clearly, spacing the labels as well as possible and joining the label to the correct point on the diagram with a neat straight pencil line.
- Always use a sharp HB pencil and a ruler with a good straight edge. Carry a spare sharp pencil with you.
- Check the marks available. This will give you some idea of the level of detail needed. There is not much point in spending 20 minutes on a work of art that carries only 2 marks for a simple sketch!

 Diagrams are important. Make them clear to the reader and remember to use labels

## 6 ⟩ GRAPHS

If you are asked to draw a graph or if you do graphs as part of your coursework then you will need to do the following to obtain the best marks:

- If the question gives you axes and scales you MUST use them.
- Always use the largest possible scale. You will lose a lot of marks if your graph is all in one corner of the graph paper and cannot be used accurately.
- Do make sure that your scales are uniform, i.e. that the number increases by the same amount across every square.
- Make sure that your axes are labelled clearly with both the quantity and its units, e.g. a cooling graph might have its axes labelled temperature/°C and time/s.
- Make sure that all of the points are plotted as accurately as you can.
- The x-axis is along the bottom or horizontal and the y-axis goes up the side or vertical.
- Put the variable that you changed, the one that goes up in regular steps, on the x-axis; e.g. this variable is often time.
- If all the points are on a straight line, or very close to one, fit the best straight line that you can as near as possible to all the points.
- If all the points are on or very close to a curve then draw the nearest smooth curve that you can – DON'T just 'join up the dots'!
- If one point is a long way out check that you have plotted it correctly. If it is correctly plotted but is not on the same line as the others then ignore it when you fit your best line. It may have been put in to see how you would deal with a 'rogue result' caused by an error in an experiment for example.

Some useful hints when drawing graphs

**7 ▷ EQUATIONS**

From the examination year of 1994 the government has decided that there are certain equations that you may not be given in National Curriculum Science examinations. Since your examination will be fulfilling part of these regulations you will have to learn them too. They are listed in Appendix 1 at the back of the book so that you can always find them easily. You should check regularly that you can remember them.

**8 ▷ NUMERICAL TECHNIQUES**

Your calculator is your greatest friend and may well prove to be your worst enemy! Make sure that you write your 'instructions to the calculator' on your exam paper.

For example, in calculating a value for a fuse to be used with a 2 kW kettle from mains supply:

| | |
|---|---|
| **State** | Power $= I \times V$ |
| **Show** | $I = \dfrac{\text{Power}}{V}$ |
| **Substitute** | $I = \dfrac{2000}{240}$ |
| **Calculate** | $I = \underline{8.3\,A}$ including units |
| **State** | Suitable fuse is 13 A |

Equally, be aware of problems involving π. Your calculator will show a large number of decimal places in its answer. You need to be aware of the number of significant figures which are *sensible* for a *particular question*. A question giving values to one decimal place only requires an answer to that number of decimal places – and no more.

Be aware of likely errors. You will be under stress in an exam and a slip of the hand can give a very silly answer. Try to *estimate* what a sensible answer will be like. A light bulb would not carry a 60 A current; a person cannot run at 20 m/s and so on. Check your numerical answers by applying common sense.

**9 ▷ WRITING UP INVESTIGATIONS**

In order to meet the new National Curriculum rules all of the assessment schemes have the **same** practical investigation section. It will count for 25% of the marks on which your final grade will be decided. Your work is therefore an important part of the final grade and it is important to present it in the best way that you possibly can. Don't hand in a piece of work that you could have improved if you had given it a little more time!! The work is marked first by your teacher using the standards set by the syllabus and the samples are sent to the Examination Board to be moderated. The *flow chart* shows a basic way to work through the investigation so that you don't miss out an important stage. You can improve on this basic idea if you understand what the marks are given for.

You will be given four marks, each being for a different part of the investigation.

**SKILL P** is *Planning Experimental Procedures* and has a maximum of 8 marks.

| What you do | Mark given |
|---|---|
| Plan a simple safe procedure | 2 |
| Plan a fair test or a practical procedure, making a prediction where appropriate.<br>*and*<br>Select appropriate equipment | 4 |
| Use scientific knowledge and understanding to plan a procedure, to identify key factors to vary, control or take into account, and to make a prediction where appropriate.<br>*and*<br>Decide on a suitable number of measurements to be made. | 6 |
| Use detailed scientific knowledge and understanding to plan an appropriate strategy, taking into account the need to produce precise and reliable evidence, and to justify a prediction where appropriate.<br>*and*<br>Use where appropriate, relevant information from secondary sources or preliminary work. | 8 |

Table 2.1

Notice that in order to get the highest marks you have to do some research or some preliminary testing on which you will base your experiments. Don't forget that you will need to record *all* of this – especially the results of any preliminary tests that you use or any calculations that you do using formulas that you have found from other sources such as text books or encyclopaedias.

- Don't forget to write down the factors that you keep the same in order to get a fair test.
- Making a prediction is not optional! – you should make one if it is possible to do so – it also makes conclusions and evaluations easier to write!!
- A suitable number of measurements will usually be at least 5 as this is the minimum needed to plot good graphs.

**SKILL O** is *Obtaining Evidence* and has a maximum of 8 marks.

| What you do | Mark given |
|---|---|
| Use simple equipment safely to make some observations or measurements | 2 |
| Make appropriate observations or measurements which are adequate for the activity. *and* Record the observations or measurements | 4 |
| Make sufficient systematic and accurate observations or measurements and repeat them when appropriate. *and* Record clearly and accurately the observations or measurements. | 6 |
| Use equipment with precision and skill to obtain and record reliable evidence which involves an appropriate number and range of observations or measurements. | 8 |

Table 2.2

To get good marks in this section you will need to repeat results, especially if they are suspect and don't fit the pattern of the other results, and take averages.

- You will also need to have a suitable range – if your results could be evenly spread over a 70°C range then you won't get much credit if your range is a set of results all clustered close to the same temperature.
- Make sure that, at the very least, all of your results and their averages are put into a neat table which shows the correct units.

**SKILL A** is *Analysing Evidence and Drawing Conclusions* and has a maximum of 8 marks.

| What you do | Mark given |
|---|---|
| Explain simply what has been found out. | 2 |
| Present findings in the form of simple diagrams, charts or graphs. *and* Identify trends and patterns in observations or measurements. | 4 |
| Construct and use appropiate diagrams, charts, graphs (with lines of best fit), or use numerical methods to process evidence for a conclusion *and* Draw a conclusion consistent with the evidence and relate this to scientific knowledge and understanding. | 6 |

| | |
|---|---|
| Use detailed scientific knowledge and understanding to explain a conclusion drawn from processed evidence.<br>*and*<br>Explain how results support or undermine the original prediction where one has been made. | 8 |

Table 2.3

Remember that you will need to put lines of best fit on your graphs – there will be no high marks if you join up the dots!!

■ To get the higher marks you will have to discuss your conclusions using the science that you have found in your research for the planning stage. You must relate your conclusion to the science that you know – a brief statement of what you have found out will get you 2 marks at best.

■ You do not have to have made a correct prediction in the first stage to get high marks here. If you were wrong, don't go back and change the prediction but explain how your results show that you were wrong, show what you now believe to be correct and support this by some clear and scientific reasons.

**SKILL E** is *Evaluating Evidence* and has a maximum of 6 marks.

| What you do | Mark given |
|---|---|
| Make a relevant comment about the procedure used or the evidence obtained. | 2 |
| Comment on the accuracy of the results or measurements, recognising any anomalous results.<br>*and*<br>Comment on the suitability of the procedure and, where appropriate, suggest changes to improve the reliability of the evidence. | 4 |
| Comment on the reliability of the evidence, accounting for any anomalous results or explain whether the evidence is sufficient to support a firm conclusion.<br>*and*<br>Propose improvements, or further work, to provide additional evidence for the conclusion, or to extend the enquiry. | 6 |

Table 2.4

Notice that this skill has a maximum of 6 marks and not 8 like the others.

■ You will not get marks in this section for statements such as "I did my best and the experiment worked OK". You need to make a proper evaluation of your investigation and its results.
Try asking yourself the following questions:
  • Were all of my results in a good pattern? – if some were not then explain what you did about them.
  • Was my range correct – should I have chosen larger or smaller values for my variable?
  • Was my graph the correct shape for the pattern that I expected? (Do remember that an inverse proportion does NOT produce a straight line graph!) – How close to the line were the results? – this is an indicator of how accurate your results were!
  • What limited the accuracy of my results? – was it the equipment ? Did I use it as precisely as possible? Were all the other possible variables controlled properly? Were repeats done under exactly the same circumstances as the first results?
    – could I have done something differently to make the results more reliable?
  • Do all the results and graphs fit in with  the theory that I researched at the start? Is my evidence  good enough to support the conclusion that I made?
  • Can I make suggestions to improve the experimental work that I did?
  • Is there further work that could be done to get more evidence for the conclusions – can you find out more from other sources and tie this in with your own results?
  • Do the results and conclusions suggest further work that could be done on the same topic?

## DOING AN INVESTIGATION

1.   List the **variables**
Make a list of all the things that would change the effect that you are investigating.

2.   Choose a variable to investigate. Make sure that you are choosing one that you can change in several steps.

4.   Give good reasons why you think that your investigation will behave as in your hypothesis. Be as scientific as possible – look up the science if you need to!

3.   The **hypothesis**
State as exactly as you can what you think your changes will do to the thing that you are investigating.

5.   Plan a **fair test**. Use your list of variables to make sure that you change only one variable and explain how you will keep all of the others the same. Write down exactly what you are going to do and what apparatus you are going to use.

6.   Check your experiment has a good range of tests and that your measurements will be accurate enough. Do a trial run if you need to. Make a **results** table. Decide if you are going to repeat all of the tests.

8.   Put all the results into a neat table and draw a **graph** or a chart of them so that you can show any pattern.

7.   Carry out the tests and *repeat* any where the results are unexpected or don't seem to fit the pattern of the others.

9.   Check over the results and discuss them. Decide what you are going to do about any rogue results that don't fit the pattern of the others.

10.  Use your results to come to **conclusions**. Say whether your original hypothesis was correct or not and give reasons using your results. If your hypothesis was wrong give new reasons why your experiment behaved as it did.

11  **Evaluate** your experiment. Were all your results in a good pattern? Were some of the results not as you expected? Explain any differences in the pattern from that you expected. How could you improve the experiment if you did it again?

Table 2.5

**10 > HOW YOUR MARKS ARE USED**

It is possible for you to do experimental work where you do not carry out all the stages of a full investigation and still be given credit in one or more of the skill areas. (e.g. If you did an experiment to determine the half life of a radioactive material you would not be allowed to do skill O but could be assessed on skills A and E if the experiment was demonstrated in an appropriate way.)

The new schemes therefore no longger allow you to simply do a set of investigations and get the best marks from them. You will need to do several investigations and marks will be taken from them which obey the following rules:

■ The skill marks must have been obtained from at least two pieces of work set in the context of the syllabus content.
■ At least one of the skill area marks must have been obtained from a whole investigation carried out by the candidate, i.e. a piece of work which covers all four skill areas.

You will need to be careful that at least one of your best marks does come from a full investigation or you will have to submit a lower mark for one of the skills that does come from a full investigation!

The total possible mark is 63 and your mark is found by adding your scores for each of the skill areas to get a mark out of 30, double the score to get a mark out of 60 and add your SPAG mark (See Chapter 1 Section 6) to get a total mark out of 63.

# IN THE EXAMINATION

📖 **Arrive fully prepared**. This doesn't just mean having done the revision! Have you got a pen, pencil, rubber and ruler? Do you have spare ones in case one stops working? Have you remembered your calculator? Does it have a good battery in it?

📖 **Fill the front part of the answer paper carefully**, including your candidate number and centre number. It is important that your paper can be correctly traced if it is mislaid later!

📖 **Read the instructions** on the front of the paper carefully. Make sure that you really do know how long the paper should take – don't assume that it will be the same as last year or the practise papers that you have been doing. Is there an information sheet with equations or other facts on it that will help you? sometimes this is the very last page so don't discover that it is there when it is too late.

📖 **Share out the time property**. Even though you have to do all the questions there will probably be more than one section and the sections will contain different types of question. In the instructions on the front of the paper there will usually be a sentence that tells you not to spend more than a certain time on each section. This is important as the sections will not all have equal total marks.

📖 **Read the first questions slowly** and begin to answer the paper. Don't begin in a rush and panic so that you make silly mistakes or miss out parts of questions that you can do.

📖 **Do have a go at *all* of the questions**. There may be some marks that you can pick up by having a go even if you don't know enough to get them all. You can't do worse than leaving a blank space which will obviously get no marks at all!!

📖 Make sure that you **answer the question that is asked** and not a similar one that you would rather have been asked. The marking scheme will be exact and aimed at only the facts that fit the question on the paper.

📖 **Do use all the help** that is built into the question paper for you. The size of the space that has been left for the answer will help you to decide how much writing you need to do and how much detail is needed. The number of marks for each part of a question is also in the margin. On a science paper this will usually be the same as the number of facts that you are expected to have in your answer. The marking scheme will then have one mark for each fact. If there are four marks available then try not to use all the space for one or two facts and have no chance of the other marks.

📖 If you are **doing a calculation** then **do** show the working. Many questions help you by asking for the equation first but try to get into the habit of following this order.

- ◆ write down the correct equation
- ◆ substitute the numbers in the correct places
- ◆ work out the answer that you need
- ◆ remember to add the correct unit for your answer.

If you do this you will have shown the examiner that you understand the science involved and have not just guessed what to do with the numbers. If you make a mistake, with the arithmetic for example, you can still get most of the marks. If you only write down a final answer you will certainly lose some marks and you will lose all of the marks if you have made a mistake.

📖 **Check that you have fully completed each question before you leave it**. It is easy to answer one part successfully and then move on thinking that you have done it all.

📖 Try to leave a little time spare at the end so that you can **check the work that you have done**. Try to find the silly mistakes before the examiner does! Don't leave questions unattempted.

📖 **If you start to run out of time** be sensible and keep your answers clear and readable. Remember that it is usually easier to get the first few marks on a new question than to continue trying to get the last few harder marks on another question.

# A FINAL WORD

Good luck, in your exam and in your studies. Use this book to help you, and use your own notes to amplify the basic information given. Remember that understanding physics is a long-term process and not something which you will be able to "cram" into a short period. Use the book as intended, as a guide through the time of your study and as a help at the time of your exam.

The **Longman Exam Practice Kit: GCSE Physics** provides further help with revision techniques and more example questions to try. The book also contains short revision notes on each of the main topics.

CHAPTER 3

# FORCES AND STRUCTURES

## GETTING STARTED

The idea of a **force** is fundamental to physics, and to engineering. The simplest way of thinking of a force is to describe it as a "push" or a "pull", but this is not very satisfactory. We cannot see a force but we can see its **effect** on an object, so we describe forces in terms of what they **do**. Forces tend to cause changes in an object's:

1 Shape or size;
2 Speed in a straight line;
3 Direction.

Forces are measured in newtons (N), using a "force-meter" (sometimes called a "newton-meter").

When several forces act on an object, they can either combine to give an **overall force** – which will change the object's shape or motion – or they could cancel each other out, giving no overall force. In this last case we would say that the forces are "balanced". If there is no force acting, or if all the forces acting on an object are balanced, then there will be no change taking place. An object at rest will remain at rest, and a moving object will continue to move, keeping the same speed and travelling in the same direction.

# ESSENTIAL PRINCIPLES

**1** **TENSION AND COMPRESSION**

Tension and compression are forces which increase or decrease the dimensions of an object or structure. In Fig. 3.1 an object under **tension** (or stretching force) has been **extended**. Its original length has been **increased**. Under **compression** the original length is **decreased** (Fig. 3.2).

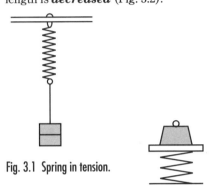

Fig. 3.1 Spring in tension.

Fig. 32 Spring in compression.

In many situations, both tension and compression exist at the same time. A simple beam or balcony will bend under its own weight (Fig. 3.3). So will a bridge or a simple doorway (Fig. 3.4). Materials such as brick or concrete are **weak under tension** but **strong when compressed**. Cracks form easily when tension is applied, but the cracks close under compression (Fig. 3.5).

Fig. 3.3 A cantilever shows both tension and compression.

Fig. 3.4 Simple bridge structure.

Fig. 3.5 Cracks open under tension and close under compression.

Reinforcing concrete makes it stronger and able to resist tension forces. The designing and building of bridges needs a careful consideration of tension and compression forces, and the use of materials in construction which can withstand tension forces.

**2** **FRICTION**

Friction is a force which opposes the movement of an object. It acts in the **opposite** direction to the way the object is being pushed or pulled (Fig. 3.6).

Friction between **solid surfaces** depends on:

1 The type of surface;
2 The size of the normal (or **reaction**) force.

It does **not** depend on:

3 The contact area;
4 The velocity of movement.

The force needed to **just start an object moving** is equal to the **static friction value** for the surfaces. The force needed to **keep an object moving steadily** (with constant velocity) on a surface is equal to the **dynamic friction value** for the surfaces. Static friction is always greater than dynamic friction.

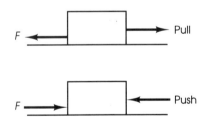

Fig. 3.6 Friction opposes the direction of motion.

Objects moving through liquids or gases (**fluids**) also have friction acting on them. This **fluid friction** does depend on the contact area and the velocity of movement. Fluid friction becomes greater as the object's surface area or its velocity increases. A reduction of surface area, or streamlining, reduces friction in planes or cars, whereas lubrication reduces friction between solid surfaces.

## 3 > MASS AND WEIGHT

> 66 These ideas are often confused. Remember WEIGHT is a force so it is measured in NEWTONS. 99

The **mass** of an object tells us how much *matter* it contains and is measured in kilograms (kg). **Weight** is a *force* caused by the pull of a planet (Fig. 3.7). All masses exert a *pull* on each other. This is one of the properties of mass. The force gets smaller as the distance between the masses increases, and gets bigger as the size of the masses increases. This effect is called **gravity** and we often refer to the "pull of gravity".

When a planet pulls on a mass the force produced is called **weight**. Near the surface of the Earth, 1 kg of mass is pulled down by a force of approximately 10 N (exactly 9.81 N). The size of the "pull on 1 kg" is called the **gravitational field strength** of a planet and is written as *g*. For the **Earth** *g* = 10 newtons per kilogram (10 N/kg). Other planets have other field strengths. These determine the

Fig. 3.7 Weight is the pull of a planet on a mass.

pull on a mass – or in other words, its *weight*. On the **moon** 1 kg weighs 1.6 N, so *g* = 1.6 N/kg. In **space**, away from a planet's pull, each kilogram has no weight. There is no pull on it from any planet and the mass is now weightless.

$$\text{weight} = \text{mass} \times g$$

## 4 > NORMAL FORCES (OR REACTION FORCES)

**Normal forces** are forces exerted *by a surface on an object*. They are the *push* of the surface on the object and act at 90° to the surface.

In Fig. 3.8 the *weight* of the object and the *normal force* are *equal and opposite* if the object is *at rest*.

In Fig. 3.9 the object is no longer "at rest". Here the *weight* of the object and the *normal force* are *not* equal and opposite. Unless there is another force acting, such as friction, the object will begin to move. Note that *weight* acts towards the centre of the Earth and the *normal force* acts at 90° to the surface.

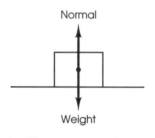

Fig. 3.8 Normal force at 90° to a surface.

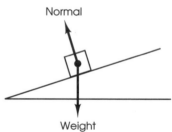

Fig. 3.9

## 5 > FIELDS

A **field** is a region in which a force is felt.
- *Gravitational field.* This is caused by a mass and acts on a mass, e.g. the moon being pulled by the Earth (Fig. 3.10).
- *Magnetic field.* This is caused by a permanent magnet or a current in a wire and acts on another magnet or another current (Fig. 3.11).
- *Electric field.* This is caused by charged objects and acts on charged objects.

In all cases the *strength* of the field *reduces* as the *distance* from the source of the field *increases*. For example, a particular object on the Earth *weighs less* up a mountain than it does at sea level; it also weighs less at the Equator than it does at the North Pole. This is because the Earth "bulges out" at the Equator and is flattened at the poles.

The strength and direction of each sort of field can be represented by *field lines*. These are rather like contour lines on maps.

Fig. 3.10 Gravitational field of the Earth extends to the moon.

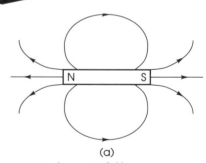

Fig. 3.11(a) Simple magnetic field;

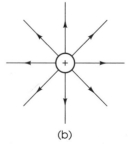

(b) electric field around a point charge.

## 6 > VECTORS AND SCALARS

Forces are *vector* quantities. They have direction *as well as* size. Quantities which *only* have size and where direction is not important (e.g. temperature, mass, volume) are called *scalars*. Force directions need care. It is important to sort out what object the force is *acting upon*. In Fig. 3.12 the forces acting on the *picture* are its weight (*W*) and the tensions (*T*) in the strings. Figure 3.13 shows the forces acting on the *hook* from which the picture is hung.

The effect of *more than one* force acting on an object depends on the *force directions*. In Fig. 3.14 these forces have the same effect on the object as a single 7 N force acting to the right. In Fig. 3.15 the two forces have the same effect as a 1 N force acting to the left. The *single force* which can *replace several forces* on an object, and still have the *same effect*, is called the **resultant force**.

> ❝ Remember to choose a large but easy scale like 5 cm = 1 Newton, and to STATE the scale in your answer. ❞

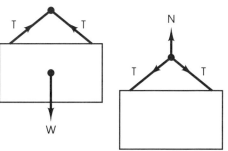

Fig. 3.12 Forces acting on the picture.

Fig. 3.13 Forces acting on the hook.

Fig. 3.14 Resultant 7 N to the right.

Fig. 3.15 Resultant 1 N to the left.

## 7 > EQUILIBRIUM

If an object remains at rest, although acted on by several forces, it is in *equilibrium*. The resultant force acting on the object is zero. The two forces in Fig. 3.16 have a resultant *R*. The body would be in equilibrium if a third force equal to *R*, but in the *opposite direction*, was also acting.

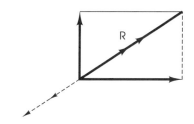

Fig. 3.16 Condition for equilibrium.

A diagram such as Fig. 3.17 is called a *space diagram*. If forces act to produce equilibrium then a scale diagram of them, taken in order, will form a *closed figure*. This is the case in Fig. 3.18. The force between two surfaces is the **contact force** between two solids. It is the *resultant* of the *normal force* and the *friction force* (Fig. 3.19).

If the forces are **coplanar** (acting in the same plane) there are two requirements for equilibrium. One is that the forces must obey the **Principle of Moments** (see next section) and secondly the resultant of all the forces in any direction must be zero. The commonest

case of this last requirement is when the forces are parallel. The total of the forces in one direction is then equal and opposite to the total in the opposite direction. Fig. 3.20 shows a bridge where the forces are the **weight W** acting downwards and the two **normal reaction forces $N_1$ and $N_2$** acting upwards. Clearly

$$W = N_1 + N_2$$

Fig. 3.17 Space diagram for three forces in equilibrium.

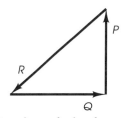

Fig. 3.18 Force diagram for three forces in equilibrium.

Fig. 3.19

Fig. 3.20 Coplanar forces in equilibrium.

## 8 > MOMENTS

The forces in Fig. 3.21 have totals that are equal and opposite (the total upward force equals the total downward force), but the 8 N force will tend to turn the beam in a *clockwise* direction. The "turning effect" of a force about a pivot or fulcrum is called the *moment* of the force.

Fig. 3.21

66 Be careful with distance measurements. The distance is FROM the force TO the pivot 99

■ *Moment = Force × Distance at 90° from the line of the force to the pivot.* Moments are measured in newton metres (N m) or newton centimetres (N cm). The moment of the 8 N force in Fig. 3.21 would be $8 \times 6 = 48$ N m.

For equilibrium, the *principle of moments* applies:

■ **Sum of clockwise moments = sum of anticlockwise moments.**

Moments can be taken about any point, but it is usual to take them about the *pivot*.

In Fig. 3.22 the moment of the 4N force is $(4 \times 6) = 24$ Nm (clockwise) and that of the 8N

Fig. 3.22

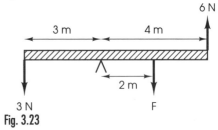

Fig. 3.23

force is $8 \times x) = 8x$ Nm (anticlockwise). For equilibrium

$$24 \text{ Nm} = 8x$$
$$3 \text{ m} = x$$

Without force $F$, both the 6 N and the 3 N forces have an anticlockwise moment about the pivot (Fig. 3.23). To obtain equilibrium, force $F$ is needed. Total anticlockwise moment about the pivot

$$= (6 \times 4) + (3 \times 3)$$
$$= 33 \text{ N m}$$

Clockwise moment $= (2 \times F)$
$$2F = 33 \text{ N m}$$
$$F = 16.5 \text{ N}$$

Remember that the distance to be used is measured from the force to the pivot in each case.

## VERIFYING THE PRINCIPLE OF MOMENTS

A metre rule is balanced on a pivot (fulcrum). Masses are hung from thin strings as shown, and their positions adjusted to achieve equilibrium, with the metre rule horizontal. Repeat for several values (Fig. 3.24).

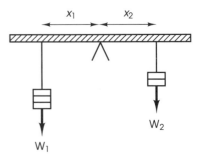

Fig. 3.24

## MEASUREMENTS

Weight added to each side
(100 g weighs 1 N)     $= W_1$ and $W_2$
Record $W_1$ and $W_2$
Distance from each weight to the pivot
$\qquad = x_1$ and $x_2$

## TREATMENT OF RESULTS

Tabulate as shown (Fig. 3.25) recording $W_1$, $x_1$, $W_2$ and $x_2$. Calculate the clockwise and anticlockwise moments.

## PRECAUTIONS

Ensure that the metre rule is initially balanced horizontally, and that it is horizontal when all other readings are taken.

| Anticlockwise | | |
|---|---|---|
| $W_1$(N) | $x_1$(cm) | Moment |
| | | |

| Clockwise | | |
|---|---|---|
| $W_2$(N) | $x_2$(cm) | Moment |
| | | |

Fig. 3.25

---

## 9 ⟩ CENTRE OF MASS

The mass of an object acts as if it is concentrated at a single point called the **centre of mass**. The object will also behave as though all its weight acts at the same place which is therefore also called the **centre of gravity** in some cases. For a regular object the *centre of mass* is the same as the *geometric centre* (Fig. 3.26).

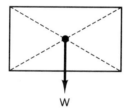

Fig. 3.26 Centre of mass.

The centre of mass of an object need **not** lie on the object. For a ring it is the centre of the ring – so the centre of mass is in space (Fig. 3.27).

Fig. 3.27 Centre of mass.

For an object to be in **equilibrium** and to be **stable** the weight, acting vertically from the centre of mass, must pass through the **base** of the object (Fig. 3.28). So to design a **stable** object, it should have a **low centre of mass** and have a **large base area**. Double-

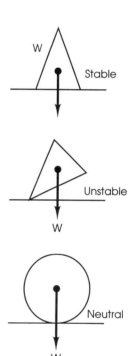

Fig. 3.28 Stable and unstable equilibrium.

decker buses are very stable – the heavy parts, such as the engine, are on the lower level. However, people are asked not to stand upstairs, because the raised centre of mass would make the bus less stable.

The first cone in Fig. 3.28 is stable because a small displacement to one side produces a moment that tips it back onto its base.

The second cone is unstable when balanced on its point because a slight push to one side produces a moment that topples it over. The third part of Fig. 3.28 shows a ball that is in the same state after a small push as it was before, so its equilibrium is neutral.

## CENTRE OF MASS OF A PLANE LAMINA

A lamina is a thin shape – usually a piece of card. Drill holes in it and suspend it from a pin held in a clamp (Fig. 3.29).

Connect a plum-line to the pin. Draw a line on the card showing the position of the plumbline. The centre of mass lies along this line. Repeat with the card suspended from Y then Z. The centre of mass is the *intersection* of the three lines.

## PRECAUTIONS

Make sure that the lamina is freely suspended. In drawing the lines mark two points behind the plumb-line carefully and join them after removing the lamina from the pin.

Fig. 3.29

---

**10> FORCE AND ACCELERATION** This is dealt with fully in the chapter on motion. However, remember that if a resultant force acts on a mass, it causes it to accelerate:

$$\text{Force} = \text{Mass} \times \text{acceleration}$$

---

# EXTENSION MATERIALS

**11> BEHAVIOUR OF MATERIALS**

The simplest behaviour under the action of a force is perhaps that of a *steel spring*. Up to a point the spring extends in a regular way as equal forces are added to it. Remembering that *extension* means "change of length", this can be written as *equal increases in force gives equal changes of extension* or as *force (F) is proportional to extension (x)*, i.e. mathematically:

$$F \, \alpha \, x$$

The graph for this behaviour is shown in Fig. 3.30. The spring would return to its original length when the forces are removed. A material which behaves in this way is called an *elastic material*.

However good the spring is, it eventually "gives" when too much force is added, and becomes permanently stretched. In this case it no longer returns to its original length. The graph now becomes like that in Fig. 3.31. Point E on the graph is the point where the force and extension *stop* going "hand in hand", i.e. where they are no longer proportional. This is called the *limit of proportionality* or the *elastic limit*. Up *to this point* the spring's behaviour is described by Hooke's law: *"Force is proportional to extension"* (provided the elastic limit is not reached).

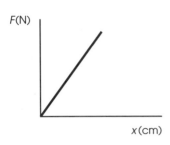

Fig. 3.30 Force-extension graph for a spring

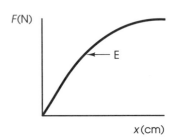

Fig. 3.31 Spring stretched beyond its elastic limit.

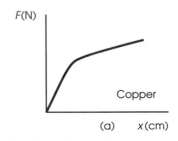

Fig. 3.32(a) Elastic behaviour of copper;

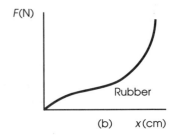

(b) Elastic behaviour of rubber.

Many materials follow Hooke's law to some extent. Two *extremes* of behaviour are shown by copper wire and a rubber band (Fig. 3.32). *Copper* suddenly gets easier to stretch and begins to flow (*plastic yielding*) until it breaks. *Rubber* gets harder and harder to stretch and finally snaps (*brittle fracture*) when it breaks.

The size of force to give a particular extension depends on the *dimensions* of the material (Fig. 3.33). A *large area* of cross-section gives a *small extension* for a *particular force* (*F*). Again longer samples extend more than short samples for a fixed force. However, the ratios

$$\frac{\text{Force}}{\text{Area}} = \text{Stress}$$

and

$$\frac{\text{Extension}}{\text{Original length}} = \text{Strain}$$

would be the same for *all* samples at their breaking points.

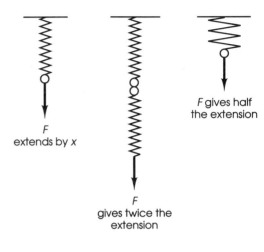

**Fig. 3.33**

---

**12> HOOKE'S LAW**

A steel spring is hung from a retort stand (Fig. 3.34). A ruler is clamped vertically near the spring. Weights are added to the spring to extend it.

## MEASUREMENTS

Original length of spring = *L*
Weight added (100 g mass weighs 1 N) = *W*
New length of spring = *l*

## TREATMENT OF RESULTS

Record weight added *W*
Record extension $x = (l - L)$

## GRAPH

Plot *W* (horizontally) against *x* (vertically) (Fig. 3.35).

## PRECAUTIONS

Make sure the ruler is vertical. Measure *l* using the same points on the spring each

time. Eliminate parallax errors by keeping the eye level with the spring when taking measurements.

**Fig. 3.34**

**Fig. 3.35**

---

**13> THE PARALLELOGRAM OF FORCES**

This is a method of adding vectors that are not in the same direction. To add together **vectors** you must add their directions as well as their sizes. This is usually done by using the parallelogram of vectors. It will probably help to think of + as meaning "followed by". Draw a scale diagram as follows:-

(i)  Choose a suitable scale for the vectors and draw one of them $v_1$ as a line of the

correct length. At its end draw the second vector $v_2$, also to its correct scale length and at the correct angle to the first one.

(ii)  The line from the start of the first vector to the end of the second vector now represents the answer that you need (in both size and direction) and is called the **resultant** R.

**Fig. 3.36**

(iii) You will make sure that your answer is correct if you "complete the parallelogram" by repeating the first two steps but use the second vector first. As the order of adding vectors does not matter, you should end at exactly the same place and therefore have a check on your resultant.

In some cases, especially the ones where the vectors are at 90°, it may be easier and more exact to draw a sketch diagram and then calculate the answer.

## EXAMPLE

A boat is following a compass bearing of 090° at 8 knots but is also in a current moving north at 6 knots. What is its true speed and direction?

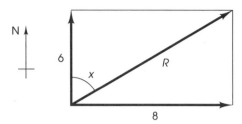

**Fig. 3.37**

You can check the following answer by doing a scale drawing with a scale of 20 mm = 1 knot. Remember that this is NOT a graph and you must use the same scale in all directions.

Using Pythagoras' rule

$$R^2 = 6^2 + 8^2$$
$$R^2 = 36 + 64 = 100$$
$$R = 10 \text{ knots}$$

also $\text{Tan } x = \dfrac{8}{6} = 1.333$

$$x = 53.1°$$

So the boat is actually moving at 10 knots on a bearing of 053.1°

---

## 14 TERMINAL VELOCITY

When an object falls in a gas or a liquid (such as a sky diver in air or a marble in a jar of oil) it has two forces acting on it. It is accelerated downwards by weight and slowed by the **drag** of the fluid through which it is passing. As it falls faster the drag force increases until it is equal and opposite to the weight. The acceleration then stops and the object falls at a uniform velocity called **terminal velocity**.

A sky diver can change the terminal velocity by altering his/her shape and therefore the air resistance but may still have a terminal velocity of 55 m/s! A parachute will produce a greater air resistance and therefore the equilibrium between the forces is achieved at a lower terminal velocity.

When a marble falls through a liquid it will accelerate at first and then fall at its terminal velocity. You can measure the terminal velocity by timing the fall over a known distance as shown in the diagram. Make sure that you only time a section *after* the acceleration has stopped. The experiment will show that the terminal velocity depends on the radius of the marble that is dropped, the viscosity of the liquid and the weight of the

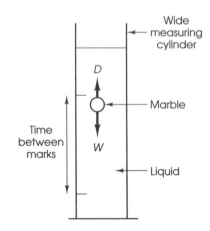

**Fig. 3.38**

marble. The viscosity is a measure of the "stiffness" of the liquid. A liquid with a bigger viscosity will flow more slowly (like treacle). The terminal velocity in water is sometimes high and oil or glycerol will give better results with ball bearings. Results may be improved if you coat the ball in some of the liquid before it is dropped to avoid air bubbles which cause errors. A longer glass tube will also improve the results.

# EXAMINATION QUESTIONS

**MULTIPLE CHOICE QUESTIONS**

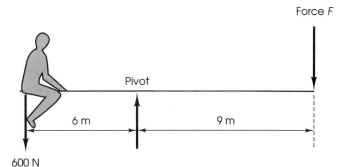

Fig. 3.40

## QUESTION 1

Three similar elastic bands are tied as shown (Fig. 3.39). One end is fixed and the other end is pulled. Which one of the following describes the new lengths of the bands?

Fig. 3.39

- A Their lengths are all equal.
- B The band nearest the wall is stretched most.
- C The middle band stretches more than the other two.
- D The band nearest the wall stretches twice as much as the other two.
- E Only the band furthest from the wall stretches.

## QUESTION 2

The force of gravity on a body is a *vector* quantity because it

- A Has size and direction
- B Acts in a vertical direction
- C Is a force of attraction
- D Has a direction but no size       (SEG)

## QUESTION 3

A steel spring obeys Hooke's law. A force of 8 N extends the spring by 40 mm. A force of 10 N will extend the spring by

- A 10 mm        C 50 mm
- B 20 mm        D 90 mm  (SEG)

## QUESTION 4

A boy, weighing 600 N, sits 6 m away from the pivot of a balanced see-saw, as shown (Fig. 3.40). What force $F$, 9 m from the pivot, is needed to balance the see-saw?

- A 300 N        D 600 N
- B 400 N        E 900 N
- C 450 N                 (ULEAC)

## QUESTION 5

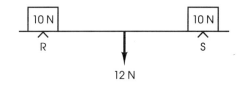

Fig. 3.41

Figure 3.41 shows two 10 N weights resting on a board of weight 12 N supported at R and S. The total upward force acting on the board is

- A 10 N        C 20 N
- B 16 N        D 32 N       (SEG)

## QUESTION 6

The diagram (Fig. 3.42) shows a man of weight 800 N standing in the middle of a uniform, rigid, horizontal plank. The plank weighs 1000 N. Which of the diagrams in Fig. 3.43 shows the forces on the plank?

(ULEAC)

Fig. 3.42

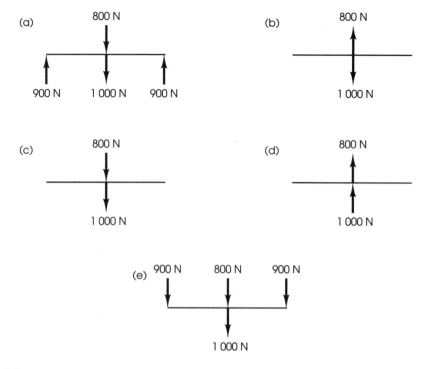

Fig. 3.43

## QUESTION 7

As it nears the moon's surface, a lunar probe of mass 10 000 kg is accelerated by the moon's gravitational field at 1.5 m/s². What force does the moon exert on the probe?

| | | | |
|---|---|---|---|
| A | 10 N | C | 1000 N |
| B | 15 N | D | 15 000 N |

(SEG)

## QUESTION 8

A force of 3 N and a force of 4 N act at right angles to each other at a point (Fig. 3.44). The magnitude of the resultant of the two forces will be

| | | | |
|---|---|---|---|
| A | 3 N | D | 7 N |
| B | 4 N | E | 12 N |
| C | 5 N | | |

(ULEAC)

Fig. 3.44

## QUESTION 9

Which of the following is not a force?

| | | | |
|---|---|---|---|
| A | Tension | C | Weight |
| B | Mass | D | Friction |

## QUESTION 10

Figure 3.45 shows designs for a double-decker bus. The symbol ⊘ represents the centre of mass. Which design will be the most stable?

(ULEAC)

Fig. 3.45

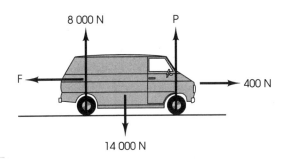

Fig. 3.46

## QUESTION 11

A front-wheel-drive car is driven at constant velocity. The forces acting on the car are shown in the diagram (Fig. 3.46). *F* is the push of the air on the car, and *P* is the total upward force on both front wheels.

(i) Name the 400 N force to the right.
(ii) Taking the weight of 1 kg to be 10 N, calculate the mass of the car.
(iii) The 400 N force to the right is suddenly doubled.
  (1) At the instant this happens, what is now the net (i.e. resultant) force moving the car forward?
  (2) Explain how this causes the car to accelerate.
  (3) Calculate this acceleration.

(ULEAC)

## QUESTION 12

An experiment is carried out to see how a steel spring stretches with the load applied. The readings are given in Table 3.1.

Table 3.1

| Load (N) | Extension (mm) |
|----------|----------------|
| 1.0 | 1.3 |
| 2.0 | 2.7 |
| 2.5 | 3.3 |
| 3.0 | 4.0 |
| 3.5 | 4.7 |
| 4.0 | 5.3 |
| 5.0 | 7.0 |
| 6.0 | 8.0 |
| 8.0 | 10.7 |

(a) On graph paper, plot a graph with extension on the vertical axis and the load on the horizontal axis. Use the points you have plotted to draw what you think is a suitable line to show how the spring behaves when it is stretched.

(b) What does the gradient of the graph tell you about the spring?

(ULEAC)

## QUESTION 13

This question is about stretching a spring. A loaded spring is mounted vertically as shown in Fig. 3.47; *h* is the height of the bottom of the load above the bench.

Fig. 3.47

(a) Describe how you would use a metre rule to measure *h*. Include the precautions you would take to make your results as reliable as possible.

(b) A student measures values of *h* for several values of load. The results are shown in Table 3.2.

Table 3.2

| Load (N) | Height h (mm) |
|----------|---------------|
| 1 | 184 |
| 2 | 172 |
| 3 | 162 |
| 4 | 150 |
| 5 | 141 |

(i) Plot a graph of *h* (*y*-axis) against load (*x*-axis).
(ii) Draw the best straight line.
(iii) Use your graph to find the load which gives a value of *h* of 180 mm.
(iv) Use your graph to find the value of *h* at a load of 1.50 N.
(v) Use your graph to find the change of load which gives a change in *h* of 1.00 mm.

(SEG)

**Fig. 3.48**

## QUESTION 14

Figure 3.48 shows a lever being used to lift a lid from a paint can.
(a) State the principle of moments.
(b) Use the principle of moments to help you calculate the force $F$ exerted by the lever on the lid. Show your working clearly.
(c) What are the size and direction of the force exerted by the lever on the pivot?
(d) State two changes which could be made to increase the size of the force $F$ if it proved to be too small to lift the lid.

(SEG)

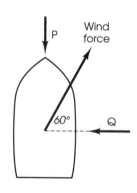

**Fig. 3.49**

## QUESTION 15

(a) (i) State the difference between a vector quantity and a scalar quantity.
   (ii) Name two vector quantities.
   (iii) Name two scalar quantities.
(b) Explain in simple language the difference between adding two vector quantities and adding two scalar quantities.
(c) A sailing boat is steered due north through the water at a steady speed. The force exerted on the boat by the wind has a magnitude of 1200 N in a direction 60 north of east. This force is balanced by two frictional forces, force $P$ opposing the forward motion of the boat and force $Q$ opposing the sideways motion of the boat (Fig. 3.49). Find by scale drawing or calculation the magnitudes of forces $P$ and $Q$.

(d) Suggest why the resistance of the water to the motion of the boat in a forward direction is likely to be much smaller than the resistance to motion in a sideways direction. The diagrams showing the shape of the boat (Fig. 3.50) may help you in your explanation.

(SEG)

**Fig. 3.50**

# OUTLINE ANSWERS

**MULTIPLE CHOICE QUESTIONS**

| Question | 1 | 2 | 3 | 4 | 5 | 6 | 7 | 8 | 9 | 10 |
|---|---|---|---|---|---|---|---|---|---|---|
| Answer | A | A | C | B | D | A | D | C | B | B |

**STRUCTURED QUESTIONS**

## ANSWER 11

(i) The force to the right is the force provided by the engine of the car. It would be named the "tractive force" or "force due to the engine".

(ii) Weight of car = 1400 N. If 1 kg weighs 10 N,

$$\text{Mass of car} = \frac{14000}{10} = 1400 \text{ kg}$$

(iii) (1) For the car to move with constant velocity, there is no resultant forward force.

$$F = 400 \text{ N}$$

At the **instant** the tractive force is doubled, $F$ is still 400 N.
Resultant forward force = (800 – 400) = 400 N.

(2) There is now a resultant force. Since $F = ma$, the car will accelerate.

(3) $F = ma$, therefore

$$a = \frac{F}{m} = \frac{400}{1400} = 0.286 \text{ m/s}^2$$

## ANSWER 12

The important point here is to draw the best straight line through the points, i.e. to show the "pattern" of the experimental values. The slope shows how "stiff" the spring is. A large slope is a weak spring – one which extends a lot for a small force applied. A strong spring would give a small slope – a lot of force would be needed to stretch the spring by a small amount.

## ANSWER 13

Graph drawing is important as stated above.

(a) **Precautions**: (1) Rule placed vertically; (2) zero of rule on bench; (3) position of load read without parallax and read at bottom of load.

(b) (iii) 1.1–1.5 N
(iv) 176–179 mm.
(v) 0.09–0.095 N

## ANSWER 14

(a) For equilibrium,

Sum of clockwise moments = Sum of anticlockwise moments about any point

(b) Moments taken about edge of tin:

Clockwise = (F × 1) N cm
Anticlockwise = (20 × 12) N cm
20 × 12 = F × 1
F = 240 N

(c) 220 N vertically downwards.

(d) (1) Increase force 20 N; (2) use longer lever.

## ANSWER 15

(a) (i) Vector – described by magnitude and direction; scalar – magnitude only.

(ii) Examples of *vectors* – force, velocity, displacement, momentum, etc.

(iii) Examples of *scalars* – mass, volume, temperature, distance, speed, etc.

(b) Scalar addition – add numbers – no direction needed; vector addition – add direction numbers or use scale diagrams.

(c) Scale diagram needed (Fig. 3.51).

$$P = 570\text{–}630 \text{ N}$$
$$Q = 1000\text{–}1100 \text{ N}$$

Fig. 3.51

(d) The forward direction is streamlined, but not the sideways direction. There is a bigger area sideways so more water to push.

# TUTOR'S QUESTION AND ANSWER

**1 > QUESTION**

Theory suggests that, when a beam is loaded at the centre, the deflection $x$ is directly proportional to the cube of $l$, the distance between the supports, provided that the same force $W$ is applied for each value of $l$ (Fig. 3.52). In other words, $x = kl^3$ where $k$ is constant.

**Fig. 3.52**

You are required to carry out an experiment to confirm that $x = kl^3$ using a metre rule as a beam. From initial checks you know that when a metre rule rests on edge supports 0.90 m apart, its centre is deflected by about 1 cm when a load of 8 N is hung from the centre. Describe:

(a) How you would set up the apparatus.
(b) How you would make your measurements.
(c) The number and range of measurements you would make.
(d) How you would use your measurements to test the theory.

**2 > ANSWER**

(a) Lay the metre rule on movable supports. Load with 8 N (800 g mass) at the centre of supports. Make sure the unloaded rule is horizontal. Measure distance using a vertical rule, eye level with the lower side of the "beam" each time.

(b) Change $l$ by moving the supports and measure the distance between the top sides of the pivots. Eye above the beam and directly over the edges of the pivots.

(c) Since a graph must be drawn, at least five sets of values of $l$ must be made. Repeat each set and take a mean value if

necessary. Vary $l$ between about 0.5 and 0.9 m.

(d) There are several possibilities:

(i) Check numbers from tabulated results. If $x = kl^3$, then doubling $l$ would give $2^3$ times the value of $x$, i.e. 8 times the value of $x$.

(ii) Plot a graph. If $x = kl^3$, a graph of $x$ against $l^3$ will give a straight line. Presumably there will be a degree of experimental error so if there appears to be such a pattern, then $x = kl^3$.

# STUDENT'S ANSWER WITH THE EXAMINER'S COMMENTS

## STUDENT ANSWER TO QUESTION 12

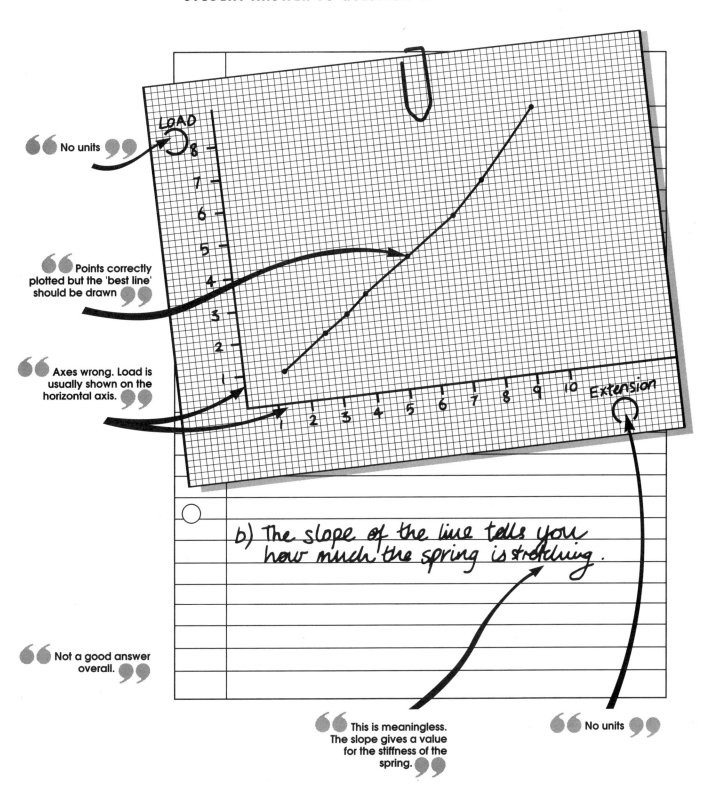

**No units**

**Points correctly plotted but the 'best line' should be drawn**

**Axes wrong. Load is usually shown on the horizontal axis.**

**Not a good answer overall.**

b) The slope of the line tells you how much the spring is stretching.

**This is meaningless. The slope gives a value for the stiffness of the spring.**

**No units**

# MORE EXAMINER'S COMMENTS
# FOUNDATION AND CENTRAL TIER

1. A girl weighing 600 N sits 2 metres away from the pivot of a uniform see-saw. The see-saw is pivoted at its centre of mass.

**Say that moment = Fd**

**Using 'Principle of Moments'?**

**Could be more clear but probably gets 2 marks**

What force, F, three metres from the pivot, is needed to balance the see-saw? Show clearly how you get your answer.

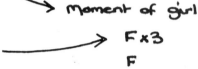

Moment of girl    = 600 x 2   = 1200

F x 3             = 1200

F                 = 400

Force F = ...**400**..... N   (2)

2. The diagram below shows a trolley on a flat bench. A string is attached to the trolley and to a spring balance as shown

When the trolley is pulled, so that the spring balance reads 0.5 N, the trolley does not move.

**1 mark**

What is the frictional force opposing the trolley's motion? ..... **0·5 N** .........

**Explain more about the forces being equal and opposite**

Explain your answer ...**The forces balance**.....................

.........................................................(2)

3. Here are two diagrams showing the same spring. In each case when the load is removed the spring returns to its original length.

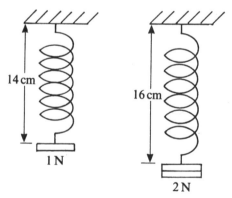

How long is the spring when no load is attached to it?

**Probably 2 marks. Not very clear but does give the correct answer. Don't be afraid to use words**

2N    = 16            1N  = 14

So 1 extra N = 2cm
So it starts at 12

Length = ......**12**........ cm
(2)

# REVIEW SHEET

■ The side of a beam that is under tension is _____ .

■ Forces can change objects in three different ways. These are

   1. _____ .

   2. _____ .

   3. _____ .

■ The force needed just to start an object moving is equal and opposite to the force called _____.

■ The force needed just to keep the object moving is less than the force to start it moving and is called _____.

■ When an object rests on a surface a force is produced that acts at _____ to the surface and is called a _____.

■ The three main types of Field are _____ , _____ and _____.

■ A vector is a quantity that has both _____ and _____.

■ The turning effect of a force about a pivot is called its _____.

■ A stable racing car will have a _____ centre of mass.

■ The total of two forces is called their _____.

■ Two vectors can be added by using a scale diagram called the _____ ____ _____.

■ Springs obey _____ law when they stretch until they reach the _____.

■ A girl pulls on a door handle with a force of 20 N. If the door is 1.2 m wide the moment of the force is _____.

■ Two boys push a box in opposite directions with forces of 100 N and 250 N. The size of the resultant is _____.

■ A teacher has a weight of 700 N. When he stands still the force of the floor on him is _____.

■ Complete the following equation

   weight = _____.

■ If your teacher weighs 600 N her mass is _____ kg.

■ The gravitational force between two objects depends directly on their _____ and inversely on _____.

■ When a falling object reaches terminal velocity its weight is equal and opposite to the _____.

■ A quantity with size but no direction is a _____.

■ A 10 N force stretches spring by 4 cm. A 5 N force will stretch the same spring by _____ cm.

■ The point where the extension of a stretched wire stops being proportional to the load on it is called _____.

■ The force F that will balance the beam is _____.

**Fig. 3.53**

# CHAPTER 4

# ENERGY, WORK AND POWER

## GETTING STARTED

Energy is a basic idea in physics; in fact you could explain what "physics" is by saying that it is a study of *energy* forms, and their relationship with each other and with matter. So an understanding of energy is essential to an understanding of physics.

The idea of **work** is inseparable from the idea of energy, because whenever work is done, energy is transformed and if an energy change takes place work is done.

**Power** is a measure of how quickly work is done (the rate of doing work, or the rate of transfer of energy).

# ESSENTIAL PRINCIPLES

## 1 ▷ FOODS, FUELS AND ENERGY

Living things need energy simply to be alive! Most plants obtain their energy directly from the sun and are able to "manufacture" food using a process called **photosynthesis** (Fig. 4.1). Many animals obtain their food by eating the *cells of plants* where energy is stored as chemical energy. Flesh-eating animals obtain their food by eating the *cells of other animals* which again are a store of chemical energy. The food in each case is not itself energy, but *energy can be released from the food during respiration*.

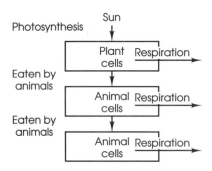

Fig. 4.1 Our energy comes originally from the sun.

In the long run all living things derive energy ultimately from the sun. This is even the case, indirectly, with non-living things which rely on *fuel* to make them run. A steam engine may need *coal*, which is a store of chemical energy. A car of a bus may need petrol or diesel, i.e. fuel products which result

from the refining of *oil*. The fuel in each case is not itself energy — it is a *store* of chemical energy — but as we shall see *energy can be released from the fuel during burning*.

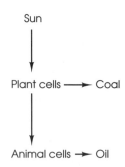

Fig. 4.2

Coal and oil were formed over millions of years by the action of pressure and heat on the decaying remains of plants and animals (Fig. 4.2). So the chemical energy in the plant and animal cells became trapped in the final products of coal and oil. These are called *fossil fuels*. The energy released today when coal or oil is burned originated from the sun millions of years ago.

We have already seen that when food is taken in by a living thing the process of *respiration* converts chemical energy to *other energy forms*. Similarly, when a fuel is *burned* the chemical energy stored in it is changed to heat *(thermal energy)*.

## 2 ▷ KINETIC ENERGY

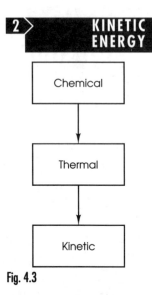

Fig. 4.3

The release of energy in the human body or in a vehicle can enable it to move. An object which is *moving* has **kinetic energy** (kinetic just means "movement"). To make a car move the energy originally in the fuel has undergone a number of changes; these can be summed up in an energy-flow diagram as in Fig. 4.3. The greater the speed required of a person, the more "fuel" has to be burned, so that a person running has more kinetic energy than when walking (Fig. 4.4).

A greater fuel consumption is needed to get a large-mass car moving at the same speed as a small-mass car. Therefore the *larger the mass* the *more kinetic energy is needed* for the same speed to be produced

Fig. 4.4 Faster speed means more kinetic energy.

(Fig. 4.5). This can be summed up as:

Kinetic energy = ½ (mass) × (velocity)²

or

$$KE = \tfrac{1}{2}mv^2$$

(See also Ch. 5.)

A dynamo can change **kinetic** energy into **electrical** energy. Electrical energy can also be obtained directly from **chemical** energy using a torch battery or a car battery. Electrical energy is a very useful form (a)

**Fig. 4.5** More mass means more kinetic energy.

because it can easily be **transported**, and (b) because it can easily be **converted** to other energy forms.

---

## 3 > POTENTIAL ENERGY

❝❝ Avoid describing potential energy as "stored" energy. This can cause confusion with other stored forms like the chemical energy stored in food. ❞❞

Electrical → Kinetic → Potential

**Fig. 4.6**

A motor converts **electrical** energy into **kinetic** energy. It can then be used to lift a mass off the ground (Fig. 4.6). Now if the mass **falls back** to the ground, the motor would run like a dynamo, turning kinetic energy back into electrical (Fig. 4.7).

Potential → Kinetic → Electrical

**Fig. 4.7**

While the mass was above the ground, it also had energy simply because it **was** above the ground. This energy is available for conversation into kinetic energy and then into electricity. The energy of an object because of its **position** (usually above the ground) is called **gravitational potential energy**.

"Potential" energy is "energy-in-waiting"; waiting to be converted to kinetic energy. It could also be described as the maximum energy reclaimable from a system.

A different type of system with potential energy is one with a **stretched** or **compressed elastic material**, like a rubber band, spring or animal muscle. A stretched catapult elastic has energy "waiting" to be released as kinetic energy (Fig. 4.8).

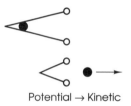

Potential → Kinetic

**Fig. 4.8**

A mass on a stretched spring will obtain kinetic energy when the spring is **released** (Fig. 4.9). This energy form is called **strain** (or elastic) **potential energy**.

Potential ⟶ Kinetic

**Fig. 4.9**

---

## 4 > CONSERVATION OF ENERGY

A number of **forms** of energy can be identified: chemical, electrical, kinetic, potential (both gravitational and strain), thermal (or internal energy), light, sound and nuclear.

Any one of these can be changed into

another energy form, but it is found that whatever change takes place the total energy available at the start is **equal** to the total at the end (taking everything in the system into account). This is called **energy conservation** and is sometimes stated as "energy cannot be created or destroyed".

In following through a sequence of energy changes it sometimes seems, however, that energy *has* been "lost". This is often due to the unwanted production of heat or sound in part of the system, where energy becomes shared among many particles, including those of the atmosphere.

Whenever we do work we change energy from one form to another. Whenever we use energy it ends up more spread out than when it started, often in the form of heat. This is called **energy degradation**.

## 5 > WORK AND ENERGY

Many laboratory examples of energy conversion involve an object moving at some time (even if the movement is the drift of electrons in a wire to give an electric current). When a force moves, it is said that *work* is being done. The greater the force, and the larger the distance, the greater the quantity of work.

$$\text{Work} = \text{Force } (F) \times \text{distance } (d)$$
$$\text{W} = F \times d$$

Work is measured in *joules* (J).

(Notice that in Ch. 3 the product, force × distance, measures the *moment* of a force, but the distance measured for a moment is at 90° to the force. In measuring *work* the distance is measured in the *same direction* as the force acts.)

If a system has energy, it can do work. If *work is done, energy is converted*. So measuring work is the same as measuring energy converted (Fig. 4.10).

💬💬 An important point. The words "Work done" and "Energy converted" mean exactly the same thing. 💬💬

Fig. 4.12 Potential energy  kinetic energy

Fig. 4.13 Energy is converted to heat when a ball bounces.

However, if the ball bounces it may only rise 0.75 m (Fig. 4.13). Its potential energy at the top of the bounce is now (5 × 0.75) = 3.75 J. According to the laws of conservation of energy the "missing" (10 − 3.75) = 6.25 J, must be present as heat in the ground and the ball, and some perhaps as sound when the ball hits the ground. This type of example can be generalised (Fig. 4.14).

To lift a mass *m* up to a height *h*:

$$\text{Force moved} = mg$$

(*g* = gravitational field strength)

$$\text{Work done} = mgh.$$

and **potential energy** = *mgh*.

Or, in words,

potential energy = weight × height.

Fig. 4.10

Fig. 4.11 Work done = energy converted.

■ *Example (a)* Suppose a motor lifts a 3 kg mass 8 m off the ground (Fig. 4.11). The *force* acting on the mass = 30 N (since *g* = 10 N/kg). Therefore the *work done* is

$$30 \times 8 = 240 \text{ J}$$

and the *energy converted* to potential energy = 240 J. If the mass now falls freely to the ground it will also have 240 J of kinetic energy just before it hits the ground.

■ **Example (b)** A football weighing 5 N dropped 2 m from the ground will have (5 × 2) = 10 J of kinetic energy just before hitting the ground. It would have 10 J of potential energy before being dropped, and 10 J of work would have to be done to lift it up in the first place (Fig. 4.12).

Fig. 4.14

## 6 ▷ POWER

Motors, engines and people can do work at different **rates** (i.e. some do the job more quickly than others). Suppose motor A lifts the weight of 40 N in 5 s and B lifts the same weight in 3 s, both through the same distance of 3 m (Fig. 4.15). Then B is more **powerful** than A, although both do the same work.

Work = (40 × 3) = 120 J

**Fig. 4.15 Comparison of two motors.**

**Power** is the work done in 1 s; it is therefore measured in joules per second or watts (W):

$$\text{Power A} = \frac{120}{5} = 24 \text{ W}$$

$$\text{Power B} = \frac{120}{3} = 40 \text{ W}$$

Since **work** is equivalent to **energy transferred**, we can say:

A transfers 24 joules of energy per second
B transfers 40 joules of energy per second

More formally, **power is the rate of doing work or the rate of transfer of energy**, i.e.

$$\text{Power} = \frac{\text{Work done}}{\text{Time}} = \frac{\text{Energy transfer}}{\text{Time}}$$

■ **Example (c)** If a person has a mass of 70 kg and climbs a flight of stairs 3 m high in 4 s, then

70 kg weighs (70 × 10) newtons

Work done = Energy transferred
= 70 × 10 × 3 = 2100 J

$$\text{Power developed} = \frac{2100}{4} = 525 \text{ W}$$

## POWER OUTPUT OF A MOTOR

The motor is connected in series to a 12 V DC supply and a rheostat (Fig. 4.16). The load is attached to a line-shaft unit coupled to the motor. In a preliminary run the rheostat is adjusted to give a suitable running speed for the motor. The motor is switched on, and a stop-clock started as the load passes a point X marked on a rule, and stopped as it passes point Y. The load is weighed and the distance XY measured with a metre rule.

**Fig. 4.16**

## RESULTS

Weight of load = $W$ (N)
Distance XY = $h$ (m)
Time = $t$ (s)

## CALCULATION

$$\text{Power} = \frac{\text{Work done}}{\text{Time}} = \frac{W \times h}{t}$$

## PRECAUTIONS

The time is likely to be short, so the distance XY should be as large as practically possible and the motor speed as slow as possible. Several runs should be made and a **mean value** of time taken.

## 7 ▷ MACHINES

The word "machine" has become a very general one – but in science it has a special meaning. An engine is a system which enables an energy conversion to take place, e.g. tractor, dishwasher, record player. A machine causes a **change** in the way the forces involved in energy conversions act. So a machine does not itself convert energy in a strict sense. The change in the way forces act can be:

1. Direction change;
2. Force increase;
3. Force reduction.

## (A) A SINGLE PULLEY

The weight $W$ being lifted is called the **load force**. The pulling force $F$ is called the **effort**

Fig. 4.17 A pulley acting as a direction changer.

*force* (Fig. 4.17). With this machine the load and effort forces are equal. But to lift this load *upwards* the effort acts *downwards*. This machine is a **direction changer**.

## (B) SIMPLE LEVER

With this arrangement a small effort force $F$ can be used to lift a larger load force $W$ (Fig. 4.18). This machine is a **force multiplier**. However, the effort has to move a large distance to make the load move a small distance, so the *work done* is the same, and there is no multiplication of energy. Other examples: nutcrackers, pulley hoists, wheel and axle, car jack, spanner, screwdriver.

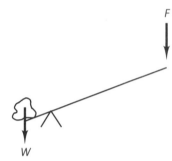

Fig. 4.18 A lever acts as a force multiplier.

You can work out the size of the forces involved by using the principle of moments. Question 14 at the end of chapter 3 illustrates this.

It is also useful to have a measure of how good a force multiplier is and this is called the **mechanical advantage** where:

$$\text{Mechanical advantage} = \frac{\text{Load force}}{\text{Effort force}}$$

## (C) GEAR SYSTEMS

As bicycle owners will realise, a gear system can act as a **force multiplier**, i.e. a small force applied gives a larger force output – this is like cycling in low gear. The "pedal" side of the gearing would need a large number of teeth and the wheel side a small number (Fig. 4.19).

Fig. 4.19 A gear wheel acting as a distance multiplier.

However, if the reverse is used (high gear) then a large force is applied and a small force results, but the distance travelled by the wheel side is increased. This is now acting as a **distance multiplier**.

A distance multiplier will change the speed that forces move at. The load usually moves more slowly than the effort. We can measure how good a distance multiplier is by its **velocity ratio**.

$$\text{Velocity ratio} = \frac{\text{distance moved by effort}}{\text{distance moved by load}}$$

## 8 EFFICIENCY

Energy is always conserved, but when energy is put into a system, like a pulley or a motor, not all the available energy turns into the energy form you require. A motor is designed to convert electrical energy into kinetic energy, but of course some heat and sound will be produced – so less kinetic energy is available at the end than there was electrical energy at the start.

$$\text{Efficiency} = \frac{\text{Energy output}}{\text{Energy input}}$$

$$= \frac{\text{Work output}}{\text{Work input}}$$

And since power is energy change per second, then efficiency is also

$$\frac{\text{Power output}}{\text{Power input}}$$

Efficiency has no units. It is a *ratio*. It can also be expressed as a percentage: e.g. if a motor is supplied at 60 W and the power output is 40 W, then its efficiency is 40/60 = 0.66 or 66 per cent.

## CAUSES OF INEFFICIENCY

### HEAT

Electrical devices must be inefficient because when a current flows a wire becomes hotter. It follows that no motor or dynamo can be 100 per cent efficient for its particular purpose. However, an immersion heater in water is close to 100 per cent efficient for its particular purpose.

### FRICTION

Friction is a force, *not* an energy form. However, friction is responsible for converting kinetic energy to heat. A rope moving over a pulley does *work* against friction – so not all the energy input is available to give potential energy to a load.

### LOADING

This is particularly true of mechanical systems. A pulley system has its own weight, so to lift a load, some energy is used in lifting the pulley system itself. It would be silly to push a single brick in a wheelbarrow because most of your energy would be given to the barrow and little to the brick. The effect of the weight of the barrow becomes smaller, in proportion, as the weight of the bricks becomes larger.

## 9 ALTERNATIVE ENERGY

### ■ Chemical energy

**Chemical energy** is contained in many chemicals by the way that their atoms are bonded together. If you react chemicals together so that their atoms are joined in a different way then the new chemicals may contain a different amount of energy. If the new chemicals need less energy to hold them together than before then the extra energy is released. This is an **"exothermic"** reaction and the energy is usually released as heat. Most fuels that we burn release chemical energy as heat in this way.

e.g. If you light a candle then the wax (which is the fuel) burns with oxygen from the air and makes carbon dioxide and water. These need less energy than the more complicated wax and the spare energy is released as heat and light energy.

e.g. Our bodies take in chemical energy as food (and store some of it as fat!). When the cells need energy they can burn some of this fuel by combining it with the oxygen that is transported by the blood stream. The new chemicals from the reaction are carbon dioxide and water vapour which need less energy. They are taken away by the blood stream and the cells get the "spare" energy.

i.e. We use an **exothermic** reaction.

Chemical energy can be both renewable (sugars grown in plants) or non-renewable (oil products).

## NON-RENEWABLE RESOURCES

### ■ Fossil fuels

**Fossil fuels** such as coal, oil and natural gas are the remains of plants and animals that have been trapped between layers of rock. They are a valuable source of many chemicals as well as fuels such as diesel, petrol (gasoline) and paraffin (kerosine). They are only present in the earth's crust in limited quantities and are running out as we use more and more. Since we cannot make more of these fuels – the natural process that formed them took millions of years – they are called **non-renewable** resources. Chemical energy in the fuel is changed into heat energy when the fuel is burned.

Another main disadvantage is the production of air pollution including carbon dioxide which increases the "**greenhouse effect**" and is therefore slowly changing the temperature of the earth's surface and its climate. Some coal and oil contains small quantities of sulphur which forms sulphur dioxide when it is burned. This dissolves in moisture in the air and leads to **acid rain** that is believed to damage plants and can accumulate sufficiently to kill plant and animal life in lakes and rivers. The plants and animals that these fossil fuels were made from got their energy from the sun – so the sun is the original source of all this energy.

### ■ Nuclear Energy

**Nuclear energy** comes from the energy released when atoms of uranium or plutonium are split into smaller pieces. The smaller pieces need less energy to hold them together and the "spare" energy is released as heat energy. This is much cleaner to use and creates much less air pollution than using fossil fuels but the new atoms created are usually radioactive. This means that some of the waste from the power station can be dangerous for many years into the future. The original fuel, uranium, is mined as uranium ore and will eventually run out like the fossil fuels although far less fuel is actually used. The sun is **not** the source of this particular type of energy as the uranium was made in the earth at the time of its formation. Many industrialised countries now produce quite a large fraction of their electrical energy from nuclear power stations.

## RENEWABLE RESOURCES

These can be put into two main groups:

Solar energy, wind power, wave power, hydroelectric power and biomass all derive their energy from the sun whereas tidal energy and geothermal energy do not.

### ■ Solar energy

This is the wide range of electromagnetic radiation that comes to us from the sun. When the radiation hits a suitable surface the energy is turned into heat energy. **Solar energy** can be used to heat water in solar panels. In some hot countries mirrors have been used to focus enough energy into one place to create a solar furnace. The energy can also be used to produce a small electric current from a solar cell. Banks of these solar cells can then be used to charge batteries and provide electrical energy. The energy per $m^2$ in colder countries is not sufficient to make large scale use practical and the weather makes it unreliable but it does have some applications in electronics where the energy required is small – calculators and radios work well on solar power with a storage or back-up battery. Solar energy is used to power satellites and a 50cm square panel should produce enough energy to run a light.

### ■ EXAMPLE

If the solar energy reaching the earth is 1250 $W/m^2$, what power can be obtained from a solar cell that measures 50 cm × 50 cm and is 12% efficient?

Area of panel = $0.5 \times 0.5 = 0.25 \text{ m}^2$

power output = area × solar power
× efficiency

$$= \frac{0.25 \times 1250 \times 12}{100}$$

$$= 37.5 \text{ W}$$

### ■ Wind power

**Wind power** can be derived from modern windmills which have rotors that are rather like the propellers of an aeroplane in shape. Large rotors can produce enough electricity by driving a generator to be economical, especially for charging batteries, but there can be problems with lack of wind – or too much – some of the time! If these windmills are to provide an alternative energy source on a large scale there would have to be a lot of them on hills facing the wind and many people would find the effect on the landscape unacceptable. The original source of energy is the sun. The kinetic energy of the wind is turned into the kinetic energy of the rotors and then into electrical energy by the generator. Denmark plans to generate 10% of its electricity from wind turbines by the year 2000. California already generates 1500 MW in this way. To give some idea of the size that a modern generator might be, there is an experimental one in England which is 45 m high, has blades 55 m in diameter and can generate 1 MW. A smaller one seen on a farm near my home has blades about 1 m in diameter and charges a 12V car battery. Several sites in the north of England, on the Pennines and the west coast are at present being set up as wind farms with between 4 and 15 large generators on each site.

### ■ Wave power

Sea waves can carry large quantities of energy as a large mass of water is being moved up and down. To exploit **wave power** involves strings of machines on the surface of the sea. As the waves go by they drive part of the machine up and down and this drives a hydraulic pump. The fluid driven by the pump in turn drives a generator. The waves emerge smaller than before meeting the machine. The main problems have been the large variation in size of the waves and the damage done by bad weather. A lot of machines are needed and suitable sites can be difficult to find. The original source of this energy is the sun – NOT the moon which produces tidal energy!!

The kinetic energy of the water in the waves is turned into electrical energy by these machines.

### ■ Hydroelectric power

**Hydroelectric power** is used in many countries where there are rivers large enough to provide the energy required. In some countries the rivers do not fall through enough height or have a large enough rate of flow to produce large quantities of energy but many are used on a smaller scale. The important factors are the mass of the water and the height that it falls through. The gravitational potential energy of the water is converted into kinetic energy as it falls and then into electrical energy by turbines. The original source of the energy is the sun which drives the water cycle, producing the rain that fills the rivers.

There are important hydroelectric schemes at several places where there are big waterfalls, e.g. Niagara Falls on the Canada–USA border and at the Victoria Falls (Zimbabwe–Zambia). In other countries large dams have created the necessary water pressure.

### ■ Biomass

**Biomass** involves using the sunlight to grow quick-growing plants with a high chemical energy content, usually in sugars. The energy is then extracted from the chemicals produced in the plants. In Brazil sugar is extracted from plants and fermented to produce alcohol. This can then be used to power engines in cars instead of petrol. In the USA a lot of the petrol has alcohol added to it (about 9%). The process is only renewable if you keep replanting the land. Burning wood is using the same process but the wood can take much longer to replace as trees are quite slow growing. If the land is poor it may be difficult to grow more trees before the soil is eroded by wind or rain, making replanting difficult and leaving the land barren. Forests used in this way must be replaced as they are part of the natural cycle that balances carbon dioxide and oxygen in the air. The original source of energy is the sun. The energy in the sunlight has been used by the green chlorophyll in plant leaves to build up more complex chemicals from carbon dioxide and water. These new chemicals therefore contain more energy. (The process is called photosynthesis.)

Carbon dioxide + water + sunlight ⟶ glucose + oxygen

We then reverse the process by burning the chemicals to get the energy back out as heat energy.

> ❝ Hydroelectric power is also a well established form in some regions, and could be included. Problems are siting and land use. ❞

A gas known as **biogas** is produced when bacteria break down the waste from farms, especially cow dung and pig slurry. For good production the bacteria need to be warm – at about 35°C – and the gas is then about 60% methane and 40% carbon dioxide. Biogas produced in this way provides energy for more than 30 million people in China.

Fig. 4.20

### ■ Tidal energy

Ocean currents contain a very large mass of moving water and so they have a lot of kinetic energy. In some countries the tides are being used as an energy source. Tidal energy is produced by the relative motion of the moon around the earth. We can use it by making the tide flow through barriers across bays or narrow straits, driving turbines as it does so. The main problem is in finding suitable sites and the large initial building costs. There are also worries about the ecological effects of the reduced tide after the barrier and visual impact of the barrier on coastal sites. The kinetic energy of the water is turned into electrical energy by the turbines driving generators.

### ■ Geothermal energy

Geothermal energy is used by pumping water under pressure down to hot rocks below the earth's surface. The water returns heated and the heat energy can be used as the alternative resource. The centre of the earth has a temperature of about 4500°C and the temperature increases by about 20°C per 100 m as you drill down into a thermally active area. The original source of the energy is radioactive decay within the earth's core which keeps the interior of the earth molten. The process is being trialled in a number of areas of the world, especially those that have volcanic areas where natural hot springs already exist. In Iceland about half of the population live in houses heated by natural hot water and there are 9 power stations of this type in Japan. About 8% of New Zealand's electricity is produced in this way from natural steam wells in the North Island.

The renewable and non-renewable resources in the previous section are all regarded as **primary sources** of energy as they are used as the fuel at the start of a series of energy changes. *Electrical energy* is different because it must always be made from one of these other sources. It is an example of a **secondary source**. The main reason why we all like to use electricity is that it is quick and easy to "transport" once a connecting cable system (a national grid) has been built to connect towns and villages. Places where there is a greater demand can be given energy almost instantly from places where the demand is less. The user also sees electricity as cleaner and more pollution free than other sources but this can be an illusion as you only see the final product and not the power station that produces it.

**11** ▷ **STORING ENERGY**

The most common way to **store** energy is as electrical energy in rechargeable batteries. These work by having a chemical reaction that goes in one direction when they are used but which can be reversed when the battery is recharged. The coiled spring in a clock or watch contains potential energy that can easily be restored. Weights are sometimes lifted so that the energy is stored as gravitational potential energy and is released as the weight is allowed to fall. This was used for many years as a way to power clocks but the same principle is now used in some power stations where it is possible to build a water reservoir both above and below the station. The system is called *pumped storage*. It is more efficient to run the generators in a power station continuously. Unfortunately we do not use the electrical energy at a constant rate and the power stations sometimes produce more energy than we require and sometimes less. When too much electrical energy is being produced it is used to pump water up into the higher reservoir where it has a lot of gravitational potential energy.

When we require more energy the water is allowed to flow back down again and the energy is converted back into electrical energy by turbines that drive generators.

Fig. 4.21

# EXTENSION MATERIALS

**12▷ MORE MACHINES**

## LEVERS

You can find the connection between the load and the effort by assuming that the forces just balance and then using the **principle of moments**. This will then tell you the **mechanical advantage**. Most levers belong to one of three types as shown in the examples in the diagram.

In each case think of the distance from the effort to the pivot as $l_1$ and the distance from the load to the pivot as $l_2$. If the effort just balances the load then, using the principle of moments

$$\text{load } l_2 = \text{effort } l_1$$

$$\text{M.A.} = \frac{\text{load}}{\text{effort}} = \frac{l_1}{l_2}$$

*Type 1*

In the case of the crow bar, $l_1$ is bigger than $l_2$ and you have a very useful M.A., i.e. the force that you put in (effort) is multiplied by quite a large number so it can move a large load. Levers often come in pairs in simple tools. A pair of scissors or pliers will have two of the first type of lever so that a small effort can act on quite a large load.

*Type 2*

In the wheelbarrow the load and effort are on the same side of the pivot but the distances still make the M.A. larger than 1 (because the effort is farther away from the pivot than the load). It will be easier to move the wheelbarrow if the load is at the front, close to the wheel, so that the M.A. is as large as

(a) A crowbar

(b) A wheelbarrow

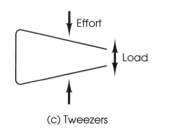

(c) Tweezers

Fig. 4.22

possible. Both of these first two types are **force multipliers**.

*Type 3*

In the tongs or tweezers the load is at a greater distance from the pivot than the effort so the M.A. is less than 1. This pair of levers is for convenience rather than for making a large force. When the muscles that we call the biceps pull on the forearm, the load in the hand is further away from the pivot (elbow) than the effort and the lever is one of the third type. This third type of lever are **distance multipliers**.

Many simple machines use levers. Some other examples are a spanner, the pedal of a cycle, a door handle and nut-crackers.

## PULLEYS

There are two common ways of using a pulley.

**Fig. 4.23**

A *fixed pulley* is only able to rotate on its axle and the axle is kept firmly in place usually on an overhead beam (see Fig. 4.23). The load hangs on the rope on one side and is supported by the effort on the other side of the pulley. The effort and the load must move through the same distance so

V.R. = velocity ratio = 1.

The tension in the rope will be the same on both sides of the pulley so that the load = effort and

M.A. = mechanical advantage = 1.

In a real case the effort has to be larger than the load so that it can overcome friction in the pulley and this will mean that the M.A. is a bit less than 1 and the efficiency is less than 100%. You might be able to improve the M.A. and the efficiency by oiling the bearings on the axle – but you will never reach M.A. = 1. In spite of this the system is often used because it is easier to use your weight to pull downwards than to pull or lift upwards.

A *moving pulley* will move up and down with its load (see Fig. 4.24). The load will only move half as far as the effort moves. Imagine pulling up the rope at the effort by 1 m. The rope on each side of the pulley will shorten by 0.5 m

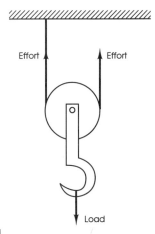

**Fig. 4.24**

and the load rises by 0.5 m. This will mean that

V.R. = velocity ratio = 2.

If the tension in the rope on each side of the pulley is the same then there will be a force equal to the effort pulling upwards on each side of the pulley. A load can be lifted that is twice as large as the effort and

M.A. = mechanical advantage = 2.

In a real moving pulley there is friction to be overcome and the pulley also has to be lifted along with the load. Each of these increase the effort needed and the real M.A. will be less than 2 so that the efficiency is less than 100%. Oil, good bearings and a lightweight pulley will all improve the M.A. The snag is that the effort may be difficult to apply because it is upwards. The two types of pulley can be combined to produce a working system with a small but useful gain in the force applied, by passing the effort rope from the moving pulley over a fixed pulley. There will still be friction in both pulleys and the moving pulley has to be lifted with the load. More pulleys can be introduced to improve the machine further.

A *block and tackle* uses one rope with several fixed and moving pulleys to produce a bigger M.A. (see Fig. 4.25). This system is often used in factories to move heavy loads and in smaller systems such as those used to lift engines out of cars.

In the system in the diagram each of the 5 lengths of rope supporting the lower pulleys and the load will have a tension equal to the effort. This means that the maximum possible M.A. is 5.

Remember that you are not getting "something for nothing" – you have produced a force larger than the effort but it will move through a distance that is smaller. In a real system the pulleys in each of the two sets would be the same size and side by side to save space and weight. The maximum M.A. will be the same as the number of ropes supporting the moving pulleys.

**Fig. 4.25**

## 13 EXPERIMENTAL WORK

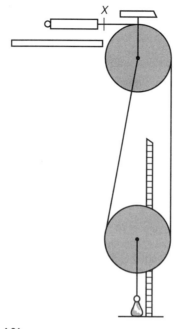

**Fig. 4.26**

the string leaving the upper pulley. The force-meter is used to raise the load, say 50 cm.

### RESULTS TAKEN

| | |
|---|---|
| Weight of load | $= W$ (N) |
| Force-meter reading | $= F$ (N) |
| Distance moved by load | $= h$ (m) |
| Distance moved by point X | $= d$ (m) |

### CALCULATION

| | |
|---|---|
| Work (*input*) done by effort | $= F \times d$ |
| Work (*output*) on load | $= W \times h$ |

$$\text{Efficiency} = \frac{\text{Work output}}{\text{Work input}}$$

$$= \frac{(W \times h)}{(F \times d)} \times 100\%$$

### EFFICIENCY OF A PULLEY SYSTEM

A simple pulley system is set up as shown (Fig. 4.26) clamped firmly at the upper pulley. A load is attached to the lower pulley. Two metre rules are fixed horizontally and vertically as shown. A marker X is attached to

### PRECAUTIONS

Rules must be horizontal or vertical. Check with set square and plumb-line. Ensure that the distance moved by X and the load are made without parallax errors.

## 14 ENERGY ARROWS AND CHAINS

Energy changes are often shown best by a diagram. If the change is a single one it is best shown by an **arrow diagram**. Begin with the original energy form and clearly label the parts of the arrow as the new forms are produced. You can try to make the width of the new parts of the arrow show the proportions of the new types of energy that are produced but this can only be approximate.

If there are several changes following one another then it is best to use a chain diagram. This sort of diagram usually only follows the energy from the source through the main

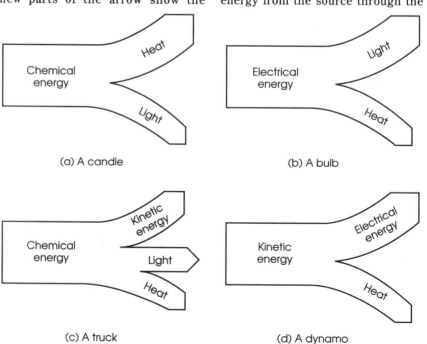

(a) A candle

(b) A bulb

(c) A truck

(d) A dynamo

**Fig. 4.27**

changes and ignores the energy "lost" into other forms on the way.

In the chain diagram for the car, energy lost as heat etc. is not shown but the overall pattern of a more complicated system would be clearer when shown this way. You can fit side arrows to show important losses if you wish.

Fig. 4.28

# EXAMINATION QUESTIONS

MULTIPLE CHOICE QUESTIONS

## QUESTION 1

Which of the following is *designed* to convert electrical energy into sound energy?

    A    Mains transformer
    B    Loudspeaker
    C    Crystal microphone
    D    Telephone mouthpiece
    E    Recording tape       (ULEAC)

## QUESTION 2

Which of the following best describes the energy changes which take place when a steam engine drives a generator which lights a lamp?

    A    Thermal–Light–Sound–Kinetic
    B    Kinetic–Light–Thermal–Electrical
    C    Thermal–Kinetic–Electrical–Thermal and Light
    D    Electrical–Kinetic–Thermal–Light
    E    Thermal–Sound–Kinetic–Electrical
           (ULEAC)

## QUESTION 3

A bullet strikes a fixed target and is brought to rest. The main energy changes when this happens are

    A    Kinetic to potential and sound
    B    Kinetic to sound and internal energy
    C    Potential to sound and internal energy
    D    Kinetic to sound and light   (SEG)

## QUESTION 4

Which one of the following statements is *untrue*?

    A    Hydroelectric power stations use water to drive turbines.

    B    In a power station turbines drive generators.
    C    Generators produce electricity.
    D    A nuclear power station generates electricity which flows as a direct current.
    E    Some energy is wasted as heat in the power station.

## QUESTION 5

Figure 4.29 shows a mass moving up and down on the end of a spring. X and Y are the highest and lowest positions of the mass. Which one of the statements in the table is true when the mass is at its highest point X?

                         (SEG)

Fig. 4.29

|   | **Kinetic energy of the mass** | **Potential energy of the mass** |
|---|---|---|
| A | Maximum | Minimum |
| B | Maximum | Zero |
| C | Zero | Maximum |
| D | Same | Same |

## QUESTION 6

Which one of the following is the meaning of power?

    A    Work done per second
    B    Velocity per kilogram
    C    Force per metre
    D    Acceleration per newton   (SEG)

## QUESTION 7

A machine such as a pulley system will have an efficiency of 100% if

    A    The load is equal to the effort.

B   The distance moved by the effort is equal to the distance moved by the load.

C   The work done by the effort is equal to the work done by the load.

D   The load is very large.

E   The load is very small.    (ULEAC)

## QUESTION 8

A force is applied to an object and causes it to move a certain distance in the direction of the applied force. The amount of work done is

A   Force × distance moved

B   $\dfrac{\text{Force}}{\text{Distance moved}}$

C   Weight of object × distance moved

D   $\dfrac{\text{Weight of object}}{\text{Distance moved}}$

E   Weight of object × force    (NISEAC)

## QUESTION 9

A boy whose weight is 400 N climbs a flight of stairs 4 m high in 5 s. His power output is

A   $\dfrac{5 \times 4}{400}$ W

D   $\dfrac{400 \times 4}{5}$ W

B   $400 \times 5 \times 4$ W

E   $\dfrac{400 \times 5}{4}$ W

C   $\dfrac{400}{5 \times 4}$ W

## QUESTION 10

Which of these quantities has the same units as energy?

A   Mass    C   Work    E   Velocity
B   Power    D   Weight

---

STRUCTURED
QUESTIONS

## QUESTION 11

This question is about **forces, work** and **energy**. A worker on a building site raises a bucket full of cement at a slow steady speed, using a pulley like that shown in the diagram (Fig. 4.30). The weight of the bucket and cement is 200 N. The force F exerted by the worker is 210 N.

(a)   Why is F bigger than the weight of the bucket and cement?

(b)   The bucket is raised through a height of 4 m.
  (i)   Through what distance does the worker pull the rope?
  (ii)   How much work is done on the bucket and cement?
  (iii)   What kind of energy is gained

Fig. 4.30

by the bucket?
  (iv)   How much work is done by the worker?
  (v)   Where does the energy used by the worker come from?    (SEG)

## QUESTION 12

In a hydroelectric generating station, water falls through pipes from a high reservoir to a turbine. The turbine drives a generator.

(a)   On the block diagram (Fig. 4.31), label the three parts of the system.

On the diagram, show clearly the main energy changes in the system.

(b)   Write down the names of *three* different sources of energy which are used for driving an electrical generating system.    (SEG)

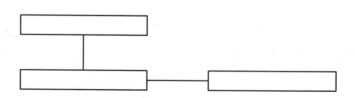

Fig. 4.31

## QUESTION 13

(a) The pie chart shows five sources of energy used by a country.

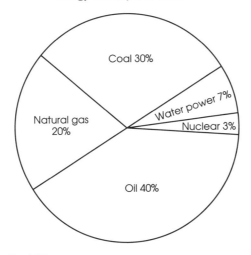

**Fig. 4.32**

The table shows the proportional use and estimated reserves of coal, oil and natural gas.

|  | Relative estimated reserves | Relative quantity used/year |
|---|---|---|
| Coal | 500 | 1.25 |
| Oil | 100 | 3 |
| Natural gas | 90 | 1.5 |

(i) Explain why it is always difficult to make accurate predictions of how long reserves will last.

(ii) Why will the pie chart be different in about 20 years time?

(iii) Explain the economic, environmental and social benefits of using nuclear energy as the main source of providing electrical power.

(b) Pumped storage power stations are used to produce electricity during periods of peak demand. Water is stored in one reservoir and allowed to fall through a pipe to another reservoir at a lower level. The falling water is used to turn turbines which are linked to generators.

In one such power station 400 kg of water passes through the turbines every second after falling through 500 m. The gravitational field strength is 10 N/kg.

Assume that no energy is wasted.

(i) What is the weight of 400 kg of water?

(ii) Calculate the decrease in gravitational energy when 400 kg of water falls 500 m.

(iii) What is the power delivered to the turbines by this falling water?

(iv) If the generator is perfectly efficient calculate the current it produces if the output voltage is 20 000 V.

(v) Why are pumped storage power stations used to produce electricity for a few hours and not for continuous generation of electricity? (SEG)

**Fig. 4.33**

**ESSAY QUESTION**

## QUESTION 14

Write a short account of the possible dangers to the environment arising from large electricity generating stations. (SEG)

# OUTLINE ANSWERS

| Question | 1 | 2 | 3 | 4 | 5 | 6 | 7 | 8 | 9 | 10 |
|----------|---|---|---|---|---|---|---|---|---|----|
| Answer | B | C | B | D | C | A | C | A | D | C |

**STRUCTURED QUESTIONS**

## ANSWER 11

(a) *F* is bigger because the worker also has to do work against friction between the rope and the pulley.

(b) (i) Distance = 4 m (the pulley only acts as a direction changer).

 (ii) Work = force × distance
 = 200 × 4 = 800 J.

 (iii) The bucket and cement gain gravitational potential energy.

 (iv) Work = 210 × 4 = 840 J.

 (v) Energy comes from his food (chemical energy).

## ANSWER 12

(a) See Fig. 4.34.

(b) There are many possibilities: burning coal or oil; nuclear fuel; wind, solar or tidal energy sources.

**Fig. 4.34**

## ANSWER 13

(a) (i) any four of – Reserves are estimated, quantity used each year can vary, environmental considerations, reserves depleted, more use of larger reserves, change of costs etc.

 (ii) oil reaching low reserves, use of other fuels/renewable sources of energy.

 (iii) Economic (large capital investment), electricity "cheap" to produce.
 Environmental – no greenhouse gases/acid rain/ ash(waste problem).
 Social – more use of electrical power in future, "clean" atmosphere.

(b) (i) weight = mass × g
 = 400 × 10 = <u>4000N</u>

 (ii) energy change = weight × height ( = grav. pot. energy)
 = 4000 × 500 = 200 000 J = <u>2 MJ</u>

 (iii) 2 MJ per second = 2 MW

 (iv) Power (watts) = volts × amps
 2 000 000 = 20 000 × I
 I = $\dfrac{2\,000\,000}{20\,000}$ = <u>100A</u>

 (v) More power used in raising water to upper reservoir hence not efficient/economic.

**ESSAY QUESTION**

## ANSWER 14

The type of problem will depend on the method used to provide the original energy supply.

■ **Coal or oil** – waste gases from burning giving rise to atmospheric pollution. Coal burning gives sulphur dioxide as by-product, which is responsible for acid rain. Both give carbon oxides with the possibility of "greenhouse effect" in the long run.

■ **Nuclear** – needs siting near the sea for optimum free cooling. Sea temperature rises causing a shift in ecology. Problem of disposal of waste, of leakage, and of control.

■ **Wind** – requires large clusters of windmills with vanes about 20 m radius. Land use and unsightliness are the main problems.

■ **Solar** – similar to wind. Land use is the main environmental consideration.

■ **HEP** – unless harnessing a natural fall, hydroelectric power may require the flooding of arable land to make the necessary reservoirs.

(*NB*. The question carries eight marks. One mark for each valid point made.)

# TUTOR'S QUESTION AND ANSWER

**QUESTION**

A student requires a small electric motor for a model crane. The crane load is raised on a single cord attached to a shaft driven by the motor through reduction gearing. At the start of the lift, one revolution of the shaft raises the load through a vertical height of 10 mm. At the end of the lift one revolution of the shaft raises the load through a vertical height of 20 mm.

(a) Assuming that the lifting shaft rotates at a constant rate of 3 rev/s, estimate the power used in raising a load of 2 N.
   (i) At the beginning of the lift;

   (ii) At the end of the lift.

(b) The rated characteristics of three possible motors, A, B and C are given in Fig. 4.35.
   (i) What is the power output of each motor?
   (ii) The motor is to be powered from a DC source giving output voltages of 3, 6 or 9 V. Given that the efficiency of the gearing system is 0.40 (40%), which motor would you recommend? Explain how you make your decision. (SEG)

| Motor | Voltage (V) | Load current (A) | Speed (rev/s) | Efficiency |
|-------|-------------|------------------|---------------|------------|
| A | 3 | 0.5 | 60 | 0.10 (10%) |
| B | 6 | 0.5 | 60 | 0.10 (10%) |
| C | 9 | 0.4 | 60 | 0.12 (12%) |

Fig. 4.35

**ANSWER**

(a) (i) At the start, 1 rev raises the load by 10 mm (0.01 m). Since the shaft rotates at 3 rev/s, the time for 1 rev = ⅓s.

$$\text{Power} = \frac{\text{Work done}}{\text{Time}}$$

$$= 2 \times 0.01 \times 3 = \underline{0.06 \text{ W}}$$

   (ii) Similarly, at the end of the lift,
   Power $= 2 \times 0.02 \times 3 = 0.12$ W

(b) (i) Input power = Current × voltage
   Output power =
   Input power × efficiency

   Therefore

   Power A = $3 \times 0.5 \times 0.1$ = 0.15 W
   B = $6 \times 0.5 \times 0.1$ = 0.30 W
   C = $9 \times 0.4 \times 0.12$ = 0.43 W

   (ii) The power output required is that calculated in (a) (ii), i.e. <u>0.12 W</u>. With gearing efficiency of 0.40, the overall output powers of the motor and gear system become
   Total power = Motor output × gear efficiency
   Therefore
   Power A = $0.15 \times 0.4$ = 0.06 W
   B = $0.30 \times 0.4$ = 0.12 W
   C = $0.43 \times 0.4$ = 0.17 W

   The calculation of power required assumed that the lift occurred at 3 rev/s for the required lifting rate, so the following factors influence the decision:

*A* The output power is too small. Therefore the speed will also be too small.

*B* The output power matches that required. Therefore the speed will also match and B should be selected.

*C* The output power and speed are too great, so while it can do the job it would be wasteful to use C.

# STUDENT'S ANSWER WITH THE EXAMINER'S COMMENTS

## STUDENT'S ANSWER TO QUESTION 14

**Good to recognise that several possible energy sources may be used.**

**The point about acid rain effects is relevant, but the long range and long term effects are also important.**

**Other, more common effects are important. Leaks ARE a danger, but are not common.**

**This is vague, it could be argued that 'empty' land is environmentally valuable.**

There might be pollution, if coal fired of smoke which can cause acid rain which damages living plants such as trees or old buildings which are considered valuable. If the power station is a nuclear reactor there is a threat of a leak which in its self kills a lot of things but would also drive away the local people making the land empty, and uncared for. There would need to be a considerable ammount of high voltage cables and pylons, which make any place look ugly, some cables might need to go underground which might mean hedges or trees must be dug up. There might be noise pollution which would discourage animals and the need for workers bringing cars would be bad news for all animals.

**An important consideration.**

**Another very valid point.**

**Weak concluding paragraph. Most planners are very environmentally aware.**

**A reasonable answer raising some valid issues, but not enough detail about any particular one. More could have been said about other alternatives.**

# REVIEW SHEET

■ If you lift a mass upwards it gains _____ energy

■ Every moving object has _____ energy

■ Name six different forms of energy

1. _____    2. _____

3. _____    4. _____

5. _____    6. _____

■ A simple lever lifts a 250 N load when the effort put in is 100 N. Its mechanical advantage is _____ . A lever like this is a _____ multiplier.

■ Draw an energy arrow for a ball that is dropped, bounces and rises to a lower height.

■ Fill in the labels on the energy diagram for a hydroelectric power station to show the energy type at each stage.

| Water in reservoir | ← _____ |
|---|---|
| Water in pipe | ← _____ |
| Rotating turbine | ← _____ |
| Generator output | ← _____ |

Fig. 4.36

■ Complete the following equations

1. Power =                              2. Efficiency =

3. Kinetic Energy =                     4. Gravitational P.E. =

■ State the units for each of the following

1. Work _____    2. Power _____

3. Energy _____    4. Force _____

■ The most common type of energy "wasted" is _____

■ Name a renewable source of energy that does NOT originate from the Sun.
_____

■ State two sources of energy that are suitable for development in hot third world countries with a few natural resources.

1. _____     2. _____

■ State two advantages and two disadvantages for the use of wind power to generate electricity.

Advantages:

1. _____

2._____

Disadvantages:

1. _____

2. _____

A lever can be used to increase *force*. Why does the lever not increase *energy* at the same time?

_____

_____

Draw a simple diagram of each of the following and mark on it the centre of mass.

1. A ball                2. A brick                3. A horseshoe

Fossil fuels are non-renewable. Explain the meaning of each of the following words:

Fossil: _____

Fuel: _____

Non-renewable: _____

# CHAPTER 5

# FORCES AND MOTION

## GETTING STARTED

The analysis of moving objects and the way that **forces** affect movement leads to the three *laws of motion* suggested by Newton. In their turn they help to explain how satellites and planets move and how jets and rockets will behave. They also help unify the motion of planets into a theory of **universal gravitation**.

To start, however, as is often the case in physics, a careful look at vocabulary (definitions) is needed. You need to be quite sure that you understand exactly what is meant when words are used in a "scientific" manner.

Most Examination Groups state that any questions set on this topic can be solved by graphical methods, but in the harder papers algebra may be needed. Both types of example are included in this chapter.

**DISTANCE, DISPLACEMENT**

**SPEED & VELOCITY**

**TICKER-TAPE MEASUREMENTS**

**INFORMATION FROM GRAPHS**

**ACCELERATION**

**COMPUTER MEASUREMENTS**

**$g$ AND ITS MEASUREMENT**

**NEWTON'S LAWS OF MOTION**

**CONSERVATION OF MOMENTUM**

**PROJECTILES**

**CIRCULAR MOTION**

**ROCKETS AND JETS**

**VELOCITY – TIME GRAPHS**

**EQUATIONS OF MOTION**

**IMPULSE AND SAFETY**

**SATELLITES**

**INERTIA**

**DETERMINATION OF $g$**

# ESSENTIAL PRINCIPLES

1 **DISTANCE, DISPLACEMENT, SPEED AND VELOCITY**

The distance from A to B in Fig. 5.1 depends on the route taken. You could travel the "long way", AXYZB, take a short cut, AXB or go directly AB. Whichever way you go the measurement would still be "the distance from A to B". **Distance** then is the total length of the journey, and it clearly depends on the route taken.

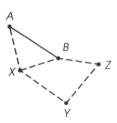

Fig. 5.1 Distance is route-dependent.

Fig. 5.2 Displacement is route-independent.

The **displacement** of B from A is the "distance as the crow flies" (Fig. 5.2). It does **not** depend on the route because there is only **one** route possible, and only **one** direction in which to travel. Displacement is the distance between two points in a fixed direction.

Distance, like mass, is a **scalar** quantity; displacement, like force, is a **vector** quantity.

To find out how "fast" you are travelling, you need to measure two things: "How far is the journey?", and "How much time did it take?". "How far?" can mean either **distance** or **displacement**, so we use two more definitions to make the meaning clear, dividing by **time** in each case.

$$\text{Speed} = \frac{\text{Distance}}{\text{Time}}$$

$$\text{Velocity} = \frac{\text{Displacement}}{\text{Time}}$$

So speed is a **scalar** quantity and velocity is a **vector** quantity. Both speed and velocity are measured in metres per second (m/s) or centimetres per second (cm/s), but velocity is measured in a **particular direction**.

2 **TICKER-TAPE MEASUREMENTS**

The problem in measuring speed or velocity is that both a length and a time are needed. In a laboratory the lengths are likely to be no more than a few metres and times will be only a few seconds or less. A **ticker-timer** is often used because it gives **both** pieces of information at once and can time to 1/50 s when run from a mains power pack. The timer taps out 50 dots on to a piece of paper tape in 1 s. So the interval between dots is 1/50 s or 0.02 s.

In Fig. 5.3 the time to travel from X to Y is (5 × 0.02) = 0.10 s. Simply pulling a tape by hand can tell you a lot about the way you moved. In Fig. 5.4:

A   Travelled with a steady speed. This is called **constant velocity** (velocity because it is in a fixed direction).

B   Started slowly and became faster and faster. This is called **accelerating**.

C   Became slower as the time went on. This is called **decelerating**.

But more information is available. Since the time interval between dots is 0.02 s, we can say **how long** it took to pull each tape:

Fig. 5.3

Fig. 5.4

Start A
A
B
C
D
E
F
Finish G

**Fig. 5.5**

A took $10 \times 0.02 = 0.20$ s
B took $4 \times 0.02 = 0.08$ s
C took $6 \times 0.02 = 0.12$ s

All are pulled in a fixed direction so we can measure the displacements with a ruler and find the velocities. In this case the lengths were as shown in table 5.1. Apart from A there is no single time when the other tapes were travelling at a fixed value for velocity, so we need to say "average" velocity, as in Table 5.1.

Table 5.1

| Tape | Displace-ment (cm) | Time (s) | Average velocity (cm/s) |
|------|------|------|------|
| A | 8 | 0.20 | 40 |
| B | 9 | 0.08 | 112.5 |
| C | 8 | 0.12 | 66.6 |

This gives another, more exact definition:

$$\text{Average velocity} = \frac{\text{Total displacement}}{\text{Total time}}$$

or

$$v_{av} = \frac{s}{t} \text{ and } s = v_{av}t$$

where $s$ = displacement and $t$ = time.

Now imagine a length of tape, as in Fig. 5.5, made in the same way, but cut into shorter lengths to make a bar chart. If each tape piece has five intervals on it, then *each piece* represents a *time* of 0.10 s.

**Fig. 5.7**

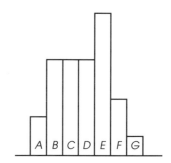

**Fig. 5.6 A tape chart constructed from Fig. 5.5.**

The information given by this type of chart is:

(i) The **type of motion** (i.e. how the pulling object moved Fig. 5.6). We can say that it began slowly, increased velocity, which then stayed constant for a while, increased velocity again and at the end rapidly slowed down.

(ii) **Total time** for the journey. Each piece has five intervals on it, i.e. 0.10 s; total time = $7 \times 0.10$ s = 0.70 s.

(iii) **Total displacement** (Fig. 5.7). Measuring each piece we have (2 + 4 + 4 + 4 + 6 + 3 + 1) = 24 cm.

(iv) **Average velocity**:

$$v_{av} = \frac{\text{Total displacement}}{\text{Total time}}$$

$$= \frac{24}{0.7} = 34.28 \text{ cm/s}$$

(v) **Average velocity** in each 0.1s (Fig 5.8) found by dividing displacement by 0.1 see table 5.2.

**Fig. 5.8**

**3 INFORMATION FROM GRAPHS**

The tape in the last section can be analysed and the data presented as a graph. Taking each individual piece of tape the average velocity for each 0.10 s time interval can be found (Table 5.2).

The same information is available:

1. Type of motion;
2. Total time;
3. Total displacement;
4. Average velocity in each time interval.

Table 5.2

| Tape | Total time from start(s) | Total displacement (cm) | Average velocity (cm/s) |
|------|------|------|------|
| A | 0.1 | 2 | 20 |
| B | 0.2 | 6 | 40 |
| C | 0.3 | 10 | 40 |
| D | 0.4 | 14 | 40 |
| E | 0.5 | 20 | 60 |
| F | 0.6 | 23 | 30 |
| G | 0.7 | 24 | 10 |

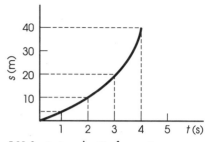

Fig. 5.11 Constant acceleration from rest.

greater in each time interval, so the **velocity is increasing**. The object is **accelerating**.

Since

$$\text{Average velocity} = \frac{\text{Displacement}}{\text{Time}}$$

the **gradient**, or slope of a displacement/time graph, is the value of the **average velocity** at that time. If the gradient is constant, then the object is travelling with constant velocity, as in Fig. 5.10. The equivalent information on a piece of **tape** would look like Fig. 5.12.

Some graphs of displacement against time can easily be understood. The object in Fig. 5.9 is **at rest**, since its displacement is the same all the time. It remains 6 m from the observer.

In Fig. 5.10 the **displacement increases in a steady way** as time goes on. So the **velocity is constant.** The displacement is 8 m after 1 s, 16 m after 2 s and so on. The velocity is constant at 8 m/s.

In Fig. 5.11 the displacement has become

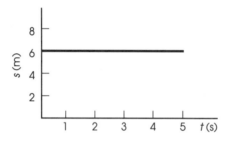

Fig. 5.9 Object at rest.

> ❝❝ A common mistake is to use both the words constant velocity *and* acceleration in the same statement. Constant velocity means NO acceleration. Constant acceleration means constant CHANGE of velocity. ❞❞

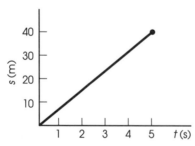

Fig. 5.10 Constant velocity from rest.

Fig. 5.12 Constant velocity.

**4> ACCELERATION**

"Accelerating" means "getting faster". A **tape chart** for acceleration would look like that of Fig. 5.13 or Fig. 5.14. Figure 5.13 represents a **constant** acceleration. The increase in velocity is the same after each time interval. There is also acceleration in Fig. 5.14, though here the velocity changes are *not* the same from one time interval to the next. This represents **non-uniform** acceleration. The same information in **graph form** is shown in Figs 5.15 and 5.16.

$$\text{Acceleration} = \frac{\text{Change in velocity}}{\text{Time}}$$

In Fig. 5.15

$$\text{Acceleration} = a = \frac{(8-0)}{5} = 1.6 \text{ m/s}^2$$

The **units** of acceleration must be units of

$$\frac{\text{(Velocity change)}}{\text{Time}} \text{ or } \frac{\text{metres per second}}{\text{seconds}}$$

Fig. 5.13 Constant acceleration.

Fig. 5.14 Non-uniform acceleration.

which is written **metres per second per second** or **m/s²**.

Figure 5.17 also represents **constant acceleration**, but not in this case starting from rest.

$$a = \frac{\text{Velocity change}}{\text{Time}} = \frac{(40 - 10)}{8} = \frac{30}{8}$$

Fig. 5.17 Constant acceleration.

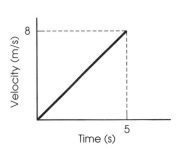

Fig. 5.15 Constant acceleration: graph.

Fig. 5.16 Non-uniform acceleration: graph.

$$a = \underline{3.75 \text{ m/s}^2}$$

Figure 5.18 represents **constant deceleration**

$$a = \frac{10 - 30}{8} = \frac{-20}{8} = -2.5 \text{ m/s}^2$$

Fig. 5.18 Constant deceleration.

Note that in a **velocity-time graph**, the **acceleration** is the **value of the gradient** or slope of the graph. Note also that the **deceleration** is given a **negative** sign.

**5 COMPUTER MEASUREMENTS**

All of the measurements that were described in the section on the ticker timer can also be done very quickly using a computer connected to a light gate sensor. This sensor will measure the time taken for a piece of card to pass through it. The computer can usually do this to at least 1/100 s accuracy. If you measure the length of the card all that is needed is to put the two numbers into the equation for velocity. In most cases you can type the length of the card into the computer and the software will work out the velocity for you.

This makes measuring the velocity of a trolley easy – all you do is attach the card to the trolley and send it through the light gate as in Fig. 5.19.

If you have two of the gates and the program to match you can measure two velocities $v_1$ and $v_2$ for the trolley as it passes down the track. The computer will also measure the time $t$ taken between the two velocities and can then calculate the acceleration from the acceleration equation:

$$\text{acceleration} = \frac{v_2 - v_1}{t}$$

**Fig. 5.19**

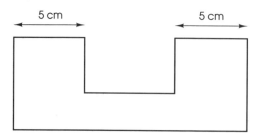

**Fig. 5.20**

This process can appear quite mysterious when all that appears is the answer on a screen. Do note that all the computer does is the same calculations that you could do by

pencil and paper! There is a better way to measure the acceleration. All that the computer is doing is finding the time for the card to go through each light gate. If you use a card shaped like the one in Fig. 5.20 and attach that to the trolley you can tell the computer to measure both times on one light gate. You will then find the average acceleration as the trolley passes through the light gate instead of the average acceleration down quite a long length of track. Note that the width of the gap between the two parts of the card need not be measured. The computer measures the *time* between the two velocities and not the distance.

## 6 ▷ *g* AND ITS MEASUREMENT

All objects fall with the same acceleration towards the Earth. (A more massive object needs its larger weight to accelerate its bigger mass.) You can measure this acceleration easily by dropping the card described in the last section through a light gate. The card will probably need a piece of plasticine on its bottom edge to stop it "fluttering" in the air. You can show that this extra weight has no real effect on the acceleration by using different sized pieces of plasticine. Although simple this method often gives better results than more complicated mechanical apparatus. *g* was described as the gravitational field strength in Chapter 3 so that

$$\text{Weight} = \text{mass} \times g$$

This acceleration is exactly the same as *g* since we also know that

$$\text{Force} = \text{mass} \times \text{acceleration}$$

More detail on this law in the next section! (See also EXTENSION MATERIAL SECTION 17)

**Fig. 5.21**

## 7 ▷ NEWTON'S LAWS OF MOTION

### LAW 1

This explains what a force is. We know that forces cause changes. Newton's first law clarifies this by saying that:

▶ **Any object will continue to do what it is already doing unless a resultant force is acting on it.**

We are used to the idea that an object on the ground which is given a push to start it

moving will come to rest quickly. Of course once it is moving, friction is a force which acts upon it to cause a change, in this case a reduction in velocity until the object stops.

*Without friction*, as in space, an object given a push will continue to move in a straight line with the velocity it had at the end of the push. You may show this "constant velocity" behaviour using an air track (Fig. 5.22) or some other method of reducing friction.

66 To summarise – constant velocity is only possible if there is **NO RESULTANT FORCE.** 99

Fig. 5.22 A linear air track gives almost frictionless motion.

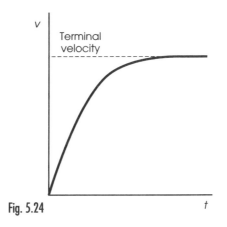

Fig. 5.23 Balanced forces produce constant velocity.

Notice that Newton's first law refers to **resultant force**. So the other way in which an object can remain in a constant state is if the resultant force acting on it is zero, i.e. all forces are "balanced". A ball-bearing in a tube of viscous liquid soon begins to travel with constant velocity, when its weight acting down is balanced by fluid friction upwards (Fig. 5.23). A free-fall parachutist experiences the same effect. On leaving the aircraft he will accelerate towards the ground. Air resistance increases as his velocity increases so while he continues to accelerate the acceleration is **less** than before. As his velocity increases so does air resistance until his weight and the resistive forces **balance**. He can accelerate no more and has reached his terminal velocity (Fig. 5.24).

Fig. 5.24

## LAW 2

This defines a force. It can be shown experimentally (see Pg. 68) that a **constant force causes constant acceleration**. The **greater the force, the greater the acceleration** for a particular body. Therefore:

**Force is proportional to acceleration**

So

$$F \propto a$$

If a particular acceleration is to be achieved, the force required to achieve it is also dependent on the mass to be moved.

So

$$F \propto m$$

Then

▶ $$F = ma$$

If we define the unit of force such that 1 unit of force will accelerate 1 kg by 1 m/s², we have the definition of the **newton**.

It also helps to think about what mass means; $m = F/a$ so the bigger the mass the less the acceleration that could be produced. One way of thinking about mass is to regard it as the "lack-of-willingness-to-move" of an object. This property is sometimes called **inertia**. The $F$ in the equation $F = ma$ is the resultant force acting on an object.

A car has a forward force due to its engine of 900 N. Friction acting while it moves is 600 N. If the car's mass is 1000 kg, its acceleration is

$$F = ma$$

$$a = F/m = \frac{(900 - 600)}{1000} = 0.3 \text{ m/s}^2$$

## LAW 3

This is about **pairs of forces**. Newton maintained that:

■ **When an object is acted on by a force, then somewhere another object is also acted on by an equal force, but in the opposite direction.**

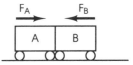

Fig. 5.25

If truck A hits truck B, then A exerts a force on B (Fig. 5.25). At the same time B exerts an equal and opposite force on A. If a tennis racquet is used to hit a ball, the racquet exerts a force on the ball, but the ball also exerts an equal and opposite force on the racquet. Note that Newton's third law refers to **pairs of forces** acting on **different objects**.

A book resting on a table has **two** pairs of Newton forces acting (Fig. 5.26):

1. Push of book on table, P;
   Push of table on book, N.
2. Weight of book W (pull of earth on book);
   Pull of book on earth W[1].

These are all equal if the system is at rest, but not if the table were in, say, an accelerating lift!

Fig. 5.26 Newton "pairs" of forces for a book at rest on a table.

## EXPERIMENTAL PROOF OF NEWTON'S SECOND LAW

Fig. 5.27

This needs a "frictionless" surface. A wood plank, slightly tilted, can be used to "compensate" for friction (Fig. 5.27). The trolley, given a push, should move along it with constant velocity. The force is provided by a rubber cord, the end of which is kept always above the end of the trolley. This means the extension of the cord is the same all the time and so also is the tension in the cord. The ticker-tape passes through a timer making 50 dots per second. The trolley is accelerated using first one rubber cord, then two cords in parallel at the same extension. Then use two similar trolleys, one on top of the other, then three trolleys.

## TREATMENT OF RESULTS

In each case the tapes are cut into 0.1 s intervals.

▶ Single trolley, one cord. The results show that a constant force gives constant acceleration (Fig. 5.28).

Fig. 5.28

▶ *Single trolley, two cords* – twice the acceleration.
*three cords* – three times the acceleration.
▶ *Two trolleys, one cord* – half the acceleration obtained initially.

## PRECAUTIONS

1. Care must be taken to friction compensate the slope.
2. The rubber cords should all be similar to ensure that the force is being doubled and trebled.
3. The trolleys should all have the same mass, or be loaded so that their masses are equal.
4. Care should be taken to ensure that the extension of the cord is the same throughout the experiment.

The law can also be demonstrated by using a computer and a light gate as in section 5 "computer measurement". Use the special double card and a single gate to determine the acceleration each time. You can use elastic cords as already described or accelerate the trolley by a thin string that passes over a pulley and has weights hanging on the end. If you do this remember that you need to keep the total mass constant – so begin with all the weights stacked on the trolley and transfer them one at a time to the end of the string to build up a set of results for force and acceleration. It may also help to remember that a 100 g mass weighs close to 1 N. A graph of force against acceleration should be straight. Using the same accelerating force on stacks of identical trolleys should also show that the acceleration is inversely proportional to the mass.

## 8 ▶ CONSERVATION OF MOMENTUM

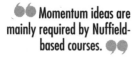
❝❝ Momentum ideas are mainly required by Nuffield-based courses. ❞❞

Newton's second and third laws combine to produce an important principle, namely, **conservation of momentum**. From law 2

$$F = ma$$

$$F = m\frac{(v - u)}{t}$$

$$F \times t = mv - mu$$

The quantity $(F \times t)$ is called *impulse* and the quantity mass × velocity is called *momentum*. The unit of momentum is kg m/s. So impulse = change of momentum. (This is only another way of stating the second law.) The units for impulse will be either kgm/s or Ns.

Now imagine again a collision process. Truck A hits truck B (Fig. 5.29).

Fig. 5.29

From the third law A exerts a force $F$ on B and B exerts the same force on A. The forces must both act for the same time.

Impulse A on B

= Impulse B on A

Change of momentum of A

= Change of momentum of B

Before

After

**Fig. 5.30 Conservation of momentum**

Suppose A and B have masses $m_A$ and $m_B$ (Fig. 5.30). **Before colliding** they travel with velocities $u_A$ and $u_B$ ($u_A > u_B$). **After colliding** the velocities are $v_A$ and $v_B$ ($v_A < v_B$). Then

$$m_A(v_A - u_A) = m_B(v_B - u_B)$$

▶ $$m_A u_A + m_B u_B = m_A v_A + m_B v_B$$

i.e. the total momentum before the collision is equal to the total momentum after the collision.

Note that momentum is a vector. It is usual to use a + sign for objects travelling from left to right and a – sign if they travel in the opposite direction.

---

# WORKED EXAMPLES

## WORKED EXAMPLE 1

A 2 kg trolley is travelling at 4 m/s (Fig. 5.31). It collides with a 3 kg trolley at rest. The two trolleys become coupled together and continue to travel together. What is their velocity?

Total momentum before collision:

$$(2 \times 4) + (3 \times 0) = 8 \text{ kg m/s}$$

Total momentum after collision:

$$(2 \times v) + (3 \times v) = 5v \text{ kg m/s}$$
$$5v = 8$$
$$v = \underline{1.6 \text{ m/s}}$$

This is an example of an **inelastic collision**.

Before

After

**Fig. 5.31**

## WORKED EXAMPLE 2

A billiard ball of mass 0.3 kg hits another stationary ball of mass 0.4 kg head on. The first ball initially travels at 3 m/s and after colliding it travels at 1 m/s. What is the velocity of the second ball?

Before collision total momentum

$$= (0.3 \times 3) + (0.4 \times 0)$$
$$= 0.9 \text{ kg m/s}$$

If the second ball then travels at $v$ metres/second:

After collision total momentum

$$= (0.3 \times 1) + (0.4 \times v)$$
$$= 0.3 + (0.4v) \text{ kg m/s}$$

i.e.
$$0.9 = 0.3 + (0.4v)$$
$$0.6 = 0.4v$$
$$v = \underline{1.5 \text{ m/s}}$$

---

**9 ▷ PROJECTILES**

Any mass falling vertically near the surface of the earth has an acceleration of 10 m/s². This acceleration does not depend on the mass.

**Fig. 5.32**

In Fig. 5.32 the larger mass has a larger force acting on it (100 N compared with 20 N) but the force has to accelerate more mass, so the accelerations are the same.

▶ $$a = F/m = \frac{100}{10} = \frac{20}{2} = 10 \text{ m/s}^2$$

(This applies as long as air resistance is negligible.)

A vertically falling mass travelling at 10 m/s² will cover distances from rest of 5 m in 1 s, 20 m in 2 s, 45 m in 3 s and so on (from $s = \frac{1}{2}at^2$). This is shown in Fig. 5.33. A mass projected "horizontally" in space will continue to move with the same velocity all the time (Newton's first law). If projected horizontally on earth, provided there is little air resistance, the same applies, and it will continue to travel equal **horizontal** distances in equal times.

The vertical and horizontal parts of the motion are independent. Vertically the object accelerates; horizontally it travels with constant velocity. The **combined** effect is

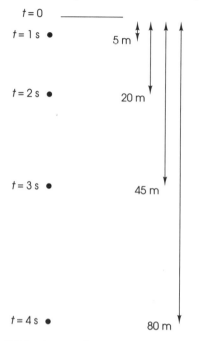

Fig. 5.33 Displacements from rest in a 1:49:16 ratio.

shown in Fig. 5.34. The dotted line shows the path taken as a result of the two motions. This means that an object projected horizontally on the earth takes the same time to reach the ground as one dropped vertically. Change in horizontal velocity only changes the horizontal displacement. The time of flight is always the same.

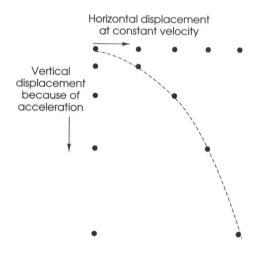

Fig. 5.34 Horizontal and vertical motions are independent.

---

**WORKED EXAMPLE**

Fig. 5.35

A ball is kicked from a cliff top with a horizontal velocity of 20 m/s. It hits the ground after 3 s. (a) How far from the base of the cliff does it land? (b) How high is the cliff?

(a) Horizontal velocity is 20 m/s and the ball travels for 3 s. Since

Distance = Velocity × time
Distance $d$ = 20 × 3 = 60 m

(b) Vertically the ball is falling under gravity for 3 s.

Use $s = \frac{1}{2}at^2$

$s = \frac{1}{2} \times 10 \times 9 = 45$ m

---

## 10 CIRCULAR MOTION

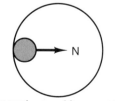

Fig. 5.36 Tension provides the centripetal force.

Fig. 5.37 The normal force provides the centripetal force.

For an object to move in a circle, a force must be acting on it, directed **towards the centre** of the circle. Such a force is called a **centripetal force**. The name centripetal is simply a "group name" for any force acting **towards the centre of a circle;** it must be provided by some real agency.

1. A stone on a string is whirled above a person's head in a circle. The **centripetal force** is provided by the **tension** (T) in the string (Fig. 5.36).
2. A ball-bearing is moved around a ring in a horizontal circle. The **centripetal force** is provided by the **normal (reaction) force** (N) of the walls of the circle on the ball (Fig. 5.37).

3. A car cornering – the **centripetal force** is provided by **friction** (Fig. 5.38).
4. Motion of the moon around the earth. The **centripetal force** is provided by the **gravitational pull** of the earth on the moon.

Experience of such forces can lead to some confusion. In whirling a stone on a string you will feel an "equal and opposite" force acting outwards on you. But **you are not moving in a circle**. The inward force on the stone **keeps it in a circle**.

In driving a car around a corner, you will start to move out, away from the centre of the circle. This is because while friction is acting on the car inwards and moving the car in a circle, you are still moving in a straight line – until either friction between you and the seat, or the reaction of the car body on you, provides you with the centripetal force needed to **move you in a circle.**

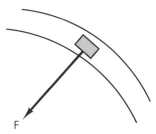

Fig. 5.38 Friction provides the centripetal force.

When an object is moving in a circle its speed (a scalar) in orbit is constant, but its velocity (a vector) is changing. The force towards the centre is not changing the speed

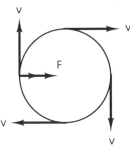

Fig. 5.39 The velocity vector changes because the object is accelerating.

at any time, but it *is* changing its **direction** – the force is causing acceleration (Fig. 5.39).

Remember that acceleration means "change of velocity" and velocity refers to speed in a fixed direction. In a straight line, acceleration can only mean "getting faster" since the direction is fixed. In **circular motion, acceleration** means **changing direction**. The force is still causing a change, but the change is now **a direction change**.

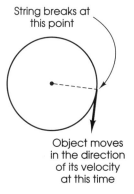

Fig. 5.40

If the force is suddenly removed (in the stone example the string may break) then the object continues to move according to Newton's first law in the direction of its velocity **at that time**, which will be at a tangent to the circular path (Fig. 5.40).

**11> ROCKETS AND JETS**

In section 7 we found that Newton's third law stated that for every force there would be an equal but opposite reaction force. If water is squirted from a hosepipe there is a reaction force pushing the pipe backwards that is equal to the force pushing the water forward. This can be a problem with large fire hoses which can be difficult to hold and direct.

A **rocket** carries with it all the fuel and oxygen that it needs. When this is burned the hot expanding gases can only leave at the back of the engine. This is then the same situation as the hosepipe and the rocket is driven forward by the reaction force which is equal to the force driving the hot gases backwards (remember that the molecules of hot gases will be moving very quickly). If a lot of fuel is being burned rapidly the force will be large.

A **jet engine** works on exactly the same principle as the rocket where hot (very fast) gases leave the rear of the engine and cause the engine to be forced in the opposite direction. The difference is that it is only designed to work in the Earth's atmosphere and does not need to carry a supply of oxygen with it. The air is taken in at the front of the

(a) A rocket

(b) A jet engine

Fig. 5.41

engine and compressed before being burned with the fuel. The compressor can be driven by a turbine placed in the path of the hot gases just before they leave the engine.

▶ NOTE Rockets and jet engines (and hosepipes!) will produce this force when obeying the third law. They do NOT need something to push against – a rocket, for example, will work just as well in a vacuum.

You can show the principle with a simple balloon driven vehicle as shown in Fig. 5.42.

You may also have a kit in your school which uses a pump to compress air behind water in a half full plastic bottle. When the air pushes the water out of the narrow neck of the bottle it is pushed forward in the same way as a rocket.

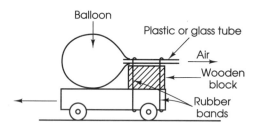

Fig. 5.42

# EXTENSION MATERIALS

## 12 DISPLACEMENT FROM VELOCITY – TIME GRAPHS

For an object moving with constant velocity of 8 m/s, the graph would look like that of Fig. 5.43. After travelling for 20 s at 8 m/s it will have travelled 160 m. This is the same as the ***area under the graph***.

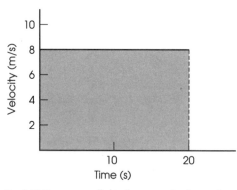

Fig. 5.43 Distance travelled is the area under the graph.

For constant acceleration the velocity is never the same from one second to the next (Fig. 5.44). But over a ***very small time interval*** the velocity would not change too much. So for the small interval around 10 s, the ***distance travelled*** is again the ***area under the graph***.

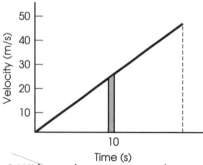

Fig. 5.44 Velocity is almost constant over a short time interval.

Adding up all such small areas is like adding up many small displacements, so the **total displacement** is also the area under the graph (Fig. 5.45).

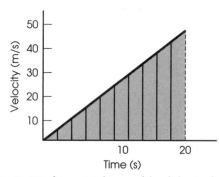

Fig. 5.45 Displacement is the area of the whole triangle.

$$\begin{aligned} \text{Area} &= \text{Area of triangle} \\ &= \tfrac{1}{2}\,(\text{base} \times \text{height}) \\ \text{Displacement} &= \tfrac{1}{2} \times 20 \times 50 = \underline{500\ \text{m}} \end{aligned}$$

It is ***always*** true that the **distance travelled** is the **area under a velocity–time graph**. In Fig. 5.46 you would have to "count squares" on graph paper to find the area. For a more complex journey, a number of pieces of information are available (Fig. 5.47):

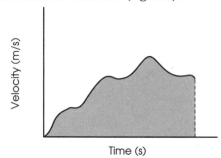

Fig. 5.46 Displacement is the area under the curve.

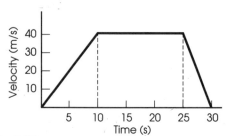

Fig. 5.47

1. ***Description of motion.*** Constant acceleration from rest for the first 10 s to a velocity of 40 m/s for a further 15 s and constant deceleration to rest in the last 5 s.
2. ***Acceleration values.*** Initially

$$a = \frac{40}{10} = \underline{4 \text{ m/s}^2}$$

Finally

$$a = \frac{-40}{5} = \underline{-8 \text{ m/s}^2}$$

3. ***Total distance travelled.*** This is the total area below the graph.

   (a) Area of first triangle = ½ × 10 × 40
   = 200 m
   (b) Area of rectangle = 15 × 40
   = 600 m
   (c) Area of last triangle = ½ × 5 × 40
   = 100 m
   Total = (200 + 600 + 100) = 900 m

The acceleration due to gravity near the surface of the earth is fairly constant at 9.81 m/s², so that 10 m/s² represents a reasonable approximation. (See Pg. 76 for a method to determine this.) For an object falling from

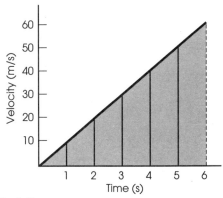

**Fig. 5.48**

rest, and accelerating at 10 m/s², a graph of velocity against time will be like that in Fig. 5.48.

By using the areas under the graph, for an object falling freely from the rest, we have:

In 1 s, displacement from rest = 5 m
In 2 s, displacement from rest = 20 m
In 3 s, displacement from rest = 45 m
In 4 s, displacement from rest = 80 m

and so on. These numbers, 5, 20, 45, 80, are in the ratio 1:4:9:16, i.e. $1^2:2^2:3^2:4^2$. ***The displacement from rest is proportional to the squares of the times.***
(See $s = ½at^2$ below).

---

## 13> EQUATIONS OF MOTION

❛❛ Equations of motion are required by only a few Examination Groups, and then only in the harder papers. Check your syllabus ❜❜

The calculations using graphs in the last two sections can be generalised into a set of equations. In each of them the following symbols are used:

$s$ = displacement          $a$ = acceleration
$u$ = initial velocity       $t$ = time
$v$ = final velocity

From the definition of acceleration we already have

$$a = \frac{v - u}{t} \quad \therefore \quad \underline{v = u + at} \quad [5.1]$$

For constant acceleration from initial velocity $u$ to final velocity $v$ over a time $t$, the ***displacement*** is the area under the graph, i.e. area of rectangle plus triangle in Fig. 5.49.

$$s = (ut) + ½(v - u)t$$

but from eq [5.1]

$$v - u = at$$
$$s = ut + ½(at)t$$
$$\underline{s = ut + ½at^2} \quad [5.2]$$

For an object accelerating uniformly from rest, this simplifies because $u = 0$, so that $\underline{s = ½at^2}$.

Combining eqs [5.1] and [5.2] gives [5.3]:

$$\underline{v = u + at} \quad [5.1]$$

$$t = \frac{(v - u)}{a}$$

$$s = ut + ½at^2 \quad [5.2]$$

$$t = \frac{v - u}{a}$$

$$2s = 2u \frac{(v - u)}{a} + \frac{(v - u)^2}{a}$$

$$2as = 2uv - 2u^2 + v^2 - 2uv + u^2$$

$$2as = v^2 - u^2$$

$$\underline{v^2 = u^2 + 2as} \quad [5.3]$$

It is also true that, with constant acceleration the average velocity is $(u + v)/2$ so that

$$s = \frac{(u + v)t}{2} \quad [5.4]$$

To summarise, the four equations for constantly accelerated motion are

$$v = u + at \quad [5.1]$$
$$s = ut + ½at^2 \quad [5.2]$$
$$v^2 = u^2 + 2as \quad [5.3]$$

$$s = \frac{(u + v)t}{2} \quad [5.4]$$

You do not need to memorise how to obtain these. You ***do*** need to be able to use them.

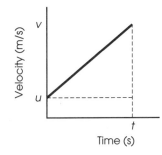

**Fig. 5.49**

## (A) WORKED EXAMPLES
## WORKED EXAMPLE 1

A train starts from rest in a station and accelerates uniformly at 2 m/s$^2$ for 1 min. What is its velocity at the end of that time? You need to decide which equation to use. Write down what you are given and what you need to find. Here

$u = 0$      $t = 1 \text{ min} = 60 \text{ s}$
$a = 2 \text{ m/s}^2$      $v = \text{unknown}$

▶ So use

$$v = u + at$$

Then

$$v = 0 + (2 \times 60)$$
$$= \underline{120 \text{ m/s}}$$

## WORKED EXAMPLE 2

An object is dropped down a deep pit from rest. The pit is 50 m deep. How long will it take to reach the bottom of the pit? ($g = 10 \text{ m/s}^2$). Here

$u = 0$      $s = 50 \text{ m}$
$a = 10 \text{ m/s}^2$      $t = \text{unknown}$

▶ Use

$$s = ut + \tfrac{1}{2}at^2$$

Since

$u = 0$      $s = \tfrac{1}{2}at^2$
$50 = \tfrac{1}{2} \times 10 \times t^2$      $50 = 5t^2$

$$t^2 = \frac{50}{5} = 10$$

$$t = \sqrt{10} = \underline{3.2 \text{ s}}$$

## WORKED EXAMPLE 3

A car is travelling with a constant velocity of 30 m/s. In order to overtake a lorry, the driver accelerates at 0.5 m/s$^2$ for 0.5 s. What is his velocity at the end of that time? How far did he travel while accelerating?

For the first part

$u = 30 \text{ m/s}$      $t = 0.5 \text{ s}$
$a = 0.5 \text{ m/s}^2$      $v = \text{unknown}$

▶ So use

$$v = u + at$$
$$v = 30 + (0.5 \times 0.5) = \underline{30.25 \text{ m/s}}$$

▶ To find the *distance* use

$$s = ut + \tfrac{1}{2}at^2$$
$$s = (30 \times 0.5) + \tfrac{1}{2}(0.5 \times (0.5)^2)$$
$$= 15 + \tfrac{1}{2}(0.125) = \underline{15.06 \text{ m}}$$

▶ Alternative solution could use

$$v^2 = u^2 + 2as$$

then

$$(30.25)^2 = (30)^2 + 2(0.5)s$$

giving

$$s = \underline{15.06 \text{ m}}$$

Many problems using these ideas involve projecting an object **upwards,** i.e. throwing a ball vertically in the air. The things to remember in these cases are:

1. The acceleration due to gravity is acting **down.** So the "acceleration" becomes **negative.**
2. At the top of the path, before the object starts to return, its velocity is *zero.*
3. The time to go *up to* the top of the path is the same as the time to *come down*.
4. Whatever velocity the object had on leaving the ground, it will have the *same* on returning. (This follows from conservation of energy since there is (almost) no energy changed to heat through work done against friction.)

## WORKED EXAMPLE 4

A stone is thrown vertically upwards leaving a person's hand at 30 m/s. (i) How high will it travel before coming to rest? (ii) How long will it take before reaching the top of its path? In this case the time is easier to calculate so start with part (ii).
You are told

$u = 30 \text{ m/s}$
$a = 10 \text{ m/s}^2$ (acceleration due to gravity)
$v = 0$ (top of path)
$t = \text{unknown}$

So use

$$v = u + at \qquad 0 = 30 + (-10)t$$

(*NB.* (–10) since decelerating.)

$$30 = 10t \qquad t = \underline{3 \text{ s}}$$

For distance travelled use

$$s = ut + \tfrac{1}{2}at^2$$
$$s = (30 \times 3) + \tfrac{1}{2}(-10(3)^2)$$
$$s = 90 + \tfrac{1}{2}(-90)$$
$$= 90 - 45 = \underline{45 \text{ m}}$$

It is again possible to use $v^2 = u^2 + 2as$ which would give the distance first, then use $s = ut + \tfrac{1}{2}at^2$. You may wish to try the solution this way.

## (B) PROOF OF FORMULA FOR KINETIC ENERGY

In Chapter 4 a formula for kinetic energy was stated as

$$\text{Kinetic energy} = \tfrac{1}{2}mv^2$$

This can be proved using the equations of motion. In Figure 5.50 a vehicle is travelling at

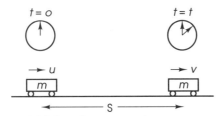

Fig. 5.50 Calculating kinetic energy change.

a velocity $u$ when a stop-clock is started. After $t$ seconds it is travelling at a greater velocity $v$. The distance between observations is $s$. The mass of the vehicle is $m$. If the vehicle accelerates uniformly then

$$a = \frac{v-u}{t}$$

In order for it to accelerate a ***resultant force F*** must be acting and

$$F = ma \qquad F = \frac{m(v-u)}{t}$$

The *work done* to move the vehicle causes a change in kinetic energy, so

$$\text{Change in kinetic energy} = F \times s$$

i.e.

$$\text{Change in kinetic energy} = m\frac{(v-u)}{t}s$$

but $s/t$ is the average velocity, $v_{av}$. Average velocity is the average of the starting velocity $u$ and the final velocity $v$, i.e.

$$v_{av} = \frac{(v+u)}{2}$$

So

Change in kinetic energy

$$= m(v-u)\frac{(v+u)}{2}$$
$$= \tfrac{1}{2}m(v-u)(v+u)$$
$$= \tfrac{1}{2}m(v^2-u^2)$$
$$= \tfrac{1}{2}mv^2 - \tfrac{1}{2}mu^2$$

If this is the *change* in kinetic energy then each term represents the kinetic energy at a *particular time*. So

$$\text{Kinetic energy at velocity } v = \tfrac{1}{2}mv^2$$

This is the usual formula, namely **kinetic energy** = $\tfrac{1}{2}mv^2$

---

## 14 IMPULSE AND SAFETY

Section 8 showed that

**Impulse = F × t = change of momentum**

In many cases where the change of momentum is large you need to make the *force* involved as *small* as possible: e.g. if an egg is dropped you will have a change of momentum when the egg hits the floor. If the egg is to be unbroken the force must be as small as possible and, looking at the equation, this means that the *time* that the force acts for should be as *long* as possible. This is done by putting eggs in boxes that *can* be crushed so

that the stopping force lasts longer.

Crumple zones in cars have the same effect. The car is designed to crumple in an impact so that the force stopping the car lasts longer and is reduced. Seat belts, apart from restraining the passengers within the car, also stretch a little and the "inertia reels" helps to make the force on your body last longer and therefore be smaller. Crash helmets and cycling helmets work on the same principle. Once such items have been deformed in an accident they will not work effectively again and should be replaced.

---

## 15 SATELLITES AND CIRCULAR MOTION

All satellites stay in their orbit because of a **centripetal** force provided by gravity. This includes the moon in its orbit around the Earth and, although their orbits are not circular, the planets rotating around the Sun.

Satellites round the Earth are of two principal types. **Polar** orbital satellites take an orbit that passes over the north and south poles. As the Earth rotates beneath the orbit

can pass over a different part of the Earth on each orbit. This can be useful for weather observation, spy satellites and for gathering information on a range of subjects from climatic changes to crop growth. The second type is called **geostationary** and rotates round the Earth once in 24 hours. Since the Earth also rotates on its axis in this time the satellite appears to be stationary when viewed from the Earth. This is especially useful in telecommunications for retransmitting telephone calls or television pictures to particular areas and for more "local" weather forecasting.

The centripetal force for any object moving in a circle is given by

$$F = \frac{mv^2}{r}$$

where $F$ is the centripetal force, $m$ is the mass of the object, $v$ is its speed around the circle and $r$ is the radius of the circle. This means that it needs a larger force to go faster round the same bend in a car. If your tyres can't provide a large enough friction force because of ice or gravel then you cannot go round the arc and you will start to go straight on, hitting the outside of the bend. A "tighter" bend has a smaller radius and therefore also requires a greater centripetal force to get you round the bend at the same speed. A heavier (and therefore more massive) lorry will also need a greater force than a light car travelling at the same speed.

The gravitational force between a satellite and the Earth also depends on the mass of the satellite and by putting the two equations together it can be shown that a geostationary satellite will need to orbit in a radius of 42 000 km from the centre of the Earth.

## 16 INERTIA

**Inertia** is a measure of how difficult it is to change the motion of a body. If an object has more inertia it will be more difficult to start or stop it moving or more difficult to change its direction. This depends on the amount of matter that the object contains, so mass is a good measure of inertia. (We have already seen in Newton's second law that the force needed to produce an acceleration depends on the mass of the object.)

## 17 DETERMINATION OF g BY A FREE-FALL METHOD

The time of the fall will be small and must be measured as precisely as possible. A millisecond or centisecond timer is needed. A steel ball-bearing is held on to an electromagnet (Fig. 5.51). The electromagnet is connected to the timer so that when the supply to the electromagnet is switched off, the timer starts. Several metres below the electromagnet is a trapdoor made of metal. Two contacts connect the trap to the timer.

When the ball hits the trap it breaks the contacts and the timer stops.

### RESULTS

Time of fall

(average of several runs)  $= t$ seconds
Distance fallen  $= s$ metres

### CALCULATION

$$s = \tfrac{1}{2}gt^2 \qquad g = 2s/t^2$$

### PRECAUTIONS

1. Measure distance s from the bottom of the ball-bearing to the top of the trap, using a plumb-line and a metre rule.
2. On switching off the supply to the electromagnet, the timer immediately starts, but the electromagnet may retain some magnetism and the ball may not release immediately. Use a soft iron core for the electromagnet and place a small piece of tissue paper between the ball and the electromagnet core.
3. Take several readings of time and use an **_average_** in the final calculation.

**Fig. 5.51**

# EXAMINATION QUESTIONS

## QUESTION 1

Which of the following is constant for an object falling freely towards the earth?

A  Velocity
B  Potential energy
C  Acceleration
D  Kinetic energy
E  Momentum

## QUESTION 2

The force of gravity on a body is a vector quantity because it

A  Has size and direction
B  Acts in a vertical direction
C  Is a force of attraction
D  Has direction but no size      (SEG)

## QUESTION 3

The graph (Fig. 5.52) shows how the speed of an object varies with time. The object is

A  Falling freely
B  Moving with constant speed
C  Moving with constant acceleration
D  Moving with constant deceleration
                                   (SEG)

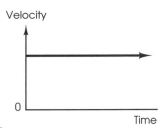

**Fig. 5.52**

## QUESTION 4

The force on a 10 kg mass is 25 N. The acceleration is

A  $0.4 \, \text{m/s}^2$
B  $2.5 \, \text{m/s}^2$
C  $25 \, \text{m/s}^2$
D  $250 \, \text{m/s}^2$          (SEG)

## QUESTIONS 5–8

The following are five physical quantities:

A  Force
B  Power
C  Pressure
D  Acceleration
E  Work

5.  Which one requires a knowledge of area?
6.  Which has the same units as weight?
7.  Which has the same units as energy?
8.  Which would be measured in newton metres per second?      (ULEAC)

## QUESTION 9

As it nears the moon's surface, a lunar probe of mass 10000 kg is accelerated by the moon's gravitational field of $1.5 \, \text{m/s}^2$. What force does the moon exert on the rocket?

A  Zero
B  1500 N
C  10000 N
D  15000 N
E  100000 N                       (ULEAC)

## QUESTION 10

Which of the following velocity-time graphs (Fig. 5.53) represents constant, positive acceleration?

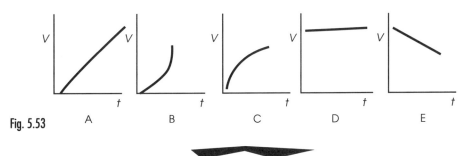

**Fig. 5.53**

## QUESTION 11

A runner and a dog of similar mass had a race. The graph (Fig. 5.54) shows how they moved during the race.

(a)  Over what distance was the race run?
(b)  How long did it take the dog to overtake the runner?

(c) How far had the dog travelled after 8 s?

(d) Describe the motion of the runner after point X on the graph.

(e) Describe the motion of the dog after point Y on the graph.

(f) Which gained the most kinetic energy during the race? Explain your answer.

(NEAB)

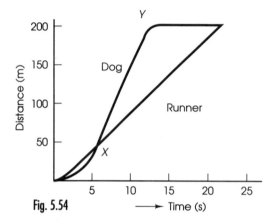

**Fig. 5.54**

## QUESTION 12

This question is about speed and acceleration. A cycle track is 500 m long. A cyclist completes 10 laps (that is, rides completely round the track 10 times).

(a) How many kilometres has the cyclist travelled?

(b) On average it took the cyclist 50 s to complete one lap. What was the average speed of the cyclist?

(c) How long in minutes and seconds did it take the cyclist to complete the 10 laps?

(d) Near the end of the run the cyclist put on a spurt. During the spurt it took the cyclist 2 s to increase speed from 8 m/s$^1$ to 12 m/s$^1$. What was the cyclist's acceleration during the spurt?

(SEG)

## QUESTION 13

This question is about force and acceleration. The driver of a car moving at 20 m/s$^1$ along a straight road applies the brakes. The car

decelerates at 5 m/s$^2$.

(a) How long does it take the car to stop?

(b) What kind of force slows the car down?

## QUESTION 14

A car engine is leaking oil. The drops hit the ground at regular time intervals, one every 2.5 s. Figure 5.55 shows the pattern of drops it leaves on part of the journey.

(a) What can you say about the speed of the car before it reaches the signs?

(b) If the car is travelling at 10 m/s$^1$ calculate the distance between the drops on the road before it reaches the signs.

(c) How can you tell the car is accelerating after it reaches the signs?

(d) After the car passes the signs, the fourth drop falls at a distance of 300 m past the signs. Calculate the acceleration using the formula $s = ut + \frac{1}{2}at^2$.

(ULEAC)

## QUESTION 15

Slow-motion photography shows that a jumping flea pushes against the ground for about 0.001 s during which time its body accelerates upwards to a maximum speed of 0.8 m/s.

(a) Calculate the average upward acceleration of the flea's body during this time.

(b) If the flea then moves upward with an acceleration, assumed constant, of 12 m/s$^2$, calculate:

(i) How long it will take after leaving contact with the ground at a speed of 0.8 m/s to reach the top of the jump?

(ii) How high it will jump after leaving contact with the ground?

(c) Why is the acceleration of the flea after leaving the ground not equal to $g$?

(ULEAC)

**Fig. 5.55**

# OUTLINE ANSWERS

**MULTIPLE CHOICE QUESTIONS**

| Question | 1 | 2 | 3 | 4 | 5 | 6 | 7 | 8 | 9 | 10 |
|----------|---|---|---|---|---|---|---|---|---|----|
| Answer   | C | A | B | B | C | A | E | B | D | A  |

**STRUCTURED QUESTIONS**

## ANSWER 11

(a) <u>200 m</u> (from graph).

(b) <u>6 s</u> (from graph).

(c) <u>100 m</u> (from graph).

(d) Runner is travelling with constant velocity (equal distances in equal times).

(e) The dog is at rest (200 m, and stays there all the time after Y).

(f) The dog. Kinetic energy = $\frac{1}{2}mv^2$. Both have the same mass. The dog has the greatest velocity shown by the greater gradient of the graph.

## ANSWER 12

(a) $500 \times 10 = 5\,000$ m = 5 km

(b) Average speed $= \dfrac{\text{Total distance}}{\text{Total time}}$

$= 500 \div 50 = 10$ m/s$^{-1}$

(c) $50 \times 10 = 500$ s

$1$ m $= 60$ s $\quad \dfrac{500}{60} = $ <u>8 min 20 s</u>

(d) Acceleration $= \dfrac{\text{Velocity change}}{\text{Time}}$

$= \dfrac{(12-8)}{2} = \dfrac{4}{2} = $ <u>2 m/s$^2$</u>

## ANSWER 13

(a) Use $v = u + at$ but remember he is decelerating so the acceleration is $(-5)$ m/s$^2$. Final velocity $v = 0$ m/s since he is at rest

$0 = 20 + (-5)t$

$5t = 20 \quad t = 4 \quad$ <u>$t = 4$ s</u>

(b) The force is friction.

## ANSWER 14

(a) Before reaching the signs the car is travelling with constant velocity.

(b) One drop every 2.5 s. At 10 m/s the distance is $(10 \times 2.5) = 25$ m.

(c) The distance between dots is greater, so the velocity is increasing and the car is accelerating.

(d) Four intervals means $(4 \times 2.5) = 10$ s to travel 300 m. Velocity before reaching the signs is 10 m/s.

$s = ut + \frac{1}{2}at^2$
$300 = (10 \times 10) + \frac{1}{2}a(10)^2$
$300 = 100 + 50a$
$200 = 50a$
$a = $ <u>4 m s$^2$</u>

## ANSWER 15

(a) Acceleration $= \dfrac{\text{Velocity change}}{\text{Time}}$

$= \dfrac{0.8}{0.001} = $ <u>800 m/s$^2$</u>

(b) In this part remember that although the question uses the word "acceleration" it is negative – pulling the flea back to the ground.

(i) Use $v = u + $ at; $v = $ final velocity at the top of the jump = 0 m/s.

$0 = 0.8 + (-12)t \quad 12t = 0.8$
$t = 0.06$ s

(ii) Use $s = ut + \frac{1}{2}at^2$.

$s = (0.8 \times 0.06) + \frac{1}{2}(-12)(0.06)^2$
$= 0.048 - 0.022 = 0.026$ m
$s = $ <u>26 mm</u>

(c) The acceleration due to gravity is 10 m/s$^2$. If the flea is experiencing a greater downward acceleration of 12 m/s$^2$ there is an extra downward force – this can only be air resistance pushing down as the flea jumps upwards.

# TUTOR'S QUESTION AND ANSWER

**QUESTION**

(a) A trolley starts from rest and runs along a straight track, about 3 m long. Describe, with the aid of a suitable diagram, how you would make measurements from which you could work out the speed of the trolley at different times from the start. Explain carefully how you would calculate the values of the speed.

(b) A car of weight 7000 N is travelling along a level road at a speed of 20 m/s when it comes to a hill which rises vertically 100 m and is 1.0 km long, the driver increases the power output of the engine to keep the speed constant at 20 m/s.

(i) How much time does it take the

car to climb the hill?

(ii) How much work does the car do against gravity as it climbs the hill?

(iii) What power is needed to do the work.

(iv) On the return journey the car crosses the top of the hill in the opposite direction at 20 m/s and the driver then disconnects the engine. Explain, in terms of energy changes, why the speed of the car increases. Include the effects of air resistance in your explanation.

**ANSWER**

(a) The track should be set up and levelled. Check using a spirit level. A 50 Hz ticker-timer is connected to a suitable power supply and tape fed through it and attached to the trolley. The trolley is started at the same time as the timer and it travels 3 m pulling the tape (Fig. 5.56).

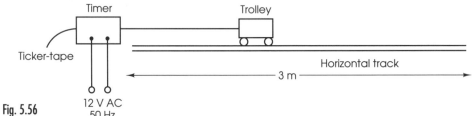

Fig. 5.56

## CALCULATIONS

The tape carries both distance and time information. If the timer is working at 50 Hz then a piece of tape with five intervals represents a time of 0.1 s. For the first 0.1 s interval measure the tape length. Suppose it is 3 cm long as shown (Fig. 5.57). Then the velocity is 3/0.1 = 30 cm/s. This can be repeated as required along the whole tape.

(b) (i) Time taken to climb the hill is the same as the time to travel horizontally at 20 m/s$^{-1}$.
Horizontal distance travelled = 1 km = 1000 m.

$$\text{Time} = \frac{\text{Distance}}{\text{Velocity}} = \frac{1\,000}{20} = \underline{50\text{ s}}$$

(ii) Work done against gravity is the same as the change in potential energy in rising 100 m above the ground.

$$\text{Work done} = mgh = 7000 \times 100$$
$$= \underline{700\,000\text{ J}}$$

(iii)

$$\text{Power} = \frac{\text{Work done}}{\text{Time}} = \frac{700\,000}{50}$$
$$= \underline{14000\text{ W}}$$

(iv) At the top of the hill the car has kinetic energy (because it is travelling at 20 m/s) and potential energy (because it is 100 m above the ground). On cruising downhill the potential energy will be converted to kinetic energy, so the velocity will increase above 20 m/s. However, not all the potential energy will convert to kinetic energy since work will be done against various friction forces, including air resistance, which will convert some kinetic energy into heat.

Fig. 5.57

# STUDENT'S ANSWER WITH THE EXAMINER'S COMMENTS

## STUDENT ANSWER TO QUESTION 15

**Better to state acceleration = velocity change ÷ time first.**

a) $0.8 \div 0.001 = 800 \, m/s^2$ upwards ✓

**No sign convention stated.**

b) i) $a = \dfrac{v-u}{t}$   downwards $a = 12 \, m/s^2$

at top of jump $v = 0$

**Extra negative introduced because unsure how to deal with motion upwards and acceleration down. This is 'faking' the answer.**

$12 = 0 - \dfrac{0.8}{t}$

**This should read −12**

$\dfrac{1}{12} = \dfrac{t}{0.8}$

$t = 1/15$ seconds ✓

**Numerically correct.**

**Could lead to problems by not using decimal form.**

ii) $s = ut + \tfrac{1}{2}at^2$

$= 0.8 \times 1/15 + 1/2 \times -12 \times 1/15^2$

$= + \dfrac{4}{75} - \dfrac{2}{75}$

$= \dfrac{2}{75}$

**Correct, and coped with the sign convention very well.**

$= 0.027 m \; (3dp)$ ✓

c) The downwards acceleration is greater than the acceleration due to gravity because air resistance turns some of the kinetic energy into heat energy.

**The idea that air resistance is responsible is correct, but Energy ideas do not relate to the acceleration change.**

# MORE EXAMINER'S COMMENTS CENTRAL TIER

In road safety tests cars are crashed into walls.

dummy **B**    dummy **A**    concrete wall

(a)  (i)  What happens to each dummy when the car hits the concrete wall?

dummy A The force of the car hitting the wall throws the dummy forward but the seatbelt locks to keep him in place

dummy B The force sent the dummy hurtling through the window screen ................................................(2)

(ii) Suggest why it is important for back seat passengers to wear seat belts.

It is important because they are subject to the force of the crash as well as the driver. So they are just as likely to die in the case of an accident ............................................(2)

(b)  The diagram shows a dummy in a test car. The dummy is not wearing a seat belt.

steering wheel

0.5m

(i)  The car is driven into a wall.
What formula links speed, distance and time?

........ Speed = $\dfrac{\text{Distance}}{\text{Time}}$ ................................................(1)

(ii) It takes 0.1 s for the dummy's head to hit the steering wheel. Use the formula to work out the speed of the car.

.... Speed = $\dfrac{D}{T}$  Speed = $\dfrac{0.5}{0.1}$ = 5 m/s ........(2)

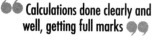 

(iii) In a crash at 10 m/s, the driver must be stopped in 0.05 s to avoid hitting the steering wheel.

Calculate the average deceleration of the driver.

Deceleration = $\dfrac{\text{Change in velocity}}{\text{Time Take}}$

.... Deceleration = $\dfrac{-10}{0.05}$  = – 200 m/s$^2$ ............(3)

it will be Decelerating at 200 m/s$^2$

# REVIEW SHEET

Define the newton by completing the following sentence.

■ A newton is a force that can _____
_____ .

■ Displacement is the distance moved in a _____ .

■ Complete the following equations

1. Average velocity = _____ 
2. Speed = _____

3. Acceleration = _____ 
4. Momentum = mass × _____

5. Force = _____ 
6. _____ = Force × time

■ To keep an object moving in a circle there must be a _____ force
acting _____ the centre of the circle.

■ A geostationary satellite is one which _____
_____ .

■ A car accelerates from 0 m/s to 30 m/s in 10 s. Its acceleration is _____ .

■ The weight of a 1 kg mass at the Earth's surface is 10 N. A 2 kg mass will have a
weight of _____ and if it is dropped its acceleration will be _____
_____ that of the 1 kg mass.

■ A satellite is kept in orbit round the Earth by a _____ force that is
caused by _____ .

■ A car of mass 100 kg moving at 5 m/s has a momentum of _____ .

■ Newton's first law says that _____
_____
_____ .

■ A rocket engine is an application of _____ law.

■ A ball has a mass of 0.2 kg and is thrown with an acceleration of 25 m/s$^2$. The
force of the throw is _____ N.

■ Cars have crumple zones to make the _____ of a crash longer so that
the _____ on the passengers is smaller.

■ In a collision the total _____ is conserved.

■ On a velocity–time graph the area under the graph is the same as _____ .

■ On a displacement–time graph the gradient is the same as the _____ .

■ Draw small sketch graphs to show the movement of each of the following objects as a velocity–time graph.

    1. constant velocity                2. constant acceleration

    3. increasing acceleration        4. stopped

■ The three equations of motion are

    1. $v =$ _____    2. $s =$ _____    3. $v^2 =$ _____.

■ A car of mass 1000 kg moves at 9 m/s. Its kinetic energy is _____

_____

_____.

■ A 1000 N force acts for 0.10 s. What is the impulse? _____.

■ Write down the units for each of the following quantities:

  Force _____    Acceleration _____   Momentum _____

  Impulse _____  Weight _____  Mass _____  Energy _____.

■ A passenger has a mass of 60 kg and is travelling at 25 m/s in a car.

  (i)   What is the momentum of the passenger? _____

_____.

  (ii)  The car stops. What is the momentum of the passenger now? _____

_____.

  (iii) What is the impulse applied to the passenger? _____

_____.

  (iv) If the car took 20 s to stop, what was the force on the passenger? _____

_____.

  (v)  If the car had an accident and stopped in 1 s what force is needed to keep the passenger in her seat? _____

_____.

    How might this be done? _____

_____.

    What would happen otherwise? _____

_____.

## GETTING STARTED

Waves are a way of transferring *energy* from one place to another, and are also a means of transferring information. This is clearly important in modern communications systems.

The way in which energy is transferred relies on **oscillations** taking place. Water waves spread out through the oscillation of water particles. Sound is transferred by the oscillation of particles in whatever material the sound is travelling, and electromagnetic waves, like radio or TV, are propagated by oscillating fields. Waves and oscillations are clearly ideas which are connected.

# CHAPTER 6

# OSCILLATIONS AND WAVES

## OSCILLATING SYSTEMS

## VARIATIONS IN PERIOD

## NATURAL FREQUENCY AND RESONANCE

## WAVES

## SOUND WAVES

## SPEED OF SOUND AND ECHOES

## WAVE BEHAVIOUR USING WATER WAVES

## ELECTROMAGNETIC WAVES

## HEARING AND THE HUMAN EAR

## HARMONICS AND OVERTONES

## A SIMPLE OSCILLATOR

# ESSENTIAL PRINCIPLES

## 1 OSCILLATING SYSTEMS

Any system which carries out a repeated "to and fro motion" is described as an **oscillator**. Simple examples are a mass on the end of a vertical spring, a pendulum, or a trolley tethered between two springs (Fig. 6.1). The **amplitude** of an oscillation is the **maximum displacement of the system from its rest position**.

Fig. 6.1 A trolley oscillator.

Once started, oscillations gradually die away. The kinetic energy of the oscillation is transferred to heat through friction, so that the amplitude gets smaller and smaller (Fig. 6.2). However, for many oscillators, the time for one complete oscillation, $T$, remains constant regardless of the amplitude. They behave like "clocks". The time $T$ is called the **period** of the oscillation. The *frequency, f,* of an oscillation is the number of complete oscillations in 1 s. It is measured in **hertz** (Hz) (1 Hz means one oscillation per second).

$$T = \frac{1}{f}$$

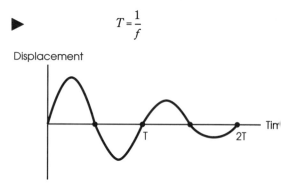

Fig. 6.2 Damped oscillations.

## 2 VARIATIONS IN PERIOD

For the simple mass and spring system (Fig. 6.3), the period can be altered in two ways:

1. **Increasing mass increases $T$.**
2. **A stiffer spring decreases $T$.**

However, **mass** has **no effect** on the **period of a pendulum system**, although the longer the pendulum, the greater the period. Pendulum swings should be measured through a small angle. Large angle swings do **not** keep constant time until the angle is less than about 15°.

Fig. 6.3

## 3 NATURAL FREQUENCY AND RESONANCE

An oscillating system once started and left to oscillate keeps constant time. The frequency of its oscillation is called the **natural frequency**. If, now, a small force is applied at the end of each swing, any energy converted during the oscillation is replaced and added to. This causes large amplitude oscillations to build up. A typical example is a child on a swing. A small push at the end of each swing builds up a large amplitude.

The **mass** on a spring behaves in the same way, if connected to a vibration generator driven at a range of frequencies (Fig. 6.4). When the frequency of the generator (**the driver**) matches the natural frequency of the system (**the responder**) then the mass makes large-amplitude vibrations. This is called **resonance**.

A car, or a large piece of machinery, has many moving parts, each with its own natural frequency. When designing such machines, it is important to take resonance into account since at particular engine frequencies some

Fig. 6.4 Apparatus for forced oscillations and resonance.

parts of the machine may begin large-scale vibrations, with possibly dangerous results.

The human body also has a sequence of natural frequencies, for example the stomach and the diaphragm. It is thought that resonance of these may be responsible for sea- or travel-sickness, the nausea being induced by strong vibrations at particular frequencies. Similarly, the eyeball is suspended in its socket like a mass on a spring. Resonance of the eyeball is a dangerous problem often experienced by helicopter pilots.

Perhaps the most famous example of resonance is the collapse of the **Tacoma Narrows Bridge** in the USA. Wind gusts at the natural frequency of the bridge caused the whole bridge to oscillate, and as the amplitude increased, the oscillations led to the eventual and spectacular collapse of the bridge.

## 4 WAVES

We have already met the idea that a **wave** carries **energy** from one place to another, and that oscillating particles or fields enable this to happen. There are two types of wave, **transverse** and **longitudinal**.

A **transverse wave** is like a wave along a string or a rope. In Fig. 6.5 the energy is being transferred from left to right, but the particles of the rope are only moving up or down. This is a transverse wave. The direction of the particle oscillations is at 90° to the direction of energy transfer. Other examples are water waves and electromagnetic waves (though for electromagnetic waves it is fields not particles which oscillate).

Fig. 6.5 Transverse wave.

> It is worth noting that these are the only two common examples of longitudinal waves. All the rest are transverse.

A spring like a "slinky" can be used to demonstrate a longitudinal wave. Here the particles oscillate about fixed points from left to right, and the energy is also transferred from left to right. Sound waves are also longitudinal waves (Fig. 6.6).

Fig. 6.6. Longitudinal wave.

The **amplitude** (A) of a **wave** has the same meaning as it has for an oscillation. It is the **maximum displacement of a particle from rest** (Fig. 6.7).

The **wavelength** is the **distance between wave crests** or **wave troughs**. It is given the symbol λ and is measured in metres (Fig. 6.8). Many other points on a

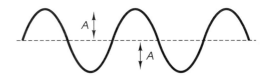

Fig. 6.7 Wave amplitude.

wave are also a wavelength apart, and some are marked in Fig. 6.9. Notice that at such points the particles are moving in the **same direction**, and with the **same speed**. They are described as being **in phase**. So **wavelength** can also be defined as the **distance between adjacent particles in phase**.

Fig. 6.8

Fig. 6.9 At points one wavelength apart, particles are in phase.

The **frequency** of a wave is the **number of complete cycles of disturbance each second**. It is measured in Hertz (Hz)

If a wave has a wavelength of 2 m and a frequency of 20 Hz then it will make 20 complete cycles of movement each second. Each cycle carries wave energy forward by one wavelength (2 m). So at the end of 1 s the energy has travelled (20 × 2) = 40 m, and the wave velocity is 40 m/s.

In general if the velocity is $v$, the frequency $f$ and wavelength λ then

 $$v = f\lambda$$

---

### EXAMPLE 1

Sound travels at 330 m/s in air. If a note of 150 Hz is struck on a piano, what is the wavelength of the sound wave? Using

$$v = f\lambda$$
$$330 = 150\lambda$$

Therefore

$$\lambda = \frac{330}{150} = \underline{2.2\ m}$$

### EXAMPLE 2

Water waves are generated at 20 Hz. If their wavelength is 2 cm what is the wave speed? From

$$v = f\lambda$$
$$v = 20 \times (0.02)\ \text{(note } \lambda \text{ in metres)}$$
$$v = \underline{0.4\ m/s}$$

---

## 5 ➤ SOUND WAVES

Sound waves are the only common example of a *longitudinal* wave. Sound can only be transferred through a material (medium). It cannot travel through space (a vacuum). This is usually demonstrated with a bell inside an evacuated jar (Fig. 6.10). The bell can be seen to be ringing but no sound can pass through the vacuum. If air is let into the jar, the sound can be heard again.

> ❝❝ The electrical pattern of voltage change is an ANALOGUE of the pattern of pressure change in the longitudinal wave. ❞❞

Fig. 6.10 Sound cannot pass through a vacuum.

Sound is transferred through air by the oscillation of molecules. Near a source of sound, molecules oscillate at the frequency of the source, causing regions of *compression*, where molecules are closer together than when the gas is undisturbed (Fig. 6.11).

Fig. 6.11 Compressions (C) and rarefactions (R) in a sound wave.

Equally there are regions where molecules are further apart than usual. These are called *rarefactions*. The sound is transferred by this sequence of compression and rarefactions. The wavelength ($\lambda$) is the *average distance* from one compression to the next, or from one rarefaction to the next.

Because it is difficult to represent a longitudinal wave, sound waves are often studied using a microphone connected to a cathode ray oscilloscope (CRO). The microphone converts the longitudinal signal into an electrical signal, which is displayed on the CRO as an equivalent transverse wave. However, the original wave was longitudinal.

A signal generator can produce the sound, if connected to a loudspeaker, so that amplitude and frequency can be easily controlled (Fig. 6.12). Using this apparatus the following effects can be seen and heard:

Fig. 6.12 A microphone gives an electrical signal corresponding to pressure changes.

1. A loud sound produces a large-amplitude wave (Fig. 6.13).
2. Higher-pitch sounds have higher frequencies and therefore shorter wavelengths (Fig. 6.14).
3. Musical instruments playing the same note produce different waveforms. This is described as producing notes of *different quality* (Fig. 6.15).

Fig. 6.13

All sounds start from a vibratioon

 Low pitch

 High pitch

 Note on tuning fork

 Same note on piano

Fig. 6.14

Fig. 6.15

## 6 SPEED OF SOUND AND ECHOES

Sound, like all waves, can be **reflected**, and the reflected wave is heard as an **echo**. This can be used as a means of finding the **speed** of sound in air.

Standing as far as possible from a smooth wall, a regular sequence of clapping noises is made. If the sequence is of low frequency, it will be followed by a sequence of echoes:

Clap—Echo—Clap—Echo—Clap

If the rate of clapping is increased, there comes a time when no echo is heard. This takes place when each echo corresponds to the next clap, i.e. in the time between one clap and the next, sound has travelled to the wall and back, a distance $2d$ (Fig. 6.16).

If, say, 20 such claps are timed, then the time between one clap and the next is known.

Time for 20 claps = $T$ seconds
Interval between claps = $T/20$ seconds
Distance travelled by sound = $2d$

Velocity of sound
$$= \frac{2d}{T/20}$$
$$= \frac{2 \times 20 \times d}{T}$$

This type of method is used in echo-sounding. The speed of sound depends on the material through which it travels. The greater the density of the material the greater the speed. Typical values for the same frequency are given in Table 6.1.

Table 6.1

| Material | Frequency (Hz) | Wave-length (m) | Velocity (m/s) |
|---|---|---|---|
| Air | 300 | 1.1 | 330 |
| Sea-water | 300 | 4 | 1200 |
| Steel | 300 | 8.3 | 2500 |

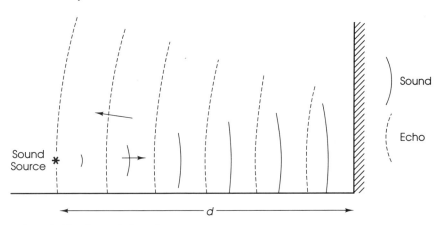

Fig. 6.16 Echo method for the speed of sound in air.

## 7 WAVE BEHAVIOUR USING WATER WAVES

Water waves are often used to examine the more general behaviour of waves because they can be seen easily, and because the velocity is small and the wavelength large for a fixed frequency. A ripple tank is normally used for this. When single water drops are pulsed regularly into a tank, a pattern is produced as in Fig. 6.17. The circular lines are called **wavefronts** and the lines with arrows

show the **direction** of energy transfer (at 90° to the wavefront).

Fig. 6.17 Wavefronts and wave direction.

## THE RIPPLE TANK

The ripple tank shows what happens to water ripples as they are reflected or refracted at different surfaces. Since these are simple transverse waves, the patterns and properties shown also apply to other types of wave. You should compare the results seen with those in the chapter on Optics and the nature of light.

(a) The ripple tank

(b) The vibrator to produce waves

Fig. 6.18

The tank is shallow and has a perspex base with sloping sides. As a ripple crosses the surface the light above the tank shows the ripple as a shadow on the screen below. (You can see this sort of shadow pattern on the bottom of an ordinary sink or bath —if you dip your finger in and out of the water you can see circular shadows of the ripples.) The sloping sides stop the waves being reflected from the sides and complicating the pattern. Straight (plane) waves can be produced by dipping a short straight length of wood in and out of the water. This is usually done by hanging the wooden beam on two rubber bands and making it vibrate up and down by means of a small electric motor driving an eccentric. (An eccentric is a small metal cylinder with the axle hole off centre so that it doesn't spin smoothly.) If circular ripples are required they are produced by raising the bar and fitting a small plastic ball as a "dipper" to it so that the ball just touches the surface.

The patterns can be made to appear stationary by viewing them through a spinning disc with a slot cut in it. If the disc spins at the correct speed the waves will have moved on by one wavelength each time the slit comes round so that the pattern always looks the same. This is the **"stroboscope effect"**. Another method is to replace the lamp with a flashing light (stroboscopic lamp) and adjust the flash rate until it is the same as the frequency at which the beam is bouncing up and down. Each time that you see the pattern it will be in the same place and looks stationary.

To make reflectors, strips of aluminium about 30 mm wide can be bent into the appropriate shape and used as mirrors by standing them in the path of the waves in the tank. You will produce patterns that show that the laws of reflection and the images produced by curved mirrors are all properties of waves.

To make the water shallower to change the speed of the ripples and get refraction you can put pieces of perspex of the correct shape into the bottom of the tank so that the perspex is only just covered by the water.

A straight-edged barrier oscillating in water in a ripple tank gives **plane** wavefronts, with the direction of energy transfer at 90° to the wavefront as before (Fig. 6.19). Continuous waves of either type can be produced using a small motor, and the waves then need to be viewed with a stroboscope (see "Applied Materials"). Just as sound can be reflected, so can any wave.

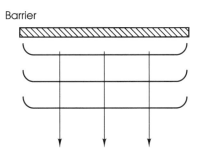

Fig. 6.19 Plane wavefronts.

In a ripple tank, a **circular wavefront** approaching a flat barrier is reflected as in Fig. 6.20. The reflected wave **appears** to have come from a point **behind** the barrier. This point is an **image** of the original source of waves and lies as far behind the barrier as the source lay in front of it (Fig. 6.21). A **plane wave** hitting a flat barrier is reflected as a plane wave. In both cases there is no change of velocity, wavelength or frequency on reflection (Fig. 6.22).

Fig. 6.20 Reflection of a barrier.

Fig. 6.21

If a plane wave approaches a barrier obliquely (i.e. at an angle) the wave **direction** follows the usual reflection rule, in that **the angle between the direction and barrier before reflection is the same as after reflection**. Again the

wavefronts are at 90° to the wave direction, and there is no change of velocity, wavelength or frequency (Fig. 6.23).

Fig. 6.22 Reflection of plane wavefronts.

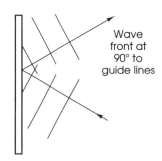

Fig. 6.23

When the waves are reflected you will often see both the incident and reflected waves. If you reflect plane waves from a straight barrier you will be able to see a pattern of parallelograms as the two sets of waves cross. If the waves hit the barrier at 45° the pattern becomes squares. At any other angle the pattern becomes parallelograms as shown in Fig. 6.24.

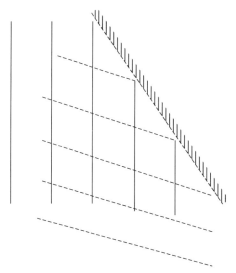

Fig. 6.24

## (A) REFRACTION OF WAVES

**Refraction** is an effect concerned with a **velocity change**. Sound waves change velocity in moving from one material to another; so does light in passing from air to glass. Water waves change velocity on moving from deep to shallow water. The effect is clearly seen in a ripple tank and the ideas can be applied to other waves.

In shallow water, waves generated at a particular frequency travel more slowly than in deep water (Fig. 6.25).

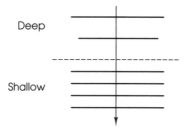

Fig. 6.25 Wave velocity is less in shallow water.

> The frequency is of course fixed by the oscillation frequency of whatever causes the original disturbance to produce the wave.

▶ Since $v = f\lambda$ and $f$ is the same in both cases then, as the velocity is reduced, so is the wavelength.

If the change of depth occurs obliquely, the change in velocity also results in a change in direction (Fig. 6.26). As the wavefronts are successively slowed down, the new fronts travel at an angle to the original fronts. See also Chapter 9.

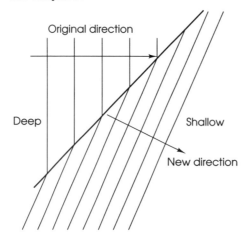

Fig. 6.26 Refraction of waves.

## (B) INTERFERENCE OF WAVES

This is a special case of the ability of waves to *superimpose*. If two **pulses** (single disturbances rather than a sequence of disturbances) are *travelling in opposite directions* they will meet and their *amplitudes add*, after which they continue as before. The sequence is shown in Fig. 6.27.

Fig. 6.27 Constructive superposition.

Similarly, if their *amplitudes were in opposite directions*, when they meet their *amplitudes subtract* (Fig. 6.28).

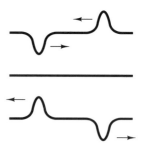

Fig. 6.28 Destructive superposition.

In the special case of *equal amplitudes*, they **combine** to give either a *maximum* of double the amplitude of one pulse or a *minimum* of zero amplitude.

**Waves** also combine in this way. If the two waves meet, and are of equal wavelength, frequency and amplitude, and are *in phase*, they combine to give a single wave of maximum amplitude $2A$ (Fig. 6.29). This is called *constructive interference*. If, however, they are *out of phase* they combine to give zero resultant amplitude. This is described as a wave minimum (Fig. 6.30). This is *destructive interference*.

Fig. 6.29 Constructive interference.

Fig. 6.30 Destructive interference.

This behaviour can again be seen in a ripple tank with two connected vibrating sources, ensuring waves of the same amplitude, frequency and wavelength. The resulting pattern is viewed through a stroboscope.

At points like X in Fig. 6.31, two wave crests (maxima) are meeting. These will at

**66** All points along a line of maximum interference are oscillating, but points along a minimum line are always at rest. **99**

some time give the maximum amplitude of 2*A*, and all points along the lines of maxima will also at some time be a maximum. The waves at a "maximum" point **combine** to give a greater value of (+2*A*) and a least value of (−2*A*). They will vary periodically between these values.

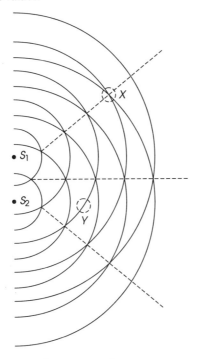

Fig. 6.31 Lines of maximum interference.

At a point like Y a maximum (crest) and a minimum (trough) are meeting. These points will always be at zero amplitude — so there is no disturbance of water, because at all times they are out of phase. The sequence is shown in Fig. 6.32. The minima are lines of zero disturbance in an otherwise moving pattern.

This can be demonstrated for sound waves using two matched speakers in a large room (Fig. 6.33). If the speakers are connected to the same signal generator then, moving parallel to the speakers, areas of "sound" and "silence" will be obvious ("silence" will not be total because of added waves caused by reflection from the walls and ceiling of the room).

Fig. 6.33 Interference of sound waves.

## (C) DIFFRACTION OF WAVES

Waves can **change the shape** of their wavefront on moving past the edge of an object or on passing through a gap in an object. They do not change velocity, frequency or wavelength. This is easily observed in a ripple tank. If plane waves approach a barrier, they spread beyond its edges. This effect is called **diffraction** (note that as in Fig. 6.34 part of the wave is

Fig. 6.34 Edge diffraction.

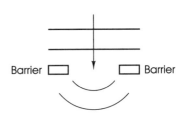

Fig. 6.35 Slit diffraction.

reflected). Similarly, diffraction also takes place on approaching a gap in a barrier with the wave being found beyond the edges of the barrier (Fig. 6.35). The amount of diffraction depends on the **size of the gap** and the **wavelength of the wave**.

▶ The **wider the gap**, as compared with the wavelength, **the less the observable diffraction** (Fig. 6.36). The gap needs to be about a few wavelengths wide for diffraction to be appreciable.

▶ The **smaller the wavelength for a fixed gap, the less the amount of diffraction**. This effect is especially important with electromagnetic waves.

Fig. 6.36 Larger gaps give less diffraction.

Fig. 6.32 The sequence of events at a minimum point.

## 8 > ELECTRO-MAGNETIC WAVES

These will also be discussed in Chapter 9 since light is a particular example of an electromagnetic wave. Here it is enough to point out the following facts about *electromagnetic waves*:

1. They are produced and propagated by changing fields and not by particles. The fields originate in accelerating charges.
2. They can travel through space since they do not require a material to transfer energy.
3. They are transverse waves, unlike sound which is a longitudinal wave.
4. They all travel at the same velocity ($3 \times 10^8$ m/s) in a vacuum.
5. They have no single wavelength. They occupy a wide band of wavelengths from $10^{-14}$ m (gamma waves) to $10^4$ m (radio waves).
6. They include visible light, which consists of a range of wavelengths from $3.3 \times 10^{-7}$ m (violet) to $6.6 \times 10^{-7}$ m (for red).

For more information on the electromagnetic spectrum see Chapter 9, "Optics and the nature of light".

## 9 > HEARING AND THE HUMAN EAR

Sound waves from a source cause compressions and rarefactions of air particles, resulting in pressure changes in the air. These pressure changes occur at the frequency of the source, causing flexible objects to vibrate strongly at the same frequency.

The human ear is based inside the skull (Fig. 6.37). The external gristle and cartilage flap (the pinna) may "collect" sound, but is thought to be a directional or warning aid. The "outer" ear is a tube leading inside the skull, and is air-filled. The ear-drum at the end of the outer ear vibrates at the frequency of pressure changes applied to it. These vibrations are passed along an interconnecting sequence of bones, the hammer, anvil and stirrup, which act as "distance multipliers" in a level system. They connect to the "oval window" which, being smaller than the ear-drum, gives a "force multiplication" rather like a car-brake system. Beyond the oval window the inner ear is liquid-filled. Vibration of fine hairs in the liquid causes nerve stimulation resulting in impulses passed to the brain and the response of "hearing".

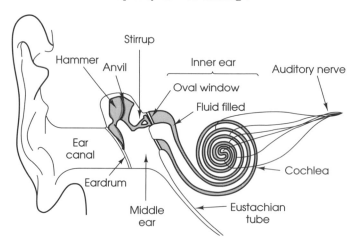

Fig. 6.37

## EXTENSION MATERIALS

## 10 > HARMONICS AND OVERTONES

### HARMONICS

A **harmonic** is a multiple of a basic (fundamental) frequency. Harmonics can be a problem when an apparatus produces harmonics that are strong enough. You would not want a radio receiver to pick up other stations transmitting on harmonics of the one that you are listening to!

### OVERTONES

These are the multiples (harmonics) of the fundamental frequency of a note that are mixed with the fundamental when the note is played on a particular instrument. These **overtones** give the note its particular quality or "timbre". Different instruments produce different overtones or different amounts of the same overtones and therefore don't sound the same, even when playing the same note. Some instruments can produce all the harmonics, some only the odd or even multiples. The overtones closest to the original fundamental frequency will be loudest.

You can display the waveshapes from different instruments by playing the instrument close to a microphone that is connected to an oscilloscope through an amplifier. You will be able to see that different instruments playing the same note display a different waveshape because of the different overtones. The wave still repeats in the same time with the same underlying wavelength and frequency. Some computers will now let you record a sound and then display its wave on the screen. This is another useful way of seeing the different shapes. Analysing the different shapes of the same basic sound is the basis for voice recognition which is starting to be used on some computers.

This example can be applied to the investigation of any oscillator. The chosen apparatus is the mass and spring oscillator. A spring is firmly fixed to a rigidly held retort stand and clamp. A mass and holder (total 100 g) are connected as shown and the equilibrium position marked on a vertical fixed metre rule (Fig. 6.38). To investigate the motion a number of repeated timings needs to be taken.

## DOES THE PERIOD DEPEND ON AMPLITUDE?

The mass is displaced from rest by, say, 2 cm and the time for five oscillations recorded. This is repeated at least three times and a *mean* taken.

The procedure is repeated for displacements of 4, 6, 8 cm, each time recording the mean of three sets of five complete oscillations.

## RESULTS

Table 6.2

| Amplitude (cm) | Time for five oscillations (s) | Mean time for five oscillations (s) |
|---|---|---|
| 2 | | |
| 4 | | |
| 6 | | |

## DOES THE PERIOD VARY WITH THE MASS ADDED?

The amplitude is initially fixed, perhaps 4 cm, and the mass is changed in equal multiples of 100 g. Timings are as before.

## RESULTS

Table 6.3

| Mass (g) | Time for five oscillations (s) | Mean time for five oscillations (s) | Period, $T$ (s) |
|---|---|---|---|
| 100 | | | |
| 200 | | | |
| 300 | | | |

## DOES THE PERIOD VARY WITH THE STRENGTH OF THE SPRING?

This is more difficult to investigate. The amplitude and mass should be kept constant, and a number of springs which are similar should be available. Two springs in *parallel* double the overall *spring constant* (stiffness). Two springs in *series* have half the overall *spring constant*. The results should be recorded as before.

## PRECAUTIONS

1. Take care not to overload the spring or otherwise to exceed its elastic limit.
2. Repeated timings will reduce uncertainty in the value of the time period.

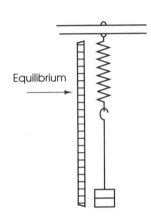

Equilibrium

Fig. 6.38

**11** **THE MOTION OF A SIMPLE OSCILLATOR**

# EXAMINATION QUESTIONS

## QUESTION 1

Which one of the following is an example of a longitudinal wave?

  A  Ripples in water in a ripple tank
  B  VHF radio waves
  C  Visible light
  D  Waves along a stretched rope
  E  Sound from a guitar        (ULEAC)

## QUESTION 2

Which one of the following would change the period of oscillation of a pendulum?

  A  Increase the length of the pendulum.
  B  Increase the mass of the pendulum.
  C  Change the thickness of the string on the pendulum.
  D  Change the density of the pendulum bob.

## QUESTION 3

A child stands some way from a high flat wall. She claps her hands and half a second later hears an echo. How far from the wall is she standing? (Take the speed of sound in air to be 320 m/s.)

  A  80 m
  B  160 m
  C  320 m
  D  670 m
  E  720 m

## QUESTION 4

Which of the following statements about waves is incorrect?

  A  The speed of a wave is how far the front of a wave travels in one second.
  B  The frequency of a wave is the time that it takes a wave to pass a point.
  C  The wavelength is the distance from crest to crest.
  D  Waves can carry energy from one place to another.
  E  Waves can carry information from one place to another.

## QUESTION 5

Figure 6.39 shows a water wave travelling in the direction of the arrow. As the wave moves forward which of the following will happen?

**Fig. 6.39**

  A  P and Q move from left to right.
  B  P will go down, Q will go up.
  C  P will go up, Q will go up.
  D  P will go down, Q will go down.

## QUESTION 6

In which of the following materials will a sound wave travel fastest?

  A  A vacuum
  B  Air
  C  Water
  D  Steel

## QUESTION 7

Figure 6.40 shows a wave diffracting through a slit in a barrier. If the frequency of the wave is made greater which of the following will happen?

  A  The wavelength increases; the amount of diffraction increases.
  B  The wavelength decreases; the amount of diffraction decreases.
  C  The wavelength increases; the amount of diffraction decreases.
  D  The wavelength decreases; the amount of diffraction increases.
  E  Both wavelength and amount of diffraction stay the same.

**Fig. 6.40**

## QUESTION 8

When water waves in a shallow ripple tank move from a shallow region to a deeper region which of the following will happen?

  A  The wavelength stays the same; the velocity stays the same.
  B  The wavelength increases; the velocity increases.
  C  The wavelength decreases; the velocity

decreases.

D  The wavelength increases; the velocity decreases.

E  The wavelength decreases; the velocity increases.

## QUESTION 9

Which of the following is not an electromagnetic wave?

A  X-rays

B  Ultrasound

C  Light

D  Radio

E  Ultraviolet                    (ULEAC)

## QUESTION 10

Which of the following is not possible for a sound wave?

A  Reflection

B  Interference

C  Travelling through space

D  Changing speed in different materials

E  Diffraction

## STRUCTURED QUESTIONS

Fig. 6.41

Fig. 6.43

## QUESTION 11

Figure 6.41 shows a fishing boat using sonar to detect a shoal of fish. A short pulse of sound waves is emitted from the boat, and the echo from the shoal is detected $^1/_{10}$ s later. The sound waves travel through sea-water at 1500 m/s.

(a)  How far has the pulse travelled in $^1/_{10}$ s?

(b)  How far below the boat is the shoal?

(c)  The reflected pulse lasts longer than the emitted pulse. Suggest a reason for this.                    (NISEAC)

## QUESTION 12

A microphone is connected to a cathode ray oscilloscope. Three sounds are made in turn in front of the microphone. The traces A, B and C produced on the screen are shown in Fig. 6.42. (The controls on the oscilloscope are not altered during this experiment.)

(a)  Which trace is the loudest sound? Explain your answer.

(b)  Which trace is due to the sound with the lowest pitch? Explain your answer.
                    (NISEAC)

## QUESTION 13

Figure 6.43 represents a wave on a rope.

(a)  Show clearly on the diagram what is meant by:

(i)  The wavelength of the wave;

(ii)  The amplitude of the wave.

(b)  State in words the equation which relates the speed of a wave to its wavelength and frequency.

(c)  Use the equation to find the speed of a water wave which has a wavelength of 4 cm and a frequency of 6 Hz.
                    (ULEAC)

## QUESTION 14

Sonar waves are emitted from a surface vessel which is determining the depth of the sea. The emitted signal and its reflection from the sea-bed are displayed on the screen of an oscilloscope as shown in Fig. 6.44.

The speed of sound in water is 1200 m/s and the horizontal speed of the oscilloscope trace is 8 cm/s. Calculate the depth of the sea at this point.

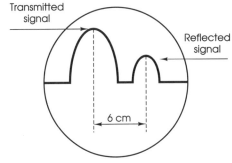

Fig. 6.44

(a)

(a)

(a)

Fig. 6.42

## QUESTION 15

Figure 6.45 shows an arrangement to observe the interference of sound waves of a single frequency from loudspeakers A and B. The microphone is placed at position P, a point at which constructive interference occurs, and then at Q at which destructive interference occurs.

Show on the diagrams (Fig. 6.46) what will be seen on the oscilloscope screen when one loudspeaker is switched on and when both are switched on. (The oscilloscope is adjusted so that the amplitude due to each wave is about 0.5 cm on the screen and so that one complete waveform may be displayed.)

(ULEAC)

**Fig. 6.45**

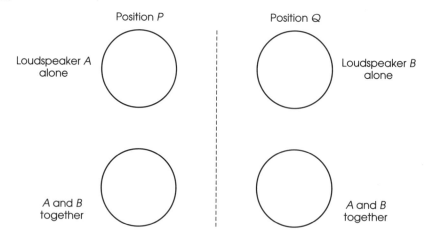

**Fig. 6.46**

## QUESTION 16

(a)  A cork is floating on water. A stone is dropped into the water.

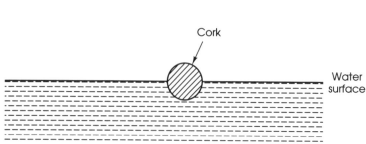

**Fig. 6.47**

(i)  After a short time the cork begins to move. Describe how the cork moves.

(ii)  What property of a wave causes the cork to move?

The graph below shows how the displacement of the cork from its original position varies with time.

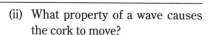

**Fig. 6.48**

(iii)  What is the amplitude and frequency of the water wave?

(iv)  The water waves have a wavelength of 0.8 m. Calculate the velocity of the water waves. Show clearly how you obtain your answer.

(b) One method of finding the velocity of sound is to use a cathode ray oscilloscope (CRO), a loudspeaker and a microphone.

**Fig. 6.49**

The loudspeaker makes a clicking noise which is detected by the microphone and displayed on the CRO.

The diagram below shows what is seen on the CRO.

For the *x* axis
1 cm = 2 milliseconds (ms)

**Fig. 6.50**

(i) The spot on the CRO starts to move across the screen from 0 just as each click is made.
How long does it take the sound to reach the microphone?
Show clearly how you obtain your answer.

When the loudspeaker is moved a FURTHER 2 m from the microphone the trace below is seen. The settings on the CRO are the same as before. Again the spot started at 0 when the first click was made.

For the *x* axis
1 cm = 2 ms

**Fig. 6.51**

(ii) Use the information in (b) (i) to find the velocity of sound. Show clearly how you obtain your answer.

(c) Loudspeakers used in theatres are arranged vertically as shown in the diagram 1 below. Explain why this is better than arranging them horizontally as shown in diagram 2.
(NISEAC Central tier)

**Fig. 6.52**

# OUTLINE ANSWERS

**1 MULTIPLE CHOICE QUESTIONS**

| Question | 1 | 2 | 3 | 4 | 5 | 6 | 7 | 8 | 9 | 10 |
|----------|---|---|---|---|---|---|---|---|---|----|
| Answer | E | A | A | B | C | D | B | B | B | C |

**2 STRUCTURED QUESTIONS**

## ANSWER 11

(a) Sound travels at 1500 m/s. In $^1/_{10}$ s the pulse travels 150 m.
(b) The pulse has travelled to the shoal and back. The shoal is 150/2 = <u>75 m</u> below the boat.
(c) The pulse will reflect off several "layers" of fish in the shoal, so that the collected reflection will have parts which have travelled further than others and will therefore last longer.

## ANSWER 12

(a) Trace C. Loudness is related to wave amplitude.

(b) Trace A. Pitch relates to frequency. Lowest frequency also means longest wavelength.

## ANSWER 13

(a) See Fig. 6.53.
(b) Speed = Frequency × wavelength.
(c) $v = 6 \times 0.04 = 0.24$ m/s.

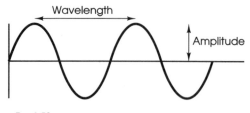

Fig. 6.53

## ANSWER 14

Time between pulses: dot on screen travels 6 cm at 8 cm/s

$$\text{Time} = 6/8 = 0.75 \text{ s}$$

Distance travelled by sound
$$= \text{Speed in water} \times \text{time}$$
$$= 1200 \times 0.75$$
$$= 900 \text{ m}$$
Sound has travelled to sea-bed and back
$$\text{Depth} = 900/2 = \underline{450 \text{ m}}$$

## ANSWER 15

See Fig. 6.54.

## ANSWER 16

(a) (i) The cork moves up and down.

(ii) The waves carry energy
(iii) Amplitude = 5 cm frequency = 0.5 Hz
(iv) Velocity = frequency × wavelength
= $0.5 \times 0.8 = 0.4$ m/s

(b) (i) Time = $2 \times 2$ ms = 4 ms
(ii) Time in second diagram = $4.8 \times 2$ ms = 9.6 ms
Time to cover additional 2 m = $9.6 - 4 = 5.6$ ms

$$\text{Velocity} = \frac{\text{distance}}{\text{time}} = \frac{2 \times 1000}{5.6} = 357 \text{ m/s}$$

(Note that the time is in milliseconds which gives the 1000 in the final equation)

(c) The sound will be diffracted more through a narrower gap. The vertical speakers will therefore diffract the sound more horizontally to reach more of the audience whereas the horizontal speakers would diffract the sound vertically.

Fig. 6.54

# TUTOR'S QUESTION AND ANSWER

Figure 6.55 shows a large-diameter steel pipe 80 m long (not drawn to scale). An experimenter at E bangs the pipe and his assistant at O listens for the sound reaching him.

(a) Explain why the assistant will hear two sounds, one arriving after the other.
(b) In an experiment to measure the time needed for sound to travel through air from E to O five values were recorded: 0.20, 0.28, 0.25, 0.27 and 0.23 s. Find
(i) The mean time;
(ii) The mean speed of sound in air.

(c) Suggest how you would attempt to measure the time needed for the sound to travel from E to O through the air.
(d) Further experiments were conducted by:
(i) Hitting the pipe harder, producing much louder sound.
(ii) Using a different pipe which gave the sound a considerably increased pitch. What would you expect to be the effect on the velocity of sound in air in each case? (UCLES)

Steel pipe

O          E

**Fig. 6.55**

**ANSWER**

(a) Sound travels fastest on the most dense material. The assistant will hear the sound wave transmitted through the steel pipe before the wave which travels through the surrounding air.

(b) Values are 0.20, 0.28, 0.25, 0.27, 0.23 s.
Sum of values = 1.23 s

$$\text{Mean} = \frac{1.23}{5} = \underline{0.25\ \text{s}} \qquad (0.246)$$

$$\text{Speed} = \frac{\text{Distance}}{\text{Time}} = \frac{80}{0.25}$$

$$= \underline{320\ \text{m/s}}$$

(c) A signal must be arranged between the experimenter E and the assistant O. At the signal, E strikes the rod and O starts a clock. When O hears the **second** sound (i.e. through air) the clock is stopped. This is clearly a crude method and many attempts would be needed to reduce the uncertainty in measurement.

(d) (i)  No change;
(ii)  No change.
Reason not required but velocity of a wave is a function of the **medium** not the mechanism by which it is produced.

# STUDENT'S ANSWER WITH THE EXAMINER'S COMMENTS

## STUDENT'S ANSWER TO TUTOR'S QUESTION

**66** Not a very helpful expression. **99**

**66** Good. By the end of the question the student has realised that it is the *difference* in velocity values which matters. **99**

**66** Good. Well set out. **99**

**66** Sensible number of figures here. **99**

**66** "Millisecond" timer. **99**

**66** Good. **99**

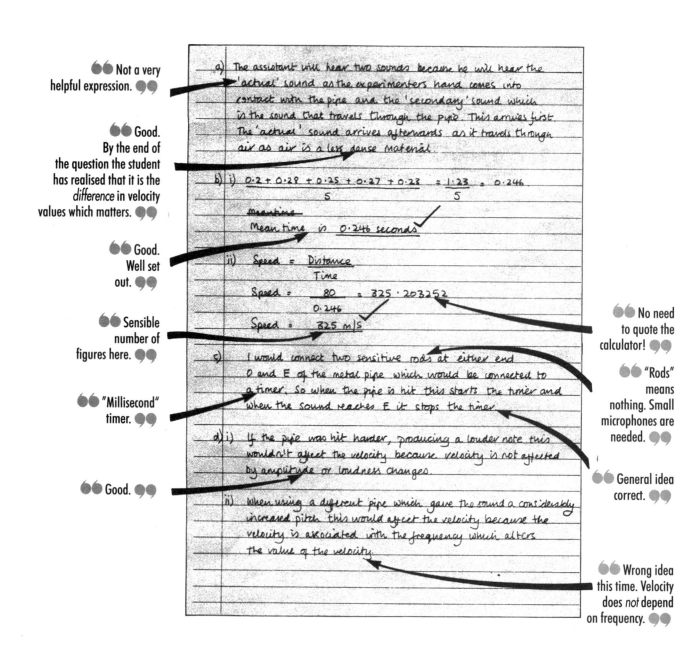

a) The assistant will hear two sounds because he will hear the 'actual' sound as the experimenters hand comes into contact with the pipe and the 'secondary' sound which is the sound that travels through the pipe. This arrives first. The 'actual' sound arrives afterwards as it travels through air as air is a less dense material.

b) i) $\dfrac{0.2 + 0.28 + 0.25 + 0.27 + 0.23}{5} = \dfrac{1.23}{5} = 0.246$

Meantime

Mean time is 0.246 seconds ✓

ii) Speed = $\dfrac{\text{Distance}}{\text{Time}}$

Speed = $\dfrac{80}{0.246}$ = 325.203252

Speed = 325 m/s ✓

c) I would connect two sensitive rods at either end O and E of the metal pipe which would be connected to a timer. So when the pipe is hit this starts the timer and when the sound reaches E it stops the timer.

d) i) If the pipe was hit harder, producing a louder note this wouldn't affect the velocity because velocity is not affected by amplitude or loudness changes.

ii) When using a different pipe which gave the sound a considerably increased pitch this would affect the velocity because the velocity is associated with the frequency which alters the value of the velocity.

**66** No need to quote the calculator! **99**

**66** "Rods" means nothing. Small microphones are needed. **99**

**66** General idea correct. **99**

**66** Wrong idea this time. Velocity does *not* depend on frequency. **99**

# REVIEW SHEET

■ Sound is an example of a _____ wave.

■ All the electromagnetic waves are _____ waves.

■ Sound always starts at something that is _____ .

■ The units for frequency are _____ .

■ Complete the wave equation

Velocity = _____.

■ Sound cannot travel through a _____.

■ Sound waves travel faster in _____ dense materials.

■ In the spaces draw a sketch of the wave pattern that you would see on a ripple tank set up as described.

1. Plane waves hit a plane barrier at an angle.    2. Plane waves hit a concave barrier.

3. Plane waves are refracted in shallower water.    4. Plane waves diffract through a narrow gap.

■ A radio wave of frequency 200 kHz has a wavelength of 1500 m. What is its velocity?

■ Two similar waves that arrive at the same place out of phase will _____. This is called _____ interference.

■ If longer waves arrive at a narrow gap they will be diffracted _____ than shorter ones. Blue light will therefore be diffracted _____ than red light at a narrow slit.

■ Fm radio waves have a higher frequency than those on the medium waveband. Their wavelength is _____ so when they pass over hills or past other barriers they are diffracted _____ This can make them more difficult to receive.

■ A ripple tank has sloping sides so that _____
_____.

■ If a wave has a frequency of 256 Hz its first harmonic will have a frequency of
_____.

■ The frequency of a pendulum depends only on its _____ .

■ A brighter light wave has a greater _____.

■ A sound with a greater frequency has a greater _____.

■ When a system vibrates at its own natural frequency because of vibrations of the
same frequency from outside it is called _____. It is important to avoid this
in the design of _____ (several possible answers for this last word!).

■ Check that you can

(i) Describe an experiment to find the speed of sound.

(ii) Label the parts of a human ear on the following diagram and explain how it
works.

Fig. 6.56

# CHAPTER 7

# CIRCUITS AND DIRECT CURRENTS

## GETTING STARTED

We all use electrical equipment, at home, at school, in offices and factories. Electricity is the most adaptable energy form, because it is easily converted into other forms which simply make life easier – light to turn "night into day", heat to change winter cold at home into all-year comfort, kinetic energy to move motors in washing machines, food mixers, vacuum cleaners. The availability of electrical energy has caused a revolution in social habits; and we take it for granted.

However, few people really understand how "electricity" *works*, many are frightened of it through their lack of understanding, and even more are confused by the terms used to describe what is going on. The aim of this chapter is to clear up some of these confusions and to deal with simple **circuits** where currents flow in one direction only.

A list of the circuit symbols that are used is in appendix 3 at the end of the book so that you can easily find and check them all.

# ESSENTIAL PRINCIPLES

## 1 > CIRCUITS AND CONDUCTORS

To make an electric current *flow*, an *energy supply* is needed – a battery, a power pack, the mains supply or some other energy source like a dynamo on a bicycle. The energy supply can cause a current flow if there is a complete route of **conducting** material for the current. All *metals* are good conductors, but carbon is exceptional because it is a non-metal and yet still conducts very well; liquids can conduct if they are ionic solutions.

Materials which do *not* conduct electricity are called **insulators**. A good insulator is usually a non-metal or a non-ionic material, like plastics, rubber and wood (Fig. 7.1).

| Conductor | Insulator |
|-----------|-----------|
| Copper | Wood |
| Iron | Sulphur |
| Aluminium | Polythene |
| Carbon | Rubber |
| Sea-water | Paraffin |
| Sulphuric acid | Propanone |

Fig. 7.1

This division into "conductors" and "insulators" is in fact a little too simple – for instance, glass conducts well near its melting-point, and even polythene allows a tiny current to flow through it. In general we shall use the term "conductor" to refer to very good current conductors and "insulator" to refer to very bad conductors.

Symbols are a useful way of drawing how a circuit is constructed. The diagrams in Fig. 7.2 show the symbols used in this chapter. Currents are assumed to flow from the ⊕ side of a battery or cell to the ⊖ side. (This is sometimes called the *conventional flow of current*.) The two lamp symbols are used to distinguish between a light deliberately used

to give illumination and one simply placed in a circuit to let you know if everything is working (indicator).

A **resistor** reduces current flow. A **variable resistor** can *change* current flow in a circuit.

**Switches** can direct *where* currents are able to flow. A switch is described as "open" when drawn like Fig. 7.3. No current will flow until it is closed (Fig. 7.4).

Single cell

Group of cells
(battery)

Lamp as indicator

Lamp for illumination

Resistor

Variable resistor

Fig. 7.2

Fig. 7.3 Open switch.

Fig. 7.4 Closed switch.

## 2 > CURRENTS

An electric current is a *flow* of charged particles. In a metal conductor these charges are *electrons*, which are part of the metal atoms and are able to move if they are given energy from a power supply. An *ammeter* is used to *measure current*, and the unit of current is called an *ampere* or amp (A).

The circuit in Fig. 7.5 illustrates an important point about currents in circuits. A

simple "loop" for current flow, with no branches, is called a **series** circuit. The current readings on all the ammeters will be the same, so *no current is used up* in flowing round the circuit. The current flowing into the bulb is the same as the current flowing out of it.

The *branching* circuit (Fig. 7.6) is called a *parallel* circuit, and the same rule applies.

Fig. 7.5 Current in a series circuit.

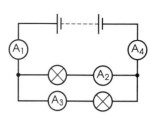

Fig. 7.6 Currents in a parallel circuit.

The currents in ammeters 1 and 4 are the same. The currents in ammeters 2 and 3 add up to the same as 1 or 4. Current is not "lost". It is only a flow of charges drifting slowly around a circuit, rather like water flowing through a group of connected pipes.

The "rule" is that the current, measured in amps, flowing *into* a point in a circuit is the *same* as the total current flowing *out* (Fig. 7.7).

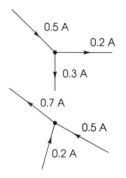

Fig. 7.7

### 3 CURRENT AND CHARGE

All materials are made up of *atoms*, and all atoms are made up of *charges*. The number of charged particles needed to make a current flow of 1 A is very large; $6.2 \times 10^{18}$ charged particles (electrons) need to flow in 1 s. So a "group word" is used to describe this large number; $6.2 \times 10^{18}$ charges is called 1 **coulomb** (C). This is like saying

12 objects = 1 dozen
20 objects = 1 score
144 objects = 1 gross

So $(6.2 \times 10^{18})$ electrons charges = 1 C

When a current of 1 A registers on an ammeter it means that 1 C of charge passes

Fig. 7.8

through the ammeter in 1 s. So 0.5 A means 0.5 coulombs per second (C/s), 10 A means 10 C/s, and for a current of 2 A to flow for 10 s means that $(2 \times 10) = 20$ C have passed through a point in a circuit.

If charge is given the symbol $Q$, current is given the symbol $I$, and time is called $t$, then

$$Q = I \times t$$

or

$$\textbf{Charge} = \textbf{Current} \times \textbf{Time}$$

This is another way of saying 1 amp means 1 coulomb per second.

### 4 ENERGY AND CHARGE – THE VOLT

In the circuit of Fig. 7.9, as we have seen, the current (flow of charge) is the same when it flows *into* a lamp, as when it flows *out*. Clearly, though, there is an *energy change* taking place as the current flows through a bulb, but this is *not* indicated by the value of the current shown on the ammeters.

If lamps X and Y were of different power, e.g. 60 W and 24 W, they would be seen to convert different amounts of energy – the 60 W lamp will be brighter than the 24 W lamp. So current, or flow of charge, is *not* the only important thing happening in a circuit. The *energy changes* matter too.

A *voltmeter* records the *energy converted* as each coulomb ($6.2 \times 10^{18}$ electrons) of charge moves from one point to another. Since voltmeters measure energy

Fig. 7.9

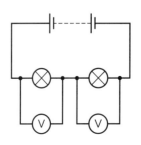

Fig. 7.10

changes between two points, they are connected *in parallel* across the points where the change in energy of a coulomb is to be detected.

▶ Just as 1 A means 1 C/s so 1 volt (V) means 1 *Joule* (J) of energy converted for each coulomb.

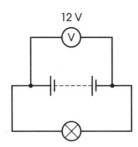

12 V

**Fig. 7.11**

The "voltage" across points in a circuit can measure two types of energy conversion. In the circuit of Fig. 7.11 the voltmeter is connected across the battery. Suppose it reads 12 V. This means 12 J of chemical energy from the battery are given to each coulomb, and converted to electrical energy.

A voltmeter connected across a bike dynamo may read 6 V. This means 6 J of energy are given to each coloumb and converted to electrical energy.

When a voltmeter records a change from some energy form to electrical, the "voltage" is described as the EMF (electromotive force) of the supply.

The circuit of Fig. 7.12 shows the voltmeter across a *lamp*. The energy change per coulomb is *from electrical to heat and light*. A voltmeter across a *motor* would record the change *from electrical to kinetic energy*.

When a voltmeter records a change from electrical energy *to another form*, the "voltage" is described as the p.d. (*potential difference*) between two points in the circuit.

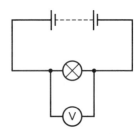

**Fig. 7.12**

---

*The energy equation*
If the p.d. in volts is the energy per coulomb then

$$V = \frac{E}{Q}$$

where p.d. = $V$, $E$ = energy in joules, $Q$ = charge in coulombs
so

$$E = V \times Q$$

and we already know that $Q = I \times t$ which means that

$$\boxed{E = V \times I \times t}$$

where $I$ is current in amps and $t$ is time in seconds.

Since $E$ is the energy released this is the equation that tells you how much heat is produced in an electric circuit and is an important equation!

---

5 ▷ **ELECTRICAL POWER**

Power has already been discussed as meaning "work done per second" or "energy transferred per second". Ammeters and voltmeters combined in a circuit can give this information about the *rate* of energy transfer.

0.2 A (A)

6 V

**Fig. 7.13**

In the circuit of Fig. 7.13 the current = 0.2 A = 0.2 C/s. The p.d. = 6 V = 6 joules per coulomb (J/C).

The *energy converted per second* is

$$6 \times 0.2 = 1.2 \text{ joules per second (J/s)}$$

$$= 1.2 \text{ W}$$

i.e.

$$\text{Current} \times \text{voltage} = \text{Power}$$

or

▶ $$P = I \times V$$

and since power is energy converted in 1 s, then

▶ $$\text{Energy} = I \times V \times t$$

where $t$ = time in seconds.

*The power equation*

You can also get this equation from the energy equation.

If power is the energy converted in 1 second then, putting $t = 1$ into the $E = V \times I \times t$ equation,

Energy per second $= V \times I$

so

$$\boxed{\text{Power} = V \times I}$$

the power will be in watts if the p.d. is in volts and the current is in amps.

---

## EXAMPLE

A lamp running normally needs a p.d. of 12 V and the current through it is 2 A.
1. What is the power of the bulb?
2. How much energy is converted in 2 minutes (min)?

1. $P = IV = 2 \times 12 = 24$ W
2. Time = 2 min = 120 s
   Energy $= IVt = 2 \times 12 \times 120$
   $= 2880$ J

When the Electricity Board sends out a bill for your electrical consumption, it is basically a bill for the energy you have used. If you run a 60 W lamp for 1 hour (h), you would use

$60 \times 60 \times 60 = 216\,000$ J

Clearly the energy measured in joules for an ordinary household would be a very large number each day. So for household or industrial measurements a *larger* energy unit is used – the *kilowatt-hour* (kWh). This is the energy converted by a 1 kW device running for 1 h. The Electricity Board calls this "1 unit"; each "unit" costs about 8p. To work out costs, then, you calculate the number of kilowatts and multiply by the number of hours, giving the number of "units". From this you can work out the cost (see Table 7.1).

---

Table 7.1

| Device | Power rating | Running time (h) | Units | Cost (p) |
|---|---|---|---|---|
| **Fire** | 3 kW | 2 | 6 | 48p |
| **TV** | 400 W = 0.4 kW | 3.5 | 1.4 | 11p approx. |
| **Reading lamp** | 100 W = 0.1 kW | 0.5 | 0.05 | 0.4p approx. |

---

## 6 MAINS ELECTRICITY, SAFETY AND FUSES

❝ Live = brown
Neutral = blue
Earth = green/yellow ❞

The mains supply is at 240 V and is an *alternating current* (AC). The wires carrying the supply are called *live* and *neutral* and wiring is colour-coded; live = *brown*; neutral–*blue*. All switches are fitted into the *live* side of a circuit. Fuses are also fitted into the live side. Power appliances are fitted with a three-pin plug (Fig. 7.14). The third wire is the *earth* wire, colour-coded *green/yellow*.

Fig. 7.14 Wiring in a mains plug.

The purpose of the *fuse* is to protect wiring from overheating because of

dangerously high currents. If the current rises *above* a safe level the thin wire in the fuse melts, causing a break in the circuit, like an automatic safety switch. It is important that the correct fuse is fitted to each appliance. Fuses are generally available as 3 A, 5 A and 13 A fuses. To find the *correct* value, you need to know the *power* of the appliance (this is marked on it by the manufacturer). For example, if a 2 kW fire is plugged into the mains (240 V): since

▶ $$P = IV$$

then

▶ $$I = P/V$$

So the working current $I = 2000/240 = 8.3$ A. The nearest fuse value would be 13 A. (3 A or 5 A would "blow" every time you switched on.)

For a 100 W table lamp, the working current is only $100/240 = 0.4$ A. And here the nearest fuse value is 3 A.

The *earth* wire is to protect you from

injury. It is connected to any metal casing on a piece of equipment. If the casing accidentally became "live" (by means of a loose wire touching it) the current flows through the earth wire, blowing the fuse at the same time.

Without the earth the current would flow through anyone who touched the metal casing.

More details about circuit wiring can be found in Section 13 below.

## 7 > RESISTANCE

A **resistor** is used to **control or reduce the current in a circuit**. The simplest form of resistor is a thin wire placed in a circuit (Fig. 7.15). The greater the **resistance** of the wire, the **smaller the current flow**.

Thin wire

**Fig. 7.15**

If the dimensions of the wire are changed, it is found that:

▶ The **longer** the wire, the **greater** its resistance.
▶ The **thicker** the wire, the **less** its resistance.

The **type** of wire also matters; for example, identical lengths and thicknesses of iron wire and copper wire can be compared.

▶ **Copper** wire has a **lower resistance than iron**.

Resistance is also affected by

▶ **temperature**. The resistance of metals is **increased** if the temperature **rises**.

Resistance is measured in **ohms** ($\Omega$); 1 $\Omega$ means that 1 V would be needed **across** the wire to drive 1 A **through** it. 100 $\Omega$ would require 100 V to drive 1 A. So in general

$$R = \frac{V}{I}$$

or

$$\text{Resistance} = \frac{\text{"Voltage"}}{\text{Current}}$$

Most resistors used in laboratories are convenient, manufactured resistors, consisting usually of carbon granules.

A **variable resistor (rheostat)** enables **different lengths of wire to be added into a circuit**, so that current can be controlled (Fig. 7.16).

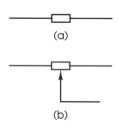
(a)

(b)

**Fig. 7.16(a) Resistor; (b) variable resistor.**

## 8 > CURRENT AND VOLTAGE RELATIONSHIPS – OHM'S LAW

Using a circuit such as Fig. 7.17, an important **general relationship** can be seen. The variable resistor is used to control the current in the circuit and the voltmeter measures how the p.d. across the resistor varies. Provided the temperature does not change significantly, the results give a graph like that in Fig. 7.18. This means that the **current is proportional to the p.d.** The relationship is called **Ohm's law**. (Note that Ohm's law only applies if the temperature is constant, and that it does not apply to all electrical components.)

We can write **Ohm's law** in symbols:

$$V \propto I$$

or

$$V = IR$$

where $R$ is the resistance of the resistor.

**Fig. 7.17 Circuit to verify Ohm's law.**

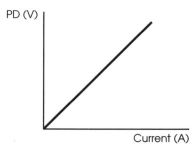

**Fig. 7.18 Current/voltage for a resistor.**

💬💬 There is often confusion here. $R = V/I$ DEFINES resistance at *all times*

$R = V/I$ AND IS CONSTANT is a statement of Ohm's Law, and is only SOMETIMES true. 💬💬

## EXAMPLE

Fig. 7.19

In Fig. 7.19 the p.d. across the resistor would be

$$V = IR = 0.5 \times 20 = 10 \text{ V}$$

Fig. 7.20

In the circuit of Fig. 7.20 the current can be found. Since

$$V = IR$$

then

$$I = V/R$$
$$I = 12/5 = \underline{2.4 \text{ A}}$$

Fig. 7.21

Finally, in the circuit of Fig. 7.21, the unknown resistance $R$ can be calculated.
Since

$$V = IR$$
$$R = V/I$$
$$R = 10/0.25 = \underline{40 \ \Omega}$$

The graph obtained (Fig. 7.22) showing current and voltage changes for a resistor is a useful way of finding an **unknown** resistance experimentally. Since $R = V/I$ it is also the slope or gradient of the graph.

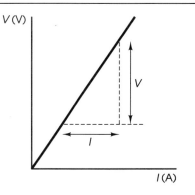

Fig. 7.22 Gradient of the graph gives the value of resistance.

▶ The **larger the resistance,** the **greater the gradient** will be.

Ohm's law **does not always apply**. A light bulb in place of the resistor in the circuit (Fig. 7.23) gives a different pattern for the current and voltage relationship, as shown in the graph (Fig. 7.24). Here the current and voltage are **not** proportional. The bulb obviously gets hotter and hotter. Since "resistance" is measured by the gradient of the graph, we have here an example where the resistance is **increasing**.

A heat-dependent resistor or thermistor gives the **opposite** pattern. Its resistance **decreases** as the **temperature rises**.

Fig. 7.23

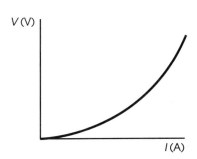

Fig. 7.24 Current/voltage for a bulb.

**9 ⟩ e.m.f.**

**e.m.f.** stands for *electromotive force*. It is the total voltage that is produced by a cell, battery or power supply. If you want to measure it you should do so when it is not supplying current i.e., not connected in a circuit because

Digital voltmeter

**Fig. 7.25**

otherwise some of the e.m.f. is used in driving current though the supply itself and you will only measure what is left. e.m.f. will usually be divided among the components of the circuit so that each component has a share of the e.m.f. called its p.d. One way to find the e.m.f. of a supply is to add all the p.d.s in a complete circuit that includes the supply.

A modern digital voltmeter will usually take so little current that the reading is very close to the e.m.f.

**10 ⟩ CELLS AND RESISTORS IN SERIES AND PARALLEL**

A "battery" is a group of cells in series. The total e.m.f. of such an arrangement is simply the sum of each individual e.m.f, provided they are connected ⊕ to ⊖. Four 1.5 V cells connected as in Fig. 7.26 gives $(4 \times 1.5) = 6$ V e.m.f. In Fig. 7.27 the second and third cells are *opposing* each other so the resulting e.m.f. is only that of cells 1 and 4, i.e. 3 V e.m.f.

**Fig. 7.26**

**Fig. 7.27**

Where *equal* value cells are connected in parallel, there is no increase in e.m.f. The resulting value is only that of *one* cell. The cells in Fig. 7.28 will still only give 1.5 V, but are able to produce more current than one cell.

1.5 V

1.5 V

**Fig. 7.28**

## (A) RESISTORS IN SERIES

The circuit of Fig. 7.29 shows two different value resistors $R_1$ and $R_2$ connected in series. They will have the same current, $I$, flowing through them both, but different p.d.s across them. They could be replaced by a *single* resistor $R$, without changing the current or total energy change in the circuit, if

▶
$$R = R_1 + R_2$$

i.e. a 10 and 20 Ω resistor in series is the same as a single 30 Ω resistor.

$R_1$   $R_2$

$V_1$   $V_2$

**Fig. 7.29**

$R_1$

$R_2$

**Fig. 7.30**

## (B) RESISTORS IN PARALLEL

The current now splits up (Fig. 7.30). The voltage across each resistor is the same. The two parallel resistors could be replaced by a *single* resistor $R$ if

▶
$$\frac{1}{R} = \frac{1}{R_1} + \frac{1}{R_2}$$

The effect of two equal value resistors in parallel gives a total resistance equal to *half* the value of *one* of them. For the two 5 Ω resistors in Fig. 7.31,

$$\frac{1}{R} = \frac{1}{5} + \frac{1}{5}$$

$$\frac{1}{R} = \frac{2}{5}$$

$$R = \frac{5}{2} = \underline{2.5\ \Omega}$$

10 Ω

5 Ω

**Fig. 7.31**

Where the resistors do *not* have equal values (Fig. 7.32), the formula is needed to find their effect. Here

$$\frac{1}{R} = \frac{1}{10} + \frac{1}{5}$$

$$\frac{1}{R} = \frac{1}{10} + \frac{2}{10}$$

$$\frac{1}{R} = \frac{3}{10}$$

$$R = \frac{10}{3} = \underline{3.3\ \Omega}$$

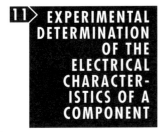

**Fig. 7.32**

So **more resistors in series increase the total resistance in a circuit,** and **more resistors in parallel decrease the resistance in a circuit**.

If a voltmeter is placed across each of a group of resistors **in parallel**, it reads the same across each of them.

However, if voltmeters are placed across resistors **in series**, the individual voltage readings depend on the resistor values. For example, the current, $I$, is the same through both resistors (Fig. 7.33).

**Fig. 7.33**

Since

$$V = IR$$

then in series

$$V \propto R$$

Therefore the larger resistor has the greatest p.d. across it. The e.m.f. of the cells (12 V) is equal to the sum of the p.d.s $(V_1 + V_2)$. The values are in proportion to the resistances, so

$$V_1 \text{ reads } \frac{500}{1500} \times 12\ V = 4\ V$$

(See also Chapter 8.)

$$V_2 \text{ reads } \frac{1000}{1500} \times 12\ V = 8\ V$$

## 11 EXPERIMENTAL DETERMINATION OF THE ELECTRICAL CHARACTERISTICS OF A COMPONENT

"Characteristics" means the way in which current and voltage are related for a particular piece of apparatus. The usual practical examples are:

1. A resistor;
2. A lamp;
3. A thermistor;
4. A diode.

In each case a circuit must be set up containing an **ammeter in series** with the component, a **voltmeter in parallel** with it, and some means of varying the current and voltage. Two possibilities are shown. In Fig. 7.34 a variable resistor is used as a rheostat (current variation). In Fig. 7.35(a) it is used as a potential divider (voltage variation). The appropriate circuit is set up, and values of full-scale deflection of the ammeter and voltmeter are chosen (usually 0–5 A and 0–15 V).

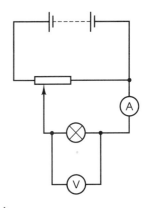

**Fig. 7.35(a)**

## MEASUREMENTS

Either the current is varied in suitable steps of about 0.2 A or the voltage is varied in, say, steps of 0.5 V. Readings should be tabulated.

| Current (A) | PD (V) |
|---|---|
| | |

If resistance variations are to be noted, the most suitable graph to plot would be $V$ (vertical) against $I$ (horizontal) since $V/I = R$, so the **gradient** of the graph gives a **resistance value**. See Fig. 7.35(b).

**Fig. 7.34**

Fig. 7.35(b)

## PRECAUTIONS

1. Check that both the ammeter and voltmeter are reading zero when the circuit is not switched on. Use a small screwdriver to adjust zero if necessary.

2. If the meters are fitted with a mirror below the indicator, use it to reduce parallax error in taking a reading.
3. Check each reading and if necessary take a **mean** value.

Some of the expected results are shown in Fig. 7.36.

Only one of these has a straight line graph and therefore the others do not obey Ohm's law as their resistance is not remaining constant. To get a full graph for the diode you will need to reverse the voltage applied to it and show that the current remains zero – there are practical limits to this and the diode will eventually fail, so take care and keep the applied p.d. down to less than 12 V.

(a) A bulb

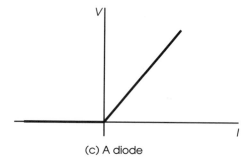

(b) A thermistor

(c) A diode

Fig. 7.36

---

<table>
<tr><td>**12** **CATHODE RAY OSCILLOSCOPE AS A VOLTMETER**</td></tr>
</table>

The CRO is increasingly used in place of a voltmeter. It has an infinitely high DC resistance, and so draws no current from a supply (Fig. 7.37). It is also able to show voltage variations as time goes on – and to show the variation on a screen. It is a visual voltmeter.

Fig. 7.37

The positions of the controls will vary from one model to another, but you should be able to identify the following:

1. ON/OFF – connecting to the mains supply:
2. Brightness.
3. Focus.

Turning on should produce a bright dot on the screen. It should be focused, and bright enough to see easily, but not so bright that the screen could be damaged.

4. X-shift will move the dot from left to right.
5. Y-shift moves the dot up and down.

To use an oscilloscope with direct current the AC–DC switch is turned to DC.

At the start of a measurement, then, the dot on the screen looks like that in Fig. 7.38. Since the oscilloscope is a **voltmeter**, any change in the position of the dot can only be caused by a voltage across the CRO. The CRO is connected **in parallel** between two points – just like a voltmeter. The dot will be moved **up** or **down**, depending on whether the applied voltage is in the **positive** or **negative** direction.

6. Use "sensitivity" to adjust the number of centimetres movement for each volt of

**Fig. 7.38**

**Fig. 7.39**

p.d.. Typical examples are shown in Fig. 7.39.

7. Finally, to show how the voltage varies with time, turn on the "time base". This

will make the dot move horizontally and draw a visual graph of volts against time (Fig. 7.40).

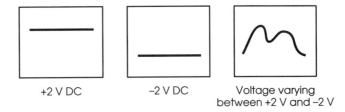

+2 V DC          −2 V DC          Voltage varying
between +2 V and −2 V

**Fig. 7.40**

## 13 ▷ RING MAINS AND HOUSEHOLD WIRING

Cables entering the home have three insulated wires within an insulated exterior sheath. The cable can be overhead or underground. On entering your home, or your place of work, the main cable is connected to:

1. The Electricity Board's main fuse;
2. The electricity meter.

   These are the property of the Electricity Board, so you are hiring property from the Board.

3. The fuse box (consumer unit) contains a switch to turn off all circuits. It will switch off both live and neutral connections by breaking the circuits. It also contains fuses to protect each circuit.

The ring main for power sockets consists of a double loop of cable beginning and ending at the consumer unit. The current therefore reaches any socket through two loops, and because the wire gauge can be reduced, it reduces the risk of overloading the circuit.

The ring main is not a series circuit. Current can only flow from live to neutral if connected with an appliance.

The fuse in the ring main will usually be 30A so that several devices can be supplied from the different sockets at the same time. A house will usually have a separate ring main for each floor. There will also be a lighting circuit for each floor, usually fused at 5A and a separate "spur" that goes directly to the cooker point in the kitchen. Since this is likely to supply more power (carry more current) than the other circuits it has its own fuse on the consumer unit.

The consumer unit may be earthed by connecting it to metal buried in the ground. An alternative (also used in caravans) is a residual current circuit breaker (**RCCB**) which detects any difference in current between that supplied on the live and that returning on the neutral and switches off the circuit. Modern consumer units have miniature circuit breakers (**mcb**) instead of fuses. These react faster and can be reset by pushing in a button (after finding the fault of course!).

Fig. 7.41

# EXTENSION MATERIALS

14> **RESISTIVITY** The resistance of a metallic conductor is proportional to the length of the conductor and is inversely proportional to the cross-sectional area of the conductor: i.e. long thin wires have more resistance than short thick ones made from the same material. (The wire should be metallic and at constant temperature or it doesn't obey OHM'S LAW anyway). This is written as

$$\text{resistance} \propto \frac{l}{A}$$

where $l$ is the length and A is the cross-sectional area. This can be changed into an equation if we include a suitable constant.

$$\text{resistance} = p \times \frac{l}{A}$$

If you put $l$ = 1 and A = 1 in the equation then

resistance = p. This means that the constant is really the resistance of a piece of the material 1 m long and 1 m² in cross-sectional area. This constant is called the resistivity of the material and it will obviously be a small number as a piece of metal that size would have a very small resistance. Some examples are shown below. Note the units are Ω m.

| Metal | Resistivity in ohm metres |
|---|---|
| copper | 0.000 000 018 |
| aluminium | 0.000 000 03 |
| invar | 0.000 000 75 |

### EXAMPLES:

1. What is the resistance of a piece of copper wire 3m long and 0.5 mm in diameter? Resistivity of copper = 1.8 × 10⁻⁸ Ω m.

$$\text{resistance} = p \times \frac{l}{A}$$

$$= \frac{0.000000018 \times 3}{\pi \times 0.00025^2}$$

$$= 0.28 \ \Omega$$

2. A piece of wire has a resistance of 4 Ω. What would be the resistance of another wire made from the same material that was twice as long and twice as thick?

   Making the wire twice as long would double its resistance. Making it twice as thick will make its cross-sectional area four times as big and quarter the resistance. When both effects are put together the resistance is halved.

---

## 15> USING METERS

### ▶ AMMETERS

Since ammeters are connected in series with the circuit (so that the current to be measured goes through the meter), the resistance must be as small as possible. A perfect ammeter would have no resistance at all so that when you put it into the circuit it wouldn't make the current smaller and give a slightly wrong reading.

### ▶ VOLTMETERS

Voltmeters are connected across the part of the circuit where you are measuring the p.d. The meter must have the largest possible resistance so that current doesn't by-pass part of the circuit by going through the meter. Modern digital meters can have a resistance of millions of ohms so that they are very accurate.

### ▶ GALVANOMETERS

A galvanometer is a sensitive meter designed

to show very small currents. You may use one to detect the small currents produced in simple electromagnetic induction experiments. (See Chapter 14.)

▶ A galvanometer can be made into an **ammeter** by connecting a *low* resistance called a **shunt** in parallel with it.

▶ A galvanometer can be made into a **voltmeter** by connecting a *high* resistance called a **multiplier** in parallel with it.

Fig. 7.42

---

## 16> INTERNAL RESISTANCE

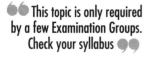 This topic is only required by a few Examination Groups. Check your syllabus

So far we have only considered a battery or other supply as an energy "provider". However, every supply has itself got some resistance (called *internal resistance*) so it is also an energy "converter".

A voltmeter connected directly across a supply draws very little current from the supply, since voltmeters have *very* high resistance. In these circumstances the voltmeter is recording the supply e.m.f. (Fig. 7.43).

Fig. 7.43 e.m.f. on open circuit.

However, if a lamp is also connected, the supply provides a lot of current, and the voltmeter reading falls (Fig. 7.44a). The reason is that the current also has to flow back through the supply – and the supply itself has some resistance; so energy is converted into heat in the supply and not all the "available" 12 V is converted at the lamp.

Fig. 7.44a Voltmeter reads terminal p.d.

Since energy is conserved, then

Energy available = Energy converted
externally
+ Energy converted
internally

or

$$E = V_{\text{in bulb}} + V_{\text{internal}}$$

The same current $I$ flows in the bulb of resistance $R$ as in the supply of resistance $r$.

$$E = IR + Ir$$

or

$$E = I(R + r)$$

The factor $(Ir)$ is sometimes called "lost volts" since it represents energy which is **not** converted usefully in the circuit.

Using the data in Figs 7.43 and 7.44, the lost volts = (12 – 9) = 3 V. Current flowing = 2 A.

$$2 \times r = 3$$

and

$$r = 1.5 \, \Omega$$

Most power packs and batteries have low internal resistance, and it is usually ignored in simple calculations.

## DOUBLE INSULATION

You may have noticed that some appliances only have two wires – the live and neutral – and are not "earthed". Mains appliances that can be connected safely in this way will be double insulated and will carry a special symbol.

The appliance will be totally enclosed in an insulating plastic body so that there is no possibility of an internal electrical component making contact with any exterior metal part. Hair driers, electric drills and vacuum cleaners are all made like this.

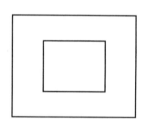

Fig. 7.44b Double insulation symbol.

## TWO-WAY SWITCHES

The sort of lighting circuit that you may have in your hall at home with a switch at each end (or at the top and bottom of the stairs) requires a different sort of switch. The switch does not turn on and off but connects to either of two wires. Two of these switches connected as shown mean that you can turn the circuit on or off at either switch.

The circuit is shown off but can be put on by setting switch 1 to A or setting switch 2 to B. Check that you can then understand how to turn the circuit off again.

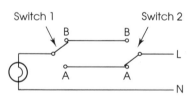

Fig. 7.44c Two way switch.

# EXAMINATION QUESTIONS

## QUESTION 1

In a correctly fused plug, the cartridge fuse is connected between the

    A  Neutral lead and live lead
    B  Live lead and live pin
    C  Neutral lead and earth lead
    D  Live lead and earth pin
    E  Neutral lead and neutral pin    (ULEAC)

## QUESTION 2

Which of the circuits (Fig. 7.45) would be suitable for measuring the resistance of a lamp?    (ULEAC)

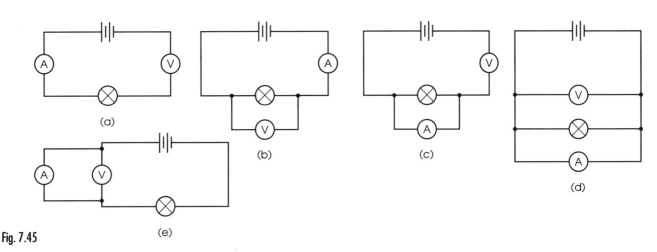

Fig. 7.45

## QUESTION 3

Two resistors, one of 3 Ω and one of 6 Ω are connected in parallel in a circuit. Which of the following is their effective resistance?

    A  2 Ω          D  9 Ω
    B  3 Ω          E  18 Ω
    C  6 Ω                  (ULEAC)

## QUESTION 4

When wiring a house, switches and fuses should be connected in one (and only one) arrangement. This one arrangement has

    A  Switches in the live side and fuses in the neutral
    B  Switches in the neutral side and fuses in the live
    C  Switches and fuses both in the live wire
    D  Switches and fuses both in the neutral wire
    E  Switches and fuses both in the earth wire    (ULEAC)

## QUESTION 5

A three-core cable is connected to a three-pin plug. The colour of the cable which should be connected to the live terminal is

    A  Brown         D  Green and yellow
    B  Black          E  Green
    C  Blue                (ULEAC)

## QUESTION 6

Electrical appliances have voltage and power ratings as listed below. Which has the largest electrical resistance?

| | Appliance | Voltage (V) | Power (W) |
|---|---|---|---|
| A | Washing machine | 250 | 3000 |
| B | Television | 240 | 160 |
| C | Kettle | 240 | 1500 |
| D | Hair curler | 250 | 20 |
| E | Car headlamp | 12 | 36 |
| | | | (ULEAC) |

## QUESTIONS 7–9

    A  Ampere        D  Watt
    B  Coulomb     E  Volt
    C  Joule

**7.** Which one of the above is a unit of energy?
**8.** Which one of the above is a unit of current?
**9.** Which one of the above is a unit of power?

## QUESTION 10

In the circuit shown (Fig. 7.46), the p.d. between X and Y is 6 V. What is the current through the resistors?

A  116 A   D  1½ A
B  ½ A    E  6 A
C  1 A          (MEG)

Fig. 7.46

## QUESTION 11

In the circuit shown (Fig. 7.47) the p.d. between X and Y is 10 V. What is the p.d. between P and Q?

A  5 V    D  100 V
B  10 V   D  210 V
C  50 V          (MEG)

Fig. 7.47

## QUESTION 12

In the circuit shown (Fig. 7.48), the lamps are each marked 12 V, 24 W. X is a 12 V car battery. What will be the reading on the ammeter?

A  1 A    D  6 A
B  2 A    E  12 A
C  4 A          (MEG)

Fig. 7.48

## QUESTION 13

In the circuit shown (Fig. 7.49), the voltmeter shows a reading of 5 V and the ammeter reads 2 A. The resistor has a value of

A  0.4    C  4.0
B  2.5    D  10.0    (SEG)

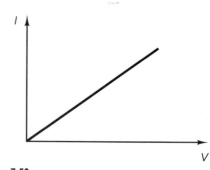

Fig. 7.49

## QUESTION 14

The graph (Fig. 7.50) shows how current $I$ changed with voltage $V$ when applied to a sample of the material. The shape of the graph shows that

A The resistance of the material decreases as the current applied to it increases.
B The resistance of the material is constant.
C The current decreases as the voltage increases
D The resistance of the material increases as the voltage increases.    (SEG)

Fig. 7.50

## QUESTION 15

Two 3 V batteries are connected as shown in Fig. 7.51. The voltage between X and Y is

A  Zero   C  3 V
B  1½ V   D  6 V

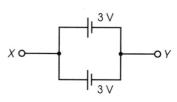

Fig. 7.51

**STRUCTURED QUESTIONS**

## QUESTION 16

The ammeters in this circuit (Fig. 7.52) have negligible resistance. Using the values shown in the circuit, calculate:

(a) The p.d. across the 6.0 Ω resistor.
(b) The current through ammeter $A_2$.
(c) The current through ammeter $A_1$.
(d) The reading of the voltmeter across the cells. (UCLES)

Fig. 7.52

## QUESTION 17

In an experiment to measure the current through a component for different potential differences across it, the following readings were obtained.

Table 7.2

| Potential difference across X (V) | Current through X (A) |
|---|---|
| 0.0 | 0.0 |
| 1.2 | 0.6 |
| 2.0 | 1.0 |
| 3.0 | 1.0 |
| 4.2 | 2.1 |
| 4.8 | 2.4 |

(a) There seems to be a mistake in one of the readings. Draw a circle around the reading.
(b) What reading would you have expected?
(c) In doing the experiment the following meters were available:

0–1 A ammeter 0–5 V voltmeter
0–5 A ammeter 0–15 V voltmeter

Which meters would you choose? Explain your answers.
(d) Why is it that teachers often ask you to repeat your readings in an experiment? (ULEAC)

## QUESTION 18

Diagram (1) of Fig. 7.53 shows the inside of a mains-operated hair drier. The fan can either blow hot or cold air. Diagram (2) is a circuit diagram of the same drier, showing how it is wired up for use.

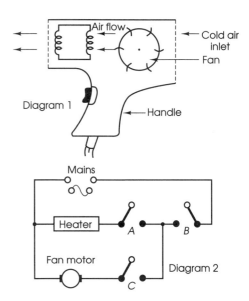

Fig. 7.53

(a) Show, by placing ticks in columns in the table which switches need to be ON to get the results shown. (You may use each switch once, more than once or not at all.)

Table 7.3

| Result | Switch A | Switch B | Switch C |
|---|---|---|---|
| A blow of hot air | | | |
| A blow of cold air | | | |

(b) The heater must not be on without the fan.
(i) Which of the switches A, B, or C must always be ON to achieve this?
(ii) Explain carefully what you would expect to happen if the heater was on, and the fan failed to work.
(c) The manufacturer wishes to include a two-speed fan. This can be done by connecting a suitable resistor across one of the switches as shown.
(i) Draw a resistor across the correct switch in the diagram (Fig. 7.53) in order to make a two-speed fan.
(ii) When this switch is open (Fig. 7.54), will it give a fast or slow speed? Explain your answer.
(d) The details of the fan are 250 V, 500 W. Calculate the current from the supply when the drier is working at its stated power.

**Fig. 7.54**

(e) Fuses for the mains of 3 A, 5 A and 13 A are available.
   (i) Which fuse would you choose for use in a plug attached to the drier?
   (ii) Which wire in the mains cable should be connected to the fuse?

(f) A girl needs to use the drier for 10 min. Calculate the energy converted during this time.

**Fig. 7.55**

(g) The manufacturer makes a different drier which will work from a 12 V car battery. You are required to find the energy taken by this new 12 V drier. Complete the circuit diargam (Fig. 7.55) to show how you would connect an ammeter and a voltmeter to do this.

(ULEAC)

## QUESTION 19

Alan was asked to set up an experiment to investigate how the current through the filament of a lamp changed with the potential difference across its ends. Alan was provided with connecting wire and five pieces of equipment.

**Fig. 7.56**

(a) (i) using the symbols above draw a circuit diagram of the apparatus Alan might use in carrying out this investigation.

(ii) Mark with an arrow on your diagram the direction in which electrons flow through the lamp.

(b) (i) Some of the results of this experiment are shown in the table below. Plot the graph of current $I$ against voltage $V$ and draw a suitable curve through the data points.

| Current $I$ through filament in amperes | 0.10 | 0.25 | 0.30 | 0.35 |
|---|---|---|---|---|
| Voltage $V$ across filament in volts | 0.10 | 0.40 | 0.60 | 1.00 |

(ii) Use your graph to find the resistance of the filament when the current flowing is 0.3 A. Show clearly how you get your answer.

(iii) In what way, if any, does the resistance of the filament increase as the current through it increases?

(iv) The lamp is at normal brightness when the current flowing through the filament is 0.3 A. Calculate the normal power of the lamp.

(v) Does the lamp obey Ohm's law? Give a reason for your answer.

(c) (i) When a house is wired it is often necessary to wire a light in such a way that it can be switched on or off from two separate switches. Draw a diagram of a bulb connected to a two way switch circuit.

(ii) The diagram shows a fused three pin plug. Label the THREE wires correctly on the diagram.

**Fig. 7.57**

# ANSWERS TO EXAMINATION QUESTIONS

**MULTIPLE CHOICE QUESTIONS**

| Question | 1 | 2 | 3 | 4 | 5 | 6 | 7 | 8 | 9 | 10 | 11 | 12 | 13 | 14 | 15 |
|---|---|---|---|---|---|---|---|---|---|---|---|---|---|---|---|
| Answer | B | B | A | C | A | D | C | A | D | C | A | D | B | B | C |

**STRUCTURED QUESTIONS**

## ANSWER 16

(a) p.d. across 6 Ω resistor is given by $V = IR$. Current in the resistor is 0.2 A.

$$V = 0.2 \times 6.0 = \underline{1.2\,V}$$

(b) The p.d. across all parallel branches is the same. p.d. across 4 Ω resistor is also 1.2 V. Resistance is given and $I = V/R$.

$$\text{Current} = 1.2/4 = \underline{0.3\,A}$$

(c) Current into a junction is the same as the current flowing out.

$$A_1 = A_2 + A_3 = (0.2 + 0.3) = \underline{0.5\,A}$$

(d) Voltage across cells (if no internal resistance) = Total in circuit.

p.d. across 3.4 Ω = $IR$ = 0.5 × 3.4 = 1.7 V
p.d. across total parallel
part of circuit = 1.2 V
Total available from cells = $\underline{2.9\,V}$

## ANSWER 17

(a) Likely mistake is the <u>second 1 A value at 3 V</u>.
(b) Resistance = $V/I$ = 1.2/0.6 = 2 from all other values. Expect current $I$ at 3 V to be $V/R$ = 3/2 = <u>1.5 A</u>
(c) Ammeter 0–5 A; voltmeter 0–5 V (in order to give greatest sensitivity within the range of readings).
(d) To eliminate uncertainty, both in terms of experimental error (the person making the readings) and inherent errors in the apparatus itself.

## ANSWER 18

(a)

| Result | A ON | B ON | C ON |
|---|---|---|---|
| A blow of hot air | ✔ | ✔ | ✔ |
| A blow of cold air | | ✔ | ✔ |

(b) (i) B must always be ON to make either part of the circuit work. C must be ON to make the fan work.

(ii) If the fan is not working, no air from outside is drawn over the heater so the temperature inside the drier rises and there is fire risk.
(c) (i) Resistor would have to be across C.
(ii) Open switch gives slow speed. Increased resistance in the circuit will reduce the current to the motor.
(d) Power = $IV$
$$I = P/V = 500/200 = \underline{2\,A}$$
(e) (i) With 2 A "safe current" a 3 A fuse is advisable.
(ii) Fuses *must* be connected into the live side.
(f) Energy = Power × time in seconds
Time = 10 × 60 = 600 s
Energy = 500 × 600 = $\underline{300000\,J}$
(g) Circuit should have a voltmeter in parallel with the drier and an ammeter in series.

## ANSWER 19

(a) (i)

**Fig. 7.58**

(ii) on the diagram – but note that electrons flow in the opposite direction to conventional flow.
(b) (i) the graph will show a smooth curve.
(ii) Using the graph voltage = 0.6 V when current is 0.3 A

$$R = \frac{V}{I} = \frac{0.6}{0.3} = \underline{2\,\Omega}$$

(iii) Resistance increases.
(iv) Power = $V \times I$ = 0.60 × 0.30 = <u>0.18 W</u>
(v) No – because the graph is curved. Increasing the voltage in equal steps does not always produce the equal increases in current.
(c) (i) See Fig 7.59
(ii) The plug will be wired as shown on Fig. 7.14 in the text.

# TUTOR'S QUESTION AND ANSWER

**THIS IS A PRACTICAL INVESTIGATION QUESTION**

You are given 100 cm of wire. How would you find the length of wire to make a 2.0 Ω resistor? You should write down details of the experiment that you wish to carry out, showing clearly what apparatus, chosen from that supplied, you wish to use. Show all results and any calculations you make to obtain your answer.                    (SEG)

**ANSWER**

The apparatus needs to be: a suitable power supply 0–12 V DC; an ammeter 0–5 A; a voltmeter 0–15 V; leads and crocs clips; 100 cm of wire provided; metre rule.

In all measurements it is important that the wire is laid straight – it is likely to be uninsulated, so a short circuit could develop leading to inconsistent results.

**Fig. 7.60**

The apparatus is set up as shown (Fig. 7.60), initially using the whole length of wire. Length is checked with a metre rule. Readings of current (ammeter) and potential difference (voltmeter) are taken. The power is turned off and the croc clip positions adjusted to give a wire length of 80 cm, and the current and p.d. are again recorded. The procedure is repeated at 20 cm intervals (10 cm intervals may be better if time is available).

The resistance is calculated from the relationship

$$\text{Resistance} = \frac{\text{Voltage (p.d.)}}{\text{Current}}$$

A graph is then plotted of resistance against length (Fig. 7.61). Draw the best straight line through the points plotted. (The examiners' instruction for this question specifies that the required 2 Ω value should need a length of wire **greater** than that provided – so the graph should look as shown.)

To obtain the "2 Ω length" the graph is extrapolated (shown by a broken line) and the required value read from the graph.

**Fig. 7.61**

# STUDENT'S ANSWER – EXAMINER'S COMMENTS

## STUDENT'S ANSWER TO QUESTION 18

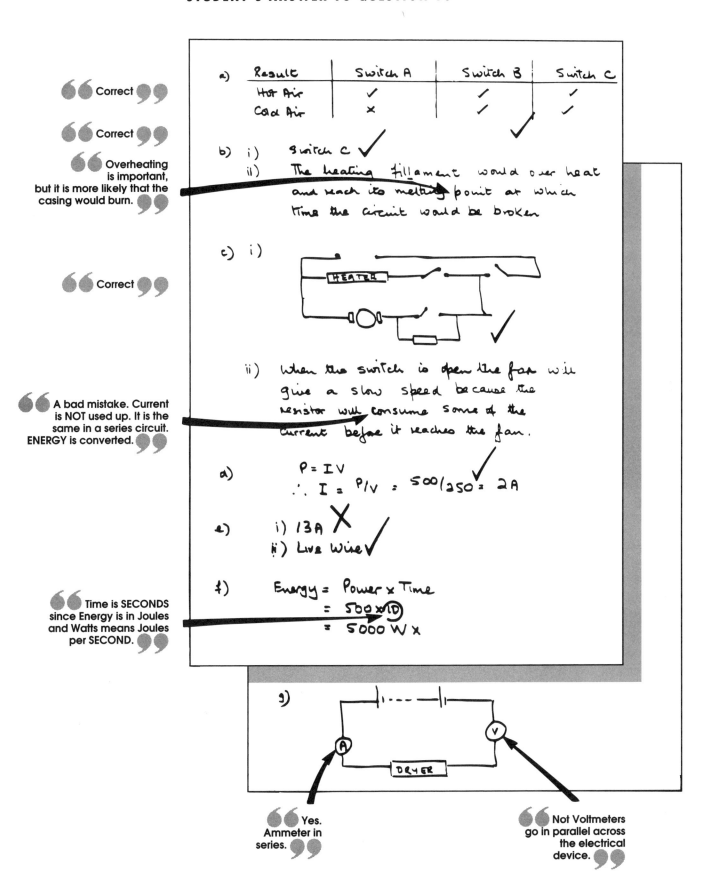

**Correct**

**Correct**

**Overheating is important, but it is more likely that the casing would burn.**

**Correct**

**A bad mistake. Current is NOT used up. It is the same in a series circuit. ENERGY is converted.**

**Time is SECONDS since Energy is in Joules and Watts means Joules per SECOND.**

a)

| Result | Switch A | Switch B | Switch C |
|--------|----------|----------|----------|
| Hot Air | ✓ | ✓ | ✓ |
| Cold Air | ✗ | ✓ | ✓ |

b) i)  Switch C ✓

ii)  The heating fillament would over heat and reach its melting point at which time the circuit would be broken

c) i)

HEATER

ii)  When the switch is open the fan will give a slow speed because the resistor will consume some of the current before it reaches the fan.

d)  $P = IV$
∴ $I = P/V = 500/250 = 2A$

e)  i) 13A ✗
    ii) Live Wire ✓

f)  Energy = Power × Time
    = 500 × 10
    = 5000 W ✗

g)

DRYER

**Yes. Ammeter in series.**

**Not Voltmeters go in parallel across the electrical device.**

# MORE EXAMINER'S COMMENTS CENTRAL TIER

(a) The diagram below shows an electrical circuit correctly set up to measure the current going through the lamp and the voltage across it.

(i) What is the effect on the brightness of the lamp when a small current flows?

.......... *it gets dimmer* ....................................(1 mark)

66 No problems – easy marks! 99

(ii) What is the value shown for the voltage across the lamp?

.......................... *3v* ..............................(2 marks)

(iii) Using these symbols, draw the circuit diagram of the arrangement in the space below. (2 marks)

battery        variable resistor        bulb        voltmeter        ammeter

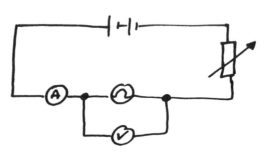

66 Correct but a neat diagram with a ruler is always better 99

(b) The following system is used in a bathroom.

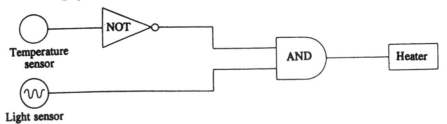

Would the heater be ON or OFF when it was:

(i) cold and dark? (1 mark)

66 Correct 99

.......................... OFF ..................................

(ii) cold and light? (1 mark)

.......................... ON ..................................

(iii) warm and light? (1 mark)

.......................... OFF ..................................

(c) Explain what would happen if someone made a mistake and put an OR gate in the system instead of an AND gate. (2 marks)

.... *it turns the heater on if it is cold or light* ......

66 Correct – but could have been expressed more clearly! 99

... *So it can turn on in the dark or if it is* ......

.... *warm and light* ..........................................

# REVIEW SHEET

- Components that follow one another in a circuit are in _____.

- Charge is measured in _____.

- Draw the circuit symbols for a battery, bulb, two wires that join, switch, ammeter, voltmeter, variable resistor.

- Complete the following equations:

  Charge =                                    Power =

  $$\frac{V}{I} =$$                           $$\frac{1}{R} =$$

- Find the total resistance in each of the two following circuits:

  100 Ω   50 Ω   25 Ω

**Fig. 7.62**

20 Ω

10 Ω

- Name two circuit components which do not obey Ohm's law.

  1. _____          2. _____

- Name the three factors that will affect the resistance of a length of wire.

  1. _____          2. _____          3. _____

- Draw a suitable circuit, including the meters, that you could use to measure the resistance of a bulb.

■ State Ohm's law

_____

_____

_____

_____

■ A bulb has a resistance of 6 Ω and carries a current of 2 A. What is its resistance?

_____

_____

■ What is the power of the bulb?

_____

_____

■ How much energy will it convert in 1 minute?

_____

■ A kilowatt hour is _____.

■ When you look at the back of a mains plug the _____ pin is on the right and the wire going to it is coloured _____.

■ In a mains circuit the fuse is always fitted in the _____ wire.

■ A fuse consists of a thin _____. When too much current flows through it _____.

■ To measure a voltage the meter is connected _____ the p.d.

■ When p.d. across a resistor is plotted against current through it, the gradient of the graph is the _____ of the resistor. What does it cost to run a 3 kW heater for 2 hours at 8p per unit?

_____

■ All good conductors are made from _____. The only exception to this is _____ which is used to make resistors.

■ The current taken by an 80 W light bulb from 240 V mains is _____.

# CHAPTER 8

# ELECTRONICS: THE COMPONENTS

## GETTING STARTED

Everyone must be aware of the importance of **electronics** in modern life, and of the way in which the so-called "new technology" has changed industry and society over the past few years. Calculators, watches, digital sound systems, the operation of industrial plant in factories . . . the list of changes caused by electronics is seemingly endless. However, despite the fact that the applications of electronics are diverse, the individual **components** involved are few, and fairly simple.

A system designed to control traffic lights and a system designed to count high-energy particles in radioactive decay will consist of essentially *similar* components. These include power supply, transistors or printed circuits with a similar function, capacitors, resistors, and some kind of indicator display. Here we consider the individual components and the way in which they operate in simple circuits.

❝❝ There is great variation in the coverage of electronics in the different syllabuses. The chapters in this book cover the needs of *all* candidates so you must check your own requirements. ❞❞

RESISTORS

VARIABLE RESISTORS

DIODES

CAPACITORS

LED

TRANSISTORS

SIMPLE SWITCHING CIRCUITS

A TIME-DELAY CIRCUIT

IMPROVING THE SWITCH

FULL WAVE RECTIFIER

CAPACITOR SMOOTHING

A POWER PACK CIRCUIT

POTENTIAL DIVIDERS

TRANSDUCERS AND DRIVERS

USING AN LED

# ESSENTIAL PRINCIPLES

## 1> RESISTORS

A **resistor** is designed to *limit* the current in a circuit or in part of a circuit (Fig. 8.1).

Fig. 8.1 Resistor.

The value of a resistor is indicated by a colour code printed in bands around the resistor, or as a value printed on its side. The resistance to current is measured in ohms ($\Omega$) and is defined as the ratio ($V/I$), so that $R = V/I$ where $R$ = resistance in ohms; $I$ = current in amps; $V$ = potential difference (PD) in volts.

Bearing in mind that $R = V/I$ this means that a 1 $\Omega$ resistor would pass 1 A of current of 1 V PD was applied. A 10 $\Omega$ resistor would need 10 V across it to allow a 1 A current, and so on. (See Chapter 7 for Ohm's Law.)

Commercial resistors obey **Ohm's law** provided they do not become too hot, so that their resistance is constant, as in Fig. 8.2 (see also the direct current section, Pg. 73).

Two types of resistor which are designed *not* to maintain constant resistance are the *light-dependent resistor* (LDR) and the **thermistor**. The **LDR** (Fig. 8.3) is a resistor whose resistance *decreases* as the *intensity of light falling on it*

Fig. 8.2 Characteristics of a resistor.

*increases*. The **thermistor** is a heat-dependent resistor whose resistance *decreases* as the *temperature increases* (Fig. 8.4). Notice that two symbols are in common use for a thermistor. The upper symbol is the "approved" one, though the lower one is often still used.

Fig. 8.3

Fig. 8.4

## 2> VARIABLE RESISTORS

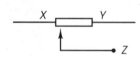

Fig. 8.5 Variable resistor.

A **variable resistor** has three connections (Fig. 8.5); X and Y connect the whole resistance into a circuit, and a sliding contact Z can allow varying amounts of resistance to be used. There are *two* ways of connecting a variable resistor into a circuit – either as a *rheostat* or as a *potential divider*.

The **rheostat** is connected as shown in Fig. 8.6. As the slider Z moves from X to Y, more and more resistance is incorporated into the circuit. The lamp becomes dimmer, and both the current and the voltmeter reading are reduced. When the slider is at Y the current is a minimum but it is not zero.

Fig. 8.6 Variable resistor as a rheostat.

The **potential divider** circuit is shown in Fig. 8.7. If the battery voltage is 6 V, then the PD across XY will be 6 V since they are in parallel. With the slider at X, the bulb is itself in parallel across the whole of the resistor, so the PD across the bulb is also 6 V and the ammeter reading will show maximum current. If Z is then moved half-way between X and Y, the PD between Z and Y will be only 3 V, so the current through the bulb will be halved. When Z is at Y there is no PD across the bulb and the current will be zero. The potential divider can therefore give *continuous variation of current and p.d. across the whole range from 0 to maximum*.

A rheostat provides variation by controlling the current in a circuit. A potential divider provides variation by controlling the voltage available across a component.

Fig. 8.7 Variable resistor as a potential divider.

### 3 ⟩ DIODES

A **diode** consists of two semiconductor slices which have low resistance in one direction, and high resistance in the other.

Fig. 8.8 Diode.

The diode symbol is shown in Fig. 8.8. The arrow in the diagram points in the direction of *low* resistance to conventional current (i.e. ⊕ to ⊖). This means that in a circuit such as Fig. 8.9 one lamp will be ON and the other OFF.

Fig. 8.9

If an ammeter and voltmeter are used to measure the current/voltage relationship for a diode, the low "forward" resistance and the high "reverse" resistance are clearly demonstrated (Fig. 8.10). The "forward" current is of the order of milliamps and the

"reverse" is a few microamps. Because larger voltages result in a very rapid current rise, diodes are usually connected in series with a high-value resistor, to protect them from the surge of current which could easily cause overheating, and the diode to burn out.

If an AC supply is connected across a circuit containing a diode, the diode will only conduct during the part of the cycle when the current flows in the positive ("forward") direction. Oscilloscopes across the supply and across the series resistor show this effect, as in Fig. 8.11. The flow of current is now in *one direction only*. This is called "half-wave rectification".

Fig. 8.11 Half-wave rectification

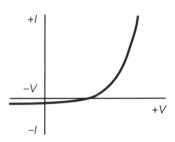

Fig. 8.10 Diode characteristics.

## 4 ▷ CAPACITORS

A **capacitor** consists of two conducting surfaces, separated from each other by an insulating layer (Fig. 8.12). The insulating material may be a polar material (in which case the capacitor must be connected with its ⊕ side to the ⊕ of the circuit) or it may be a material such as waxed paper or air where the direction of connection does not matter. If a capacitor is connected as in the circuit of Fig. 8.13, and the "flying lead" is connected to X, nothing appears to happen. However, if the lead is now touched at Y, the bulb will light briefly.

Electrolytic capacitor

Non-electrolytic capacitor

**Fig. 8.12**

**Fig. 8.13 Charging and discharging a capacitor.**

Touching the lead at X caused electrons to flow on to the negative plate of the capacitor. These would repel electrons from the other plate, leaving it **positively** charged. As more and more charge builds up on the capacitor, so does the voltage across it. When the voltage across the capacitor is **equal** to the battery voltage, no more electrons will flow and the capacitor is charged to the supply voltage. It is now storing energy. The graph in Fig. 8.14 shows how the voltage, and therefore the charge in the capacitor, builds up as time goes on.

**Fig. 8.14 Capacitor charging.**

When the lead is then touched at Y, the capacitor voltage is able to push charges around the completed circuit. As more and more charge leaves the capacitor, the p.d. across it drops, until eventually there is no longer any charge on the capacitor plates, and therefore no p.d. across it. The capacitor has **discharged**.

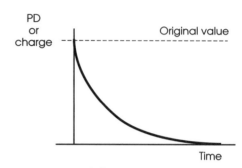

**Fig. 8.15 Capacitor discharging.**

The graph of Fig. 8.15 shows how the voltage, and therefore charge, decays away with time. The time taken to charge or discharge depends on the value of resistance in the circuit, and the "size" of the capacitor. The **more charge** a capacitor can store at a given supply voltage, the **greater its capacitance**.

**Capacitance** is defined as

▶
$$C = \frac{Q}{V}$$

where $Q$ = charge and $V$ = voltage.

Capacitance is measured in **farads** (F) so a 1 F capacitor would store 1 C of charge when connected to a 1 V supply. The farad is a very large unit, and practical capacitor values are usually expressed as microfarads (µF) where $1\ \mu F = 10^{-6}$ F.

The charge and discharge graphs shown in Fig. 8.16 illustrate the effect of varying the values of resistance and capacitance. A **large-value capacitor** and a **large resistance** cause a **slow charge build-up** and a **slow discharge**. In contrast, small values of resistance and capacitance cause a rapid charge build-up and a rapid discharge.

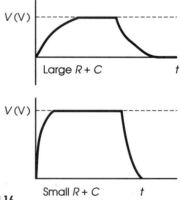

**Fig. 8.16**

## 5 LIGHT EMITTING DIODE

A light emitting diode (LED) gives out light when a current flows in a positive (forward) direction (Fig. 8.17). As with a diode, the LED must be connected with a protective resistor in series with it. LEDs are often used in electronics circuits because they require less power than an ordinary indicator lamp.

Fig. 8.17 LED.

## 6 TRANSISTORS

This semiconducting device has three connections. They are called the **base, collector** and **emitter** (Fig. 8.18). Currents in a transistor circuit are likely to be small, so an indictor should be either a low-power lamp (e.g. 6 V, 0.06 A) or an LED.

Fig. 8.18 Transistor.

In the circuit of Fig. 8.19 there is a complete path for current flow through the collector to the emitter, but the lamp will not light. This suggests that the route from collector to emitter is a high-resistance route. If, however, a second battery is connected between the base and the emitter, and a large-value resistor is incorporated, as in Fig. 8.20, the lamp will light. The flow of current in the "base" circuit (through the base to the emitter) appears to change the resistance in the collector-emitter path and a larger current can now flow, enough to light the lamp.

Fig. 8.19

Fig. 8.20

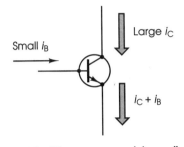

Fig. 8.21(a) Small base current controls large collector current;

When a current flows in the collector, the transistor is described as being "ON" or "OPEN". It is effectively an electronic switch, with the base current acting as the switch operator. It is not necessary to use two sets of batteries as in Fig. 8.20. In Fig. 8.21(b) there will be a PD of 6 V between X and Y and this can be used to provide the voltage necessary to give the base current.

Fig. 8.21(b)

A potential divider circuit, Fig. 8.22, could be incorporated. The PD across XY is then 6 V and the slider Z can vary the voltage between the base and the negative side. A voltmeter in the base circuit will show that a minimum voltage between the base and the negative side of 0.6–0.7 V is needed for the transistor to "switch" ON.

Placing ammeters in the circuit at X and Y shows that the base current is very small (usually microamps) compared with the collector current (milliamps). So a small base current controls the larger collector current. The current in the base circuit must be in the direction shown in Fig. 8.20. This is called **"forward biasing"**! The base current must also be limited by using the large-value series resistor in the base to protect the transistor from over-heating.

> ❝❝ 1 microamp = $10^{-6}$ amp
> 1 milliamp = $10^{-3}$ amp
> i.e. 1 million microamps in 1 amp.
> 1000 milliamps in 1 amp. ❞❞

Fig. 8.22

**SIMPLE SWITCHING CIRCUITS**

Fig. 8.23

Fig. 8.25

The potential divider in Fig. 8.22 could be replaced by two fixed resistors as in Fig. 8.23. Suppose $R_1$ is a 1 k $\Omega$ resistor and the PD across $(R_1 + R_2)$ is 6 V. A minimum voltage across $R_2$ of 0.6 V is needed to switch the transistor, so the voltage across $R_1$ would be a maximum of 5.4 V.

For series resistors, the voltage is proportional to the resistance, since the current is the same through both, and $V = IR$. Therefore, $V \propto R$.

$$\frac{R_1}{R_2} = \frac{5.4}{0.6}$$

$$R_2 = \frac{0.6R_1}{5.4} = \frac{0.6 \times 1000}{5.4} = \underline{111\ \Omega}$$

If $R_2$ is any smaller than this value the transistor would remain OFF. (The statement that the "current in $R_1$ is the same as in $R_2$" is not quite correct. A small current (µA) is tapped off through the base resistor – but this is so small it can be ignored.)

If $R_1$ is now replaced with a thermistor of resistance 1 k $\Omega$ and $R_2$ is 90 $\Omega$ the circuit will cause the transistor to be OFF. The voltage across the thermistor and $R_2$ together is always 6 V, and this is shared between the two resistors in proportion to their resistances (Fig. 8.24). If the thermistor is warmed, its resistance falls, and the PD across it will fall, causing that across $R_2$ to rise and the transistor to switch ON.

Fig. 8.24

The system could act as a fire alarm. In practice $R_2$ is usually a variable resistor, whose value is adjusted so that at room temperature the transistor is OFF, but with switching occurring when the temperature

rises beyond an acceptable level (Fig. 8.25).

Reversing the positions of the two resistors (Fig. 8.26) would cause the system to switch ON when the temperature *drops* significantly, like an "icing-up" warning device. When the temperature falls the thermistor has a bigger resistance and therefore gets a larger share of the voltage. When this is equal to 0.7 V the transistor is switched on.

Fig. 8.26

In the same way an LDR can be used to make a transistor circuit switch ON when the level of light changes (Fig. 8.27). The resistance of an LDR rises when the light intensity drops. If the resistance of $R$ is adjusted so that the circuit is OFF in daylight, then a reduction in intensity of light will increase the resistance of the LDR, raising the base voltage above 0.7 V and switching the transistor ON.

Remember that in these circuits the collector current is only a few milliamps, so to use any circuit practically to operate a bell, motor or other device using large currents, it is likely that a *relay* would have to be incorporated (see P. 231).

Fig. 8.27

Remember that for resistors in series the voltage across each one is proportional to the value of the resistance – so that the larger the resistance the bigger the voltage across it.

8 > **A TIME-DELAY CIRCUIT**

When the switch is open there is no PD between the base and the negative line, so the transistor is closed (OFF). On closing the switch, charge flows on to the capacitor, building up a voltage across it. When this exceeds 0.7 V the transistor "switches ON" and the lamp lights (Fig. 8.28). The delay before this happens will be increased if the resistor $R$ has more resistance so that the current charging the capacitor is smaller and it takes longer to reach the 0.7 V.

If the manual switch is opened again the lamp remains ON for a time. The capacitor is discharging and maintains the base voltage above 0.7 V for some time (Fig. 8.29). The delay is increased if the capacitance or the base resistor are increased in value.

Fig. 8.28 Capacitor delay circuit.

Fig. 8.29

9 > **IMPROVING THE SWITCH**

The circuits so far only turn on a low power lamp or an LED (with a series resistor). Putting a relay (see Chapter 13) in the collector lead enables the circuit to switch much larger currents on or off. The circuit in Fig. 8.30 will switch on a "mains" lamp when it gets dark.

The NO on the relay symbol shows that it is "normally open" –off until current passes through the coil – and the box represents the coil of the relay. There are hidden dangers when using relays and a diode may be needed to protect the transistor – see Chapter 14.

Fig. 8.30

# EXTENSION MATERIALS

10 > **FULL WAVE RECTIFICATION – THE BRIDGE RECTIFIER**

A single diode in an AC circuit gives a *half-wave rectified output*, since the dioide will only conduct when the current flow is ⊕ to ⊖ (conventional current flow). Clearly energy supplied to the input is not made available at the output for half of the time for one cycle of AC. A more useful circuit to deliver "one-direction" current would need to produce current *over the entire cycle of energy delivery*. The circuit requires a bridge

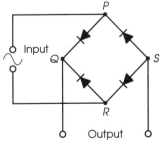

Fig. 8.31 Bridge rectifier.

rectifier and is shown in Fig. 8.31. On the positive part of the cycle, current flows in the direction P → Q. On the negative part, the flow is R → Q. Point Q is always at the start of positive current flow, so the output is always in the same direction.

An oscilloscope across the input and another across the output show the patterns of Fig. 8.32. This gives "direct" current in the sense that it remains in the positive direction but it clearly has a varying value. The next section shows how a capacitor can keep the output at a fairly constant level.

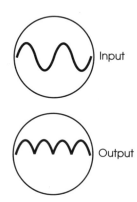

Fig. 8.32 Full wave rectification

## 11 > CAPACITOR SMOOTHING CIRCUIT

The output from a bridge rectifier is shown again in Fig. 8.33. Remember that a circuit containing a capacitor and a resistor takes time to charge and discharge, so this type of circuit would not respond as rapidly to changes as the basic bridge rectifier circuit.

Fig. 8.33

When the voltage rises across both $C$ and $R$ the capacitor is charging (Fig. 8.34). When the bridge rectifier output drops rapidly to zero the capacitor, which is fully charged, discharges slowly, supplying the energy to maintain the current at a fairly constant value until the bridge output is high again.

The **greater the value of capacitance and resistance, the longer the effect lasts** and the **smaller the reduction of voltage from the maximum value**.

Fig. 8.34 Capacitor smoothing circuit

## 12 > LOW-VOLTAGE POWER PACK CIRCUIT

The ideas incorporated in this section can be gathered together to explain how a low-voltage power pack works (Fig. 8.35). You have probably used a power pack many times and will be aware that either AC or DC is available. The requirements of the pack are as follows:

1. Mains AC at 240 V and 50 Hz are transformed to 2–12 V AC or DC. This clearly needs a step-down transformer.
2. If DC is required the low-voltage AC must be made into a "one-direction" supply – a bridge rectifier will do this.
3. The output should be as "smooth" as possible giving a fairly constant DC voltage.

Fig. 8.35

4. Safety needs consideration since the original supply is from the mains. The circuit is shown in Fig. 8.36. The transformer has a fuse and switch in the live side and the core is earthed.

Fig. 8.36 Simple circuit for a DC low-voltage power supply.

## 13 MORE ABOUT POTENTIAL DIVIDERS

It is possible to calculate the output voltage from a voltage divider provided that the current taken is very small; i.e. you can assume that the current through both resistors is the same. The voltage across each resistor is then proportional to its resistance, and for Fig. 8.37:

$$V_{out} = V_{in} \times \frac{R_1}{(R_1 + R_2)}$$

where the symbols represent the values shown in the diagram.

Fig. 8.37

## 14 TRANSDUCERS

Devices that change energy from one form to another are called **transducers**. Bulbs are transducers, as are heaters, fans, loudspeakers and microphones. You might want to switch one of these transducers by the transistor switch but the current needed is often too large for the simple transistor to carry. One way is to use a relay as shown in section 9. The voltage at the collector could also be connected to the base of a transistor that *can* carry a larger current and this will in turn switch your transducer. This transistor is known as a transducer driver. It is often used so that the low-power transistor circuits in logic gates can switch transducers (see chapter 16).

## 15 USING AN LED

An LED can only pass a small current of about 10 or 20 mA. You must fit a series resistor to protect it.

Fig. 8.38

If you can use Ohm's law you can find the size of the resistor needed.

The diode will work with a p.d. across it of about 2 V. If the supply is from a 9 V battery

then the voltage across the resistor

$$V_R = 9 - 2 = 7 \text{ V}$$

The LED will be quite bright if it carries a current of about 15 mA. This same current flows through the resistor. Applying Ohm's law:

$$R = \frac{V_R}{I}$$

$$R = \frac{7}{0.015}$$

$$R = \underline{467 \ \Omega}$$

The nearest value to this that you can buy is 480 Ω. Larger supply voltages will require larger value resistors. The resistors can be very small (low power) because they carry so little current.

# EXAMINATION QUESTIONS

MULTIPLE CHOICE QUESTIONS

## QUESTION 1

The trace on an oscilloscope is shown in Fig. 8.39(a). A student then alters one of the oscilloscope controls and obtains the trace in Fig. 8.36(b). Which one of the controls did the student alter?

A The Y gain
B The Y shift
C The X shift
D The time base frequency          (SEG)

(a)

(b)

**Fig. 8.39**

## QUESTIONS 2–4

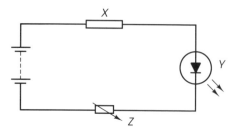

**Fig. 8.40**

Figure 8.40 refers to questions 2–4. The answer code is:

  A  Resistor
  B  Transistor
  C  LED
  D  Capacitor
  E  Variable resistor

2. Which one of the above is component X?
3. Which one of the above is component Y?
4. Which one of the above is component Z?

## QUESTION 5

One-millionth of a volt is known as a

  A  centivolt      D  microvolt
  B  kilovolt       E  millivolt
  C  megavolt           (ULEAC)

## QUESTION 7

When a capacitor is charged from a battery, which of the following cannot take place?

  A  Electrons move in the circuit.
  B  Energy is stored in the capacitor.
  C  The capacitor acquires a steady voltage across it.
  D  The current in the circuit is constant.

## QUESTION 6

In which one of the circuits (Fig. 8.41) will the lamp light?

(a)

(b)

(c)

(d)

(e)

**Fig. 8.41**

## QUESTION 8

This question is about the voltages across devices connected in series.

  (a) Figure 8.42 shows a 500 Ω resistor and a 1000 Ω resistor connected in series across a constant 3 V DC supply.

  (i) What is the total resistance across the supply?
  (ii) What is the current through the circuit?

Fig. 8.42

(b) When a voltmeter is connected across LN as in Fig. 8.43 it shows a voltage of 3 V. The voltmeter is then connected across MN as shown in Fig. 8.44. What voltage will it now show?

Fig. 8.43

Fig. 8.44

(c) The 1000 Ω resistor is then taken out of the circuit and a well-lit light dependent resistor (LDR) is put in its place, as shown in Fig. 8.45.

Fig. 8.45

(i) The voltmeter now shows a reading of 1.5 V. What is the resistance of the LDR?

(ii) What would happen to the voltmeter reading if no light were allowed to fall on the LDR (by wrapping it in black cloth for example)?

(iii) Explain why this would happen.

(SEG)

## QUESTION 9

The circuit diagram (Fig. 8.46) shoes how a transistor may be used to make a lamp come on in the dark.

(i) Complete the circuit (Fig. 8.46) by

Fig. 8.46

adding in the spaces the symbols and labelling as Fig. 8.47:

A  A light-sensitive resistor;
B  A variable resistor;
C  An electromagnetic relay.

 (a)  A light sensitive resistor

 (b)  A variable resistor

 (c)  An electromagnetic relay

Fig. 8.47

(ii) Explain how the circuit will operate the relay, and hence switch a bulb on in the dark.

(iii) Why is a variable resistor preferable to a fixed resistor?

(iv) Why is a relay preferred to inserting a bulb directly into the circuit?

(v) What is the purpose of resistor $R$?

(ULEAC)

## QUESTION 10

Name the component whose circuit symbol is shown in Fig. 8.48.

Fig. 8.48

(i) Name _____

(ii) The trace on an oscilloscope with the time base turned on and no input to the Y plates is shown in Fig. 8.49(a). For each of the circuits in Fig. 8.49(b), use the blank circle on its right to sketch the trace that would be seen on the oscilloscope screen.

Fig. 8.49(a)

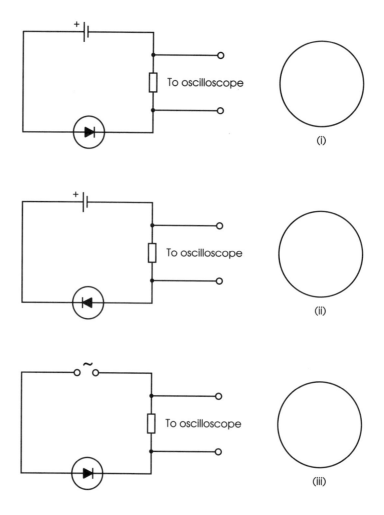

**Fig. 8.49(b)**

## QUESTION 11

Sensing, responding and controlling.

A building engineer was asked to design a system for keeping an office cool in summer. She decided to install a cool air fan and control it electrically using a transistor as a switch. The switch was set to turn the fan on when the sensor temperature rose above 23°C.

The graph shows how the air temperature in the room changed during an hour at midday.

(a) Explain what the fan was doing at the following times.

   (i) 11.00
   (ii) 12.00

(b) Explain why the air temperature did not rise far above 23°C.

The thermistor was connected to a 1000 Ω resistor and a 6 V battery as shown. The resistance of the thermistor is 1000 Ω when its temperature is 16°C.

(c) Show that the input to the transistor would be 3 volts when the temperature was 16°C.

(d) The 1000 Ω resistor was then replaced by a variable resistor. What advantage would this have?

(e) Explain how feedback was achieved in this situation. (ULEAC)

**Fig. 8.51**

**Fig. 8.50**

# OUTLINE ANSWERS

**MULTIPLE CHOICE QUESTIONS**

| Question | 1 | 2 | 3 | 4 | 5 | 6 | 7 |
|----------|---|---|---|---|---|---|---|
| Answer   | D | A | C | E | D | B | D |

**STRUCTURED QUESTIONS**

## ANSWER 8

(a) (i) Total resistance $R = R_1 + R_2 = 1500\ \Omega$.
   (ii) Current $= V/R = 3/1500 = 0.002$ A.

(b) Voltage divides in proportion to resistances

$$V = \frac{1000}{1500} \times 3 = 2\ \text{V}$$

(c) (i) Since there must be 1.5 V across each resistor, they must be of equal value:

Resistance of LDR = 500 $\Omega$

   (ii) Voltmeter reading increases.
   (iii) The resistance of the LDR is greater in the dark; voltage across it is greater.

## ANSWER 9

(i) See Fig. 8.52.

+9 V

B

C

A

0 V

**Fig. 8.52**

(ii) B is adjusted so that in bright light the transistor is OFF. When it gets dark, the resistance of the LDR increases and the voltage between the base and O volts rises, switching the transistor ON. This energises the relay coil and a second circuit is switched causing a light to turn ON.

(iii) The variable resistor will give greater sensitivity.

(iv) The current in the collector is too small to power a large lamp. The relay will

control a circuit with a high-power lamp in it.

(v) Resistor $R$ is to limit the current to the base, protecting the transistor.

## ANSWER 10

(i) The component is a diode.
(ii) See Fig. 8.53.

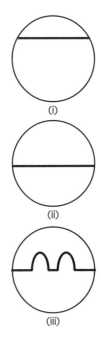

(i)

(ii)

(iii)

**Fig. 8.53**

## ANSWER 11

(This is an intermediate level question.)

(a) (i) fan off.
   (ii) fan on.

(b) As room temperature goes greater than 23°C the sensor switches the fan on and the room cools. As room temperature goes less than 23°C the sensor switches the fan off and the room warms up.

(c) The two equal resistors in the potential divider will each have the same share of the voltage – i.e. 3 V each.

(d) Feedback happens when the fan blows cold air across the room to the sensor and changes its state.

# REVIEW SHEET

■ Draw the symbols for

    1. LED                     2. LDR                     3. Thermistor

    4. Transistor                       5. Electrolytic capacitor

■ A diode only allows current to flow _____.

■ A LED will only light when it is _____ biased and takes a _____ current from the circuit.

■ A circuit that connects across an a.c. supply so that current can only leave it flowing in one direction is called a _____.

■ The simple type uses one _____ to control the current flow.

■ Write down the equation that connects charge, capacitance and voltage.

■ The unit for capacitance is the _____.

■ Name a use for a capacitor _____.

■ When two resistors of equal value are put in series across a supply voltage the voltage at the junction of the two is _____.

■ A 900 Ω resistor and a 100 Ω resistor are connected in series across a 24 V supply. The p.d. across the smaller resistor is _____.

■ Write down the names of the three connections to a transistor.

    1 _____.     2 _____.     3 _____.

■ A time delay circuit uses a capacitor charged through a resistor. What could you change to make the time delay longer?

_____
_____
_____
_____

■ A transistor uses a small current through its _____ to switch on a larger current that flows through its _____ and _____. The voltage at the base must be at least _____ before the transistor turns on.

■ Draw a transistor switch circuit that will turn on a small warning lamp if the temperature outside falls to freezing point. (Use a thermistor as the sensor and make sure that you put it in the correct place!)

■ A 200 μF capacitor is charged up to 9 V. Use the equation to work out the charge on it. If it is discharged in 0.5 s what is the *average* current that flows? (You will find the equation for charge in chapter 7 if you have forgotten it! Note that the current will be bigger than this at the start and zero at the end.)

_____

_____

_____

_____

_____

# OPTICS AND THE NATURE OF LIGHT

## GETTING STARTED

This chapter is closely linked to the earlier one about oscillations and waves (Ch. 6). **Light**, in common with the whole electromagnetic wave spectrum, is a ***transverse wave***, consisting of oscillating electric and magnetic fields. The wavelength of light is so small that the effects normally associated with waves are only apparent under very carefully controlled conditions.

It is convenient to discuss light in terms of "rays" emitted from a luminous object. A light ray as such does not really exist. It is a ***guideline*** drawn to indicate the direction of travel of a wavefront. However, the use of the ray idea is simpler than drawing wavefronts and still leads to correct predictions.

# ESSENTIAL PRINCIPLES

Around a small light source, waves travel out as spherical wavefronts. The ***direction*** in which the wavefront travels (or the "ray" of light associated with it) is at 90° to the wavefront. We therefore say that light "rays" travel from a source in straight lines (Fig. 9.1). This idea is useful in explaining the behaviour of light in a simple pinhole camera experiment.

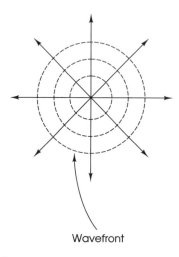

Wavefront

Fig. 9.1

The pinhole camera is a light-proof box with a translucent screen at one end, made of tracing paper. The other end has a small pinhole made in the otherwise light-proof front. Observations are made from behind the screen (Fig. 9.2). Since little light enters the "camera" a source of light, like a bright filament in a lamp, must be observed.

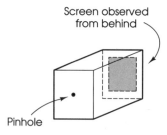

Fig. 9.2 Pinhole camera.

The following are typical observations and results:

1. With a small pinhole, and observing a filament lamp "object", an inverted image is seen on the screen (Fig. 9.3). The image is sharply focused for all distances of the object from the camera. The image is larger when the camera is moved closer to the object.

Object        Image

Fig. 9.3 Image in a pinhole camera.

2. If the single hole is made larger, the image remains the same size for a given camera distance, but it is brighter (since more light can enter) and blurred (Fig. 9.4).

Object        Image

Fig. 9.4

3. A number of small pinholes give an equal number of images, all inverted, and overlapping if the original holes are close together (Fig. 9.5).

Object        Image

Fig. 9.5 Overlapping images with three pinholes.

The image is inverted because of the straight line path taken by the light rays. A ray leaving the top of the object carries that information to the bottom of the screen and vice versa (Fig. 9.6).

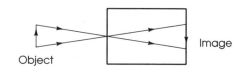

Object        Image

Fig. 9.6 Ray diagrams for a pinhole camera.

In drawing ray diagrams, it is important to show the ***ray direction*** by putting an ***arrow*** on the ray. For the pinhole camera, rays leaving the object and forming the image all across at the pinhole.

## 2 ▷ REFLECTION OF LIGHT

Most objects can only be seen because they reflect light into the eye, since they are not themselves luminous. A plane mirror reflects in a special way (**specular reflection**). A simple experiment with light rays illustrates this (Fig. 9.7). The arrangement of the lamp with a single slit and a lens enables a narrow single parallel beam of light to be used, and this arrangement should be used in all such experimental arrangements where rays are

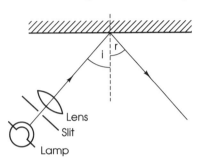

**Fig. 9.7** Reflection at a plane mirror.

being studied. If the positions of the two rays are marked on paper, and a reference line called the **normal** is marked at 90° to the reflecting surface, the following rule is apparent:

▶ **The angle of incidence (*i*) = the angle of reflection (*r*)** where the angles are the angles between the rays and the normal (Fig. 9.8).

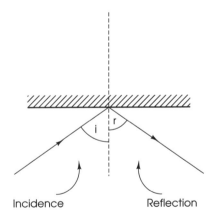

**Fig. 9.8** Law of reflection i = r

Reflection at any surface follows this rule, even when the surface is not smooth (**diffuse**

**Fig. 9.9**

**reflection**). It is because of its smooth surface that an image can be seen in a plane mirror. Experiment shows that the image lies **as far behind the mirror as the object is in front of it**. The reason for this is shown by the geometry of the rays reflected in Fig. 9.10.

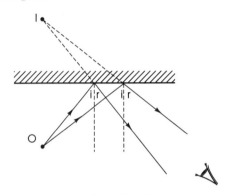

**Fig. 9.10** Virtual image formed by a plane mirror.

All rays leaving the object and hitting the mirror are reflected such that their angles of incidence (*i*) are equal to their angles of reflection (*r*). Rays entering the eye are therefore diverging and are seen as coming from a point behind the mirror. The **image** is the point from which the rays **appear** to have come; only two rays are shown in the diagram. There are of course many of them, all appearing to have started at the image I.

The image in a **plane mirror**, unlike that in a pinhole camera, cannot be put on a screen, since it does not exist in space. It is a **virtual image**. However, the image in a **pinhole camera** is called a **real image**. A real image can always be formed (**focused**) on a screen.

The image in a plane mirror is also the **right way up (erect)** but it is **laterally inverted (left and right are interchanged)**.

## 3 ▷ REFRACTION

Light travels at a unique speed of $3 \times 10^8$ m/s in a vacuum. It travels slightly more slowly in air, and much more slowly in glass, water or other transparent materials. It is because its speed changes that it also changes direction if it enters a transparent material at an angle.

This change of direction is called **refraction**. This is a property of waves and is also described in Section 7 of Chapter 6.

A ray of light entering a glass block at 90° to a surface passes straight through with no direction change, as in Fig. 9.11.

66 Look back to the section on "Oscillations and waves", Chapter 6, to see how light refraction and water wave refraction are similar 99

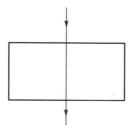

Fig. 9.11 No refraction for light normal to a surface.

But if the ray approaches at an angle to the normal, its direction changes on entering and leaving the glass block (Fig. 9.12).

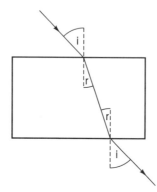

Fig. 9.12 Path of a light ray through a glass block.

On moving from air to a more dense material, the ray refracts towards the normal. It refracts away from the normal on moving from the denser material to a less dense one. Notice that for a parallel-sided block the incident and emerging rays in the air are parallel. The angles made with the normal by the ray are called the angle of incidence ($i$) and the angle of refraction ($r$). The angle of refraction in a denser material is always less than the angle of incidence in a less dense material.

The amount of angular change in direction depends on an optical property of the material called the **refractive index**. It is a measure of how much the speed of light has changed.

$$\text{Refractive index} = \frac{\text{Speed of light in air}}{\text{Speed of light in material}}$$

Refraction can also be seen in a glass prism and follows the same rules for direction change, though the path of light looks very different (Fig. 9.13). Light refracts towards the normal on entering the prism and away from the normal on leaving the prism. (This is best shown using single-colour light, not white light, to avoid complications with spectra.) It is because of refraction that objects viewed below a glass block or under water, appear closer to the surface than they really are.

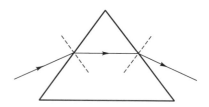

Fig. 9.13 Refraction with a prism.

Rays from an object, O, under a water surface (Fig. 9.14) are refracted away from the normal when they leave the water and enter the air. An observer sees an image, I, where the rays appear to have come from. This again is a **virtual** image and cannot be put on to a screen.

The distance from the surface of the water to the object is called the **real depth** (RD) and the distance from the surface to the image is called the **apparent depth** (AD).

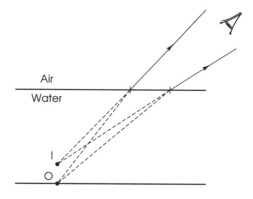

Fig. 9.14 Real and apparent depth

---

4> **TOTAL INTERNAL REFLECTION**

66 Remember to send the ray along a radius to the centre of the straight side 99

This is an effect which can occur when light travels from a denser material to a less dense one. To illustrate it experimentally a semicircular glass block is used, because any light ray travelling along a radius of a semicircle will cross the boundary circumference at 90° and will not therefore be refracted. This enables angles such as $r$ inside the block to be measured.

The block is placed on paper and its position is marked by drawing around it. The

**incident ray** and **refracted ray** are also marked, so that when the apparatus is removed the drawing on the paper shows the block and the ray directions, as in Fig. 9.15. The diagram has added to it the usual arrangement of a lamp, slit and lens which give a single parallel ray of light.

If angle $r$ **inside** the block is gradually increased, then angle $i$ **outside** will also increase until eventually the emerging ray just grazes the edge of the block (Fig. 9.16).

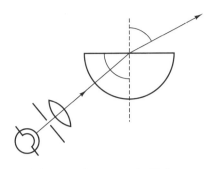

Fig. 9.15 Refraction with a semicircular block.

Fig. 9.16

Fig. 9.17 Total internal reflection.

Eventually, if *r* is made bigger, the light can no longer escape from the far surface, but is reflected, and the usual law of reflection applies (Fig. 9.17). This is called *total internal reflection*. The position of the ray between refraction and total internal reflection occurs at a particular angle for each material. It is called the *critical angle* (Fig. 9.18) and depends on the *refractive index* of the material. The *larger the refractive index*, the *smaller the critical angle*. For glass the critical angle is about 42° and for water it is about 48°.

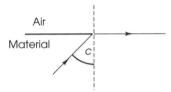

Fig. 9.18 Critical angle.

**To summarise:** Total internal reflection can only take place if light travels from a denser to a less dense material, and if the angle it makes with the normal inside the denser material is *greater than* the critical angle. With water, and a critical angle of 48°, light could only leave an underwater lamp through a narrow cone, since any light rays hitting the water surface at greater than 48° will be reflected back again (Fig. 9.19).

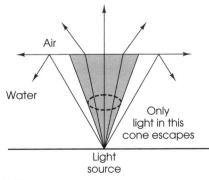

Fig. 9.19

With glass, and a critical angle of 42°, the effect can be made use of with the help of prisms. If the prism angles are 45°, 45°, 90° then, as in Fig. 9.20, light entering one face at

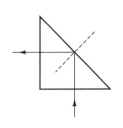

Fig. 9.20 Internal reflection with a 45° prism.

right angles will hit the opposite face at *more than* 42°, and reflect internally, turning the ray through 90°.

A second prism can be used to make a *prism periscope*. This is often used in preference to mirrors because there is no lateral inversion (left and right on the image are the same as on the object) and because there are no problems with poor silvering of glass surfaces. An internal reflection acts as a perfect reflector. Notice that the image in Fig. 9.21 is the same way up (erect) as the object.

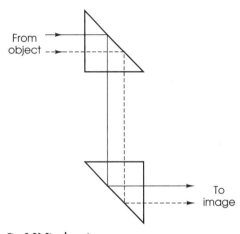

Fig. 9.21 Simple periscope.

Used in a different way, a 45° prism can be used to erect an inverted image. This is used in *binoculars* (Fig. 9.22).

Fig. 9.22 45° prism as an inverter.

While it has been stated that light rays travel in *straight lines*, there are certainly times when it would be useful to see around corners. This is particularly so in internal surgical operations. Optical fibres overcome this problem by using total internal reflection (Fig. 9.23).

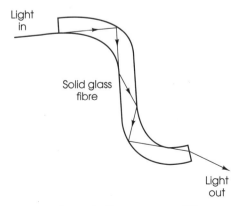

Fig. 9.23 Total internal reflection in an optical fibre.

A bundle of the very thin fibres can be used. Some of these carry light down to illuminate the inside of the patient's body whilst the others each pick up some of the reflected light so that each fibre carries one dot of the final picture. The instrument is called an **endoscope**.

Another use is in telecommunications.

Telephone calls can be sent down a fibre by converting the signal into a digital signal so that it can be sent as a series of light flashes. The fibres are lighter and cheaper and less liable to corrosion than copper wires. Computer networks can also be connected in a similar way.

## 5 LENSES

Lenses refract light, but because of their continuously curved surfaces they show some new effects. The most common lenses are

Convex  Concave

**Fig. 9.24**

convex and concave (Fig. 9.24). A simple experiment with a "fan" of rays shows the effect of each type. A **convex lens** brings rays of light together (causes them to **converge**) while a **concave lens** spreads them further apart (causes them to **diverge**) as in Fig. 9.25.

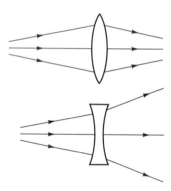

**Fig. 9.25 Action of lenses on a beam of light.**

If a convex lens is set up several centimetres from an appropriate small luminous object, an image of the object can be focused on a screen, if the position of the screen is adjusted. The image is real (exists in space) and inverted. If the object is now moved further from the lens, the screen must be moved closer to the lens to focus the image again (Fig. 9.26), i.e. the **closer an object is** to a convex lens, the **further away from the lens is the image**. The further an object is from a convex lens, the closer to the lens is the image.

When an object is very far away from a lens, the rays arriving at its surface are

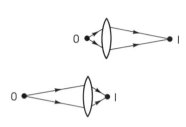

**Fig. 9.26 The further the object is from the lens, the closer the image.**

effectively parallel, and the image is formed as close to the lens as is possible. The closeness of the image will depend on how strong the lens is (i.e. how good it is at converging rays of light).

If the "distant" rays are also parallel to the main axis of the lens (called the **principal axis**) the image will lie **on** this axis. This point is called the **principal focus** (F) of the lens. The distance from the centre of the lens to the principal focus is called the **focal length** ($f$) of the lens. These are marked in Fig. 9.27.

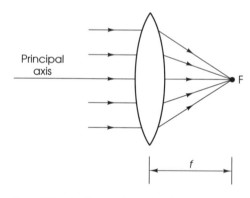

Principal axis

F

$f$

**Fig. 9.27 Principal focus and focal length.**

All parallel rays are focused at a distance away from the lens **equal** to the focal length (Fig. 9.28). This is so whether or not they are parallel to the lens axis, but they only focus at F if they are parallel to the axis.

F

**Fig. 9.28 Focusing in the focal plane.**

The focal length of a convex lens can easily be measured using a "distant object". In a laboratory an object outside the window is far enough away for rays leaving it to be parallel at the lens surface. If the image is "caught" on a paper screen, the distance from the lens to the screen can be measured and this is the focal length (Fig. 9.29).

A powerful lens has a short focal length because it can converge rays more readily than a weaker lens.

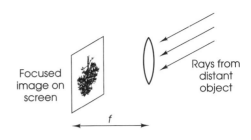

Fig. 9.29 Measurement of focal length.

## 6 DISPERSION

A prism has been shown to refract light of one colour (red, green or blue – Fig. 9.30). If white

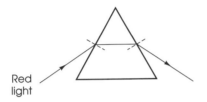

Fig. 9.30 Effect of a prism on monochromatic light.

light is shone in a similar way on to a 60° equilateral prism, a spectrum of coloured light will be seen on a screen on the far side of the prism. Seven colours have been identified; starting at the top of the screen they are: red, orange, yellow, green, blue, indigo, violet. This effect, where white light is split into a sequence of colours, is called *dispersion*. When the colours are mixed in the right proportion and enter the eye, they give a white impression.

Each colour corresponds to a different wavelength of light – and since refraction depends on velocity changes, this suggests that each wavelength travels through the prism at a different speed – blue being slower than red since its refraction is greater.

A white light source also emits invisible waves – infra-red which is detectable because it produces heat when absorbed, and ultraviolet which causes fluorescence of certain chemicals.

A heat-sensitive detector placed at X in Fig 9.31 will show that despite visible light being present, there is a heating effect due to the infra-red waves. Fluorescent paper will fluoresce at Y through interaction with the invisible ultraviolet waves at Y.

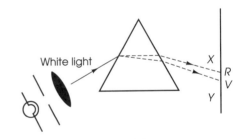

Fig. 9.31 Prism disperses white light.

## 7 IS LIGHT A WAVE?

Light can be reflected *and* refracted. White light can be dispersed into a *spectrum*. This is not, however, evidence that light actually *is* a wave, though in this chapter a wave picture has been used to explain these effects. The only properties which distinguish waves from particles like electrons or ions are interference and diffraction. So if light is a wave, then, like sound, it should give situations where *interference* occurs (see Ch. 6). Interference takes place when waves of equal amplitude, frequency and wavelength, and which are initially in phase, superimpose to give regions of maximum and minimum intensity. This was illustrated with water waves earlier (Fig. 9.32).

**Such waves are described as arriving from COHERENT sources.**

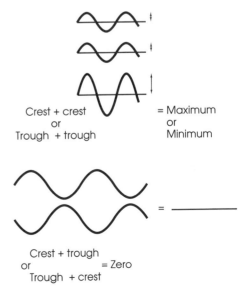

Fig. 9.32 Constructive and destructive interference.

The equivalent statement for light would be

Light + light = Extra intensity

or

Light + light = Darkness

The wavelength of light is very small, so the conditions for this to be observed are difficult to obtain. No two individual sources of light will provide exactly the same amplitude or be exactly in phase. To overcome this problem experimentally **one** source of light is used which is split into two sources by a finely ruled pair of slits on a blackened glass slide. A lens in front of the source provides parallel plane wavefronts, and diffraction at the slits causes a spread of light from the two sources (Fig. 9.33). The width of each slit must not be too much greater than the wavelength of light, and the distance between the slits must be small, so there is in practice very low light intensity and a small spread of light.

The optical arrangement is shown in diagram (Fig. 9.34). The light falling on the screen is viewed from behind with an

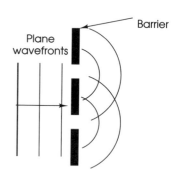

Fig. 9.33 Interference between two diffracted wavefronts.

eyepiece and dark and bright bands are seen spread over a few centimetres.

The spreading is caused by diffraction at the slits and the dark areas are caused by destructive interference where

Light + light = Darkness

i.e. a wave crest and trough have superimposed to give zero amplitude. These effects would not be possible unless light was a wave. (For further discussion see "Extension Materials", p. 157.)

Fig. 9.34 Young's double slits.

## 8 > POLARISATION

This is another property which shows that light is a wave. The waves in a beam of light will be vibrating in all the directions that are at 90° to the direction of travel of the wave. If the beam is sent through a sheet of **_polaroid_** the structure of the solid only allows through those waves that have a vibration in a particular direction and blocks the others. (It may help to think of the crystal structure of the polaroid as being like the parallel bars of a

grille. Only the waves vibrating parallel to the bars can get through the gaps between them.)

If two pieces of polaroid are used, the light can get through both if their structures are parallel. If one is then turned through 90° the waves are all blocked by one sheet or the other and no light gets through. Rotating one of the sheets takes you steadily from light to dark and back again. This effect is used in polaroid sun-glasses.

Fig. 9.35

## 9 > THE ELECTRO-MAGNETIC SPECTRUM

Light is only one part of a family of waves called *electromagnetic waves*. They are similar in that they all travel at the same speed in a vacuum, and all are transverse. The only difference is in the wavelength. Their characteristics are outlined in Fig. 9.36.

| Name | λ (m) | Effect |
|------|-------|--------|
| Radio | 0.01–3 000 | Cause electrical oscillation in circuits |
| Infra-red | $7 \times 10^{-6}$ | Cause heating on absorption |
| Visible | $5 \times 10^{-7}$ | Response of human eye |
| Ultraviolet | $<3 \times 10^{-7}$ | Fluorescence |
| X-rays | $10^{-10}$ | Affect photographic plates. Penetrate some materials |
| γ–waves | $10^{-14}$ | Cause ionisation |

Fig. 9.36

# EXTENSION MATERIALS

An image which can be focused on a screen is called a *real image*. Images formed using convex lenses can be predicted by using *scale diagrams* which incorporate two rays of light which have special features:

1. A ray *parallel to the principal axis* always passes through the principal focus, F.
2. A ray *passing through the centre of a lens* does not change direction.

In drawing ray diagrams the thickness of the lens is not included. The changes are assumed to take place at the **centre** of the lens, so the special rays would be drawn as in Figs 9.37 and 9.38.

The *principal focus* is marked on both sides of the lens. Since the lens is symmetrical, it does not matter if the light is travelling from right to left or left to right. So by knowing the focal length of the lens, the position and size of the image can be found from a suitable scale diagram.

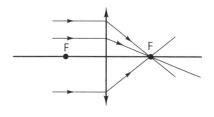

Fig. 9.37                    Fig. 9.38

The following diagrams (Figs 9.39, 9.40, 9.41(a)) are drawn to scale. The lens has a focal length of 10 cm.

> ❝ Lenses must be thin. They can be shown as a line. The "arrow heads" show convex or concave lenses ❞

Fig. 9.39

Fig. 9.40

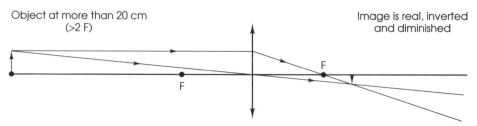

Fig. 9.41(a)

For an object placed at F no image is formed (Fig. 9.41(b)). Light rays become parallel and do not converge to form an image.

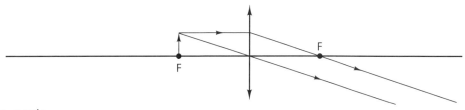

Fig. 9.41(b)

The ***magnification*** of the image can also be found if the diagrams are drawn to scale.

$$\text{Magnification} = \frac{\text{Height of image}}{\text{Height of object}}$$

Notice also in the previous group of diagrams that as the ***object distance decreases*** the ***image distance increases***, and ***so does the magnification***.

In a camera, the image is often a ***diminished one*** (magnification less than × 1). This happens if the object is further away from the lens than twice the focal length. A projector, on the other hand, is designed to give an enlarged image so the object film or slide must be as close as possible to the lens but not closer than the focal length or no real image will be formed.

## VIRTUAL IMAGES WITH CONVEX LENSES

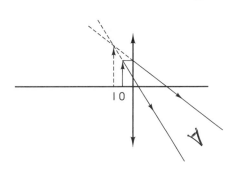

Fig. 9.42 Convex lens as a magnifying glass.

A convex lens will always give a real image when the object is ***further*** from the lens than its focal length. The same lens can be used as a magnifying glass if the object is closer to the lens than the focal length (Fig. 9.42). Rays entering the eye are now diverging rather than converging and the image is seen as the point where the rays appear to come from.

The image in this case is ***virtual, erect*** and ***enlarged***. Notice that in this diagram, the same two rays have been used; the "parallel" one which passes through F and the one passing through the centre which is not deviated. Once these two are established and the image is located any other rays can be drawn since any ray from any point on the object has to arrive at the point on the image as in Fig. 9.43.

Fig. 9.43

## EXPERIMENTING WITH A SIMPLE PROJECTOR SYSTEM – MAGNIFICATION

### METHOD

The apparatus is set up as shown in Fig. 9.44, carefully lined up using a metre rule, and with each component in a suitable holder to give vertical alignment. The lens position is initially adjusted to give a sharp image of the slide on the screen. The distance from the object to the lens (object distance, $u$ centimetres) is measured, as is the image distance ($v$ centimetres). The original height of the slide is measured with a millimetre scale and the corresponding height of the image recorded. This is repeated for a number of object distances, the screen being moved each time till a focused image is obtained.

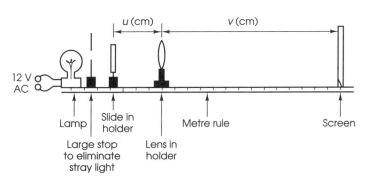

Fig. 9.44

## RESULTS

| Object distance $u$(cm) | Image distance $v$(cm) | Height of object | Height of image |
|---|---|---|---|

## TREATMENT OF RESULTS

Magnification is calculated in each case as

$$\frac{\text{Image height}}{\text{Object height}}$$

It is also found that magnification is

$$\frac{\text{Image distance}}{\text{Object distance}}$$

So in practical projector, image distances are large and the distance of the object from the lens must be small (but not smaller than the focal length of the lens).

## A PRACTICAL PROJECTION SYSTEM

The slide or film is placed upside down so that the final image is erect (Fig. 9.45). The projection lens and slide are slightly further apart than the focal length of the lens, fine focusing is obtained by screwing the projection lens in and out of the projector casing. The condenser lens converges light evenly over the whole of the slide. The mirror reflects all light leaving the lamp towards the condenser lens.

Fig. 9.45

### 4 LENS CAMERAS

A pinhole camera gives a focused image regardless of the object distance, but since little light enters, the exposure time using a pinhole camera with film in it would be long (typically about 15 min). A lens focuses all light passing through it, but it will only focus on a fixed screen for one particular object distance. A lens camera needs to give a lot of light intensity on a screen and to focus at many distances.

The following are some features of a ***lens camera***:

1. The shutter is a spring-loaded blind covering the film, except when a photograph is taken. The shutter speed can change the exposure time and affect how much light reaches the film.
2. The diaphragm adjusts the size of the aperture, which also affects the light reaching the film. Since small apertures (as in pinhole cameras) give sharp focusing for all distances, the aperture also has an effect on focus.
3. The lens converges light to the film forming an image. The lens position relative to the film can be changed with the focusing ring, moving the lens further from the film for a close-up object and towards the film for a distant object.

### 5 THE HUMAN EYE

The main structures of the eye (Fig. 9.46) can be compared with those in a lens camera. The curved cornea begins the focusing process, which is completed by the lens, forming an image on the retina. The pupil (black part at the front of the eye) is a hole, acting like the aperture in a camera. The iris (coloured part at the front of eye) is like the camera diaphragm, controlling the amount of light entering the pupil by opening and closing and therefore changing the pupil diameter.

When light falls on the retina, nerve endings are stimulated and a "message" is sent along the optic nerve to the brain which interprets the message into a sensation of seeing. The lens cannot move in and out to give fine focusing as in a camera. Instead it is made of a flexible material, and muscles surrounding it change its shape, making it more powerful to focus on near objects and less powerful for distant objects. This change of lens power is called ***accommodation***.

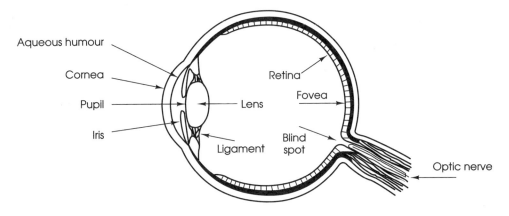

Fig. 9.46

## 6 YOUNG'S DOUBLE SLIT EXPERIMENT – SOME THEORY

The experiment and result were discussed under "Essential Principles", p. 152. Light emerges from the double slit and a pattern of light and dark "fringes" is seen on a screen. The fringes are evenly spaced (Fig. 9.47). The two slits are arranged to give coherent light, same phase, wavelength, amplitude and frequency.

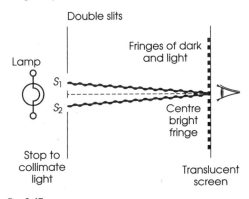

Fig. 9.47

*At the centre bright fringe:* waves from $S_1$ and $S_2$ have travelled the same distance. If they leave in phase they will arrive in phase,

Fig. 9.48

giving a maximum response. There is no path difference between them (Fig. 9.48).

At some other maximum position the wave from $S_2$ has travelled further to point X than the wave from $S_1$. There is a path difference of $S_2X - S_1X$. If the point X is a maximum the waves must be in phase at X. This can only occur if the path difference is a whole number of wavelengths:

$$S_2X - S_1X = (\text{whole number} \times \lambda)$$

$$= n\lambda$$
$$(n = \text{any whole number})$$

For a point Y which is a minimum, the path difference must have an odd half-wavelength in it, so that the waves arrive exactly out of phase:

$$S_1Y - S_2Y = (n + \tfrac{1}{2})\lambda$$

The geometry of the situation gives the following equation which can be used to obtain the value of the wavelength of light:

$$\frac{\text{Separation of fringes}}{\text{Wavelength}}$$

$$= \frac{\text{Distance from slits to screen}}{\text{Distance between slits}}$$

The fringes separation is therefore wavelength dependent (smallest for blue and greatest for red), so the experiment is best done with single-colour light. The greater the distance from slits to screen, and the smaller the distance between slits, the bigger the fringe separation.

## 7 COLOUR

We have already found that light of a different wavelength is seen as a different colour. Surfaces look coloured because they reflect those colours and absorb the others. A red rose reflects red light but absorbs the other colours of the spectrum. A white surface will reflect all the colours of the spectrum and a black surface will absorb them all and reflect none.

When different colours of light are shone onto a white screen we see their addition as they are all reflected. The ***primary colours*** red, green and blue cannot be made by mixing other colours. When the primaries are mixed we get the secondary colours and white is obtained by mixing all three primaries.

red + blue = magenta
red + green = yellow
green + blue = cyan
red + blue + green = white

A similar result is obtained by switching on the coloured dots on a TV screen and these are again red, green and blue.

Remember that only the colours in incident light can be reflected. Reflecting surfaces don't produce their own light. A red rose in white light or in red light will appear red. In blue light it will appear black because it absorbs the blue and there is no red light to reflect.

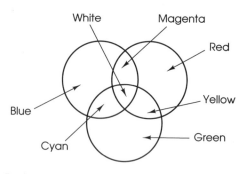

Fig. 9.49

Colour filters also work by absorbing some colours and transmitting the ones that we can see. A blue filter transmits blue light but absorbs all the other colours. If filters follow one another you should remember that the process this time is subtraction and not addition.

Fig. 9.50

**8 THE PHOTOELECTRIC EFFECT**

Light is emitted from atoms in short bursts of waves called *photons*. Each photon carries an exact amount of energy that depends on the frequency of the light.

Energy = constant × frequency.

The constant is called **Planck's constant.** The greater the frequency the greater the energy.

Fig. 9.51

Some of the evidence for this comes from the *photoelectric effect*. When you shine light on the surface of some metals electrons are released. This can be done with a zinc plate but UV light is needed to release the electrons.

The basic effect can be seen by charging a gold leaf electroscope negatively with a clean zinc plate on its cap. When the plate is illuminated with UV light the electrons are emitted and the electroscope loses its negative charge and the leaf falls. More detailed experiments show that:

- A *brighter* light does NOT give more energy to the electrons.
- A brighter lamp does release *more* electrons with the *same energy*.
- Light with a *greater frequency* gives *more energy* to the electrons.
- There is a **threshold frequency** $f_o$. Light below this frequency cannot release electrons from the metal, no matter how bright the light source.

## EXPLANATION

The light arrives in photons. *All* the energy from *one* photon is absorbed by an electron when it is emitted. For the electron to leave the metal a certain amount of energy called the **work function** is needed. If the photon energy is less than the work function the electron is not emitted. If the photon energy equals the work function then its frequency is the threshold frequency $f_0$ and the electron is just able to leave the surface. If the photon energy is greater than the work function the electron emitted has the "extra" energy as its kinetic energy. Making the light brighter doesn't change the energy of the individual photons; there are more of them but their energies can't be added to reach the threshold energy as they all behave individually.

For most materials visible light does not have sufficient energy to cause ionisation in this way. X-rays do have the energy needed and are usually absorbed when a photon causes ionisation of an atom of the absorber. In cell tissue the ejected electron might have sufficient energy to cause further damage. Remember that the photons are either absorbed or pass through unchanged. The energy of the individual photons is fixed and cannot be partly reduced.

---

## 9 THE LENS FORMULA

To find the position of an image more accurately than by using scale drawing you can use the lens formula.

$$\frac{1}{f} = \frac{1}{v} + \frac{1}{u}$$

$f$ = focal length, $v$ = distance of image from lens. $u$ = distance of object from lens. This equation uses the "**real is positive**" sign convention:

- All distances to real objects, images and focuses are positive.
- All distances to virtual objects, images and focuses are negative. The focal length of a convex lens will be + and the focal length of a concave lens will be −.

You can also find *linear magnification*.

$$\text{Magnification} = m = \frac{\text{object size}}{\text{image size}} = \frac{v}{u}$$

### EXAMPLES

1. Find the position, size and nature of the image produced by an object 5 mm high placed 200 mm in front of a convex lens of focal length 150 mm.

From the question, $f$ = +150 mm

$u$ = +200 mm

$$\frac{1}{f} = \frac{1}{v} + \frac{1}{u}$$

$$\frac{1}{150} = \frac{1}{v} + \frac{1}{200}$$

$$\frac{1}{v} = \frac{1}{150} - \frac{1}{200}$$

$$= \frac{4-3}{600} = \frac{1}{600}$$

$$v = 600 \text{ mm}$$

$$\text{magnification} = \frac{v}{u} = \frac{600}{200} = 3$$

size of image = size of object × magnification

$$= 5 \times 3 = 15 \text{ mm}$$

Looking at the signs of the answers you should be able to see that the image is real, inverted, 600 mm from the lens on the opposite side to the object and 15 mm high. You will always find it helpful to draw a sketch diagram to ensure that you have got the correct answer and not made an arithmetic mistake.

2. An object is placed 40 cm from a diverging lens of focal length 10 cm. Find the position, nature and magnification of its image.

From the question, $f$ = −10 cm

$u$ = +40 cm

$$\frac{1}{f} = \frac{1}{v} + \frac{1}{u}$$

$$\frac{-1}{10} = \frac{1}{v} + \frac{1}{40}$$

$$\frac{1}{v} = \frac{-1}{40} - \frac{1}{10}$$

$$= \frac{-1-4}{40} = \frac{-5}{40}$$

$$v = 8 \text{ cm.}$$

$$\text{magnification} = \frac{v}{u} = \frac{8}{20} = 0.4$$

The image is 8 cm from the lens on the same side as the object, virtual, and erect. Compare this with the expected answer from a sketch diagram.

**10** **DEFECTS OF VISION**

A normal eye can focus objects from infinity (its **far point**) down to about 25 cm (its **near point**) without being strained. The distance from the eye to its near point is also called the **least distance of distinct vision**. As we grow older the ciliary muscle becomes less able to change the shape of the lens and many older people are unable to focus on objects that are either very far away or very close. Bifocal lenses in spectacles correct this, the lower part of the lens for the near objects and the rest, with a different lens shape, for those farther away.

### ■ SHORT SIGHT (MYOPIA)

In this case the eyeball is too long or the lens is too powerful and the image is focused in front of the retina so that it is not clear – Fig. 9.52(a). The far point of this eye is not at infinity but is closer to the lens.

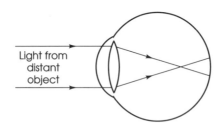

Fig. 9.52(a)

The light from an object close to the eye can be focused. The correction is therefore to wear a diverging lens so that the light from the distant object appears to come from the

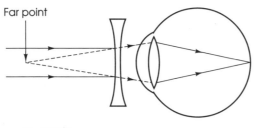

Fig. 9.52(b)

far point of the eye – Fig. 9.52(b) – and can be focused.

### ■ LONG SIGHT (HYPERMETROPIA)

In this case the eyeball is too short or the lens is not powerful enough and the image is focused behind the retina – Fig. 9.53(a). The near point of this eye is farther away than is normal. Light from a more distant object can be focused.

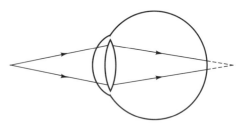

Fig. 9.53(a)

The correction is to wear a converging lens to help the eye lens focus the light. The lens makes the light seem to come from the near point of the eye so that it can be focused – Fig. 9.53(b).

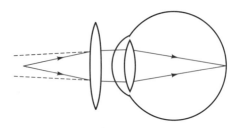

Fig. 9.53(b)

### ■ ASTIGMATISM

In this case the eye lens is slightly cylindrical instead of being spherical. This makes one plane of vision less clear. The correction is a cylindrical lens to help the eye lens in its "weak" plane. It is not possible to use contact lenses to correct for this as they rotate on the eye when in use.

# EXAMINATION QUESTIONS

**MULTIPLE CHOICE QUESTIONS**

## QUESTION 1

A ray of light is incident on a plane mirror. The mirror is then turned through an angle of 30°. The reflected ray will be turned through

A 15°   C 60°   E 90°
B 30°   D 75°                    (ULEAC)

## QUESTION 2

A clear erect image can be obtained from a prism periscope only if the prisms are correctly positioned. Figure 9.54 shows five possible arrangements of two prisms, with rays of light drawn. Which is the correct arrangement for prisms and light?   (ULEAC)

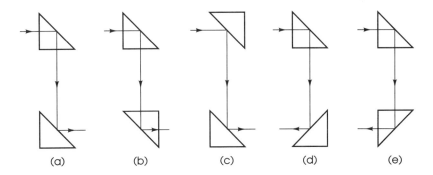

Fig. 9.54

## QUESTION 3

A magnified and inverted image is obtained by placing an object in front of a converging lens. The distance of the object from the lens must be

A  Less than one focal length
B  Equal to one focal length
C  Between one and two focal lengths
D  Equal to two focal lengths
E  Greater than two focal lengths

## QUESTION 4

Which one of the diagrams in Fig. 9.55 correctly shows the path of a ray of light through a glass block? (ULEAC)

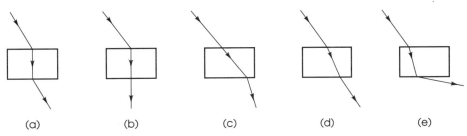

(a)          (b)          (c)          (d)          (e)

Fig. 9.55

## QUESTIONS 5 AND 6

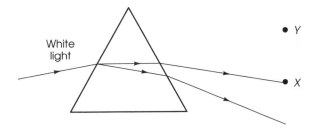

Fig. 9.56

Figure 9.56 represents a narrow beam of white light passing through a glass prism and forming a spectrum on the screen. The points X and Y are on the screen and the rays drawn show the limits of the visible spectrum.

5. The colour of light appearing at X will be

A  Red          D  Blue
B  White        E  Green
C  Violet                    (ULEAC)

6. A thermometer placed at Y records a rise in temperature from the radiation produced. The correct name for this radiation is

A  Ultraviolet
B  X-rays
C  Gamma rays
D  Alpha particles
E  Infra-red                 (ULEAC)

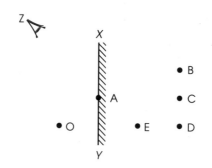

**Fig. 9.57**

## QUESTION 7

An object O is placed in front of a plane mirror XY (see Fig. 9.57). At which of points A–E will an observer at Z see an image of the object?

(ULEAC)

## QUESTION 8

In each of the diagrams in Fig. 9.58, two parallel rays of light enter the left-hand side of a box and leave the right-hand side as shown. Which box contains the most powerful convex lens?          (MEG)

## QUESTION 9

A ray of light is incident on a thin convex lens as shown in Fig. 9.59. In which of the directions A–E will the ray emerge?  (ULEAC)

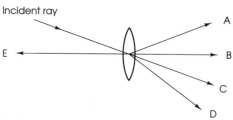

**Fig. 9.59**

## QUESTION 10

A lamp 6 cm high is placed 24 cm in front of a small hole in a pinhole camera. The distance from the hole to the screen is 8 cm (Fig. 9.60). What is the size of the image on the screen?

A  24 cm          D  2 cm
B  8 cm           E  1 cm
C  3 cm

**Fig. 9.60**

**Fig. 9.58**

**STRUCTURED
QUESTIONS**

## QUESTION 11

(a) The diagrams in Fig. 9.61 show four lenses made from glass. Complete the ray paths through the lenses.

(b) In this part of the question you are going to compare a pinhole camera and a lens

camera. Each is to be used to photograph a tree.

(i)  Complete the paths of any rays which go through the pinhole in Fig. 9.62(a). Mark on the film the "image" produced by the pinhole camera.

(ii) Name the type of lens used in the lens camera.

(iii) Complete the paths of any rays hitting the lens in Fig. 9.62(b). Mark on the film the image produced by the lens camera.

(iv) State two ways in which the images produced on the film in these cameras are different from the tree itself. (2 lines)　　　(ULEAC)

Fig. 9.61

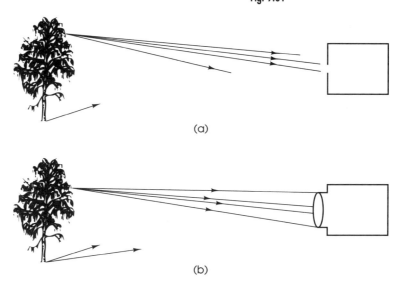

Fig. 9.62

## QUESTION 12

(a) Figure 9.63 shows a narrow beam of light, incident on a 90°– 45° glass prism. Complete the diagram showing the path of the ray in and out of the prism.

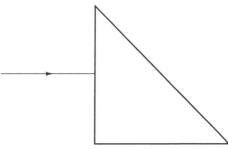

Fig. 9.63

(b) Figure 9.64 shows plane waves of light incident on the same prism. (Let 2.0 cm represent the wavelength of light.)

(i) Make an exact copy of the diagram, and complete it to show the path of the waves into, and out of, the prism.

(ii) What, if anything, happened to the wavelength and frequency of the light waves as they enter the prism?

Fig. 9.64

(c) Figure 9.65 refers to an optical dipstick which causes an alarm to operate when the level of liquid in a tank is below F.

(i) By referring to the diagram describe in words how the light reaches the photocell when the liquid level is below F.

(ii) Explain, with the aid of the diagram, why the photocell will not operate when the liquid level is above GE.

(iii) Explain whether or not the detector will work when the liquid level is between GE and F.         (ULEAC)

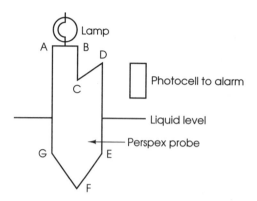

Fig. 9.65

## QUESTION 13

Figure 9.66 shows a ray of light, A, being refracted as it passes from air into a glass block.

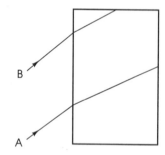

Fig. 9.66

(i) What causes the ray to change direction as it enters the glass?
(ii) Draw on the diagram the ray as it emerges from the glass.
(iii) Draw on the diagram the path of ray B, after it meets the top of the block until it emerges into the air.

## QUESTION 14

Some students are preparing spotlights for the school play. Fig. 9.67 shows the spotlight arranged in two groups: PRIMARY colours and SECONDARY colours.

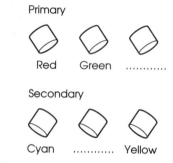

Fig. 9.67

(a) (i) Complete the labelling of the PRIMARY colour spotlights.
    (ii) Complete the labelling of the SECONDARY colour spotlights.
(b) Which of the three primary colours of light has
    (i) the shortest wavelength.
    (ii) the longest wavelength.
The students set up the three primary colour spotlights as shown in Fig. 9.68.

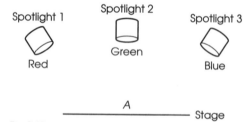

Fig. 9.68

(c) What colour of light is seen on the stage at A when
    (i) spotlights 1 and 2 are switched on.
    (ii) spotlights 2 and 3 are switched on.
    (iii) all three spotlights are switched on.
(d) What is
    (i) a primary colour?
    (ii) a secondary colour?

# ANSWERS TO EXAMINATION QUESTIONS

| Question | 1 | 2 | 3 | 4 | 5 | 6 | 7 | 8 | 9 | 10 |
|---|---|---|---|---|---|---|---|---|---|---|
| Answer | C | B | C | D | A | E | E | B | C | D |

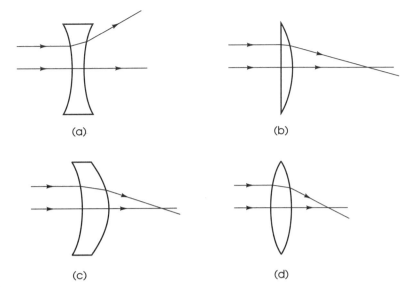

Fig. 9.69

## ANSWER 11

(a) See Fig. 9.69. Explanation: The lower ray in each case hits the lenses at 90°, so there is no change of path. (A is a diverging lens; B has less curvature than D so it is weaker, less converging; C is a concave lens at one surface and convex at the other.)

(b) All rays from a point on an object which pass through the lens contribute to the same point on the image. Rays 1 and 2 pass through the centre of the lens, placing the positions of the top and bottom of the image.

(i) See Fig. 9.70.

(ii) The lens is a convex (converging lens).

(iii) See Fig. 9.71. Pinhole cameras require a long exposure time since they allow only a little light to enter. Pinhole cameras cannot take good photographs of anything likely to move a little – it would result in several blurred images. A lens camera has a short exposure time so this is possible.

(iv) Image is diminished and inverted.

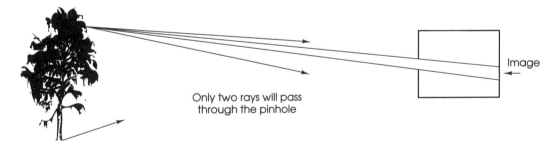

Only two rays will pass
through the pinhole

Image

Fig. 9.70

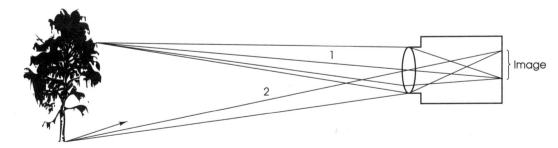

Fig. 9.71

## ANSWER 12

(a) See Fig. 9.72.

**Fig. 9.72**

(b) (i) See Fig. 9.73. Explanation: "Rays" in Fig. 9.72 are the line at 90° to the wavefronts.

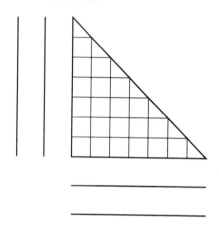

**Fig. 9.73**

(ii) As shown in Fig. 9.73, wavelength is reduced in the prism and frequency remains the same.

(c) (i) Light rays enter AB normal to the surface so there is no direction change and they travel to GF. If there is air outside GF the rays hit GF at an angle greater than the critical angle so total internal reflection takes place with reflection to FE. Again there is total internal reflection sending the ray to CD. A further internal reflection sends light out normally to the photocell.

(ii) With liquid outside GF the refraction relationship is changed, and so is the critical angle. The refractive index is.

$$\frac{\text{Velocity in material 1}}{\text{Velocity in material 2}}$$

so with liquid in place of air the refractive index is less, the critical angle is greater and light hitting GF is refracted out into the liquid.

(iii) If the liquid level is very close to F, internal reflection will take place; if

very close to G it will not. So a small, and gradually increasing amount of light will reach the cell as the level falls from G to F.

## ANSWER 13

(i) Light changes direction because it enters the block at an angle, and it then changes speed. The wavefront as a whole changes direction because of this.

(ii) and (iii) See Fig. 9.74, and 9.75.

**Fig. 9.74**

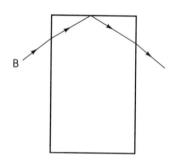

**Fig. 9.75**

Ray A emerges parallel to the starting direction, refraction having taken place each time the medium changes.

Ray B hits the top surface at an angle greater than the critical angle, so total internal reflection occurs.

## ANSWER 14

(This is a basic level question)

(a) (i) Blue (ii) Magenta
(b) (i) Blue (ii) Red
(c) (i) Yellow (ii) Cyan (iii) White
(d) (i) one that cannot be made by mixing other colours

(ii) one that is made by mixing two primary colours

# TUTOR'S QUESTION AND ANSWER

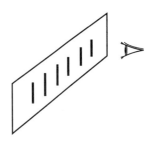

**Fig. 9.76**

**QUESTION**

To observe Young's fringes, a blackened microscope slide with two slits ruled close together is placed between a lamp and a screen in a dark-room (Fig. 9.76). Bright and dark bands (fringes) are seen on the screen.

(a) What property of waves does this experiment demonstrate?

(b) Explain, with aid of diagrams, what causes the bright bands on the screen.

(c) Why are there several bright bands?

(d) Explain the cause of the dark bands.

(e) Describe what measurements you would make to find the wavelength of light.

(f) Blue light has a shorter wavelength than red light. What would happen to the fringe separation if a blue filter were used instead of red? Explain your answer.

(g) What would happen to the fringe width if the slits were replaced by two slits closer together? (ULEAC)

**ANSWER**

(a) Interference.

(b) Waves spread out at the slits (Fig. 9.77). When they reach the screen there are regions of overlap. If waves meet in phase a bright patch is produced. This happens when the path difference between the two sets of waves is a whole number of wavelengths.

Wave 1
Wave 2

**Fig. 9.77**

(c) There are several bands because constructive interference is possible for path differences of 0, λ, 2λ, etc.

(d) Dark bands happen where waves arrive out of phase and amplitudes are equal and opposite causing destructive interference (Fig. 9.78). It happens if the path difference is $(n + \frac{1}{2})\lambda$.

**Fig. 9.78**

(e) $$\frac{\text{Fringe separation}}{\text{Wavelength}} = \frac{\text{Distance from slits to screen}}{\text{Distance between slits}}$$

Need to measure separation – use several fringes – say 10. Mark the start and end of 10 fringes on the screen. Measure the separation of 10 fringes with a millimetre scale and divide by 10. Measure distance from slits to screen with a metre rule. Measure slit distance using a microscope with a scale.

(f) The fringes would be closer. Smaller path difference is needed to get a wavelength difference.

(g) The pattern is wider. Greater separation of fringe.

# STUDENT'S ANSWER – EXAMINER'S COMMENTS

## STUDENT ANSWER TO QUESTION 13

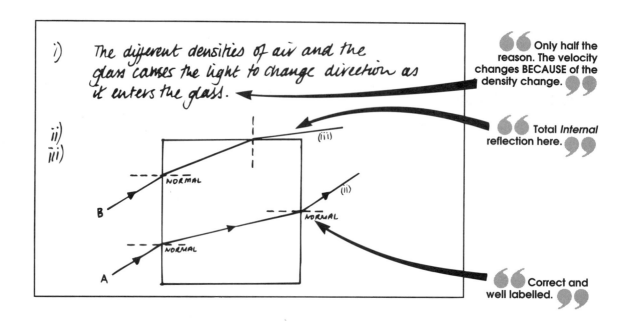

i) The different densities of air and the glass causes the light to change direction as it enters the glass.

**Only half the reason. The velocity changes BECAUSE of the density change.**

**Total *Internal* reflection here.**

**Correct and well labelled.**

# REVIEW SHEET

■ All angles of incidence, reflection and refraction are measured from the _____.

■ All waves reflect so that the angle of reflection = _____.

■ An object is placed 20 cm in front of a mirror. The image will be _____ from the mirror and will be _____ inverted.

■ An image which cannot be found on a screen is a _____ image.

■ Waves refract when their _____ changes as they go from one material into another.

■ When a ray of light inside a more dense material meets the surface at more than the _____ _____ it is _____ reflected.

■ Name two uses for optical fibre.

1. _____. 2. _____.

■ A lens that is thicker in the middle is a _____ lens and will make parallel light converge to a _____.

■ A lens used as a magnifying glass will be a _____ lens and the object will be _____ to the lens than the focus. The image that is produced is magnified, _____, and erect.

■ The distance from the centre of a lens to its focus is called the _____ _____.

■ Name the colours the spectrum formed from white light in order of their wavelength.

_____

■ In a projector the two lenses that make sure that the slide is evenly illuminated are called _____.

■ Label the parts of the eye in the following diagram.

Fig. 9.79

■ If two waves arrive at the same place at the same time they will _____.

If the two waves are in phase they will cause _____.

■ Briefly explain what is meant by "in phase".

_____

_____

_____

■ Light can be seen to cause interference patterns. What does this tell you about the nature of light?

_____

_____

■ Describe the difference in the ways in which the eye and the camera focus on objects at different distances.

_____

_____

_____

■ Complete the paths of the light rays in the following diagrams.

Fig. 9.80

■ Name the three primary and the three secondary colours.

_____

_____

_____

# GETTING STARTED

One of the questions which concerns a scientist is "Why do materials behave in a particular way?" There is often no conclusive answer to the question, because the particles which make up the material are very small, and cannot be observed directly. We can, however, see *large-scale effects* and it is these that are often used as the basis for a "model". To a physicist a *model* is a mental picture of what is actually going on. It is an attempt to explain how small-scale interactions can combine to cause large-scale behaviour. The model is sometimes expressed in words or pictures or by using the language of mathematics. This chapter considers the ways in which *solids, liquids* and *gases* behave and tries to explain the *differences* in their behaviour in terms of *atoms* and *molecules*.

The word "particle" will be used throughout this chapter, with no attempt being made to distinguish atoms, molecules or ions.

# STRUCTURE OF MATTER AND KINETIC THEORY

STATES OF MATTER

DENSITY

A MODEL FOR MATTER

DIFFUSION

BROWNIAN MOTION

KINETIC THEORY AND
  KINETIC ENERGY

CHANGE OF STATE

EVAPORATION

THE BEHAVIOUR OF
  GASES

DETERMINING DENSITIES

REFRIGERATORS

BOILING POINTS

SURFACE TENSION

# ESSENTIAL PRINCIPLES

## 1 STATES OF MATTER

**Matter** is a general word used to describe any piece of material. The material could be a solid, a liquid or a gas, and these are described as the **states of matter**.

Any substance can, under the right conditions of temperature and pressure, exist in **any** of the three states. For example, we are used to seeing mercury at room temperature as a liquid metal. However, if mercury is cooled enough it becomes a silvery solid, and it vaporises easily to become a gas. In a similar way water can exist as ice or as steam.

The obvious differences between the three states are:

1. **Solids** have a fixed volume, and a fixed shape. They are not easily expanded or compressed by mechanical means.
2. **Liquids** have a fixed volume, but no fixed shape. They take up the shape of their container. They pour easily and are not easily compressed.
3. **Gases** have neither fixed volume nor fixed shape. They can take up any volume available to them. They flow easily and are easily compressed.

Because both liquids and gases can **flow** they are sometimes referred to as **fluids**, so "fluid" can mean either a liquid or a gas.

## 2 DENSITY

Solids, liquids and gases show very different **densities**. The **density** of a material is large if a **large mass** of it occupies a **small volume** (e.g. lead, mercury, steel). A small density means that a large volume of material has a small mass (e.g. all gases at normal temperatures and pressures, cotton wool, expanded polystyrene).

Density is calculated using the ratio

■ $$\text{Density} = \frac{\text{Mass}}{\text{Volume}} \text{ or } D = \frac{M}{V}$$

It is measured in kg/m³ or g/cm³. It sometimes helps to remember that a material can only float on top of a *more* dense material – so oil is less dense than water!

### EXAMPLE 1

A piece of glass has a mass of 40 g and a volume of 16 cm³. Calculate the density of the glass.

$$D = \frac{M}{V} = \frac{40}{16} = 2.5 \text{ g/cm}^3$$

or

$$D = \frac{M}{V} = \frac{40 \times 10^{-3}}{16 \times 10^{-6}} = 2500 \text{ kg/m}^3$$

### EXAMPLE 2

Expanded polystyrene has a density of 1.6 kg/m³. What volume does it occupy of its mass is 400 g?

400 g = 0.4 kg

$$D = \frac{M}{V} \quad \text{so} \quad V = \frac{M}{D}$$

$$\text{Volume} = \frac{0.4}{1.6} = 0.25 \text{ m}^3$$

The densities of some common materials are given in Table 10.1. It is worth noting that air and other gases have values of density which are much less than those of solids and liquids.

Table 10.1

| Material | Density (kg/m³) | Material | Density (kg/m³) |
|----------|-----------------|----------|-----------------|
| Water | 1000 | Turpentine | 1362 |
| Air | 1.2 | China | 2800 |
| Mercury | 13 600 | Iron | 7860 |
| Concrete | 2400 | Hardboard | 900 |
| Lead | 11 340 | Helium | 0.09 |

If we assume that all matter is made up of particles, then the density data suggest that the particles are packed more closely together in solids and liquids than in gases. It follows that a larger mass of particles is occupying a smaller volume in solids and liquids than in gases.

## (a) SOLIDS

***High-density*** materials such as metals, must have a ***closer packing*** arrangement than low-density materials such as expanded polystyrene. The closest packing of all would be achieved if the particles were arranged as in Fig. 10.1 with each particle ***stacked*** in three dimensions.

Fig. 10.1 Close-packed particles in a high-density solid.

However, since all materials show different densities, the arrangement must vary slightly from material to material. There may, for example, be gaps in the close-packed structure, and the particles of some material may vary in size, e.g. for alloys such as steel. The idea of an orderly arrangement does, however, seem to fit the large-scale density data for metallic solids.

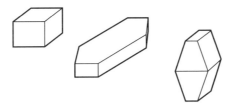

Fig. 10.2 Crystal shapes.

***Compounds*** which form ***crystals*** also show an orderly arrangement (Fig. 10.2). Typical crystals have a regular ***geometric*** shape, which suggests that the internal arrangement of particles may also be an orderly one. Metallic solids tend to have high-density values. High density, therefore, suggests a close packing of particles.

***Non-crystalline and low-density solids*** are thought to show little orderliness. Their particles might be arranged in a more ***random*** way (Fig. 10.3).

Fig. 10.3 Low-density solid or liquid.

## (b) LIQUIDS

***Liquids*** must also be arranged in this random way. Liquids and solids both reveal low-density values, and both are difficult to compress. Although the arrangement of particles is similar for liquids and solids, there remains a basic difference. Liquids can flow and pour, so their particles must have greater freedom to move. The models have, up to this point, taken no account of the ***forces*** holding the particles together.

## (c) FORCES AND PARTICLES

Forces between particles are ***electrical*** in nature, because within each particle there are positive and negative charges. Two types of forces are therefore possible, ***attraction*** and ***repulsion***. A picture of this would be along the lines of Fig. 10.4, where two trolleys are linked by a ***spring (attraction)*** but mounted with repelling ***magnets (repulsion)***. They will stay at rest, separated from each other, when the two sets of forces are in ***equilibrium (balance)***.

Fig. 10.4 Forces of both attraction and repulsion.

The following provides some evidence of the nature of these two sets of forces:

1. Solids are difficult to pull apart – this suggests that there are attracting forces holding the particles together.
2. Solids are difficult to compress – there are repelling forces stopping the particles from getting too close together.
3. Liquid droplets hold together – attracting forces.
4. Liquids are difficult to compress – repelling forces.

Since solids maintain their shape and liquids do not, this suggests that the ***forces in a solid are stronger than those in a liquid***. The forces in liquids are weak enough to allow some movement of the particles.

### (d) GASES

Gas densities are about 1000 times less than solid or liquid densities. This suggests than on average gas particles are further apart than solid or liquid particles. 1 cm³ of water will expand to give about 1000 cm³ of steam. This gives a figure of about 10 times the particle distance in a gas compared with solids or liquids (since $10^3 = 1000$). A particle model for a gas would therefore look something like Fig. 10.5.

Gases are easily compressed, and can expand to fill any volume. The forces between particles at these distances must therefore be very weak. They are effectively non-existent except when a gas is greatly compressed and the particles are moved closer together.

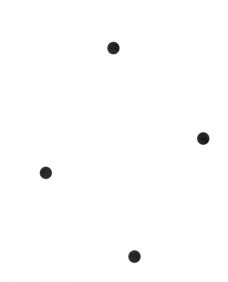

Fig. 10.5 Model for a gas.

---

### (a) GASES

***Gases*** like ammonia and hydrogen sulphide, which have unpleasant smells, can be quickly detected at one end of a room after a little has escaped at the other end. This strongly suggests that gas particles are moving.

Clearer evidence for this can be provided by the following experimental demonstrations:

1. ***Ammonia*** is an alkaline gas. It will turn damp red litmus paper blue. A long tube containing pieces of damp red litmus paper and with an ammonia-soaked piece of cotton wool in one end can be used to show that ammonia particles are moving. The pieces of litmus paper turn blue in succession (Fig. 10.6).

Fig. 10.6 Diffusion of ammonia.

2. ***Bromine*** liquid vaporises easily at room temperature. If bromine liquid is introduced into a gas jar, the brown gas colour slowly moves up the jar (Fig. 10.7).
3. ***Carbon dioxide*** placed in the lower tube can be detected in the upper tube after several minutes, despite being denser than air (Fig. 10.8).

### (b) LIQUIDS

***Liquids*** also show diffusion. A large copper sulphate crystal, placed in a gas jar of water, dissolves slowly. The blue colour of the solution gradually develops throughout the jar over the course of a few days (Fig. 10.9).

Water

Copper sulphate

Fig. 10.9

All these diffusion experiments take time, because diffusion is a random process. Indeed our model of gases and liquids explains why this is the case. In a gas, the particles are moving. A single bromine particle in a gas jar has around it many air particles. It is ***not*** simply able to move from one end of the jar to the other by a ***direct route***. It will collide

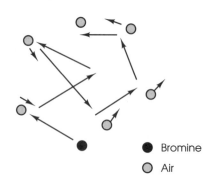

Bromine

Air

Fig. 10.10 Diffusion of bromine.

❝❝ Bromine is a highly dangerous substance. It should only be used in a fume cupboard. Your answer to a question should mention this hazard. ❞❞

Fig. 10.7 Bromine diffusion.

Air

Carbon dioxide

Fig. 10.8

many times with air particles and make a *random journey* (Fig. 10.10). The distance between collisions is called the "mean free path". A typical particle may experience $10^9$ collisions per second!

Liquid particles, because of their weak forces, are also able to move. However, they are unable to escape from the total liquid volume unless they have a lot of extra energy (see *evaporation*).

Applying these ideas to a *solid* suggests that even in a solid some movement is possible, but that the movement is confined by the strong forces. Particles in solids can only move by vibrating about fixed positions, so that the solid shape is maintained. The theory which suggests that particles in solids, liquids and gases are in constant motion is called the *kinetic theory.*

## 5 ▷ BROWNIAN MOTION

This is a much more direct piece of evidence for the movement of particles. It is best observed using a smoke cell. The smoke cell is a small container, like a test-tube, about 1 cm high (Fig. 10.11). Smoke can be poured into it using a burning piece of string or a drinking straw. A cover slide placed on top of the cell prevents the smoke from escaping.

Light from a strong light source can be focused with a lens into the cell. The light is scattered by the smoke particles. When viewed with a microscope the smoke particles appear as bright specks against a

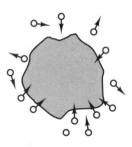

Fig. 10.12 Smoke particle is bombarded by air molecules.

darker background. They are seen to be in *continuous random* motion.

Smoke particles are very large (as particles go) and in the cell they are surrounded by small (invisible) air particles in motion. Air particles hit the smoke particles on all sides and at random. If enough air particles hit in one particular direction, thereby providing a large enough resultant force on the massive smoke particle, it will move (Fig. 10.12).

The movement of the smoke particles, caused by the random movement of the air particles, is called Brownian motion. Brownian motion can be observed using any fluid (liquid or gas) with suitable particles. The original discovery was with pollen grains in water. It can also be seen with Indian ink in water, and with milk (fat globules) in water. However, the movement is seen most clearly with smoke in air.

> ❝❝ Randomness is a recurring idea in Physics. It refers to a process which seems to occur only by chance. Check that you understand which other processes are random, and list them. ❞❞

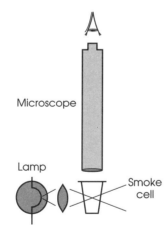

Fig. 10.11 Smoke cell to show Brownian motion.

## 6 ▷ KINETIC THEORY AND KINETIC ENERGY

The hotter a gas becomes, the greater the internal energy of its particles. We can interpret this in the model for matter if we assume that the greater the internal energy of a material, the greater the average kinetic energy of its particles. So the hotter a gas becomes, the faster, on average, is the movement of its particles.

Temperature is directly linked to the kinetic energy of particles. It can be looked on

as a rough measure of kinetic energy. This raises the important point that at the same temperature the average kinetic energy of all particles is the same. The effect of having a particular amount of kinetic energy will, however, depend on the mass of each particle and the forces restraining them.

## 7 > CHANGE OF STATE

If ice is taken from a deep freeze so that its temperature is well below 0 °C and heated with a constant and controlled energy supply, like a small immersion heater, its temperature gradually rises to 0 °C (melting-point). We continue to supply heat at the same rate until all the water obtained when the ice melts, boils and turns to steam. The temperature is recorded at one-minute intervals during this process. A graph similar to that in Fig. 10.13 would be obtained.

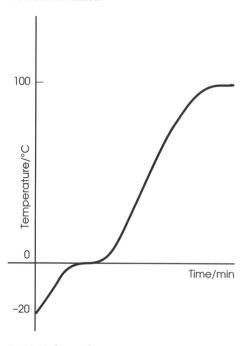

Fig. 10.13 Change of state: ice–water–steam.

While the ice was below 0 °C, the heat energy supplied raised its temperature to its melting-point. Since temperature is related to the mean kinetic energy of particles, this can be interpreted as saying that the ice particles vibrate more rapidly as they gain energy.

At 0 °C, heat was still being supplied, but while the ice is melting, no further temperature rise is observed. Since there was no temperature rise, the applied energy can no longer be increasing the kinetic energy of the particles. Instead it is being used to do work, namely to break the bonds holding the particles in the solid state.

Once the bonds are broken, and the ice has turned to water, the temperature rises again, and the heat supplied increases the kinetic energy of the particles in the liquid.

The energy applied to cause a change of state without a change of temperature, is called the ***latent heat*** of the material (see Ch. 12). There is a similar effect when water boils. The temperature remains steady, with the energy provided now being used to do work in removing particles from the liquid to the gas state. Once all the particles are in the gas state the temperature rises again. The energy has been used in separating the particles against their attracting forces. The same quantity of latent heat is released when the gas condenses back to a liquid.

In a laboratory demonstration, the reverse process is usually shown, where a hot liquid is allowed to cool and solidify. Stearic acid crystals are suitable for this with a melting-point around 40 °C. A hot solution will give a cooling curve like that in Fig. 10.14.

As the liquid begins to solidify the temperature remains steady. Bonds are reforming as the particles join together in the solid state, and in the process energy is released. This release of energy maintains the temperature, until the whole of the mass is solid and then cooling takes place. The kinetic energy of the particles drops, and the temperature is again seen to fall.

Fig. 10.14 Cooling curve for a liquid changing to a solid at 40° C.

## 8 > EVAPORATION

Unlike boiling, evaporation of a liquid can take place at any temperature. The ***rate of evaporation*** depends on a number of factors. It can be ***increased*** by the following:

1. Increased temperature;
2. Decreased pressure on the surface;
3. Increased surface area;
4. Draughts over the surface.

In terms of kinetic theory, increased temperature means an increased average

kinetic energy of the particles. The term "average" has been used throughout since not all particles have the same kinetic energy at a particular temperature. Some have above-average energies, some below average. The overall picture follows a ***normal distribution curve*** (Fig. 10.15).

If a particle has above-average kinetic energy, it has a greater chance of removing itself from the forces holding it in the liquid and therefore of entering the gas state. This

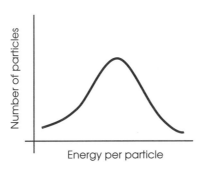

Fig. 10.15 Normal distribution of energy among particles.

change is further increased if it is also at the *surface* of the liquid. So greater tempera-

tures and larger surface areas give greater rates of evaporation.

The surface is, of course, being bombarded by gas particles which can collide with an escaped liquid particle, forcing it back into the liquid. Reduced pressure or a draught across the surface helps prevent this taking place.

If the rest of the liquid loses "above-average kinetic energy" particles, then the remaining particles in the liquid have now a reduced average kinetic energy, and the liquid temperature falls. So evaporation results in the cooling of the original liquid.

## 9 THE BEHAVIOUR OF GASES

❝ The ideas have often formed the basis of examination questions. It is worth checking that you understand and can remember all the points raised here. ❞

Gases, because their particles are much further apart than in liquids and solids, have extremely small forces acting between the particles. For this reason, gases respond more noticeably to changes in pressure and temperature. These changes can be explained in terms of gas particles using kinetic theory.

The following are explanations of typical gas behaviour, using the kinetic theory model.

### (a) GASES EXERT A PRESSURE

Gas particles are in constant, random motion. They collide with other particles and with the walls of their container. Each collision exerts a force on the container. Since many collisions take place, a fairly constant force is exerted. A constant force on an area is described as a constant pressure since pressure is defined as force ÷ area.

### (b) FOR A GAS AT CONSTANT VOLUME, AN INCREASE IN TEMPERATURE CAUSES AN INCREASE IN PRESSURE

Increased temperature increases the average kinetic energy of the particles, so the average velocity increases. Therefore in a fixed volume, the time between each collision is reduced, and there are more collisions with the walls per second. This increases the average force exerted and therefore increases the pressure.

### (c) A VOLUME REDUCTION AT CONSTANT TEMPERATURE INCREASES THE GAS PRESSURE

A reduced volume means smaller distances between collisions and therefore more collisions per second. This increases the average force exerted and again increases the pressure. There is more detail about the gas laws in Chapter 12.

# EXTENSION MATERIALS

## 1 EXPERIMENTAL DETERMINATION OF DENSITY

Density is defined as mass/volume. Modern electronic balances present no problem in measuring masses very precisely to about 0.1 g or less, but measuring volume is more difficult.

### (a) REGULAR SOLIDS WITH A CUBOID SHAPE

These can be directly measured using a ruler with a millimetre scale (Fig. 10.16). Volume = $a \times b \times c$.

Fig. 10.16

Fig. 10.17

Fig. 10.18

## (b) SPHERICAL OBJECTS

These need their radius determined. This could be done using string to find the circumference (Fig. 10.17). The circumference is $2\pi r$, which establishes the radius. Then volume is $\frac{4}{3}\pi r^3$. Alternatively, vernier callipers can be used to find the diameter.

## (c) CYLINDRICAL OBJECTS

These need their length and radius determined (Fig. 10.18). A millimetre scale on a ruler can be used for the length and vernier callipers for the radius. Volume = $\pi r^2 l$.

## (d) IRREGULAR SOLIDS

Volumes have to be found indirectly by displacement of water. A measuring cylinder is filled to a known volume with water, e.g. 25 cm³. The volume is read with the eye level with the bottom of the meniscus (Fig. 10.19).

The solid is lowered into the liquid on a thread and the water-level rises to say 35 cm³ (Fig. 10.20). The volume of the solid is therefore 10 cm³. For larger solids a displacement can is used.

## (e) LIQUIDS

Their volumes can be determined directly using a measuring cylinder.

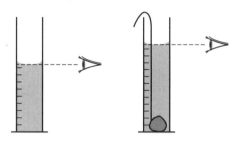

Fig. 10.19 Volume measurement: the eye is level with the bottom of the meniscus.

Fig. 10.20 Volume of an irregular solid by displacement.

## 2 > REFRIGERATORS

The inside of a refrigerator is cooled by evaporation. A liquid called **Freon** is circulated inside the refrigerator through a system of pipes by a pump. Evaporation of the Freon occurs inside the refrigerator, which has several loops of pipe inside the freezer cabinet. The pump helps evaporation by pumping vapour out of the "evaporator" pipes and reducing pressure. The latent heat for the Freon to evaporate is removed from the air and food inside the refrigerator, making them cold (Fig. 10.21).

The compressor pump compresses the freon vapour inside the condenser pipes which are at the back of the refrigerator and surrounded by air. Pressurising the vapour helps it condense, and causes it to give up its latent heat of vaporisation to the surrounding air.

The refrigerator is an example of a heat pump, removing heat energy from the air and food inside the cabinet and transferring it to the air outside.

Fig. 10.21

## 3 BOILING POINTS

A liquid will boil when the pressure of its vapour is the same as the pressure in the space above it. Standard ***boiling point*** is measured when the pressure is one standard atmosphere (760 mm mercury pressure). The vapour that is formed is then able to form bubbles in the liquid. Water will normally boil at about 100 °C because that is the temperature at which the vapour pressure of water becomes equal to the pressure of one atmosphere. A liquid can therefore boil at almost any temperature depending on the pressure above it. A modern car will have a pressurised cooling system where the vapour is not released so that the water will not boil even though the temperature rises above 100 °C.

A pressure cooker also works on this principle. The steam can only escape through the valve when its pressure has been raised. Since the pressure is greater than one atmosphere the boiling point is raised and the food cooks faster. Reducing the pressure above a liquid will enable it to be boiled at a lower temperature. Dissolved substances will also change boiling point (salt raises the boiling point of water). Chemists use this to check the purity of chemicals.

Fig. 10.22

## 4 SURFACE TENSION

We have already seen that the particles of a liquid attract each other. A particle in the liquid will be attracted in all directions by the surrounding particles and the forces will therefore cancel leaving it free to move. This is not true for a particle at the surface where there are no particles above it and the particle will need quite a lot of energy to move out above the surface because of the downward attraction of the other particles (as we found in the section on evaporation). The *sideways attraction of the particles at the surface* produces the surface tension effect. (Note that there is NOT a "skin" on the surface!)

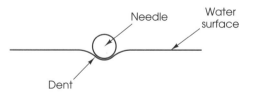

Fig. 10.23

If a needle is placed gently on the surface of water its weight will not be sufficient to push apart the surface particles and it will rest *on* the surface. If you look closely you can see that it makes a dent in the surface. Note that the needle is NOT floating. If you put the needle onto the water point first its weight will be acting on fewer particles and it can push them apart and sink. Detergents make the forces between the particles smaller. If you add a drop of detergent to the water the needle will break through the bonds and sink.

In a glass container water molecules are attracted more to the glass than to each other and are pulled up the side of the glass. We see this as a ***meniscus***.

Fig. 10.24

If the container is narrow (a capillary tube) the liquid will be pulled up the tube until the attractive force from the glass is balanced by the weight of water being lifted. The same effect is the reason why water soaks up through your bath sponge or tea soaks up through a sugar cube. This is known as *capillary action*. Damp will rise through brickwork in this way and is stopped by a non-porous damp proof layer between the bricks. Blotting paper and wicks use the effect to move ink or the fuel upwards.

In some cases, such as mercury in a glass container, the liquid molecules attract each other more than the glass and the effect is reversed so that the meniscus curves the other way.

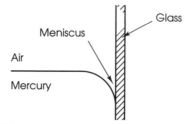

Fig. 10.25

Water molecules attract each other but are repelled by some other materials such as waxes. Water will therefore "bead" on a waxed surface rather than soak in. This is why we polish coffee tables and car bodywork. When the polish wears off the water is attracted to the surface and spreads out into a large thin layer. This same attraction between molecules can make two wet microscope slides or two wet plates difficult to separate.

The attraction of the molecules in soap film will make it take up the smallest possible area (spherical bubbles have the smallest possible area for their volume). This can be investigated by making soap bubbles in a wire frame crossed by a cotton loop. When the bubble is burst on one side of the loop the cotton is pulled into an arc by the remaining soap film.

A soap film formed at the wide end of a clean glass funnel will move towards the narrower end so that it has a smaller area.

Fig. 10.26

# EXAMINATION QUESTIONS

**MULTIPLE CHOICE QUESTIONS**

## QUESTION 1

Which of the following statements about the volume, density and mass of a metal cube is true, when the cube is heated?

A The volume decreases, the density decreases, but the mass remains the same.

B The volume, density and mass all increase.

C The volume increases, but the density and mass remain the same.

D The volume increases, the density decreases, but the mass remains the same.

E The volume remains the same, but the density and mass both increase.

(ULEAC)

## QUESTION 2

Which of the following describes particles in a solid at room temperature?

A Close together and stationary

B Close together and vibrating

C Close together and moving about at random

D Far apart and stationary

E Far apart and moving about at random

(ULEAC)

## QUESTION 3

A material has a density of 2 g/cm³. What would be the mass of a block of it 3 cm × 2 cm × 1 cm?

A 2 g      D 8 g
B 3 g      E 12 g
C 6 g              (NISEAC)

## QUESTION 4

When air in a closed container of fixed size is heated, which of the following statements is true?

  A The molecules move more slowly.
  B The pressure of the air increases.
  C The velocity of the molecules stays the same.
  D The molecules expand.
  E The force between the air molecules increases.

## QUESTION 5

A cube has a side of 2 cm, a volume of 8 cm³ and a density of 8 g/cm³. The mass of the cube is

  A 1 g          C 32 g
  B 16 g        D 64 g    (SEG)

## QUESTION 6

Small particles of smoke in air in a well-lit glass box are seen making small jerky movements. These movements are due to

  A Energy from the light source making the particles expand
  B Energy from the light source causing convection currents in the box
  C Static electricity on the particles
  D The motion of molecules of the air in the box        (SEG)

## QUESTION 7

The phrase "latent heat of fusion" is used to describe the amount of heat required to change

  A A liquid into a gas without raising its temperature
  B A liquid into a gas with a rise in temperature
  C A solid into a liquid without raising its temperature
  D A solid into a liquid with a rise in temperature.

## QUESTION 8

In a room at 20 °C, liquid naphthalene (melting at 80 °C) is allowed to cool from 100 °C. Which one of the graphs (Fig. 10.27) best shows the cooling?

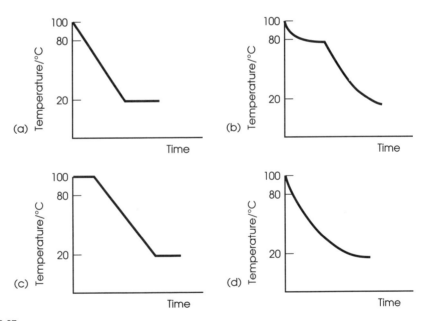

Fig. 10.27

## STRUCTURED QUESTIONS

## QUESTION 9

(a) In the diagram (Fig. 10.28), the bottom circle represents the molecules in a liquid. Complete the top circle to represent the molecules in a gas.
(b) With reference to the diagram, explain why gases can be compressed easily but liquids cannot. (2 lines)
(c) Brownian motion is usually shown in a school laboratory by looking at smoke specks under a microscope.
  (i) Describe the motion of the smoke specks. (1 line)

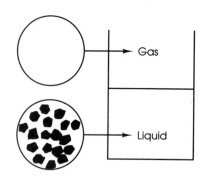

**Fig. 10.28**

(ii) What causes this motion? (2 lines)

(NEAB)

## QUESTION 10

(a) Assuming air is made up of molecules, which are always moving, how do we explain why the pressure of the air increases as its volume decreases. (2 lines)

(b) (i) How could you increase the pressure of air in a sealed container without changing its volume? (1 line)

(ii) Explain your answer to (i) in terms of the motion of the molecules. (2 lines)

## QUESTION 11

(a) Complete the following table:

1 kilogram = _____ grams
1 metre = _____ centimetres
1 cubic metre = _____ cubic centimetres

(b) (i) Place the following in order of increasing density. The least dense and the most dense are shown.

Hydrogen    Air    Aluminium    Gold
Water    Iron    Oil

(ii) State the density of water. Give the units.

(c) You are provided with a box of ball-bearings (small steel spheres, all of equal size). Describe how you would find, as accurately as possible, each of the following:

(i) The mass of one sphere;

(ii) The volume of one sphere;

(iii) The density of steel. (ULEAC)

## QUESTION 12

(a) A light cotton loop can rest on a soap film which has been formed on a metal ring.

**Fig. 10.29**

(i) Draw arrows on the diagram to show the forces acting on the thread.

(ii) What name is given to the forces acting on the cotton thread?

(iii) Why do these forces seem to have no effect on the surface of the soap film?

(b) The diagram below shows what happens when the soap film inside the thread is punctured and the thread is drawn out into a circle. Explain why this should happen.

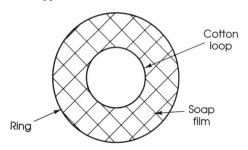

**Fig. 10.30**

(c) Explain in terms of the forces between molecules why the surface of a liquid behaves like a stretched elastic skin that is always trying to shrink. Your answer should include a diagram. (SEG)

# ANSWERS TO EXAMINATION QUESTIONS

**MULTIPLE CHOICE QUESTIONS**

**STRUCTURED QUESTIONS**

| Question | 1 | 2 | 3 | 4 | 5 | 6 | 7 | 8 |
|----------|---|---|---|---|---|---|---|---|
| Answer | D | B | E | B | D | D | C | B |

## ANSWER 9

(a) See Fig. 10.24. Gas particles are about $10 \times$ further apart than particles in a liquid.

Fig. 10.31

(b) There are no gaps between the particles of a liquid even though they are free to move. The liquid cannot be compressed as the particles themselves cannot be squashed smaller and there are no spaces to push them into. A gas has lots of space between the particles and can therefore be compressed easily. As the volume is reduced the particles will hit the walls more often and the resulting increase in pressure makes further compression harder.

(c) (i) Smoke specks move continuously in a random way in three dimensions.

    (ii) Motion is caused by collisions of air molecules. Enough collisions in a particular direction exert a resultant force on the smoke particle.

## ANSWER 10

(a) Decreased volume means smaller distances moved between collisions with the walls of a container. Each collision exerts a force so more collisions per second gives a greater force on the container and therefore greater pressure.

(b) (i) Increase the temperature.

    (ii) Increased temperature raises kinetic energy of the molecules. Therefore more collisions per second and greater pressure.

## ANSWER 11

(a) 1 kilogram    = 1000 grams

    1 metre       = 100 centimetres

    1 cubic metre = $10^6$ cubic centimetres

                            ($1\,000\,000\,cm^3$)

(b) (i) Hydrogen, Air, Oil, Water, Aluminium, Iron, Gold.

(ii) Density of water is $1000\ kg/m^3$ or $1\,g/cm^3$.

(c) (i) Count out a known number of ball-bearings (say 20). Find the mass of 20 spheres using a top-pan electronic balance. Divide the mass by 20 to find the mass of one sphere.

Fig. 10.32

    (ii) Several possibilities: (a) Lay 20 spheres in a line. Measure total length. Divide by 20 to find average diameter and therefore average radius. Volume is $^4/_3\,\pi r^3$. (b) Measure a known volume of water with a measuring cylinder. Record its volume $V_1$. Drop in 20 spheres, displacing some water. Record the new volume $V_2$. Here $(V_2 - V_1)$ is the volume of 20 spheres. $(V_2 - V_1) \div 20$ is the volume of one sphere. (Fig. 10.32.)

    (iii) Density = mass of one sphere ÷ volume of one sphere.

## ANSWER 12

This is a higher level question.

(a) (i) Show a pair of equal and opposite forces acting perpendicular to the thread.

    (ii) Surface tension.

    (iii) The forces will act equally on both sides of any line in the surface.

(b) The forces pulling the thread outwards are no longer counterbalanced and the film tries to reach a minimum area.

(c) Your diagram and explanation should show that the forces on the molecules in the liquid are balanced but those at the surface are not. The attractive forces between the molecules are greater than the repulsive ones. This will mean that the attractive forces from neighbouring molecules will put the surface into a state of tension.

# STUDENT'S ANSWER – EXAMINER'S COMMENTS

## STUDENT ANSWER TO QUESTION 11

**No. A common er**
**1m**
**(100 × 100 × 100) c**
**= 10⁶ cm³.**

a)
I Kilogramme = 1000 grammes ✓
I metre = 100 centimeters ✓
I cubic metre = 100 cubic centimeters

b)
i) Hydrogen, Air, Oil, Water, Aluminium, Iron, Gold. ✓

ii) Density of water = 1g/cm³ or 1000 kg/m³ ✓

**Should make clear the likely range.**

c)
i) Use a set of electronic scales and use the sensitivity gauge so the mass can be measured as accurately as possible.

**In both parts the student has missed the idea of finding values for *several* bearings.**

ii) Place a ball near the end of a ruler with a millimeter scale, then find the diameter. Divide by 2 to get the radius Then use Vol. of a sphere = $4/3\pi r^3$ to get the volume.

iii) Use the formula $D = M/V$
We know the values of mass and volume. Plug them into the formula and get the density of steel.

**Not a very good statement**

# REVIEW SHEET

■ The three states of matter are _____, _____ and _____.

■ _____ and _____ are both called fluids because they can flow.

■ Write down the equation for density and state suitable units for the density of a liquid.

■ Four steel balls displace 25 cm³ of water and have a mass of 210 g. Their average density is _____.

Clear water

Blue copper
sulphate solution

Fig. 10.33

■ The diagram (Fig. 10.33) shows water which has been carefully floated on top of some blue copper sulphate solution.

1. What will you see happen? _____

2. How long do you think this will take? _____

3. What does this tell you about particles in a liquid?

_____

4. Why would the process be much faster in a gas mixture?

_____

_____

■ The energy taken in at constant temperature to change the state of a material is called _____.

■ When two solids are pushed tightly together there is no diffusion because the particles _____.

■ Write down four factors that can increase the rate of evaporation of a liquid.

1. _____          2. _____

3. _____          4. _____

■ Explain briefly how a gas produces a pressure on the walls of its container.

_____

_____

■ Put the following in order of increasing density.

| ice water petrol wood aluminium concrete |
|---|

_____

■ When a liquid evaporates it is the _____ particles that escape. Separating the particles uses _____ heat so the liquid that is left is _____.

■ To make a liquid boil at a higher temperature you could _____ the pressure on it.

■ When a gas is heated in a closed container it can be very dangerous because the particles move _____ when they are given more kinetic energy and hit the walls _____ often. This is an increase in _____ which might cause the container to _____.

■ If a gas is slowly pushed into a smaller space so that its temperature stays the same its _____ will increase because the _____ hit the walls _____ often.

# PRESSURE AND HYDRAULICS

## GETTING STARTED

Pressure and force are ideas which are often confused. **A force** is applied at a particular point, and causes a change of some sort; **pressure** is the result of the force acting on an area. Pressure effects are noticeable when a solid rests on a surface, when a liquid is compressed, or when a gas changes its volume or its temperature. The air around us exerts a large pressure on our bodies, and the fluids in our bodies are able to withstand this pressure. Weather forecasts depend on the ability of a meteorologist to predict how pressure changes will affect patterns in the atmosphere, and many technological applications depend on pressure changes in gases and liquids. This chapter will try to explain some of these ideas.

# ESSENTIAL PRINCIPLES

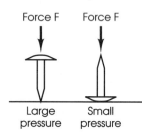

**1> FORCE AND PRESSURE**

66 Force and pressure are often confused. Make sure that you clearly understand the difference between the terms and can use them correctly. (What are their units?) 99

## (a) FORCE

A *force* is only definable in terms of its effects. It is anything which changes or tends to change the motion of an object (see Ch. 3). The same force can cause different effects if it acts on different areas.

In Fig. 11.1 a 1 kg mass is placed above a wood block resting on Plasticine. The force on each block is 10 N. The Plasticine will be more deformed in (a) than (b) because in (a) the force is exerted on a smaller area; another way of saying this is that "the pressure in (a) is greater".

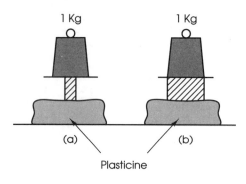

Fig. 11.1 Pressure depends on area.

## (b) PRESSURE

*Pressure* is the effect of a force on an area. The same force acting on a small and a large area will give a larger pressure for the smaller area. Simple examples of this are:

1. There is a greater pressure under the point of a drawing pin than under the head, when the same force is applied (Fig. 11.2).
2. Animals with a large weight tend to have feet with a large surface area, reducing the pressure they exert on the ground (e.g. elephants, camels; Fig. 11.3).

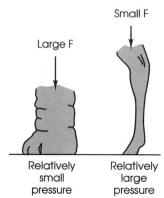

Fig. 11.3

3. Knives, saws, chisels, etc., have a small area of cross-section so that the application of a small force gives a large pressure (Fig. 11.4).

Fig. 11.4

These and many other examples suggest that when a force is applied, the pressure which results from it depends on the area over which it is acting, i.e.

▶
$$\text{Pressure} = \frac{\text{Force}}{\text{Area}}$$

The units are therefore $N/m^2$ or $N/cm^2$; 1 newton per square metre ($1\ N/m^2$) is called 1 Pascal (1 Pa). This enables us to calculate how much pressure is exerted, and to compare pressure effects if forces and areas are known.

---

### EXAMPLE 1

An average grown person weighs about 650 N (has a mass of 65 kg). A typical area below one shoe would be about $170\ cm^2$. To calculate the pressure on the ground, we need to convert the units.

$$1\ cm^2 = (10^{-2} \times 10^{-2})\ m^2$$
$$= 10^{-4}\ m^2$$

$$170\ cm^2 = 170 \times 10^{-4}\ m^2$$
$$= 1.7 \times 10^{-2}\ m^2$$

Then

$$\text{Pressure} = \frac{\text{Force}}{\text{Area}} = \frac{650}{3.4 \times 10^{-2}}$$

$$= 1.9 \times 10^4\ Pa$$

If the same person stood on one foot, the force exerted would be the same (650 N) but the area would be halved, so the pressure is doubled. The same person standing on stilts, where the area is even smaller, would exert an even bigger pressure. Clearly pressure increases as the area over which the force is acting becomes smaller.

---

Force F    Force F

Large      Small
pressure   pressure

Fig. 11.2

## 2 ▷ PRESSURE IN LIQUIDS – THEORY

We have defined pressure as force ÷ area. It is clearly more difficult to define this for a liquid where forces and areas are not as obvious as in the case of a solid. A little thought and some theory helps solve the problem.

Imagine an object below the surface of a liquid. All the liquid above it has a weight and will exert a force, since weight is itself a force caused by the pull of a planet. If the object has an area, $A$, and is $h$ metres below the surface, the situation is rather like that of Fig. 11.5.

The object is lying under a weight of liquid, which is exerting a force on its area. Then

$$\text{Pressure} = \frac{\text{Force (weight)}}{\text{Area}}$$

Weight of the object = (Mass) $\times g$
($g$ = gravitational field strength)

but

$$\text{Mass} = \text{Volume} \times \text{Density}$$
$$= \text{Height} \times \text{Area} \times \text{Density}$$
$$\text{Pressure} = \frac{g \times \text{Height} \times \text{Density} \times \text{Area}}{\text{Area}}$$
$$= \text{Height} \times \text{Density} \times g$$

or in **symbols**

▶  $$\text{Pressure} = \rho g h$$

where $\rho$ = density, $g$ = gravitational field strength and $h$ = depth of liquid. This means that:

1. Pressure increases with fluid depth.
2. Pressure increases with fluid density.

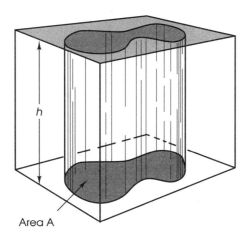

Fig. 11.5 Pressure below a liquid column.

## 3 ▷ MEASUREMENT OF PRESSURE

While pressure below a solid or a liquid is easily determined, a gas presents more of a problem. Gas pressure in a laboratory is usually measured with a manometer (Fig. 11.6). This is a U-tube containing a suitable liquid.

Before connecting to the gas supply the level of liquid in each tube is the same. The pressure along a horizontal line below the liquid is the same, since pressure is proportional to depth. Above the surface of the liquid, the pressure is that of the atmosphere, $P_A$.

So the pressure at X or Y = $P_A$ + pressure due to height of liquid above X or Y. On connecting to a gas supply (e.g. the outlet of the mains gas supply in a lab) the manometer liquid levels change (Fig. 11.7). Since the gas pressure is greater than atmospheric pressure, the liquid in the right-hand column of the manometer is pushed upwards. The pressure on X is now the pressure of the gas supply. This is the same as the pressure at Z (same level).

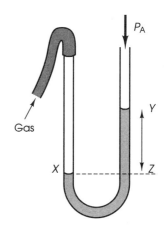

Fig. 11.7 Manometer used to measure gas pressure.

Pressure at Z = $P_A$ + Pressure due to liquid column YZ
($h$ centimetres)

Gas pressure = $P_A + h$ centimetres of liquid

It is common for pressures to be expressed in liquid column equivalents, but they can be converted to pascals using $P = \rho g h$.

Fig. 11.6 Manometer.

**Fig. 11.8 Variation of pressure with depth.**

The manometer can be used to check the idea that pressure in a liquid depends on depth and density using apparatus as in Fig. 11.8. A funnel with a rubber membrane over one end is lowered into a long tube of liquid. The depth of liquid and pressure can be measured and the relationship verified. Similarly, using different density liquids, with the funnel at a fixed depth, proves that pressure is proportional to density.

If the funnel is arranged as in Fig. 11.9 and lowered to a fixed depth it can also be shown

**Fig. 11.9**

that the pressure at a given depth is the same in all directions.

The liquid used in a manometer will depend on the pressure difference to be measured. Small values of pressure will be more sensitively measured if the manometer liquid has a low density (water or an organic liquid); larger values of pressure may require a high-density oil or even mercury.

A more direct reading of pressure can be obtained using a Bourdon pressure gauge.

When the pressure of the gas is *less* than atmospheric the liquid will move the other way so that it is higher in the arm of the manometer that is connected to the gas. Measure the height difference $h$ as before and the gas pressure is $P_A - h$ cm of liquid.

## 4 > ATMOSPHERIC PRESSURE

This has already been mentioned in connection with the measurements using a manometer. We live underneath a large air mass (the atmosphere) and it exerts pressures on us. The size of this pressure can be gauged from the "collapsing can" experiment (Fig. 11.10), where a tin can connected to a vacuum pump collapses and crumbles as air is removed from it.

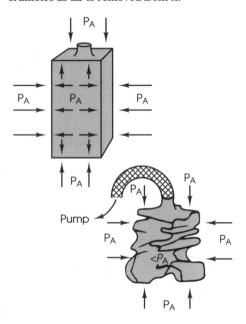

**Fig. 11.10 The "collapsing can" experiment.**

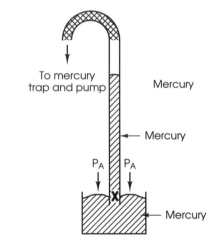

**Fig. 11.11 Mercury rises 76 cm.**

Under ordinary conditions the atmosphere exerts pressure on the can from all directions and the air inside also exerts an equal pressure on all walls of the can. The pump removes air from the can, and the pressure inside it is reduced. The can's walls are pushed in on all sides by the pressure of the atmosphere. To obtain a clearer idea of the size of the pressure of the atmosphere we can use the apparatus of Fig. 11.11. A long (1 m) thick-walled glass tube is connected to a vacuum pump with a mercury trap to prevent mercury entering the pump, and is then

Fig. 11.12 A mercury barometer.

placed in a trough of mercury (Fig. 11.11). The pump is turned on and mercury rises up the tube. It rises because the pump removes air, reducing the pressure in the tube. The atmosphere pushes on the surface of the mercury in the trough, forcing it up the tube until the pressure at X is equal to the atmospheric pressure. It is found that the maximum height the mercury rises is about 76 cm. Therefore atmospheric pressure is equivalent to the pressure below a column of mercury 76 cm high.

The mercury barometer uses the same principle. A 1 m long tube, closed at one end, is filled with mercury. Holding a finger over the open end, the tube is inverted into a mercury trough (gloves should be worn!). The mercury level falls to about 76 cm (Fig. 11.12). Above the mercury there is now a vacuum. Again it is seen that the atmosphere can support a column of mercury 76 cm high. The pressure at X below the column is equal to the atmospheric pressure, $P_A$. The pressure below this column is given by

$$P_A = \rho g h$$
$$= 13\,600 \times 10 \times 0.76$$
$$(\rho_{mercury} = 13\,600 \text{ kg/m}^3)$$
$$= \underline{103\,360 \text{ Pa}}$$

The figure 76 cm varies from time to time as the atmospheric pressure varies, and this gives an indication of prevailing weather conditions.

A more common barometer is an aneroid barometer (see "Extension Materials").

## 5 > HYDRAULIC MACHINES

Hydraulic machines use liquid pressure to transfer a force from one place to another, using the following properties of liquids:

1. They are incompressible.
2. At the same depth, liquid pressure is the same in all directions.
3. Any change in liquid pressure is transmitted instantly to all parts of the liquid

$$\text{Pressure} = \frac{\text{Force}}{\text{Area}}$$

$$\text{Force} = \text{Pressure} \times \text{area}$$

Force applied at the larger cylinder

$$F_2 = P \times A_2 = \frac{F_1 \times A_2}{A_1}$$

Since $A_2$ is greater than $A_1$, a small force applied at the smaller cylinder is multiplied to become a large force applied at the larger cylinder. Although the force is made greater, energy is still conserved and at best work done by $F_1$ = work done by $F_2$. In Fig. 11.14

$$F_1 \times d_1 = F_2 \times d_2$$

So if the force is increased 10 times, the distance moved is decreased in the same proportion.

This is the basic principle behind hydraulic jacks and hydraulic brakes. Obviously if air entered the hydraulic fluid, the system would not work well since gases can be compressed and pressure would not be transmitted instantly from one side of the system to the other.

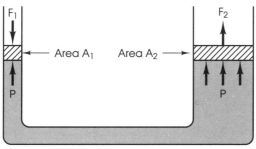

Fig. 11.13 Principle of hydraulic systems.

The basic idea is shown in Fig. 11.13. If a force $F_1$ is applied to the smaller piston whose area is $A_1$ the pressure below the surface is $P = F_1/A_1$. This pressure is transmitted through the liquid and is now applied at the larger piston, area $A_2$,

Fig. 11.14

## 6 PRESSURE AND UPTHRUST IN A LIQUID

An object immersed in a fluid has a force on it which tends to push it upwards out of the liquid. This is called "upthrust". The reason for it is based on pressure differences.

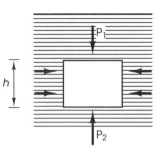

**Fig. 11.15 Pressure is greater below the block than above it.**

Pressure increases with depth, so for an object below a liquid surface (Fig. 11.15), the forces on the sides will balance out, since pressure is the same at any horizontal level. The pressure $P_2$ below the object must, however, be greater than the pressure $P_1$ above it.

For an object height $h$ in a liquid of density $\rho$, the pressure difference

■ $$P_2 - P_1 = \rho g h$$

The upthrust force is equal to the pressure difference multiplied by the base area of the object (Force = Pressure × Area)

$$\text{Force} = (P_2 - P_1)A = A(\rho g h)$$

but $A \times h$ is the volume of the object

$$\text{Force} = \rho g \,(\text{Volume})$$

and since Volume × Density = Mass of liquid

■ $$\text{Force} = \text{Mass} \times g$$

■ Force = Weight of liquid equivalent to the volume of the object immersed

i.e.

Upthrust force =
 Weight of liquid displaced by the object

This is known as ***Archimedes principle***. See also "Extension materials".

An object will float if the upthrust force is equal to its own weight. This means that if a large enough weight of liquid can be displaced (e.g. by a liner) then an object will float.

## 7 PRESSURE AND VOLUME OF GASES – BOYLE'S LAW

❝❞ This idea is often used in experimental work with fluids. Volume = Area × length of tube ∴ If area is constant Volume ∝ length of tube. Make sure you understand this use of proportionality in drawing graphs. ❞❞

The molecular explanation of pressure and volume changes in a gas is discussed in Chapter 10. This section is concerned with the large-scale behaviour of a gas. One laboratory version of an apparatus to investigate pressure and volume changes is shown in Fig. 11.16. Air is enclosed in a thick-walled tube by a light oil. The tube is attached to a centimetre scale. By pumping air above the oil in the reservoir, pressure is transmitted through the oil and the air in the tube can be compressed. The pressure is recorded on the Bourdon pressure gauge.

**Fig. 11.16 Boyle's law apparatus.**

Since the tube is of uniform cross-section the volume of gas trapped in the tube is proportional to the length of gas read from the scale.

The pressure is increased in stages and the length of gas (proportional to volume) is recorded. The tap on the reservoir enables the pressure to be reduced and a "check" set of readings can be taken as the pressure is reduced.

A graph of pressure against "volume" (or length of air) shows the pattern of Fig. 11.17, i.e. volume decreases as pressure increases. This is an inverse relationship. If now the pressure is plotted against inverse volume (1/volume) the graph is a straight line (Fig. 11.18), i.e.

■ $$\text{Pressure} \propto \frac{1}{\text{Volume}}$$

or

■ Pressure × Volume = Constant

This is described as "Boyle's law". It holds true at normal pressures provided that the mass of gas remains constant, and the temperature remains constant. If a gas at pressure $P_1$ and volume $V_1$ has its volume changed to $V_2$, the pressure will change to $P_2$. Since

Pressure × Volume = Constant

Then

■ $$P_1V_1 = P_2V_2$$

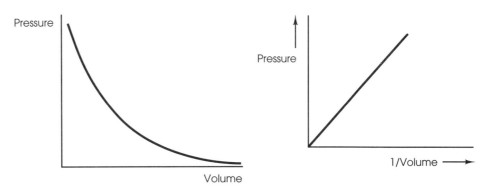

Fig. 11.17 Variation of pressure and volume.

Fig. 11.18 Pressure ∝ 1/volume.

---

### EXAMPLE 2

A gas at 76 cm of mercury pressure occupies a volume of 2 litres. What pressure is required to reduce the volume to 0.25 litres?

Using

$$P_1V_1 = P_2V_2$$

$$76 \times 2 = P_2 \times 0.25$$

$$P_2 = 608 \text{ cm mercury}$$

(Notice that provided the units are consistent on both sides of the equation there is no need to convert to the SI system.)

---

# EXTENSION MATERIALS

**1 ANEROID BAROMETER AND ALTIMETER**

This consists of a thin-walled metal box, the air inside of which has been partly removed, leaving low-pressure gas inside it (Fig. 11.19). It is prevented from collapsing by a strong spring. Changes in atmospheric pressure will compress the box slightly, and if the pressure is reduced the box will recover its shape. The small movements are amplified by a lever system which moves a pointer over a scale, calibrated against a mercury barometer.

The same device can be used as an altimeter in an aircraft. The pressure of the atmosphere changes with height above sea-level and the scale can be calibrated to read height rather than pressure.

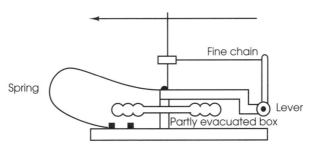

Fig. 11.19 Aneroid barometer.

## 2 › WEATHER MAPS

Barometers kept at the same height above sea-level show daily variation in atmospheric pressure. These variations are shown on weather maps (Fig. 11.20) and used to predict weather changes. Places of equal pressure are joined by lines called *isobars*. There is more detail about weather in chapter 17.

Fig. 11.20 Isobars on a weather map.

## 3 › ARCHIMEDES PRINCIPLE

### Upthrust = weight of fluid displaced

This relationship was shown in section 6 and is equally true for both liquids and gases.
In many cases the weight displaced is *less* than the weight of the object and the upthrust is less than the weight of the object.

The object then moves *downwards*, e.g. a stone in water. The apparent weight of the object is still less than the real weight and when objects are recovered from underwater they seem to become much heavier as they leave the water and the upthrust is removed. You might notice this if you lift up another person in the swimming baths.

If an object displaces a weight of fluid that is *greater* than the weight of the object then the upthrust is greater than the weight of the object and it moves *upwards*. This would be the case for a cork in water or a balloon filled with hydrogen or hot air. In a few cases the weight of fluid displaced is *equal* to the weight of the object so that there is no overall force acting up or down and the object *floats* or *hovers* at the same level. A submarine can do this by adjusting the amount of air and water in its ballast tanks. A ship will float when the upthrust is equal to its weight, so it settles into the water until it displaces its own weight of

water. When the ship takes on cargo it gets heavier and settles further into the water to restore the balance.

The principle is also used in a *hydrometer*. This is a small weighted float with a density scale on its side. When it is floating in a liquid it must displace its own weight of the liquid. It will sink to different depths in liquids of different density in order to do this and the density can be read from the liquid level on its scale. The scale is not uniform (i.e. not equally spaced) and will have smaller values at the top.

Fig. 11.22

Fig. 11.21

## 4 ▷ FLUID FLOW AND PRESSURE

When a fluid passes through a narrower tube its velocity increases and its pressure gets smaller.

Fig. 11.23

The pressure at B in the diagram will be less than that at A or C.

If you blow between the two sheets of paper in Fig. 11.24 they move towards each other because of the reduced pressure between them. The idea that the faster flowing

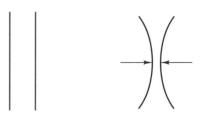

Paper strips in still air

Paper strips with air flow between them

Fig. 11.24

stream of fluid has a lower pressure is called *Bernoulli's Principle*.

## 5 ▷ PRINCIPLES OF FLIGHT

An aeroplane will be subject to four basic forces: *thrust* (T), *drag* (D), *lift* (L) and *weight* (W).

Fig. 11.25

For level flight at constant velocity the forces must be in equilibrium so that thrust = drag and lift = weight. Forward acceleration will happen when thrust > drag and the aeroplane will rise when lift > weight.

The forward thrust will usually be obtained from the engines and drag is the result of the air resistance and *turbulence* in the air behind. Streamlining reduces the drag by making the turbulence less. The weight is caused, as always, by the pull of gravity on the mass of the plane.

Lift is produced by the shape of the wing and its angle into the air (called the *angle of attack*). The shape of the wing causes the air flow above the wing to be faster than that below so that the pressure is less above the wing obeying Bernoulli's principle. If the wing has a large enough surface area the pressure difference will produce the required lift.

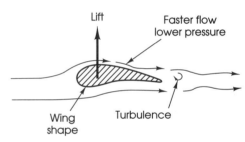

Fig. 11.26

Increasing the angle of attack increases lift until it reaches about 15° when the pressure lowering effect suddenly starts to disappear. This is called *stalling* and is caused by a sudden increase in turbulence.

A glider will normally get its thrust by falling fast enough to overcome drag. A glider can also get lift by being in a rising current of warm air (a *thermal*). It can then also get thrust by falling forward *relative to the rising air* so that drag is overcome without a loss of height.

# EXAMINATION QUESTIONS

MULTIPLE CHOICE QUESTIONS

## QUESTION 1

The instrument shown in Fig. 11.27 is used to measure gas pressure. It is called a

A Barometer
B Bourdon gauge
C Manometer
D Thermometer                    (SEG)

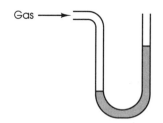

Fig. 11.27

## QUESTION 2

Pressure can be calculated from

A $\dfrac{\text{Mass}}{\text{Area}}$      D $\dfrac{\text{Force}}{\text{Volume}}$

B $\dfrac{\text{Force}}{\text{Area}}$      E $\dfrac{\text{Force}}{\text{Density}}$

C $\dfrac{\text{Mass}}{\text{Volume}}$          (ULEAC)

## QUESTION 3

One side of a water-filled manometer is connected to the laboratory gas supply as shown in Fig. 11.28. The vertical difference in the levels is $h$. The distance $h$ could be increased by

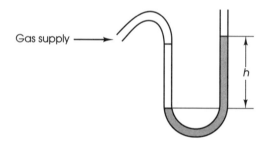

Fig. 11.28

    A Use of an oil of lower density than water
    B Use of mercury instead of water
    C Tilting the tube clockwise
    D Tilting the tube anticlockwise.
    E Increasing the cross-sectional area of
       the tube.       (ULEAC)

## QUESTION 4

If a mercury barometer is taken to the top of a mountain the level of mercury in the tube will fall provided that the temperature remains constant. This is because the

    A Tube expands
    B Tube contracts
    C Mercury weighs more
    D Air pressure decreases
    E Force of gravity increases    (ULEAC)

## QUESTION 5

Fig. 11.29

Figure 11.29 shows a piston and a cylinder, of such a design that trapped air cannot pass the piston. The top of the piston moves from A to B, without affecting the temperature of the enclosed air. As a result of this, the air pressure is

    A Reduced to a third     D Doubled
    B Reduced to a half      E Trebled
    C Unchanged           (ULEAC)

## QUESTION 6

Figure 11.30 shows a simple mercury barometer. Which one of the distances A–E should be measured to determine the atmospheric pressure?

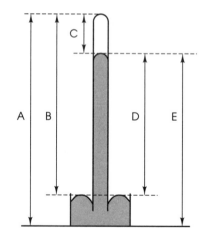

Fig. 11.30

## QUESTION 7

An empty aerosol can may "explode" if left in strong sunlight, because the molecules inside

    A Are attracted towards each other
    B Collide more frequently with each other
    C Collide more frequently with the walls
    D Completely fill the can     (ULEAC)

## STRUCTURED QUESTIONS

## QUESTION 8

(a) Figure 11.31(a) shows a mercury barometer.
  (i) What is the average value of the height $H$ above sea-level? (1 line)
  (ii) Why is it important that the space above the mercury contains no air? (2 lines)
  (iii) Explain why the diameter of the tube does not affect $H$. (3 lines)

(a)

**Fig. 11.31**

(b) Figure 11.31(b) shows an aneroid barometer.
  (i) What is part Z? (1 line)
  (ii) What is the purpose of part Z? (2 lines)

(b)

(c) While washing up, a boy lifted a tumbler full of water to the position shown in Fig. 11.31(c). Explain why the water stayed in the glass. (2 lines)

(c)

(d) A motorist attached her wing-mirror to the windscreen of her car with a suction disc as shown in Fig. 11.31(d).
  (i) Explain what holds the disc to the body of the car. (1 line)
  (ii) In hot sunshine the car was parked in the sun. The mirror and disc fell from the screen. Suggest two reasons for this. (4 lines) (ULEAC)

(d)

## QUESTION 9

(a) (i) Draw a labelled diagram of the apparatus you would use to show that the atmosphere exerts a pressure.
  (ii) Explain how you would carry out the experiment.
  (iii) Explain carefully how the experiment shows that the atmosphere exerts a pressure.

Cap $C_1$ Cap $C_2$ Measure

20 cm

Base 20 × 10 cm

**Fig. 11.32**

(b) Figure 11.32 shows a plastic container for liquid fertiliser as used by gardeners. The container has a built-in measure so that the liquid can easily be used in the correct amount. (Throughout the question you are to assume that the density of the liquid is the same as that of water.) In order to fill the measure, the sides of the container are squeezed.
  (i) State which of $C_1$ and $C_2$ should be tightly closed at this stage. (1 line)
  (ii) Explain why. (2 lines)
  (iii) Calculate how much extra pressure, measured in pascals (over and above atmospheric), will be needed in the container in order to fill it with liquid. (3 lines)
    (Use $g$ = 10 m/s$^2$ and density of water = 1000 kg/m$^3$.)
  (iv) Name the type of energy the liquid would gain by being pushed up into the measure. (1 line)
  (v) In fact the person squeezing the container in order to fill the measure would probably have to supply more energy than that accounted for in (iv) above. Give a reason for this. (3 lines)

(c) Suppose the container shown in Fig. 11.32 has a negligible weight and contains 2 litres of liquid. Given the dimension of the container as shown in Fig. 11.32, calculate the pressure which it exerts on the ground. (4 lines)
  (Use $g$ = 10 m/s$^2$ and density of water = 1000 kg/m$^3$ or 1 kg/l.) (ULEAC)

Fig. 11.33

## QUESTION 10

(a) The diagram shows part of the hydraulic braking system of a motor car.
  (i) Mark with an arrow, on the diagram, the direction in which the piston in the slave cylinder moves when the driver presses down on the brake pedal.
  (ii) Explain why the downward force on the brake pedal causes the piston in the slave cylinder to move.
  (iii) The driver pushes down on the brake pedal with a force of 100 N. Calculate the force that this causes on the piston in the master cylinder. Show clearly how you obtain your answer.
  (iv) Find the pressure in pascals in the brake fluid when the force on the master cylinder piston is 300 N. Show clearly how you obtain your answer. The master cylinder has an area of 20 cm².

  (v) The piston in the master cylinder has an area 10 times that of the piston in the slave cylinder. What is the force on the slave cylinder piston when the force on the master cylinder piston is 300 N? Show clearly how you obtain your answer.

(b) The graph below shows the motion of a car of mass 1000 kg over a period of 30 seconds.
  (i) Find the acceleration of the car.
  (ii) Calculate the resultant force acting on this car to produce this acceleration. Show clearly how you obtain your answer.
  (iii) Calculate the average speed of the car over the 30 seconds. Show clearly how you obtain your answer.

(NICCEA)

Fig. 11.34

# ANSWERS TO EXAMINATION QUESTIONS

**MULTIPLE CHOICE QUESTIONS**

| Question | 1 | 2 | 3 | 4 | 5 | 6 | 7 |
|---|---|---|---|---|---|---|---|
| Answer | C | B | A | D | E | D | C |

**STRUCTURED QUESTIONS**

## ANSWER 8

(a) (i) The average height $H$ = 76 cm (0.76 m).

(ii) If air is present, pressure will be exerted on the top of the mercury column, which will reduce the height which can be supported by the atmospheric pressure and give a reading which is too small.

(iii) Pressure is the same at all points on the same horizontal level. The mercury in the tube is balancing the pressure of the atmosphere on the top of the mercury in the trough. The area does not matter. (Or pressure = $\rho g h$ – does not concern area.)

(b) (i) Z is a strong spring.

(ii) It prevents the can from collapsing and restores it to its original shape if pressure falls.

(c) Atmospheric pressure pushing on the water surface is greater than the pressure below the column of water in the tumbler.

(d) (i) When the suction disc is pressed on to the car body some air escapes below the pad. Under the pad the air pressure is therefore reduced, so atmospheric pressure outside the pad holds it to the body of the car.

(ii) Air under the pad gains kinetic energy. The volume is restricted so the pressure rises until it is equal to or above atmospheric pressure. The car body expands, allowing air under the rubber pad, and restoring pressure.

## ANSWER 9

(a) This part will depend on your choice of experiment. There is no one correct answer, but parts (ii) and (iii) must refer to the diagram in part (i).

(b) (i) $C_1$ must be closed.

(ii) Otherwise squeezing the can will simply expel air from $C_1$ and have no effect on the liquid.

(iii) Pressure = Height × density × $g$

$$= 0.2 \times 1000 \times 10$$

(0.2 m = 20 cm)

$$= \underline{2000\ Pa}$$

(iv) (Gravitational) Potential energy.

(v) Energy will be needed to deform the plastic can.

(c)

$$\text{Pressure} = \frac{\text{Force}}{\text{Area}} = \frac{\text{Weight of liquid}}{\text{Area}}$$

$$= \frac{2 \times 10}{0.2 \times 0.1} = \underline{1000\ Pa}$$

## ANSWER 10

This is a further level question.

(a) (i) An arrow on the diagram near the slave cylinder pointing outwards.

(ii) The liquid transmits pressure from master cylinder to slave cylinder because the liquid cannot be compressed.

(iii) Take moments about the pivot (see chapter 3)

$$25 \times 100 = 5 \times F$$

$$F = \underline{500\ N}$$

(iv) $\text{Pressure} = \dfrac{\text{Force}}{\text{Area}} = \dfrac{300}{20}$

$$= \underline{15\ N/cm^2}$$

(= 15 × 10 000 = 150 000 Pa)

(v) Force = Pressure × Area

$$= 15 \times 2 = \underline{30\ N}$$

(b) (i) $\text{Acceleration} = \dfrac{\text{Change in velocity}}{\text{Time taken}}$

$$= \frac{35}{10} = \underline{3.5\ m/s^2}$$

(ii) Force = Mass × Acceleration

(See chapter 5)

$$= 1000 \times 3.5 = \underline{3500\ N}$$

(iii) Distance moved

$$= 0.5 \times 10 \times 35 + 20 \times 35$$

$$= \underline{875\ m}$$

$$\text{Average speed} = \frac{\text{Distance travelled}}{\text{Time}}$$

$$= \frac{875}{30} = \underline{29.2\ m/s.}$$

Note how some questions can include work from several topics.

# STUDENT'S ANSWER WITH THE EXAMINER'S COMMENTS

## STUDENT ANSWER TO QUESTION 9

"Diagrams illustrate the general idea but are poorly labelled. The can must be thin-walled (since the pressure change is not likely to be very great). The tubing thick walled (or it will collapse itself)"

"The pump removes air molecules and causes a pressure difference. Bad explanation – but mainly because the diagram contained so little information.

"They both exert pressure. "Push" is a weak term here."

"Again the use of "force" is not useful in a question about pressure. Remember that Pressure = Force ÷ Area. So Pressure and Force are quite different."

"This answer shows some understanding, but seems to forget that the question is about atmospheric pressure – it hasn't been mentioned."

"Yes. This does account for it."

"Lucky to get the right answer. Wiser to show the steps in a calculation."

a) i)

To vacuum pump

To vacuum pump

before

after

ii) Well you use the can and just suck out the air.

iii) There is air in the can at the start, and there is air outside it. They both push on the sides of the can, so it stays upright. If you take air out there's more force outside than inside so it collapses.

b) i) Cap C.

ii) Otherwise the liquid will not get into the measure.

"This doesn't explain why $C_1$ is closed."

iii) Pressure = 20 × 1000 × 10
= 200 000 Pa

"Forget to convert 20 cm into metres."

iv) Potential energy.

v) Some energy goes into making the person's muscles move.

c) Pressure = force ÷ area
= 1000 Pa

# REVIEW SHEET

■ Complete the equations

Pressure =                    Pressure in a liquid =

■ The pressure of the gas supply can be measured with a _____.

■ Atmospheric pressure can be measured using a _____.

■ Boyle's law states that _____
_____
_____

■ In a hydraulic system the pressure is the _____ under each piston. If the areas
are different then the _____ will be different on each piston. The piston
that has the largest _____ on it will also have the largest _____ but will
move through a smaller distance so that the work done at each piston is the same.

■ When a bubble expands to twice its original volume the pressure inside it will
_____ provided that the _____ stays the same.

■ A stone will sink in water because its weight is greater than
_____.

■ When a hot air balloon stays at a constant height its weight will be equal to the
_____.

■ Pressure in a fluid acts in all _____.

■ A standard atmosphere pressure is the same as _____ mm of mercury.

■ A pressure of 1 N/m$^2$ is called 1 _____.

■ A man who weighs 700 N stands on an area of 200 cm$^2$. The pressure caused is
_____ N/cm$^2$ or _____ Pa.

■ What depth of water will have the same pressure as one atmosphere? (*Hints* –
remember the depth of mercury that has the same pressure as one atmosphere
and that mercury is 13.6 times as dense as water.)

■ Briefly explain why ladies with high-heeled shoes are sometimes banned from
rooms with wooden floors.
_____
_____
_____

■ An isobar is a line which joins _____
_____.

■ Describe an experiment which will show that the pressure of the atmosphere is large.
_____
_____
_____
_____

■ Name the four forces that act on an aeroplane

1. _____        2. _____
3. _____        4. _____

■ What do you understand by "Boyle's Law"?

_____

_____

_____

_____

■ Draw a graph to show how pressure varies with volume

■ Upthrust = _____.

■ Using the idea of "upthrust" explain why each of the following occurs, using a diagram in each case

    a) A stone sinks

    b) A cork rises

    c) Wood floats

■ Explain the workings of a *hydrometer,* using a diagram

■ What must be true to achieve level flight at constant velocity?

_____

_____

CHAPTER

# 12

# HEAT ENERGY

## GETTING STARTED

Changes of temperature have a considerable effect on the behaviour of materials, and many aspects of design have to take account of fluctuations in temperature. A temperature change indicates that heat energy has either flowed into or out of a material. There is a clear distinction between the ideas of heat and temperature. Heat is an *energy form*, like kinetic and potential energy, or electricity. Temperature is a measure of the kinetic energy of the particles of the material and gives an indication of the direction in which heat energy will flow – usually from high temperature to low temperature. This section deals with the distinction between heat and temperature, and with the ways in which the properties of solids, liquids and gases are changed by heating.

# ESSENTIAL PRINCIPLES

Any property of a material can be used as a thermometric property, provided that it varies in a *uniform* way. The most common property used is the *expansion of a liquid*, like mercury or alcohol, in a uniform glass tube. However, the *pressure changes of a gas*, the *resistance changes of a metal* and *thermoelectric EMF in a thermocouple*, are all suitable changes for measuring temperature. Apart from a property which is temperature-dependent, two fixed points are required in defining a temperature scale. The most common are:

1. The freezing-point of pure water, 0 °C.
2. The boiling-point of pure water, 100 °C, at a fixed pressure (76 cm mercury).

The values 0 °C and 100 °C are arbitrary. It is convenient to adopt a scale of 100 intervals. To calibrate a thermometer, the lower fixed point 0 °C is marked when the thermometer is placed in pure melting ice; the ice must be pure since impurities lower its melting-point (Fig. 12.1). The upper fixed point, which is correctly called the steam point, is the temperature of steam *just above* the surface of boiling water. The thermometer bulb is not placed in the water because impurities raise the boiling-point. Equally the pressure above the water must be 76 cm of mercury since pressure changes affect the temperature at which water boils (Fig. 12.2). The interval between the fixed points is then divided into 100 equal parts (degrees).

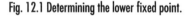

Fig. 12.1 Determining the lower fixed point.

Fig. 12.2 Determining the upper fixed point.

The most obvious effect is *expansion*. Solids and liquids expand on heating because more energy is applied to their particles, which in turn respond by increasing their kinetic energy. This results in the bulk of the solid or liquid taking up a *larger volume*. (The particles themselves do not expand, but since they are moving faster they occupy more space.)

Solids only expand a little with each °C temperature increase, and liquids expand rather more than solids. A useful application of *solid* expansion is a *bimetal strip*. This consists of two metals welded together, which have different expansions for a given rise in temperature. Copper and iron are often used. Copper expands more for a given temperature

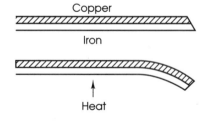

Fig. 12.3 A bimetallic strip.

rise than does iron. On heating, the strip therefore curves, as shown in Fig. 12.3. This property can be used to make or break a contact in an electrical circuit.

The circuit in Fig. 12.4 would act as a fire alarm, the bimetal strip bending to complete the circuit when the temperature rises. Similarly, bimetal strips can "break" a circuit, and as such are used in thermostats.

*Melting* and *evaporation* are also associated with the heating of solids and liquids. These are dealt with in Chapter 10 when considering kinetic theory.

Liquids expand much more than solids for similar temperature rises.

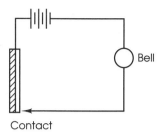

Fig. 12.4 Bimetallic strip as a fire alarm.

## 3 ▷ GASES – THE EFFECTS OF TEMPERATURE CHANGES

Temperature changes cause larger effects in gases than in solids or liquids because the particles are so mobile. Heat energy applied to a gas sample will always change the kinetic energy of the particles, but the effect of this change will depend on the conditions which apply to the gas. Assuming that the mass of gas is constant, there are two *extreme* situations:

1. Keeping the *volume fixed* – in which case the pressure of the gas will increase as the temperature rises.
2. Keeping the *pressure fixed* – in which case the volume of gas will increase as the temperature rises.

The molecular explanation of these effects is again dealt with in Chapter 10.

### (a) WITH A FIXED VOLUME OF GAS

Here there will be a change in *pressure* if the *temperature* rises. A suitable apparatus to investigate this is shown in Fig. 12.5. A water bath is used to heat a flask of air. The temperature of the water bath is the same as the air in the flask, and is recorded on a thermometer. Pressure changes of the gas are

recorded on the Bourdon gauge. The temperature can be raised in suitable steps, about 10–20 °C, and the pressure recorded. When the water reaches boiling-point, allow the apparatus to cool and during cooling take a second set of readings of pressure at each temperature selected. A mean value of pressure can be found from these two sets of readings. A graph can be drawn of *pressure* against *temperature*. It will look like that in Fig. 12.6. The graph shows that there is a numerical relationship between the pressure and the temperature of the gas at constant

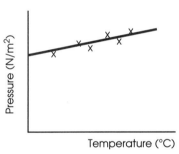

Fig. 12.6 Variation of gas pressure with temperature.

volume. This relationship is *not* a proportional one – the graph does not pass through point (0, 0) – and this means that a doubled temperature change will *not* give a doubled pressure change. "Proportion" means that when one quantity changes in a particular way, another quantity changes in the same way (doubling one thing causes the doubling of another). This would also mean that a graph of the two quantities must pass through (0, 0). Of course temperature, on the Celsius scale, is a number chosen in an arbitrary manner, assigning 0 °C as the temperature at which pure ice melts. Since the value is assigned in this manner it is little wonder that other materials behave in rather different ways.

The axis of the pressure and temperature graph is placed where it is because the zero of temperature is taken as the melting-point of ice. However, a more rational "zero" for temperature in this context is where the *pressure of a gas is zero*, and where the molecules stop moving. If the experimental

Fig. 12.5 Variation of gas pressure with temperature at constant volume.

graph is taken to **this** point it is found to be at –273 °C. This is called absolute zero – there being no movement of particles at this temperature (Fig. 12.7). This temperature – the point where particles have no kinetic energy – is designated the zero of the "Absolute scale" which is named after its discoverer, Lord Kelvin. The point –273 °C is called 0 K (zero Kelvin): the ° sign is left out because there is no decision to be made about where "zero" is, since it is the same for **all** materials.

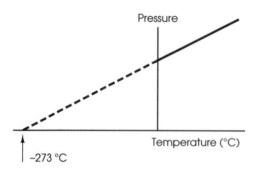

**Fig. 12.7**

## (b) WITH A FIXED PRESSURE

Here there will be a change in **volume** of the gas if the temperature rises. This is experimentally much more difficult to demonstrate. The standard apparatus is shown in Fig. 12.8.

**Fig. 12.8 Variation of gas volume with temperature at constant pressure.**

In order to keep the pressure constant the capillary tube has an open end, so that the pressure above the tube is atmospheric pressure. The air is trapped in the capillary tube by two droplets of sulphuric acid, which absorbs moisture and keeps the small air sample dry. The capillary tube is fixed to a millimetre scale so that the volume changes can be noted. The tube, being of uniform cross-section, permits length measurements to be made that will be proportional to volume.

The **temperature** is raised by heating the water bath and the corresponding change in

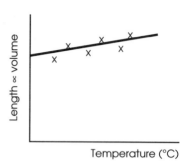

**Fig. 12.9**

length (and therefore volume) of the air column is noted. This is done both on **raising** the temperature, and on **cooling**, giving two sets of readings from which the **mean** value is taken. A graph plotted of **volume** against **temperature** gives the pattern of Fig. 12.9. This is similar to the pressure and temperature graph and it would again cut the temperature axis at –273 °C if it were extrapolated (taken further back), as in Fig. 12.10. The absolute zero of temperature is –273 °C or 0 K.

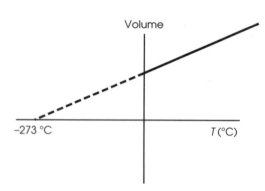

**Fig. 12.10**

Both pressure and volume of an ideal gas are zero at 0 K. This leads to the two relationships, where ∝ means **proportional**, namely:

■ $P \propto T$   (measured in kelvins)

■ $V \propto T$   (measured in kelvins)

Since

$$0 \text{ K} = -273 \text{ °C}$$

Then

$$0 \text{ °C} = +273 \text{ K}$$

and

$$100 \text{ °C} = +373 \text{ K}$$

The volume/temperature and pressure/temperature relationships can also be

expressed as

| Charles' Law | The Pressure Law |
|---|---|
| $$\frac{V_1}{V_2} = \frac{T_1}{T_2}$$ | $$\frac{P_1}{P_2} = \frac{T_1}{T_2}$$ |
| (if mass and pressure constant and temperature is in kelvins) | (if mass and volume constant and temperature is in kelvins) |

**4 ▷ HEAT ENERGY MEASUREMENT – SPECIFIC HEAT CAPACITY**

The difference between "heat" and "temperature" has already been discussed. It is clear that if 100 W of power (energy per second) is applied to a small mass and to a large mass, then the **smaller mass** will show a **larger temperature** change, although the heat energy applied to both masses will be the same (Fig. 12.11).

Fig. 12.11 Heat energy depends on mass.

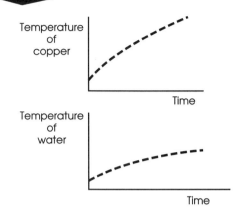

Fig. 12.12

Apart from the effect of mass, the **material** also affects the way in which added joules of heat energy change the temperature of an object. If 1 kg of **copper**, in the form of a solid block, and 1 kg of **water** are both heated with the same immersion heater, supplying the same power over the same time, then the temperature changes will work rather like those in Fig. 12.12. The two materials have **different** heat capacities – the same energy supply causes a different temper-

ature change. This suggests that a change in heat energy depends on the **mass** of material heated, the **temperature** rise produced and a factor which depends on the **type of material**. This factor is called the **specific heat capacity** of the material. It is defined as **the heat energy required to raise the temperature of 1 kg of the material by 1 °C or 1 K**.

The specific heat capacity of **water** is 4200 joules per kilogram per kelvin (J/kg K). This means that 4200 J of energy are needed to raise the temperature of 1 kg of water by 1 degree (Celsius or Kelvin). The specific heat capacity of **copper** is 380 J/kg K. This means that only 380 J of energy are needed to raise the temperature of 1 kg of copper by 1 degree (Celsius or Kelvin).

The **measurement** of specific heat capacity is dealt with in "Extension Materials". However, a few sample calculations should illustrate the idea.

**EXAMPLE 1**

A tank contains 160 kg of cold water at 20 °C. Calculate (a) the energy needed to raise the temperature of the water to 60 °C, and (b) the time this will take using a 5 kW electric immersion heater.

(a) The specific heat capacity of water is 4200 J/kg K.

To raise 1 kg by 1 °C needs 4200 J

To raise 160 kg by 40 °C needs 160 × 4200 × 40

Energy required = 26 880 000 J

This part of the example introduces a simple equation for finding heat energy changes:

**Heat energy = Mass × specific heat capacity × change in temperature**

(It applies to heat gained by a mass, or to heat lost from it.)

(b) A 5 kW heater provides 5000 J/s. Since 26 880 000 J are needed, then

$$\text{Time} = \frac{26\ 880\ 000}{5000} = 5376 \text{ s}$$

(which is about 1½ h).

## 5 LATENT HEAT

When a solid melts to form a liquid, it undergoes the change of state **without** any temperature change. All the energy supplied goes to breaking bonds in the solid. The energy required to convert 1 kg of a solid at its melting-point into liquid, without any change of temperature, is called the **specific latent heat of fusion** of the solid.

Similarly, a liquid at its boiling-point requires energy to change to a gas, without a change of temperature. The energy needed to change 1 kg of liquid at its boiling-point to gas without any temperature change is called the **specific latent heat of vaporisation** of the liquid. When a liquid cools and solidifies the latent heat of fusion is released as bonds re-form, which maintains the liquid–solid medium at its melting-point until all has solidified. Similarly a gas condensing gives out its latent heat of vaporisation. The energy supplied or evolved on changing state is therefore simply given by:

$$\text{Energy} = \text{Mass} \times \text{specific latent heat}$$

### EXAMPLE 2

A kettle contains 1.6 kg of water. After the water starts to boil, the kettle is left on. (a) How much energy is needed for all the water to boil away? (b) How long will it take to boil dry if the kettle is rated as 2.5 kW. (The specific latent heat of vaporisation of water is $2.3 \times 10^6$ J/kg.)

(a)  Energy = Mass × specific latent heat
    $= 1.6 \times 2.3 \times 10^6 = \underline{3\,680\,000 \text{ J}}$.

(b)  The kettle provides 2500 J/s. Therefore

$$\text{Time needed} = \frac{3\,680\,000}{2500} = \underline{1472 \text{ s}}$$

Some more difficult examples use both the specific heat capacity and specific latent heat ideas. These need step-by-step calculations of the quantities of energy involved at each stage.

### EXAMPLE 3

Calculate the heat required to convert 5 kg of ice at –20 °C into steam at 100 °C.

Specific heat capacities:    Water 4200 J/kg K
                             Ice 2100 J/kg K

Specific latent heat of
        fusion of ice = 340 000 J/kg

Specific latent heat of
vaporisation of water = $2.3 \times 10^6$ J/kg

***Step (i)*** Ice at –20 °C heating to 0 °C:

Energy  = Mass × specific heat capacity ×
            temperature rise

        $= 5 \times 2100 \times 20 = \underline{210\,000 \text{ J}}$

***Step (ii)*** Ice at 0 °C turning to water at 0 °C:

Energy  = Mass × specific latent heat of
            fusion
        $= 5 \times 340\,000 = \underline{1\,700\,000 \text{ J}}$

***Step (iii)*** Water at 0 °C heating to 100 °C:

Energy  = Mass × specific heat capacity ×
            temperature rise
        $= 5 \times 4200 \times 100 = \underline{2\,100\,000 \text{ J}}$

***Step (iv)*** Water at 100 °C changing to steam at 100 °C:

Energy  = Mass × specific latent heat of
            vaporisation
        $= 5 \times 2.3 \times 10^6 = \underline{11\,500\,000 \text{ J}}$

The total energy is the **sum** of steps (i)–(iv), i.e. $\underline{15\,510\,000 \text{ J}}$.

## 6 CONVECTION IN LIQUIDS AND GASES

This is the main method of **transfer of heat energy** in a fluid. A heated liquid or gas expands, so its particles occupy a greater volume than when it was cold. This in turn means that there is a **decrease** in density.

The effect can be seen by filling gas jars with hot and cold water, and adding a drop of dye to the hot one. With care the hot liquid can be inverted over the cold. The hot, less dense, liquid floats above the cold, denser liquid (Fig. 12.13).

If the **reverse** is tried, the hot, less dense liquid travels upwards, warming the cold

Fig. 12.13 Hot liquids are less dense than cold liquids.

liquid and giving an even temperature distribution (Fig. 12.14). This is the principle of **convection**. Hotter, less dense liquids and gases move **upwards** through colder denser fluids.

Fig. 12.15 Convection.

Fig. 12.14 Hot liquid floats upwards giving an even temperature distribution.

Fig. 12.16 Convection currents.

A **convection current** is the continuous movement of the fluids; this is usually studied by tracking the liquid movement with a few crystals of dye (Fig. 12.15). The dye shows the path of warm, less dense liquid. At the same time cooler liquid is taking its place, and the whole mass of the liquid is warmed (Fig. 12.16).

The use of a so-called "radiator" to warm a room is an example of a large-scale convection

current. Near the heater, warm, less dense air rises, colder air takes its place and this is heated in turn. The heat energy is transferred **throughout** the room by the movement of the whole mass of air. This happens on a large scale over land masses, giving rise to convection currents called thermals, which are made use of by glider pilots.

> It is useful to be able to state typical schemes for insulating a home and the reasons why a particular method is effective.

## 7 CONDUCTION IN SOLIDS

Fig. 12.17 Comparison of conductivity.

Rods of different materials, heated as shown, can illustrate the idea of rates of **conduction** (Fig. 12.17). The rods have a matchstick sealed to one end with wax. If they are equally heated, the matchsticks fall at different times. Heat is flowing along the rods **without the material itself moving**. This is an example of conduction. Generally, metals are good conductors, and non-metallic solids tend to **conduct badly**, and are called **insulators**.

The mechanism of conduction relies on the passing of kinetic energy from one vibrating particle to another, so a good conductor will

have strong linkages between particles. Since the inter-particle linkages are **not** as strong in liquids as in solids, and are almost non-existent in gases, liquids and especially gases are very poor conductors. These properties are put to good use in house insulation – cavity walls and window double glazing make use of the insulating properties of air. The types of solid material used in loft insulation are those which are both poor conductors and which help trap a still layer of air which acts as a very effective insulating layer.

Metals have a lot of electrons which can move quite freely from one atom to another throughout the piece of material. These electrons can carry the energy quite rapidly through a metal and are the main reason why all metals are good conductors. Solids such as plastics have none of these "free" electrons and also have long molecules which are difficult to vibrate. They may be such poor conductors that the plastic will melt and burn because the heat remains concentrated in one place.

## 8 HEAT RADIATION

This important mechanism of **heat energy transfer** does not rely on particles at all. It is the means by which we receive heat energy from the sun, across space, by means

of electromagnetic waves in the infra-red region of the spectrum. The waves are **not** heat carriers, but their **absorption** by matter causes an increase in molecular kinetic energy, and a heating effect is produced.

An electric fire filament emits both visible light and invisible infra-red waves, and can be used to test two important properties. A heater placed midway between two sheets of metal, one blackened and one silvered, will deliver the same energy on to each surface (Fig. 12.18). If a metal disc is secured on to each metal sheet with wax, the one attached to the blackened sheet falls off *before* the other. This is because radiated energy is absorbed better by the blackened sheet – a large proportion of energy is reflected by the silvered one.

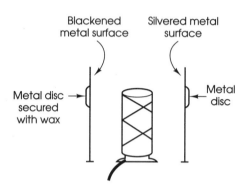

Fig. 12.18 Blackened surfaces are good absorbers of radiation.

Black and roughened surfaces are good *absorbers* of heat radiation.

Another metal sheet, but with one side silvered and the other blackened (Fig. 12.19), can be used to show another property if initially heated with Bunsen burners. The two surfaces must be at the same temperature, but the black surface emits more radiation than the silvered one.

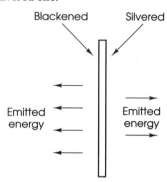

Fig. 12.19 Blackened surfaces are good emitters of radiation.

This can be simply felt by holding the hand near each surface in turn, or more precisely observed using a thermopile. Aluminium beakers filled with the same quantity of hot water from a kettle will also show this if one has been polished and the other painted dull black. The temperature of the water in the dull black container falls faster.

Black and roughened surfaces are better *emitters* of heat radiation than are silvered surfaces.

# EXTENSION MATERIALS

## 1 MEASUREMENT OF SPECIFIC HEAT CAPACITY

The apparatus used for this determination is often a solid block of the material, drilled with holes into which can be fitted a small electrical immersion heater and a thermometer. In the case of a liquid, the liquid is placed in a well-insulated container.

### METHOD

The mass of the block is found, and its initial temperature noted. The circuit is set up as shown (Fig. 12.20) and values are adjusted with the rheostat to give suitable current and PD. (The rheostat also enables these values to be held steady during the experiment.) A stop-clock is started and the current turned on for a given time – enough to give about 20 °C temperature increase. At the end of this time the current is switched off and the final temperature taken.

Fig. 12.20 Determining specific heat capacity.

## READINGS TAKEN

| | |
|---|---|
| Mass of block | $= M$ kilograms |
| Starting temperature | $= T_1 \,^{\circ}C$ |
| Final temperature | $= T_2 \,^{\circ}C$ |
| Current | $= I$ amps |
| PD | $= V$ volts |
| Time | $= t$ seconds |

## CALCULATION

Energy supplied
electrically $= IVt$ (joules)

$\qquad$ = Mass × specific heat capacity

$\qquad\qquad$ × temperature rise

Therefore

$$\text{Specific heat capacity} = \frac{IVt}{M(T_2 - T_1)}$$

**"GREENHOUSE EFFECT"**

Radiation from the sun contains a mixture of wavelengths, including visible, ultra-violet and infra-red. Just as visible light is a band of wavelengths and not a single one, so too infra-red is a band containing many wavelengths. The wavelengths of infra-red emitted by a hot object depend on its temperature – hotter objects emit smaller wavelength, high-frequency waves, which penetrate glass in the same way that visible light passes through glass (Fig. 12.21). Infra-red from the *sun* has

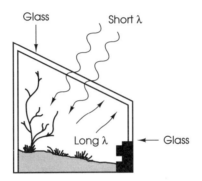

Fig. 12.21 The "greenhouse effect".

both small and large wavelengths present, and the larger wavelengths cannot pass through glass. The inside of a greenhouse therefore

becomes heated by these low-wavelength rays when they are absorbed. The temperature of *objects* inside the greenhouse rises and *they also* emit infra-red radiation. However, as these rays have a longer wavelength, they are trapped *inside* the glass and the temperature rises even more. This principle is used in the case of *solar panels* for heating. A glass or transparent cover traps heat by the "greenhouse" effect. The absorber is blackened to assist absorption of thermal radiation. Water circulated through the panels is therefore heated and pumped to the domestic supply (Fig. 12.22).

The Earth's atmosphere has some gases which behave in a similar manner to the greenhouse glass. They allow through the shorter wavelengths from the Sun that heat the surface of the Earth but absorb and radiate back the longer wavelengths that the Earth's cooler surface emits. The heat energy is therefore trapped and the average temperature of the outer surface of the Earth and the atmosphere is raised. These gases (such as carbon dioxide from the burning of fuels) could upset the delicate temperature system which controls the weather. Note that this is NOT the same effect as either holes in the ozone layer or acid rain.

Fig. 12.22 Solar heating panel.

## 3 ▷ THE GENERAL GAS EQUATION

Provided that the mass of gas remains the same there are three main factors that can change: pressure, volume and temperature. In this chapter and the previous one you will have met the three gas laws that tell you what happens when each of these is kept constant and the connection between the other two is determined. The laws are for a constant mass of gas.

**Boyle's law** at constant temperature

$$P_1V_1 = P_2V_2$$

**Charles' law** at constant pressure

$$\frac{V_1}{V_2} = \frac{T_1}{T_2}$$

**The pressure law** at constant volume

$$\frac{P_1}{P_2} = \frac{T_1}{T_2}$$

We can combine all three of these together into one equation to see what happens when all three factors are changed. The law is only really true for a perfect gas and is sometimes known as the **ideal gas** equation. It gives correct answers for real gases provided that the particles are not compressed too close together that the forces between the particles becomes significant.

$$\frac{P_1V_1}{T_1} = \frac{P_2V_2}{T_2}$$

Where $P_1$ = first pressure, $V_1$ = first volume and $T_1$ – first temperature. $P_2$ = second pressure, $V_2$ = second volume and $T_2$ = second temperature. The temperatures MUST be in kelvin.

### EXAMPLE

A gas has a volume of 300 ml at 6 atmospheres pressure and 327 °C. What will its volume become at 1 atmosphere pressure and 27 °C?

$$T_1 = 273 + 327 = 600 \text{ K}$$
$$T_2 = 273 + 27 = 300 \text{ K}$$

$$\frac{P_1V_1}{T_1} = \frac{P_2V_2}{T_2}$$

$$\frac{6 \times 300}{600} = \frac{1 \times V_2}{300}$$

$$V_2 = \frac{6 \times 300 \times 300}{600} = \underline{900 \text{ ml}}$$

## 4 ▷ HEAT INSULATION

We have already seen that gases are poor conductors of heat. If they are trapped in small bubbles or thin layers so that they cannot move and transfer heat by convection then they will be good insulators. Most **warm clothing** works on this principle, trapping layers of warm air between layers of clothing and pockets of air between the fibres of the material. Several layers of clothing will be warmer than one thick layer.

House insulation uses similar principles.

**Double glazing** works because an extra layer of insulating air is trapped between the layers of glass. **Roof/loft insulation** is made from thick layers of fibreglass matting or mineral wool and **hot water tanks** are covered with a fibreglass blanket or have about 25 mm of rigid plastic foam bonded to the outside. **Cavity walls** can be filled with mineral wool and **water pipes** covered with plastic foam. The gas bubbles trapped in closed cells of plastic foam make it a good insulator.

(a) Loft insulation

(b) Cavity wall insulation

(c) Hot water storage

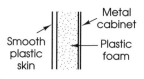

(d) Wall of refrigerator

Fig. 12.23

## 5 EXPANSION OF LIQUIDS

Most liquids expand steadily as temperature rises. If you investigate this remember that the container will also be expanding. Water is unusual in that it contracts from 0°C to 4°C and then expands. This means that the water has its minimum volume and maximum density at 4°C. When pond water cools below 4°C in the winter the water becomes less dense and floats above the water at 4°C which sinks to the bottom. Ice will therefore form from the top downwards and plants and animals in the water can survive.

## 6 U-VALUES

This is a practical way to determine the heat loss through the walls, windows, roof and doors of a building.

A *U-value* is the power loss through a square metre of the material when the temperature difference across it is 1 °C (or 1 K) The U-values can be obtained from standard tables and have been determined by experiment in real situations. If you find the total power loss from a room or building you will know the power of the heating system needed to maintain the temperature.

Power loss = U-value × area × temperature difference.

Fig. 12.24

Some U-values are given in the table.

| Material | U-value in W/m² °C |
|---|---|
| Double brick cavity wall | 1.7 |
| Double brick wall with cavity insulation | 0.6 |
| Single glazed window | 5.6 |
| Double glazed window | 3 |
| Tiled roof | 2.2 |
| Insulated roof | 0.5 |

### EXAMPLE

Find the power loss through a double glazed patio door that measures 2.2 m by 3 m if the room temperature is 20 °C when the temperature outside is –2 °C.

Area $= 2.2 \times 3 = 6.6 m^2$
Temperature difference $= 22°C$
U-value $= 3 W/m^2 °C$

Power loss = U-value × area × temperature difference.
$= 3 \times 6.6 \times 22 = \underline{436 \text{ W.}}$

(So almost 0.5 kW is being lost through this window alone!)

## 7 EXPANSIVITY

When solids expand they do so by a small amount but with a very large force. This expansion must be allowed for in many engineering designs or there will be severe damage. A steam pipe for example may change considerably in length when turned off and a desert oil pipeline may have considerable temperature changes from midday to the middle of the night.

← Bend allows changes in length

Fig. 12.25

For the same reason gaps must be left at the ends of bridges and railway lines to allow for expansion and contraction.

Metal parts can be permanently fitted together by machining the outer piece very slightly too small. If the inner is then cooled (liquid nitrogen), or the outer heated, they will fit and then cannot be parted when allowed to return to normal temperature.

A metal bottle top may be unscrewed more easily after being put in running hot water for a short time so that it expands. A glass may break when suddenly put into very hot water. It is a poor conductor and the outside is expanding faster than the inside! Rivets may be put in hot so that they pull the materials together when they contract on cooling.

The *linear expansivity* of a solid is the expansion of 1 m of the solid when its temperature rises by 1 °C. It is sometimes given the symbol α and the units will be /°C. The value will be small some examples are as follows:

| Material | Expansivity/°C | Material | Expansivity/°C |
|---|---|---|---|
| steel | 0.0000150 | aluminium | 0.0000230 |
| copper | 0.0000170 | invar* | 0.0000009 |
| brick | 0.0000090 | concrete | 0.0000120 |
| glass | 0.0000080 | PVC | 0.0001500 |

## EXAMPLE

A concrete bridge is 80 m long at –10 °C on a cold night. How much will it have expanded on a hot day when its temperature is 30 °C? Using the value of expansivity from the table,

$$\text{Expansion} = \text{linear expansivity} \times \text{orig. length} \times \text{temp. change}$$
$$= 0.000012 \times 80 \times 40$$
$$= \underline{38 \text{ mm}}$$

# EXAMINATION QUESTIONS

**MULTIPLE CHOICE QUESTIONS**

## QUESTION 1

Energy may be transmitted through a vacuum by

- A  Conduction only
- B  Convection only
- C  Radiation only
- D  Convection and radiation        (SEG)

## QUESTION 2

Cold — Brass / Iron

Hot — Brass / Iron

Fig. 12.26

The strips of brass and iron are firmly fixed together as shown in Fig. 12.26. The bar is straight when cold. When heated the bar bends as in the diagram. This is because

- A  The brass has expanded more than the iron.
- B  Iron is a poor conductor of heat.
- C  The iron has expanded more than the brass.
- D  Both metals have expanded by equal amounts.        (SEG)

## QUESTION 3

Two liquids are spilt on the hand. One is alcohol, one is water, and both are at the same temperature. The alcohol feels colder than the water, because

- A  Alcohol has a higher boiling-point than water.

- B  Alcohol is a worse conductor of heat than water.
- C  Alcohol has a higher specific latent heat of vaporisation than water.
- D  Alcohol evaporates more readily than water.        (ULEAC)

## QUESTION 4

The temperature of pure melting ice is

- A  –273 K      C  100 K
- B  0 K         D  273 K        (SEG)

## QUESTION 5

Which of the following does **not** work by expansion?

- A  Mercury thermometer
- B  Bimetallic strip fire alarm
- C  Vacuum flask
- D  Cut-out on automatic kettle (ULEAC)

## QUESTION 6

A metal cap was found to be so tight that it could not be unscrewed from its bottle. After directing a stream of hot water on to the cap, it became possible to remove it. This is because

- A  The hot water acted as a lubricant between the glass and the bottle.
- B  The increased air pressure in the bottle caused the cap to expand.
- C  The glass in the neck of the bottle contracted.
- D  The pressure of the air trapped in the screw threads caused the cap to expand.

E   The metal cap expanded more than the glass.                    (ULEAC)

## QUESTION 7

In cold weather, the metal handlebars of a bicycle feel colder to the hands than the plastic handgrips. This is because

A   The metal is at a lower temperature than the plastic.

B   The plastic material contains more heat energy than the metal.

C   The metal is a better conductor of heat than plastic.

D   The shining metal does not reflect radiated heat well.

E   The plastic material is a good radiator of heat.           (ULEAC)

## QUESTION 8

Which of the following is *not* due in some way to the movement of molecules?

A   Convection of heat

B   Pressure of a gas

C   Transfer of heat by radiation

D   Thermal conduction

E   Transmission of sound

## QUESTION 9

A beaker contains water, initially at room temperature. It is continuously stirred while a hot object is immersed in it. Which one of the graphs (Fig. 12.27) best shows the temperature changes which follow?

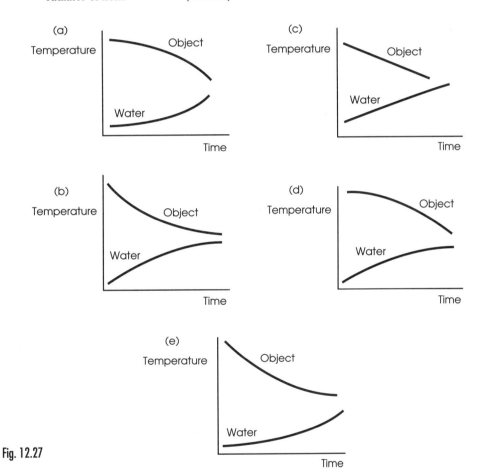

**Fig. 12.27**

## QUESTION 10

Figure 12.28 shows a section through a particular type of building board. Which line in the following table shows why such boards provide good heat insulation?

| | **Aluminium foil is** | **Expanded polystyrene is** |
|---|---|---|
| A | A poor conductor | A good reflector |
| B | A poor reflector | A poor conductor |
| C | A good reflector | A poor conductor |
| D | A good conductor | A good reflector |

Compressed paper boards → | Aluminium foil
← Expanded polystyrene
← Aluminium foil

**Fig. 12.28**

## QUESTION 11

Fig. 12.29(a)

Fig. 12.29(b)

Figure 12.29(a) illustrates an instrument used to measure the time that the sun shines during a day. The blackened glass bulb contains mercury and is supported inside an evacuated glass case. Figure 12.29(b) shows how the connecting wires are arranged inside tube A.

(a) How does energy from the sun reach the mercury? Explain your answer. (3 lines for answer)

(b) Explain why the clock starts when the sun shines? (2 lines for answer)

(c) Why is the tube A of small cross-sectional area? (2 lines for answer)

(d) Explain why blackening the bulb ensures that the mercury level falls rapidly when the sun ceases to shine. (3 lines for answer).

Fig. 12.30

## QUESTION 12

This question is about solar panels, devices that are sometimes seen on the roofs of houses and are used to provide hot water. An example is shown in Fig. 12.30.

(a) State the purpose of the following:
 (i) The insulation behind the absorber panel. (1 line)
 (ii) Having the absorber painted black. (1 line)
 (iii) Having a glass cover on top of the panel. (3 lines)

(b) (i) Name suitable materials for making the absorber panel and water-ways (do not use brand names). (1 line)
 (ii) Give your reasons for the choice of such materials. (4 lines)

(c) The pipe connecting the water outlet from the panel to the hot water storage pipe is kept short. Why is this desirable? (2 lines)

(d) The angle of tilt of the solar panel greatly affects the amount of energy it receives at different times of the year. Figure 12.30 shows what is meant by angle of tilt. The table of data (Fig. 12.31) shows the effect of different angles of tilt for the summer months. Use the table of data to answer the following questions:
 (i) What angle of tilt would be ideal for a solar panel in April? (1 line)
 (ii) Is it better to have the panel tilted at 40 all the summer, or at an angle of 50 all the summer? Show your working. (3 lines)
 (iii) What is the maximum amount of energy a 4 $m^2$ panel could receive during a day in July? (2 lines)

(ULEAC)

| Energy in Megajoules to a 1 $m^2$ panel | | | | | | | | | | |
|---|---|---|---|---|---|---|---|---|---|---|
| Month | Angle of tilt | | | | | | | | | |
| | 0° | 10° | 20° | 30° | 40° | 50° | 60° | 70° | 80° | 90° |
| Apr. | 20.5 | 22.3 | 23.8 | 24.9 | 24.8 | 24.1 | 22.7 | 20.5 | 18.4 | 15.1 |
| May | 26.3 | 27.7 | 28.4 | 28.8 | 27.4 | 25.2 | 23.0 | 19.8 | 16.6 | 13.0 |
| June | 28.4 | 28.8 | 29.2 | 29.2 | 27.4 | 25.2 | 22.3 | 19.1 | 15.1 | 11.2 |
| July | 28.1 | 28.4 | 28.8 | 29.2 | 27.4 | 25.6 | 23.0 | 20.2 | 16.2 | 12.2 |
| Aug. | 23.0 | 24.8 | 25.6 | 25.9 | 26.3 | 24.8 | 22.7 | 20.5 | 17.3 | 13.7 |
| Sept. | 16.2 | 18.7 | 20.5 | 21.6 | 22.3 | 22.7 | 21.6 | 20.5 | 18.7 | 16.2 |

Fig. 12.31

## QUESTION 13

A saucepan of water is put on the hotplate of an electric cooker. The hotplate is *then* switched on and the temperature of the water is recorded every minute until the water boils. The temperature each minute is shown in the table.

| Time (min) | 0 | 1 | 2 | 3 | 4 | 5 | 6 | 7 | 8 |
|---|---|---|---|---|---|---|---|---|---|
| Temperature (°C) | 15 | 20 | 33 | 49 | 64 | 79 | 93 | 100 | 100 |

(a) Plot a graph of the temperature (vertical axis) against time (horizontal axis) on the graph paper. Join the points by a smooth line.

(b) Explain why the rise in temperature of the water is slower at first. (2 lines)

(c) What is the boiling-point of water? (1 line)

(d) From your graph, determine how many seconds it takes for the water to boil. (1 line)

(e) If the power of the hotplate is 1000 W, how much energy is used to bring the water just to the boil? (3 lines)

(f) Some energy is lost from the sides of the saucepan to the surrounding air. What is the best type of surface for the outside of the saucepan if it is to lose the least amount of heat? Give a reason for your choice. (2 lines)

(g) In a similar experiment with a second saucepan of water it took twice as long for the water to boil. Suggest possible reasons for this. (2 lines)

(NICCEA)

## QUESTION 14

(a) To compare the rate at which two different types of surface absorb radiant heat, the apparatus shown below was set up. Can X has a polished surface and can Y has a dull black surface. The starting temperature of the water in each can was 20 °C.

Fig. 12.32

(i) To make this a fair comparison state *two* things that should be the same for each can.

(ii) Which can will show a greater rise in temperature? Explain your answer.

(b) The loss of heat from a house can take place through the roof, through the floor and through the walls. For each of these ways suggest how the heat loss can be reduced.
In each case name the method of heat loss that is being reduced.

(c) (i) A single glazed window has a U value of 5.0 W/m² °C. Explain in detail what this means.

(ii) A house has a total window area of 15 m². Calculate the heat energy, in megajoules, saved in one hour if the owner replaced all the single glazed windows with double glazing of U value 2.8 W/m² °C. The temperature inside the house is 20 °C and the outside temperature is 10 °C. Show clearly how you obtain your answer.

(iii) The house is heated by electricity. One unit of electricity costs 7.5p and is equivalent to 3.6 MJ. Calculate the saving per day of installing the double glazing.

(d) In a steel rolling mill, hot steel comes out of a set of rollers and is cooled under jets of water before being formed into a coil as in the diagram.

(i) Give ONE reason why water is suitable as a coolant in this case.
The mass of steel passing out from the rollers per second is 380 kg. The steel leaves the rollers at a temperature of 1250 °C and it is coiled at a temperature of 600 °C.

(ii) Calculate the heat lost by the steel each second. Give your answer in kilojoules (specific heat capacity of steel = 500 J/kg °C).

Fig. 12.33

# ANSWERS TO EXAMINATION QUESTIONS

| Question | 1 | 2 | 3 | 4 | 5 | 6 | 7 | 8 | 9 | 10 |
|---|---|---|---|---|---|---|---|---|---|---|
| Answer | C | A | D | D | C | E | C | C | B | C |

## ANSWER 11

(a) The mechanism is radiation. The tube is enclosed in a vacuum. No other mechanism transmits across a vacuum (i.e. conduction and convection require a material).

(b) Heat energy is transferred to the mercury. Its temperature rises and it expands up tube A. Since it is a metal it is an electrical conductor, and makes connection with the wires, completing the circuit.

(c) Small cross-section means large change in length for a small volume change. The device is therefore sensitive to small changes in temperature.

(d) Black surfaces are good emitters of heat radiation so the temperature of the mercury will fall more rapidly.

## ANSWER 12

(a) (i) Insulation to prevent heat loss through the back of the panel.
(ii) Painted black to absorb infra-red radiation – black surfaces are good absorbers.
(iii) Glass helps trap long-wave infra-red – rather like the greenhouse effect, so the temperature rise is greater.

(b) (i) and (ii) *Panel* – aluminium; aluminium – light, cheap, good conductor. *Waterways* – copper; copper – good conductor.

(c) Shorter pipe reduces surface area for heat loss by conduction through the pipe and convection in the air around the pipe.

(d) (i) 30°
(ii) At 40° total energy received all summer = 155.6 MJ.
At 50° total energy received all summer = 147.6 MJ.
Therefore 40° is better.
(iii) Maximum July value is 29.2 MJ (for 1 m² panel). Therefore (4 × 29.2) = 116.8 MJ.

## ANSWER 13

(a) Graph – four points to note:
1. Label axes correctly;
2. Units on axes;
3. Points plotted correctly;
4. Points joined with a smooth curve.

(b) At first the electricity supply has to heat the hotplate to the required temperature, so less energy is transferred to the water. Equally conduction through the base of the saucepan takes time.

(c) 100 °C.

(d) 400 seconds (from graph).

(e) $1000 \times 400 = 400\ 000$ J.

(f) Shining outside – poor radiation emitter.

(g) Possibly twice the mass of water used or half the power of the hotplate.

## ANSWER 14

This is a further level question.

(a) (i) Same distance from heater, same volume/mass of in each can, same metal for each can etc.
(ii) Can Y because dull surfaces are better absorbers of radiant heat.

(b) roof – fibreglass matting or mineral wool
floor – carpet and foam underlay
walls – mineral wool fibre.
in all of these the process in conduction.

(c) (i) 5 J of heat are lost each second for every 1 m² and every 1 °C temperature difference.
(ii) *For single glazing*
Power loss = U-value × area × temperature difference.
Power loss = $5 \times 15 \times 10 = \underline{750\ W}$.

*For double glazing*
Power loss = U-value × area × temperature difference.
Power loss = $2.8 \times 15 \times 10 = \underline{420\ W}$
Energy saved per second = power saved = $750 - 420 = 330$ J
Energy saved per hour = $330 \times 60 \times 60 = 1\ 188\ 000$ J = $\underline{1.2\ MJ}$
(iii) Energy saved in one day = $1.2 \times 24 = 28.8$ MJ.
Number of units saved = $28.8/3.6 = 8$
Saving = $8 \times 7.5 = \underline{0.60}$

(d) (i) Water has a high specific heat capacity and a high specific latent heat capacity.
(ii) Heat = mass × specific heat capacity × temperature change
$= 380 \times 500 \times 650 = 123\ 500\ 000$ J
$= \underline{123\ 500\ kJ}$

# TUTOR'S QUESTION AND ANSWER

**QUESTION**

(a) Many domestic oil-fired central heating systems operate by pumping water through a boiler, and circulating the heated water through pipes to radiators. The same water is recirculated continuously through the system. In one such system, water flows at a rate of 0.6 kg/s. Water enters the boiler at a temperature of 35 °C and leaves the boiler at a temperature of 75 °C. Each kilogram of oil provides $3 \times 10^7$ J to heat the water. The density of oil is 850 kg/m³. The specific heat capacity of water is 4200 J/kg K. *Calculate*:

(i) The energy absorbed by the water per second as it passes through the boiler.

(ii) The mass of oil which would provide this energy.

(iii) The time required to consume 1 m³ of oil if the system runs continuously.

(b) In practice the action of the boiler is a little more complicated. The water inlet and outlet temperatures are not constant, and when the outlet temperature exceeds a given pre-set value, the burner is switched OFF. The burner is switched ON again when the outlet temperature falls below a second, and lower, pre-set value.

(i) State and explain the factors which would determine the fraction of the time in which the oil would be burned.

(ii) State and explain the steps a householder might take to keep this fraction to a minimum.

(iii) Outline the principle of operation of a device which might be used to turn the burner ON or OFF. (SEG)

**ANSWER**

(a) (i) Energy per second
= Mass per second × specific heat capacity × temperature rise
= $0.6 \times 4200 \times 40$ = <u>100 800 J</u>

(ii) Mass of oil = $\dfrac{100\,800}{3 \times 10^7}$ = <u>0.003 kg</u>

(iii) Mass of 1 m³ of oil = 850 kg. 0.003 kg are burnt per second. Therefore,

Time required = $\dfrac{850}{0.003}$ s

= 283 333 s = 78 h

(b) (i) Obviously the pre-set temperatures determine how much energy is needed to produce a given energy change in the water (and therefore a rise in temperature). The number of radiators used will affect the overall house temperature, as will the surface are of the radiators. The time for the fuel burning to be OFF will depend on how quickly the rooms cool. A large heat loss through an uninsulated ceiling will give a larger fraction of time when the boiler is operating.

(ii) Insulation of loft, walls, windows. Draught exclusion, double glazing, etc.

(iii) The device used might operate rather like a bimetallic strip, or something similar, which uses expansion to control switching. There would need to be a valve or switch to provide ON/OFF control.

# STUDENT'S ANSWER WITH THE EXAMINER'S COMMENTS

## STUDENT ANSWER TO QUESTION 13

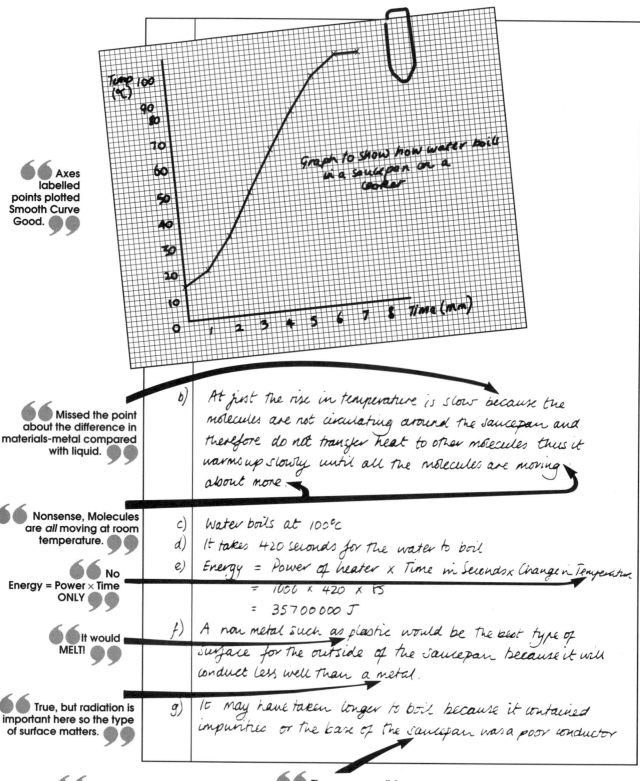

66 Axes labelled points plotted Smooth Curve Good. 99

*Graph to show how water boils in a saucepan on a cooker*

66 Missed the point about the difference in materials-metal compared with liquid. 99

b) At first the rise in temperature is slow because the molecules are not circulating around the saucepan and therefore do not transfer heat to other molecules thus it warms up slowly until all the molecules are moving about more.

66 Nonsense, Molecules are *all* moving at room temperature. 99

c) Water boils at 100°c
d) It takes 420 seconds for the water to boil

66 No Energy = Power × Time ONLY 99

e) Energy = Power of heater × Time in Seconds × Change in Temperature
= 1000 × 420 × 85
= 35 700 000 J

66 It would MELT! 99

f) A non metal such as plastic would be the best type of surface for the outside of the saucepan because it will conduct less well than a metal.

66 True, but radiation is important here so the type of surface matters. 99

g) It may have taken longer to boil because it contained impurities or the base of the saucepan was a poor conductor

66 The graph is well done, as is the information obtained from it. The other parts are weak, suggesting poor understanding of the topic, and not enough practice in answering questions. 99

66 These are possible, but unlikely to result in a *doubled* time to boil. 99

# REVIEW SHEET

■ Write down briefly how the upper and lower fixed points are determined on a Celsius thermometer.

Upper fixed point

_____

_____

Lower fixed point _____

_____.

■ Which will expand most when heated at constant pressure: solid, liquid or gas?
_____

■ Name the three ways in which heat can be transmitted from one place to another.

1. _____    2. _____    3. _____

■ Write down the following equations

1. Boyle's law                                    2. Charles' law

_____          _____

3. The pressure law                            4. The ideal gas equation

_____          _____.

■ In the gas laws the temperature MUST be in _____.

■ 20 °C is the same as _____ K,    400 K is the same as _____ °C.

■ Heat energy gained or lost when a material changes temperature is found by using the specific heat of the material. Complete the equation:

Energy gained or lost = specific heat capacity × _____ × _____

■ The greenhouse effect in the atmosphere depends on the fact that cooler objects radiate at _____ wavelengths which are absorbed and radiated back by gases in the air but the gases will transmit the _____ wavelengths from the hot Sun.

Complete the following table

| Object to be insulated | Insulating material |
|---|---|
| Hot water tank | |
| Cold water pipe | |
| Cavity wall | |
| | Layers of clothing |

■ To keep heat in, the outside of a pan should be _____ but to release heat quickly a car radiator should be _____.

■ The U-value of a double glazed panel will be _____ than the value for a single glazed panel.

■ Convection cannot occur in a _____. The only way the energy can reach us from the sun is by _____.

■ How much heat is needed to raise the temperature of 1 kg of water from 20 °C to 100 °C ? (specific heat capacity of water is 4200 J/kg K).

_____

_____

_____

■ Two metals such as _____ and _____ can be bonded together to make a _____ strip which will bend when its temperature changes.

■ Describe an experiment you might use to help you measure *specific heat capacity*.

_____

_____

_____

_____

_____

_____

_____

_____

_____

_____

_____

_____

_____

■ What is meant by "linear expansivity".

_____

_____

_____ .

# 13

# MAGNETISM AND ELECTRO-MAGNETISM

## GETTING STARTED

Magnetic effects have been known and used for centuries, particularly in navigation. However, it is the link between electric currents and magnetic effects which is important both in theory and in practical application. Magnetic sensing devices such as relays make circuit switching possible by remote control. Microphones and loudspeakers also use magnetic effects and, perhaps most importantly, so does the electric motor.

# ESSENTIAL PRINCIPLES

A **magnetic material** is one which can be attracted to a permanent magnet, and which could **itself be magnetised**. Iron, nickel and cobalt are metals which show this behaviour, and so do alloys of them, like steel.

A single, freely suspended, permanent magnet will line itself up in the magnetic field of the earth, so that one particular end of it points towards the earth's magnetic north pole. This end is called the **north-seeking** (N-seeking) **pole** of the magnet. The other end is the **south-seeking pole** (Fig. 13.1).

Fig. 13.1 Establishing the polarity of a magnet.

If two N-seeking poles of magnets are brought together they **repel** each other, as will two S-seeking poles. But a N-seeking pole **attracts** a S-seeking pole. The rule is:

▶ **Unlike poles attract.**
▶ **Similar poles repel.**

But note that either type of pole will attract a piece of magnetic material (which has no poles). **Repulsion** only takes place between **similar poles of magnetised materials**.

A magnetic compass is itself a small horizontally mounted magnet. Its N-seeking end can be identified by holding it well away from magnetic materials and noticing which end points to the north of the earth (Fig. 13.2). In future diagrams the **N-seeking end of a compass** will be drawn as the **head of an arrow**.

Fig. 13.2

If a compass is brought near a permanent magnet, the N-end of the needle is **repelled** from the N-seeking end of the magnet. The pattern, as the compass is moved around the magnet, is shown in Fig. 13.3. The force on the N-seeking end of the compass is away from the north pole of the magnet and

Fig. 13.3 The N-seeking end of a compass used to establish a pattern.

towards its south pole. The region around a magnet where a force is experienced can be shown using iron filings or by careful plotting with compasses. The region is called the **magnetic field** of the magnet.

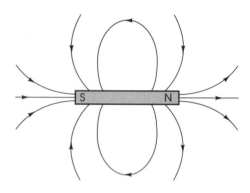

Fig. 13.4 The pattern of flux for a bar magnet.

The **pattern** revealed by filings or compass plotting shows **lines** along which a compass needle would line up. These are called **lines of magnetic force** or **lines of magnetic flux**. The lines of a flux for a single bar magnet are shown in Fig. 13.4. The **direction** is the way an N-seeking pole would point in the field, i.e. **away from the north pole** of the magnet and **towards its south pole**.

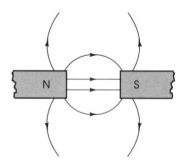

Fig. 13.5 Flux pattern between attracting magnetic poles.

Other typical patterns are also shown. Figure 13.5 is the **field between attracting poles**. This gives a fairly uniform (steady strength) field in the region between the two poles. Figure 13.6 is the **field for**

Fig. 13.6 Flux pattern for repelling poles.

*repelling north poles*. There is no field at point X (sometimes called a *neutral* point). A *horseshoe magnet* is like a bar magnet bent at the centre. It gives a field *between its poles*, as in Fig. 13.7. Notice that *field lines do not cross*, and that they *begin or end on the magnet*.

Magnets with curved pole pieces are sometimes used to give a very uniform field (Fig. 13.8) when used with a soft iron armature.

Magnetic materials which are difficult to magnetise but are also difficult to demagnetise are suitable for making permanent magnets. Such materials are called *hard* magnetic materials. Some uses, such as

Fig. 13.7 Flux pattern for a horseshoe magnet.

Fig. 13.8

electromagnets, the centre cores of relay coils and transformer cores must magnetise and demagnetise quickly and easily. The materials to do this are called *soft* magnetic materials.

## 2 MAGNETISING AND DEMAGNETISING

A piece of iron placed in contact with a permanent magnet will, for the time they are in contact, produce magnetic poles and can then itself attract magnetic materials (Fig. 13.9). This is described as *induced magnetism*, and is the reason why iron filings can be used to reveal the lines of flux in a magnetic field. Each filing becomes temporarily an induced magnet.

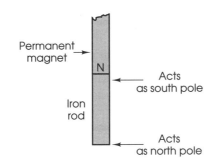

Fig. 13.9 Induced magnetic poles.

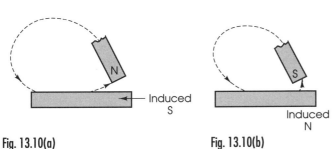

Fig. 13.10(a)          Fig. 13.10(b)

### (a) DIRECTION OF MAGNETISM

The *direction* of induced magnetism follows the usual rules. The end closest to the north pole of the magnet becomes a south pole. A sample can be permanently magnetised by induction if a permanent magnet is repeatedly stroked over the sample from one end to the other, and lifted clear of the sample before the next move along it. The directions of magnetism are shown in Figs 13.10(a) and (b).

### (b) ELECTRICAL METHODS OF MAGNETISING

A more effective method of magnetising is an *electrical* one.

Fig. 13.11 d.c. method of magnetising.

### (c) DEMAGNETISING

*Demagnetising* can occur if a sample is *heated above a critical temperature*, called the *curie temperature*, and *then rapidly cooled. Repeated hammering* also causes demagnetising. A non-destructive demagnetising method uses a.c. in a different way. The sample is placed in the coil in an east–west direction, and *while the current is still flowing in the coil, the sample is rapidly removed*.

If this procedure is repeated a few times the sample is demagnetised (Fig. 13.12).

## (d) MAGNETIC MATERIALS SHOW VARIATIONS IN MAGNETIC PROPERTIES

*Soft iron* is easily magnetised, but it loses its magnetism easily as well. It is called a soft magnetic material. This makes it very suitable as the core of an electromagnet, in a relay or bell circuit or in the core of a transformer,

where rapid magnetising and demagnetising are important (Fig. 13.13). However, *steel*, a hard magnetic material, is more difficult to magnetise, though once it is magnetised it retains it. It is therefore ideal as a permanent magnet or a compass needle (Fig. 13.14).

Fig. 13.12 a.c. method of demagnetising.

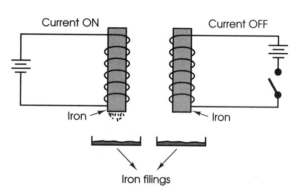

Fig. 13.13 Soft iron gains and loses magnetism easily.

Fig. 13.14 Steel retains some magnetic properties.

**3 › ELECTRO-MAGNETISM**

Whenever an electric current flows in a wire, there is a magnetic field produced around the wire. A single straight wire carrying a current will affect a compass needle. If the compass is placed *below* the wire (Fig. 13.15), the needle points *across* the wire, *out of* the plane of the page. A needle *above* the wire points *across* the wire *into* the plane of the page.

If the current direction is *reversed*, the compass needle directions also reverse. The pattern of the magnetic flux can be seen more easily if the current flows up a wire through a horizontal piece of card. If a compass is moved on the card, the needle directions show that the force is at right angles to the current flow, and the flux lines form a

Fig. 13.15

*circular* pattern around the wire (Fig. 13.16). Again reversing the current reverses the field direction.

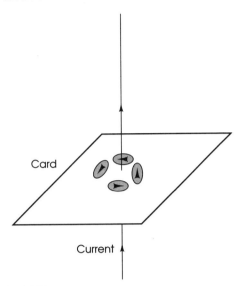

Fig. 13.16

The pattern is usually illustrated as if the card were viewed from above. The *dot* in the centre of Fig. 13.17 represents a current in a wire moving *upwards*, *out of* the plane of the page. The *cross* in Fig. 13.18 represents a current moving *downwards*, *into* the plane of the page.

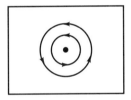

Fig. 13.17 Flux patterns for a single wire carrying current.

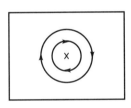

Fig. 13.18 Flux patterns for a single wire carrying current.

The further away from the wire, the weaker the magnetic force. This is represented by drawing flux lines further apart.

The directions can be worked out using the *right-hand grip rule*. Point your thumb (right hand) in the direction of the current. Curl your fingers. Your fingers give the direction of the lines of flux.

The magnetic effect of a current in a single wire is weak. Stronger fields can be obtained using a coil of wire (a solenoid). This gives the same field pattern as a single bar magnet, and

**Another way of finding the direction is to use the 'Maxwell Corkscrew Rule'**

it is very uniform along the centre of the coil (Fig. 13.19).

Fig. 13.19 Flux through a solenoid.

The *strength* of the field is increased if:

1. The current is increased;
2. The number of turns of the coil is increased;
3. A soft iron core is placed in the coil.

The *direction* of the field depends on two factors:

1. The direction of the current flow;
2. The direction in which the wire is coiled.

Figure 13.20 shows current flowing in a *clockwise direction* around end X of the core. This makes this end a *south pole*. (A letter S with clockwise arrows helps in remembering this.)

Fig. 13.20 South pole for a clockwise current.

In Fig. 13.21 the current flow at end X is *anticlockwise*, giving a *north pole*. Once again, having fixed the winding of the coil, the polarity can be changed simply by reversing the current direction.

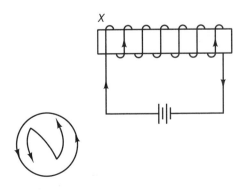

Fig. 13.21 North pole for an anticlockwise current.

**4** **FORCES ON CURRENTS IN MAGNETIC FIELDS**

> ThuMb = Movement
> First finger = Field
> SeCond Finger = Current
> and remember it's the motor rule
> – so LEFT hand – we drive a
> motor car on the left! ""

A long strip of aluminium foil placed in the field of a strong permanent magnet has no force acting on it, since aluminium is not a magnetic material. If a current is then passed through the aluminium, there is a larger force and the strip moves upwards, at 90° to the magnetic field direction (Fig. 13.22).

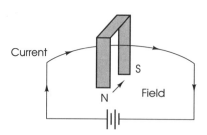

Fig. 13.22 A catapult field.

If the current direction is reversed, the force on the current is reversed, and so therefore is the movement direction (Fig. 13.23).

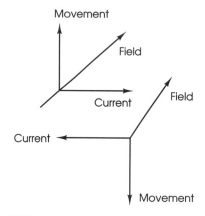

Fig. 13.23

The movement direction can also be changed by **changing the field direction**. Unlike effects in electric or gravitational fields, a magnetic field exerts a force on a current which is at 90° to both the current and the field. This can also be shown with a free-moving piece of copper wire on two rails carrying current (Fig. 13.24). A magnetic field

Fig. 13.24

exerts a force on the current at 90° to it. In this case the wire moves along the track. Reversing the field would make the wire shoot off the end of the track. The easiest way to remember which way the force acts is to use **Fleming's left-hand rule** (Fig. 13.25):

■ If the thumb, first finger and second finger of the left hand are held at 90° to each other, and

■ the first finger is pointed in the direction of the **field**, and

■ the second finger is pointed in the direction of the **current**, then

■ the **thumb** indicates the direction of **movement**. (This does require a certain amount of contortion for some arrangements!)

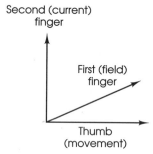

Fig. 13.25

The reason for this movement comes from the interaction of two magnetic fields, that of the permanent magnet and that due to the current. In the arrangement shown in Fig. 13.26, Fleming's rule predicts that the wire will move inwards.

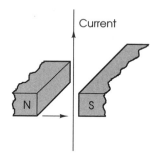

Fig. 13.26

Now think about the **fields**. The field of the magnet is shown (from above) in Fig. 13.27(a) and that of the current in Fig. 13.27(b).

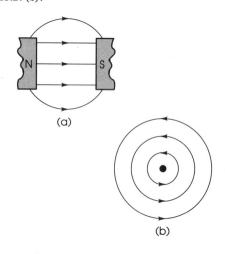

Fig. 13.27(a) and (b) Components of a catapult field.

If the two fields are superimposed on each other, the result is that *below* the wire the two sets of flux *combine* in the *same direction*, whereas *above* the wire they are *opposing*. This result is shown in Fig. 13.28.

In consequence the wire moves from the stronger field to the weaker field – or referring back to Fig. 13.26, *into* the plane of the paper as predicted by Fleming's rule. This combined field is sometimes referred to as a *catapult field*.

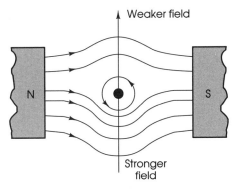

Fig. 13.28 Effect of the combined fields.

# 5  THE SIZE OF THE "CATAPULT" FORCE

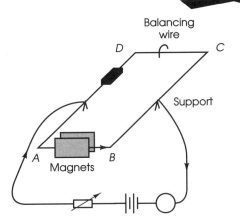

Fig. 13.29 A current balance.

This can be investigated using a *current balance*. This is a wire frame with an insulating portion fixed in it and balanced on two conducting supports. Current can therefore be passed around the frame, *in at one support* and *out at the other* (Fig. 13.29). If the current flow is along AB, and the magnetic field is out of the plane of the paper, then the force on AB is *downwards* (Fig. 13.30).

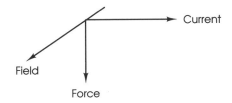

Fig. 13.30

Small lengths of wire placed on arm CD can be used to restore the balance. Since the weight of the wires is equal to the magnetic force, the size of the force is found.

If the current is varied using the variable resistor it can be shown how the force depends on the current. The magnetic field can also be changed if electromagnets are used in place of permanent magnets. It is found that the force depends on:

1. The size of the current;
2. The size of the field:
3. The length of the wire in the field.

In practice the length of wire is increased by having several turns of wire in the field. A coil carrying current in a field is a good way of illustrating this. A wood frame, free to move about on an axle, can be wound with insulated wire to form a coil. Current is then let in and out of the coil through wires wound like loose springs at each end of the axle (Fig. 13.31).

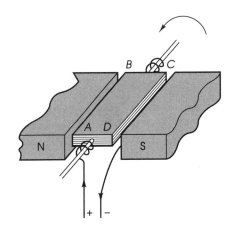

Fig. 13.31 Rotation of a coil in a uniform field.

Current flows in the direction ABCD. The direction of force on AB is downwards and the force on CD is upwards, so an *anticlockwise* rotation is produced, which is *opposed* by the forces produced in the springs (Fig. 13.32). The effect of changing the number of turns, the current and the field can be shown by the change in the angle of rotation produced.

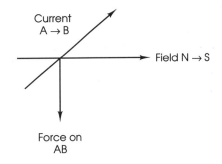

Fig. 13.32

6 d.c. ELECTRIC MOTOR

The movement of the coil described in the last section is restricted by the springs. If the springs were ***removed***, the movement is still restricted to a single turn through a maximum of 180°. This is because the force on AB is ***always downwards*** and the force on CD is ***always up***, so that when the coil is vertical, as in Fig. 13.33, the forces will keep it there.

Fig. 13.33

A motor needs ***continuous*** rotation through 360°. This is achieved by making the current reverse every time the coil passes through the vertical position, by using an arrangement called a ***split-ring commutator***. This is shown attached to the coil in Fig. 13.34, with an end-on view shown in Fig. 13.35. When AB reaches the bottom of its rotation the two half-rings reverse the $\oplus$ and $\ominus$ sides of the circuit. As a result the current in AB now flows from B to A and the force on it is upwards. Similarly, BC moves down so that constant rotation is achieved.

Fig. 13.34 d.c. motor arrangement.

A practical motor may have many coils each with its own commutator to increase the force on each 360° turn.

Fig. 13.35 Commutator with contacts.

7 THE LOUDSPEAKER

Fig. 13.36

The coil is attached to the centre of the cone and is in the field between the poles of a circular magnet.

The input is a current of the same frequency as the sound that is to be produced. The current goes through the coil and an electric motor effect is produced. As the current alternates the coil is pushed backwards and forwards at the same frequency and the card cone sends out the soundwaves. The edge of the cone is corrugated so that it can flex many times per second without cracking and splitting. Strong permanent magnets are needed to produce loud clear sound with little distortion.

# EXTENSION MATERIALS

**1 > RELAYS AND RELAY CIRCUITS**

❝ Relays are often used in transistor circuits. A small current flows in the transistor circuit but it is enough to switch the relay and operate a second circuit. ❞

A **relay** is an electromagnetic switch. In its simplest form it has two circuits. The *input circuit* supplies current to a coil. Only a small current is needed for the electromagnet in this circuit to become magnetised. The electromagnet then attracts a soft iron rocking armature which closes the contacts connected to the *output circuit*, where a high current may flow (Fig. 13.37). A small input current controls a larger output current. The circuit symbol for a relay is shown in Fig. 13.38.

Fig. 13.38 Circuit symbol for a relay.

If the thermistor in circuit (Fig. 13.39) has a large enough resistance when it is cold, then the current in the coil will be *less than* that needed to switch the relay. If the temperature rises, the thermistor resistance falls, the current rises, thereby switching the relay and operating the bell.

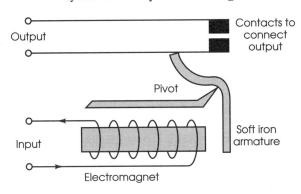

Fig. 13.37 Magnetic relay.

There is a certain *minimum current* needed to make the relay *switch*, and this can be used to make the relay act as a *sensor*.

Fig. 13.39 Thermistor to control relay switching.

**2 > MAKE AND BREAK CIRCUITS – THE ELECTRIC BELL**

This circuit causes the bell to ring continuously by automatically switching the current ON and OFF (making and breaking the circuit). When the switch is closed, current flows, and the electromagnet is magnetised. The soft iron armature is attracted to the electromagnet and the hammer hits the bell gong (Fig. 13.40). This breaks contact with the contact screw and the current stops flowing. The electromagnet loses its magnetism. The springy metal pulls the armature back and contact is made again, so the process repeats as long as the switch is closed. (*NB*. If the electromagnet core and armature were made of steel they would *not* lose their magnetism and the hammer would stay in contact with the gong after only one ring of the bell.)

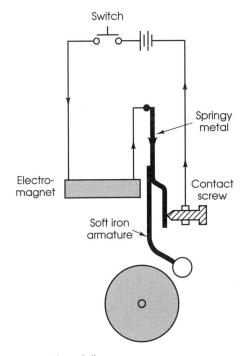

Fig. 13.40 Electric bell circuit.

## 3 > TAPE RECORDERS

The sound is recorded on a narrow strip of plastic tape which has a thin coating of magnetic material bonded to its surface.

**Recording** is carried out by changing the sound wave into an electric current of the same frequency using a microphone. This is made stronger by an amplifier and then sent into a small but powerful electromagnet called the **record head**. As the current changes the field of the magnet also reverses at the same frequency and records the changing pattern on the tape which is moving past the head.

**Fig. 13.41**

**Playback** is done by moving the tape, at the same speed as it was when recorded, past a coil called the **replay head**. The changing magnetic field in the coil induces a current (see chapter 14) of the same frequency. This current is amplified and sent to the loudspeaker which produces sound of the same frequency as the original sound wave. On some recorders the same coil is used as the replay head and record head.

**Erasing** is done by passing the tape by an electromagnet called an **erase head** that has a high frequency alternating current in it. The magnetic field from this is changing so rapidly that the original pattern on the tape is removed.

This process will given an **analogue** recording which may become distorted after a time and is difficult to transmit (see chapter 16).

A **digital recording** is obtained by turning the analogue signal into a series of numbers that represent its amplitude. The numbers are then recorded onto the tape. The quality of the recording will depend on two factors: how often the sound is sampled and how accurately the amplitude is measured. The first is usually stated as a frequency. The bigger the frequency the better the recording. The second is decided by the maximum number of digits (bits) in the binary number that is recorded. If a bigger number with more bits is used the "steps" between the possible amplitudes that can be recorded become smaller. The recording on a compact disc is similar in that a number is recorded but it is as a series of small dents that reflect a laser beam instead of being magnetic.

# EXAMINATION QUESTIONS

## MULTIPLE CHOICE QUESTIONS

## QUESTION 1

Which of the following materials could be used to make the needle of a pocket navigating compass?

A  Magnesium
B  Soft iron
C  Aluminium
D  Steel
E  Brass

(ULEAC)

## QUESTION 2

Two bar magnets are placed so that their north poles are 2 cm apart. Which diagram in Fig. 13.42 best represents the resulting magnetic field?

(ULEAC)

## QUESTION 3

Which one of the following must be made from a material which maintains its magnetism?

A  The commutator for a d.c. motor
B  The magnet in a moving coil meter
C  The core of a transformer
D  The core of an electromagnet
E  The slip rings of an a.c. generator

## QUESTION 4

In Fig. 13.43, the two rectangles represent two light, cylindrical iron cores, about 1 cm apart. The two circuits are identical except that the left-hand one contains a switch. When the switch is closed, the gap labelled X

A  Tends to increase
B  Remains the same
C  Tends to decrease
D  Increases then decreases
E  Decreases then increases

(ULEAC)

Fig. 13.42

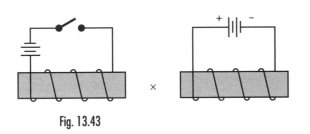

Fig. 13.43

A  From N to S
B  From S to N
C  In the direction of the current
D  Vertically upwards                    (SEG)

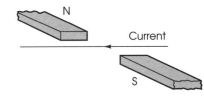

Fig. 13.44

## QUESTION 5

A horizontal wire carries a current in the direction shown in Fig. 13.44 between the magnetic poles N and S of two magnets. The direction of the force on the wire is

STRUCTURED
QUESTIONS

## QUESTION 6

Two metal rods are placed in a long coil as shown in Fig. 13.45. When a direct current flows through the coil the rods move apart. When the current is switched OFF the rods return to their original positions.

Explain your answer.          (NICCEA)

Fig. 13.45

(a)  Why did the rods move apart?
(b)  From what metal are the rods likely to be made? Give a reason for your answer.
(c)  If alternating current from a mains transformer is passed through the coil, what effect, if any, will it have on the rods?

Fig. 13.46

## QUESTION 7

The circuits in Fig. 13.46 show two ways of

(b) Describe a situation where circuit 2 is better than circuit 1 for controlling the motor. (3 lines) (ULEAC)

## QUESTION 8

(a) A bar magnet is supported by a cork so that it floats in a tank of water with its north pole uppermost (Fig. 13.47(a)). A second bar magnet is placed on the side of the tank.

**Fig. 13.47(a)**

**Fig. 13.47(b)**

(i) The fixed magnet will cause two forces to act on the floating magnet when it is held in position A. Add arrows to Fig. 13.47(b) to show the directions of these two forces.

(ii) The floating magnet is now released. Show on the plan view (Fig. 13.47(b)) the subsequent movement of the magnet.

(b) A bar magnet, a piece of soft iron and a compass are all placed on a horizontal bench as shown in Fig. 13.48.

**Fig. 13.48**

(i) State and explain which way the compass needle will turn. (2 lines)

(ii) The soft iron bar is now reversed, end for end, and the experiment repeated. Explain why the compass needle will turn in the same direction as before. (3 lines) (ULEAC)

## QUESTION 9

This question is about converting an analogue signal to a digital signal.

(a) Explain how you know that the signal is analogue.

(b) A digitiser records the voltage every 0.4 ms. Write down the first five voltages in the second column of the table.

**Fig. 13.49**

| Time | Voltage | Code |
|------|---------|------|
| 0 | | |
| 0.4 ms | | |
| 0.8 ms | | |
| 1.2 ms | | |
| 1.6 ms | | |

(c) Convert these voltages into integer codes using the graph (Fig. 13.50). Enter the values in the third column of the table.

**Fig. 13.50**

(d) This code is then recorded onto a compact disc. Draw the output of the CD player when the code is converted back into a voltage signal using the same code again. (MEG)

**Fig. 13.51**

# ANSWERS TO EXAMINATION QUESTIONS

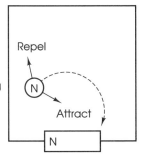

**MULTIPLE CHOICE QUESTIONS**

| Question | 1 | 2 | 3 | 4 | 5 |
|----------|---|---|---|---|---|
| Answer   | D | D | B | C | D |

**STRUCTURED QUESTIONS**

## ANSWER 6

(a) The rods move apart because each has been magnetised in the same direction by the current in the coil. The polarity of a given end is the same for each rod and they repel.

(b) The rods are likely to be made of soft iron. One reason is that when the current is turned off, the rods quickly lose their magnetism and return to their original positions. They must be made of a "soft" magnetic material.

(c) The rods will vibrate, moving away and returning at the frequency of the supply. On each part of the a.c. cycle the rods repel. As the current passes through zero the rods come together again.

## ANSWER 7

(a) When current flows in the relay coil the electromagnet in it becomes magnetic. This attracts the metal in the switch which, in moving, closes the contacts to the second circuit, and turns the second circuit on.

(b) If the motor ran on a high voltage or required a large starting current, the relay would isolate the "used" side of the circuit from the dangerously high value side. Only a small current is needed to activate the relay coil.

Fig. 13.53

## ANSWER 8

(a) (i) and (ii)  Two forces – repelled by N, attracted by S. Pole moves along resultant force direction. See Fig. 13.52.

Fig. 13.52

(b) (i) The needle turns as shown in Fig. 13.53. The soft iron becomes an induced magnet as indicated. The N-seeking end of the compass is repelled.

(ii) The soft iron will not retain this polarity. When it is reversed end Y becomes induced south and X induced north – so no change in the compass needle.

## ANSWER 9

This is a further level short question.

(a) The signal is smooth and continuous.

(b) 0, 0.3, 0.55, 1.05, 0.75.

(c) 0, 3, 6, 11, 8.

(d) Points (not a line) marked correctly with the same values as in (a).

# TUTOR'S QUESTION AND ANSWER

**QUESTION**

Figure 13.54 shows the switching of a high-voltage circuit by a relay operated by a 12 V supply.

(a) Calculate the current flowing in the relay coil if its resistance is 48 $\Omega$.

(b) Calculate the energy transformed in the coil in 2 min.

(c) The relay is wound on a metal core.

(i) State a suitable metal for the core.

(ii) Explain why you think this metal suitable.

(iii) What would happen if the core was made of copper?

(d) Give a reason why the high voltage is switched in this way rather than by inserting a switch directly into the high-voltage circuit. (MEG)

Fig. 13.54

**ANSWER**

(a) $V = IR$, therefore

$$I = \frac{V}{R} = \frac{12}{48} = \underline{0.25 \text{ A}}$$

(b) Energy $= IVt = 0.25 \times 12 \times 2 \times 60$

$= \underline{360 \text{ J}}$.

(c) (i) Soft iron.

(ii) Soft iron is easily magnetised so a small current can operate the coil

and switch the relay on. It easily loses its magnetism so the relay can also switch off.

(iii) Copper is ***not*** a magnetic material so the only field would be that of the coil itself which would not be enough to attract the switch armature.

(d) Safety – the circuit to be switched by a manual operation is isolated from the dangerous high-voltage system.

# STUDENT'S ANSWER WITH THE EXAMINER'S COMMENTS

## STUDENT ANSWER TO QUESTION 7

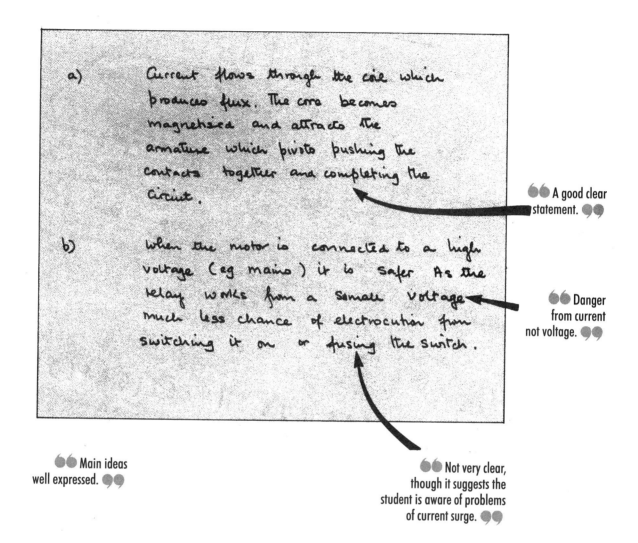

a) Current flows through the coil which produces flux. The core becomes magnetised and attracts the armature which pivots pushing the contacts together and completing the circuit.

**66** A good clear statement. **99**

b) When the motor is connected to a high voltage (eg mains) it is safer. As the relay works from a small voltage much less chance of electrocution from switching it on or fusing the switch.

**66** Danger from current not voltage. **99**

**66** Main ideas well expressed. **99**

**66** Not very clear, though it suggests the student is aware of problems of current surge. **99**

# MORE EXAMINER'S COMMENTS CENTRAL/HIGHER LEVEL

The diagram shows some of the parts in a cassette tape recorder.

tape

record/replay head

erase head    coils

The record/play head consists of a coil of wire wound around a core. When making a recording, an electrical signal passes through the coil to produce a magnetic field. This field leaves a magnetic pattern on the tape.

(a) Explain why recorded tapes should not be stored in a strong magnetic field.

........ *The tapes get wiped* ........................................

.........................................................(1)

*66 The question says explain 99*

(b) When replayed, the magnetic tape passes over the record/replay head.

(i) What effect will this produce in the coil of wire?

......*A charging current is produced*............(1)

*66 Correct 99*

(ii) The signal from the coil of wire is amplified and passes to the loudspeaker. Why does the signal need to be amplified to make the loudspeaker work?

....*So that it has enough energy to drive*...(1)
     *the loudspeaker*

*66 Correct 99*

(c) The pattern on the tape can be destroyed by passing the tape over the erase head. An alternating current passes through a coil around the erase head.

(i) What is an alternating current?

........*It goes to and fro*............................

.........................................................(1)

*66 Very vague! The current flows first in one direction and then the other. This is then repeated. 99*

(ii) How does an alternating current destroy the recording on the tape?

........*It makes a magnet*...........................

.........................................................(1)

*66 The a.c. makes it a changing magnetic field. This new, high frequency pattern is recorded on the tape instead of the original magnetic pattern 99*

# REVIEW SHEET

■ All magnets have _____ poles.

■ Name the three magnetic metal elements.

1. _____.      2. _____.      3. _____.

■ Lines of force are also called _____.

■ Lines of force show the direction that would be taken by a __ pole and therefore often go from a __ pole to a __ pole. The lines will be _____ when the field is stronger.

Fig. 13.55

■ The end A of the iron bar in the diagram will be a _____ pole.

■ Name a use for a relay. _____.

■ The wire in the diagram carries a current as shown by the arrow.

Fig. 13.56

What is the direction of the force on the wire? _____.

What is the name for the sort of magnetic field that produces this force? _____.

State two things that you could do to make the force on the wire greater.

_____  _____.

■ A d.c. motor must have a split ring commutator. Explain *why* the split ring commutator is needed.

_____

_____.

■ Draw a diagram of the split ring commutator.

■ Name three things that you could increase in order to change the design of an electric motor and make it turn faster.

1. _____. 2. _____. 3. _____.

■ Name suitable materials for

1. The coil of a motor. _____

2. The brushes of a motor. _____

3. The permanent magnet of a motor. _____

4. The core of the coil for a relay. _____

5. The armature of an electric bell. _____

6. The core of an electromagnet for lifting ferrous scrap. _____

7. The core of a tape recorder read/write head. _____

■ Which of the above materials will be a soft magnetic material.

_____

■ Write down two advantages and two disadvantages of a digitally recorded signal when compared with an analogue recording.

Advantages: 1. _____

2. _____

Disadvantages: 1. _____

2. _____

■ Using an appropriate diagram explain the working of the electric bell

_____

_____

_____

_____

_____

_____

_____

_____

# INDUCED EMF & AC

## GETTING STARTED

Electricity and magnetism are closely linked. An electric current gives rise to a magnetic field, and current flowing in a magnetic field is acted upon by a force. This can be put to useful effect in the d.c. motor, converting electrical energy to kinetic energy. This section explores the *reverse effect*, obtaining electrical energy from kinetic energy using magnetic flux changes. This has application in various devices including dynamos and transformers. Many such effects rely on a changing or alternating current, and some properties of alternating currents will also be considered.

# ESSENTIAL PRINCIPLES

❝❝ Be careful of using the expression induced CURRENT. Induced currents can occur *as a result of* an induced e.m.f. if a circuit is complete – but the e.m.f. comes FIRST. ❞❞

A single wire connected to a sensitive galvanometer, and moved in a magnetic field as shown (in Fig. 14.1), causes a movement on the galvanometer. This means that a small current flows. The flow occurs **only** when the wire moves, and only then if it **moves across** the magnetic field, **not** when it moves in the same direction as the field.

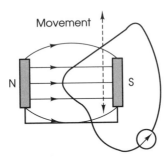

Fig. 14.1 Moving a wire in a field induces an e.m.f.

For current to flow, there must be a source of e.m.f. The e.m.f. is induced in the wire. Current then flows because there is a complete circuit. The e.m.f. can also be induced if a magnet moves relative to a stationary wire. However, the effect is more noticeable if the wire is in the form of a coil or solenoid (Fig. 14.2). Again the e.m.f. only occurs when the magnet moves.

It can be shown, by adapting the experimental arrangement that the **greatest deflection** occurs when:

Fig. 14.2 A magnet moving relative to a coil induces an e.m.f.

1. A large number of turns of coil is used;
2. The magnet is very strong;
3. The magnet moves very quickly.

A **magnetic field** can be pictured as consisting of **lines of magnetic flux**. Figure 14.3 shows the relation between the coil and the magnetic flux of the magnet as the magnet moves towards the coil. The flux linking the coils is changing. The e.m.f. induced is **greatest** when the "flux linkages" are **changing fastest**. The same applies on withdrawing the magnet.

The rule can therefore be simply stated as the **induced e.m.f. is proportional to the rate of change of magnetic flux linking the coil**. In other words, the **more flux** (stronger magnet), the **more links** (more coils) and the **faster speed** (bigger change), the **greater the e.m.f.** This is called **Faraday's Law**. An e.m.f. is induced, whether or not a current flows – current **will** flow if the circuit is complete.

 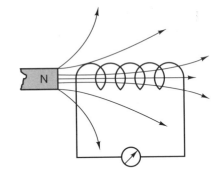

Fig. 14.3 Changing flux "linking" a coil.

In moving a magnet towards or away from a coil, the **direction** of the galvanometer deflection will depend on which way the movement occurs. Consider Fig. 14.4. As the north pole of this magnet moves **towards** the coil, the current flow and therefore the direction of induced e.m.f. are noted to be as

Fig. 14.4

shown, namely *anticlockwise* at end X of the coil. This means that the magnetic field produced by the *induced current* has made end X like a north pole itself – *opposing* the approach of the magnet.

Fig. 14.5 Direction of induced e.m.f.

If the north end moves *away*, the current is *reversed*, and X behaves like a south pole opposing the departure of the north pole (Fig. 14.5). Similarly an approaching south pole gives rise to current making end X like a south pole itself. A south pole leaving the coil makes X like a north pole. **The direction of induced e.m.f. is such as to oppose the motion producing it.** This is called **Lenz's Law.** This sounds very odd, but imagine what

would happen if this were not so. Imagine the north pole of a magnet mounted on wheels and given a small push towards the coil (Fig. 14.6). If the current flowed to make end X a south pole, instead of as really happens, a repelling north pole, then the magnet would be attracted, and accelerate to X. The flux change would be greater, giving a greater induced e.m.f., more current, a stronger attracting field, more acceleration, etc. One small push, and a little work done would produce a huge energy conversion. Energy can only be converted if work is done, so the direction rule for e.m.f. is only a *consequence of energy conservation*.

Fig. 14.6

## 3 GENERATING AN e.m.f. – THE DYNAMO

The e.m.f. induced in all previous examples have been very small, and only occur when a wire moves in a field or a magnet moves relative to a coil. To produce a *continuous source of e.m.f., continuous motion in a field* is required.

### (a) GENERATING AN e.m.f. IN ALTERNATING DIRECTIONS

A coil is wound on a wooden or soft iron armature, and is rotated in a magnetic field provided by the poles of permanent magnets. As side AB moves upwards it cuts the flux of the magnet and an e.m.f. is induced (Fig. 14.7).

The direction of induced e.m.f. in a wire is given, as in a motor, by *Fleming's rule*, but using the *right* hand. Therefore e.m.f. induced is from A to B. Similarly there is an e.m.f. induced from C to D and, if the external circuit is complete, current flows in the direction ABCD. The ends of the coil are in contact with carbon brushes through slip rings, so that side AB of the coil is always in contact with brush X and CD is always in contact with brush Y (Fig. 14.8). When BC is vertical, side AB moves down, and the e.m.f. and current in AB are now in the *opposite direction* to when AB was moving upwards.

Fig. 14.7 a.c. dynamo system.

Fig. 14.8 A slip-ring commutator.

An oscilloscope connected across XY shows that the e.m.f. is continuously changing in size and direction (Fig. 14.9). The maximum e.m.f. occurs when there is the

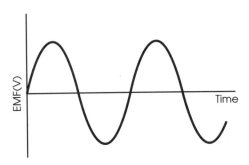

Fig. 14.9 Output waveform from a dynamo.

greatest rate of flux change. When the coil is horizontal as in Fig. 14.10 there is no flux cutting through the coil. A small movement of the coil will "capture" flux, resulting in a *large change* in the situation and the *maximum induced e.m.f.*

Fig. 14.10

Fig. 14.11

With the coil vertical (Fig. 14.11) the maximum flux is linking the coil. However, a small movement will *not* change the linkage by a lot, if at all. There is now zero induced e.m.f.

If the dynamo is rotated more quickly, two effects are noted. Figure 14.12 shows the

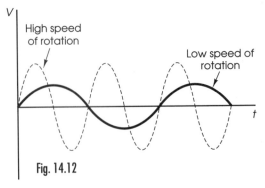

Fig. 14.12

output of a dynamo driven at two speeds. The *faster the rotation* the *greater the*

*frequency of the voltage change*, and the *greater the amplitude of the maximum e.m.f.*, since flux is now being cut more rapidly. This form of dynamo gives an alternating output, the e.m.f. and current change both size and direction.

## (b) GENERATING AN e.m.f. WHICH REMAINS IN THE SAME DIRECTION

It is sometimes convenient to generate an e.m.f. which remains in the *same* direction. There are two ways of achieving this:

Fig. 14.13 Split-ring commutator.

1. *Use of split rings*. If split rings (Fig. 14.13) are used in place of slip rings, then when AB and CD change their direction of induced e.m.f., they also change output contacts X and Y. In this way the output from X and Y are always in the same direction, though the e.m.f. will still vary in size. The waveform of the output is shown in Fig. 14.14. This is called a *full-wave rectified output*.

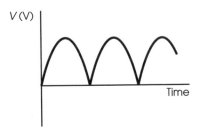

Fig. 14.14 Full-wave rectification.

2. *Bridge rectifier.* This also gives full-wave rectification and is discussed in Chapter 8.

A bicycle dynamo is similar to the a.c. dynamo discussed in this section, except that magnets are usually made to rotate within fixed coils in order to produce the necessary changing flux. The output is, however, the same.

## 4 DYNAMOS AND MOTORS

A dynamo is designed to convert kinetic energy into electrical energy, and a motor converts electrical energy into kinetic energy. The same design applies in each case – both have a coil, magnets and a commutator of some sort contacting carbon brushes. When a dynamo is turned by hand with no external circuit (i.e. no current is drawn) it can be turned easily. However, if it is required to light a bulb, and therefore to supply current, it is much harder to turn. In lighting a bulb,

> 🌑🌑 This is again a consequence of conservation of energy. 🌑🌑

current is flowing in the coil. The force on the current is **opposed** to the original force turning the dynamo, so more **work** must be done to overcome this force.

Similarly when a motor is running, the coil is turning in a magnetic field and flux is being cut. The motor has an e.m.f. induced in its coil which *opposes* the original supply. This is called a **back e.m.f.** and it limits the current flow in the motor.

## 5 A DIFFERENT WAY OF CHANGING FLUX

Fig. 14.15 "Mutual" change of flux.

Figure 14.15 shows two separate circuits containing coils, and wound on to the same piece of soft iron rod. If the switch in circuit 1 is closed, there is a momentary current flow in circuit 2. The same thing happens when circuit 1 is switched OFF, but the flow in circuit 2 is in the *opposite* direction to the way

it flowed before. There is no current in circuit 2 except on switching circuit 1 ON or OFF.

This is a **different** way of inducing an e.m.f. Originally there is no magnetic flux in the soft iron. When the current first flows in circuit 1 flux builds up in the iron, to a steady value. This means that flux is changing in the other circuit, so an e.m.f. is induced while the change is taking place. When the current flow is steady and the flux remains constant there is no induced e.m.f.

On switching circuit 1 OFF, the flux in the iron collapses, again causing a flux change, but in the opposite direction, in circuit 2. If the flux in the first circuit could change continuously, then there would be a continuous e.m.f. induced in the other circuit. This can be achieved using alternating current, and is the principle behind the **transformer**.

## 6 THE TRANSFORMER

Fig. 14.16 Simple transformer.

The circuit is shown in Fig. 14.16. It consists of a central closed soft iron core, which itself is made of laminations, rather than one solid piece of iron. Two coils of insulated copper wire, called the **primary coil** and the **secondary coil**, are wound on the core as shown. If an alternating e.m.f. is applied to the primary coil, an oscilloscope across the secondary shows an alternating e.m.f. across the secondary. If the secondary circuit is completed with a bulb, it will light continuously.

The explanation for transformer action is best split into a **sequence** of **statements**,

explaining what is happening at each stage:

1. The applied alternating e.m.f. drives alternating current through the primary.
2. The alternating current in the primary causes alternating magnetic flux in the core.
3. Changing flux in the core links with the secondary coil and induces an alternating e.m.f.
4. The secondary e.m.f. drives alternating current in a completed secondary circuit.

The size of the induced e.m.f. in the secondary depends on the primary e.m.f., and also on the relative number of turns of wire in the primary and secondary coils.

With 120 turns on the primary side and 240 turns on the secondary side, 6 V a.c. applied to the primary gives about 12 V a.c. at the secondary output (Fig. 14.17). This is called a **step-up transformer**.

Fig. 14.17 Step-up transformer; circuit symbol.

With 240 turns (primary) and 120 turns (secondary) at 6 V input gives about 3 V output; a **step-down transformer** (Fig. 14.18).

Fig. 14.18 Step-down transformer.

The ratio of voltages is the same as the turns ratio, or

$$\frac{V_p}{V_s} = \frac{N_p}{N_s}$$

where $V_p$ = primary voltage;
$\quad V_s$ = secondary voltage;
$\quad N_p$ = number of primary turns;.
$\quad N_s$ = number of secondary turns.

However, the **actual** number of turns must be enough to prevent a coil burning out; 20 on the primary and just 2 on a secondary would result in too much heat generated. There must be enough turns to give reasonable resistance of a few ohms. Although a step-up transformer will give a greater output voltage than its supplied input, it does not multiply energy. **Energy is still conserved** as the following circuit shows.

In order to measure the energy supplied to the primary and secondary circuits, readings of current and voltage are required. This means that **a.c. meters** are necessary, or in the case of voltage measurements a calibrated oscilloscope could be used.

A resistor, or a lamp, is used as a "load" in the secondary to complete the circuit (Fig. 14.19). If the input voltage is 6 V a.c., and the turns ratio is 120 : 240, the output will be near 12 V. If the current in the primary is 0.5 A, then it is found that the secondary current will be about 0.25 A.

Fig. 14.19 Measurement of power in a transformer circuit.

- Power is energy per second.
- Power in primary = $I_p V_p$.
- Power in secondary = $I_s V_s$.
- It is found that **approximately** $I_p V_p = I_s V_s$.
- **Always** $I_p V_p \geqslant I_s V_s$.

So energy is conserved. If the voltage rises, the current **falls** in the same proportion. Stepping down the voltage **increases** the current.

**7  TRANSFORMER EFFICIENCY**

Values quoted in the last section have always been qualified by the words "about" or "approximately". An **ideal** transformer would be one for which

$$\frac{V_p}{V_s} = \frac{N_p}{N_s}$$

and

$$V_p I_p = V_s I_s$$

However in reality, while transformers tend to be very efficient indeed, there are ways in which the energy supplied is converted into other unwanted forms, which leads to **less than** 100 per cent efficiency of conversion. These "losses" can be reduced by good design.

## WAYS OF REDUCING LOSSES IN EFFICIENCY

### 1 ENERGY CONVERTED TO HEAT IN THE COILS

Whenever a current flows, heat is produced, given by $I^2R$. The use of **low-resistance wire** helps minimise this wasted energy.

## 2 HEATING OF THE CORE-EDDY CURRENTS

The core is a magnetic conductor, but also a conductor of electric current. Changing flux in the core induces e.m.f. in the core itself which causes surges (eddies) of current in the core, and produces heat. This is reduced by **laminating the core**.

## 3 FLUX LOSS

The transformer depends, for efficient action, on all flux produced in the primary arriving at the secondary. A square core with sharp edges leads to flux leakage to the air. A *good core design* (e.g. a circle with the secondary wound on top of the primary) can eliminate the source of inefficiency.

## 4 HYSTERESIS

During a cycle of magnetic reversal there is a loss of energy to the magnetic material. *Soft iron* suffers less from this than steel, and is therefore more appropriate as a core material.

## 8 POWER TRANSMISSION

Energy converted at a power station from chemical or nuclear energy to electrical (in most cases) has to be transmitted over long distances through the National Grid system. This means that it has to be transmitted through wires, which have resistance, and which cause wasteful energy conversion into heat.

The fact of energy conversion into heat during transmission is easily illustrated in a laboratory, if a short length of high-resistance wire is used to model the large resistance of many kilometres of wire used in transmission.

The 12 V lamp connected in parallel across the supply glows brightly, indicating that there is a large energy conversion. The lamp at the right-hand side of the high-resistance line only glows dimly. Energy is "lost" from electrical energy to heat and is not available to the lamp (Fig. 14.20). Since energy = power × time the total energy can be found by considering the power at the input and output ends of the line:

$$Power = IV$$

Therefore

$$P_{IN} = P_{OUT} + P_{LOSS}$$

and

$$IV_{OUT} = IV_{IN} - IV_{LOSS}$$

The circuit is a series circuit so the current is the same throughout. This suggests that losses can be reduced by using low currents, because $IV_{LOSS} = I^2R$.

The same arrangement of apparatus driven at 240 V a.c. has two lamps of the same power as before at about the same brightness, so less energy loss is occurring (Fig. 14.21).

At the higher voltage, the current is smaller, and the energy loss is smaller. However, in practice, it is not possible to use a high voltage transmitted directly to a consumer. The answer is to use an alternating

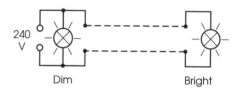

Fig. 14.21 High-voltage power line.

supply which can be transformed to give a high-voltage transmission at low current, and therefore low power loss.

At the generating end the voltage is raised by a factor of 1 : 20, so the current is reduced (Fig. 14.22). Smaller current flows in the wires to the delivery end, so there is less heat loss. Since there is less energy converted to heat, there is more energy conversion at the end of the wires.

*Note*: This experiment produces high voltage and should *not* be carried out by students.

Fig. 14.20 Low-voltage power line.

Fig. 14.22 Use of transformers to reduce power losses.

# EXTENSION MATERIALS

**1** **POWER STATIONS**

In the UK the majority of our electrical energy is generated using oil or coal as a fuel, though there is increasing use of nuclear energy and some additions to the National Grid from "alternative" sources. The sequence produced in a power station is as follows:

1. Heat energy is produced by burning coal or oil, or from fission in the core of a reactor.
2. Water is heated and converted to high-temperature steam, which is also maintained at high pressure.
3. The steam is allowed to expand into a low-pressure region and in doing so it turns the blades of a turbine, after which it is condensed back to water, for use again in the boiling. Condensing the steam requires large cooling towers, and a lot of heat is lost to the atmosphere.
4. The moving turbines rotate generators, producing electricity by electromagnetic induction. The voltage is stepped up by a transformer before transmission. The flow diagrams (Fig. 14.23) show the process, and the energy conversion.

Fuel → Furnace or reactor → Steam generator → Turbine → Generator

chemical → heat → potential → kinetic → electrical

Fig. 14.23

**2** **THE NATIONAL GRID SYSTEM**

The generators at a power station are slightly different from the simple dynamo described earlier. They are designed with a set of coils, producing three separate supplies of a.c. known as a ***three-phase supply***. Each supply is out of phase with the other two, so that there is always current in two of the three wires. Heavy-duty machinery is usually run on a three-phase supply, while an ordinary household has only one phase supplied to it. The supply is generated at 25 kV and stepped up to 400 kV for transmission. A series of transformers, called substations, steps the voltage down for consumption. Industrial users receive the three-phase supply at 33 kV or 11 kV. Households receive one phase at 240 V, with one house in three receiving a particular phase from the three available.

**3** **DIODE PROTECTION**

As we have seen earlier in this section a rapidly changing current in a coil causes a rapid change of flux linkage and an e.m.f. is induced. If there is only one coil the e.m.f. is said to be ***self induced*** and will either oppose a growing current when it is switched off or will help maintain a decreasing current that is being switched off. (This is another illustration of Lenz's law.) This can be quite important when the current to the coil of a relay is switched off. The collapse of the magnetic field is sudden and quite large voltages can be induced. The resulting current, though lasting a short time, can be sufficient to permanently damage transistors or other low voltage hardware.

The transistors can be protected by connecting a diode across the coil as shown in the diagram. The diode is normally reverse biased and does not conduct until the p.d. is self induced in the coil, at which point it conducts the current as shown by the arrow so that the current does not pass down through the transistor but takes the low resistance route through the diode.

Fig. 14.24

# EXAMINATION QUESTIONS

## QUESTION 1

Power losses in the National Grid system are reduced by using

    A   Thin cables
    B   High cables
    C   Underground cables
    D   High voltages       (SEG)

## QUESTION 2

A step-down transformer changes 240 V a.c. to 48 V a.c.. There are 2000 turns on the primary coil. The number of turns on the secondary coil is

    A   40
    B   400
    C   5000
    D   10000       (SEG)

## QUESTION 3

On electricity bills 5p is charged for each "unit" used. This means 5p for each unit of

    A   Electric charge
    B   Electric current
    C   Electrical energy
    D   Electrical voltage      (SEG)

## QUESTION 4

When 24 V is applied across the primary of a transformer, the current in the primary is 2 A. The output voltage from the secondary is 12 V. What is the ratio of the number of turns in the secondary to the number of turns in the primary?

    A   1 : 4
    B   1 : 2
    C   1 : 1
    D   2 : 1
    E   4 : 1       (ULEAC)

## QUESTION 5–7

Signals are applied to the Y-plates of an oscilloscope. Which one of the diagrams in Fig. 14.25 shows the trace obtained in each case?

   5. An alternating voltage with the time base switched OFF.
   6. The same alternating voltage with the time base switched ON.
   7. A voltage from a 1.5 V cell with the time base switched ON.      (ULEAC)

## QUESTION 8

In the National Grid system the transmission

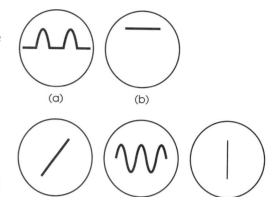

**Fig. 14.25**

of electrical energy is by means of overhead conductors. These conducting wires carry

    A   Alternating current at high voltage
    B   Alternating current at high frequency
    C   Alternating current at low voltage
    D   Direct current at high voltage
    E   Direct current at low frequency
         (ULEAC)

## QUESTION 9

Figure 14.26 represents a simple transformer with 20 turns on the primary coil and 80 turns on the secondary. If 4 V a.c. is supplied to the primary coil, what voltage would you expect across the secondary coil?

20 turns      80 turns

**Fig. 14.26**

  A  4 V        C  100 V
  B  16 V      D  240 V    (ULEAC)

## QUESTION 10

Karen sets up the circuit shown in Fig. 14.27. Which of the traces shown in Fig. 14.28 might be seen on the oscilloscope screen?    (SEG)

To oscilloscope

**Fig. 14.27**

(a)          (b)          (c)          (d)

Fig. 14.28

## QUESTION 11

This question is about supplying a consumer with electrical power from the National Grid system. The voltage across the power lines supplying alternating current to an isolated house is 120000 V (Fig. 14.29). The device D changes the voltage of the supply to 240 V.

(a) What do we call the device D? (1 line)
(b) Why is the supply not transmitted all the way at 240 V? (2 lines)
(c) Why cannot 120 000 V be used, unchanged, in the house? (Give two reasons)
(d) Why is alternating current used? (1 line)          (ULEAC)

Fig. 14.29

Fig. 14.30

## QUESTION 12

An a.c. generator is connected to the Y-inputs of an oscilloscope, as shown in Fig. 14.30. The time base of the oscilloscope is on so that a horizontal line is seen on the screen when the coil is not turning.

(a) Sketch what might be seen on the screen (Fig. 14.31) if the coil is turned at steady speed.
(b) Sketch what you might see on the screen (Fig. 14.32) if the coil is turned at a faster speed.
(c) State two ways in which the generator could be changed so that it would produce a greater e.m.f. (voltage) (2 lines)

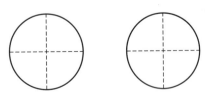

Fig. 14.31          Fig. 14.32

(d) The large a.c. generators used in power stations use electromagnets instead of permanent magnets. They are driven by turbines. Suggest reasons for these differences. (3 lines) (NEAB)

## QUESTION 13

Figure 14.33 shows a power station which generates 100 MW of power. The voltage is stepped up to 400 kV and then power is transmitted by the National Grid over a large distance. The voltage is stepped down before the power is used by industry and homes in a town.

(a) Given that 100 MW is fed into the transmission line at 400 kV, calculate the current flowing in the transmission line. (3 lines)

(b) If the resistance of the transmission line is 100 Ω calculate the potential drop along the line due to the current. (1 line)

(c) Calculate the power "lost" along the transmission line. (2 lines)

(d) Calculate what fraction of the power is "lost". (2 lines)

(e) What happens to the "lost" power? (2 lines)

(f) Explain why less power is "lost" when a given amount of power is transmitted at high voltage and low current, rather than high current and low voltage. (4 lines)

(g) Why is there a saving on the cables when the current is low? (2 lines)

(h) The Electricity Board normally transmits power over long distances using overhead power lines, but the general public would often prefer power lines to be put underground.

(i) Give one advantage of having overhead power lines. (1 line)

(ii) Give one advantage to the general public of having the power lines underground. (1 line)

Fig. 14.33

# ANSWERS TO EXAMINATION QUESTIONS

**MULTIPLE CHOICE QUESTIONS**

| Question | 1 | 2 | 3 | 4 | 5 | 6 | 7 | 8 | 9 | 10 |
|----------|---|---|---|---|---|---|---|---|---|----|
| Answer | D | B | C | B | E | D | B | A | B | D |

**STRUCTURED QUESTIONS**

## ANSWER 11

(a) Device D is a transformer.

(b) The current would be higher to transmit the same power. This would result in greater power losses. Equally, heavier duty cable would be needed, which would be more expensive.

(c) Voltage would be dangerously high for a person to use with safety – equally for a given power appliance the current would be very high indeed.

(d) Alternating current is used because the voltage can easily be stepped up for transmission with low power losses and stepped down for domestic uses.

Transformers do NOT work on direct current.

## ANSWER 12

(a) See Fig. 14.34(a).
(b) See Fig. 14.34(b).

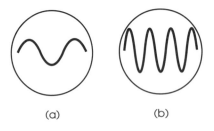

(a)          (b)

**Fig. 14.34**

(c) Possible changes: more turns of wire, stronger magnets, larger area of coil.
(d) Electromagnets are stronger and more easily constructed than large permanent magnets. Turbines are needed because a lot of energy is required to turn the generators.

## ANSWER 13

(a) Power = $IV$. Therefore

$$100 \times 10^6 = I \times 400 \times 10^3$$

Therefore

$$I = \frac{100 \times 10^6}{400 \times 10^3} = \underline{250 \text{ A}}$$

(b) $V = IR$. Therefore

$$V = 250 \times 100 = \underline{25 \text{ kV}}$$

(c) Power = $IV$. Therefore

$$\text{Power} = 25\,000 \times 250 = \underline{6.25 \text{ MW}}$$

(d) Fraction is

$$\frac{6.25}{100} = \underline{0.0625} \text{ or } \underline{6.25\%}$$

(e) Power "loss" is through heat developed in the transmission lines.
(f) For a given amount of power to be transmitted, the higher the voltage the smaller the current. Power losses are given by $I^2R$, so small current results in smaller power loss.
(g) Low current can be transmitted using thin cables thus causing a saving in outlay cost.
(h) (i) Easier repair and maintenance if calbes are overhead.
    (ii) More attractive and unspoiled environment if cables are underground.

# TUTOR'S QUESTION AND ANSWER

**QUESTION**

(a) (i) Draw a labelled diagram of a transformer suitable for converting the 240 V main supply to 12 V a.c.
(ii) If the transformer is ideal and has 80 turns on its secondary (12 V) winding, how many turns should it have on its primary winding?

(b) Explain how the transformer works.
(c) Transformers are not usually 100 per cent efficient. Give a full explanation of two ways in which energy losses occur.
(d) Explain the part played by transformers in the distribution of electrical energy around the country.    (UCLES)

**ANSWER**

**Fig. 14.35**

(a) (i) See Fig. 14.35.
(ii) With a turns ratio of 20 : 1, the primary needs $20 \times 80 = \underline{1600 \text{ turns}}$.

(b) The alternating supply drives alternating current through the primary coil. This produces alternating magnetic flux. The flux passes through the soft iron core, and links with the secondary coil. Since the flux is continuously changing there is an induced e.m.f. in the secondary (alternating) coil which can drive alternating current in a load in the secondary circuit.

(c) The current in the coils will cause a heating effect, which causes the "loss" of some energy. Heating depends on $I^2R$ so low currents and low-resistance wire help eliminate this. Flux changing in the core will induce e.m.f.s in the core itself, so currents, called eddy currents, flow in the core and cause core heating. This is reduced by laminating the core – preventing currents from having a path to flow throughout the core.

(d) Transmission over long distances uses high voltage and low current to prevent excessive power losses (loss through heating proportional to $I^2$). A transformer at the power station is used to give the high voltage (step-up) and at a substation a step-down transformer converts the high voltage to a suitable safe value for household or industrial use.

# STUDENT'S ANSWER WITH THE EXAMINER'S COMMENTS

## STUDENT ANSWER TO QUESTION 13

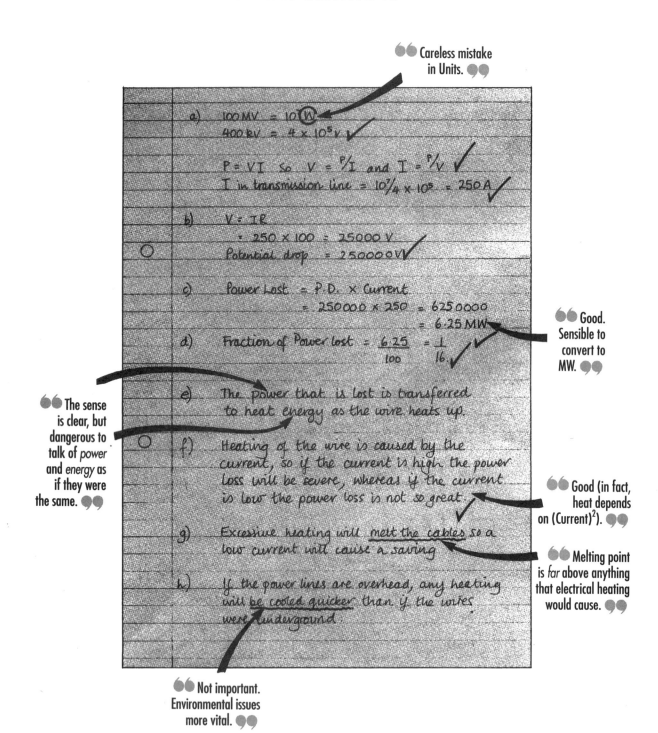

**Careless mistake in Units.**

a) $100 \, MV = 10 \, W$
$400 \, kV = 4 \times 10^5 \, V$ ✓

$P = VI$ so $V = P/I$ and $I = P/V$ ✓
I in transmission line $= 10/4 \times 10^5 = 250 \, A$ ✓

b) $V = IR$
$= 250 \times 100 = 25000 \, V$
Potential drop $= 250000 \, V$ ✓

c) Power Lost $= P.D. \times$ Current
$= 250000 \times 250 = 6250000$
$= 6.25 \, MW$

**Good. Sensible to convert to MW.**

d) Fraction of Power lost $= \dfrac{6.25}{100} = \dfrac{1}{16}$ ✓

e) The power that is lost is transferred to heat energy as the wire heats up.

**The sense is clear, but dangerous to talk of *power* and *energy* as if they were the same.**

f) Heating of the wire is caused by the current, so if the current is high the power loss will be severe, whereas if the current is low the power loss is not so great.

**Good (in fact, heat depends on (Current)²).**

g) Excessive heating will melt the cables so a low current will cause a saving

**Melting point is *far* above anything that electrical heating would cause.**

h) If the power lines are overhead, any heating will be cooled quicker than if the wires were underground.

**Not important. Environmental issues more vital.**

# REVIEW SHEET

■  State Faraday's law: _____

_____.

■  State Lenz's law: _____

_____.

■  Complete the following equations for an ideal transformer.

$V_p I_p =$                                           $\dfrac{V_s}{V_p} =$

■  Power is transmitted at _____ voltage on the National Grid system to avoid

_____ _____.

■  The core of a transformer will be _____ to avoid heat losses.

■  A transformer that increases voltage is a Step _____ transformer.

■  A transformer with 2000 turns on the primary coil and 200 turns on the secondary
coil will be a _____ transformer.

■  Name three ways to increase the output voltage from a generator

1. _____.          2. _____.

3. _____.

■  Sketch the output waveform from a simple a.c. generator

■  A transformer has 240 V a.c. applied to its 1200 turn primary coil. The secondary
coil consists of 5 thick turns of copper. What is the secondary voltage?

_____

_____

_____.

■  If the ends of the secondary coil are joined by an iron nail it becomes red hot.
Explain briefly why this happens.

_____

_____

_____.

■  There are hints here about how electric welders work!

Complete the following table for four transformers.

| Primary volts | Secondary volts | Primary turns | Secondary turns |
|---|---|---|---|
| 240 | 12 | 12 000 | |
| 240 | 2400 | | 1000 |
| | 24 | 120 | 240 |
| 110 | | 200 | 400 |

■ Write under each stage the form of *energy* involved.

■ A magnet is pushed into a coil. Write down three ways in which you could *increase* the e.m.f. produced.

1. _____.     2. _____.

3. _____.

■ A transformer is used to light a 12 V 24 W bulb. If the primary voltage is 240 V what is the current in the primary coil?

_____

_____.

■ Draw a diagram of a simple a.c. generator and label the main parts.

# ATOMIC STRUCTURE AND RADIOACTIVITY

## GETTING STARTED

The model used for a "picture" of a particle of matter so far is a *submicroscopic sphere with no particular structure*. This serves to explain the packing of particles in a solid or the behaviour of gases in Brownian motion or diffusion. It does *not* explain why some materials are good conductors of electricity or of heat, and will certainly not serve to explain the strange behaviour of *radioactive materials*. A revised model is needed to cover these aspects, and to help make accurate future predictions. We need, therefore, to think how the simple "atom" model of kinetic theory should be *adapted* to account for electrical phenomena. This means that we must consider carefully the notion of "moving charges". Equally the discovery that some materials have properties described as "radioactive", means that new ideas about atoms have to be thought through. This section attempts to link the three notions – **atoms** have a substructure which can account for **electrical** properties; within that structure there are **energy** considerations which cause some atoms to be unstable; these ideas give some insight into what an atom may be like.

NO investigation of ionising materials should be carried out by students with this level of knowledge and experience. Experiments on radioactive materials may only be carried out by more experienced students and there are strict rules about supervision, safety, and disposal of waste.

# ESSENTIAL PRINCIPLES

**1 > IDEAS ABOUT CHARGES**

**Charge**, like mass, is a fundamental idea in physics, and yet it is difficult to say what it is! The only way of approaching the idea of charge is to look at what charges **can do**.

## "RUBBING" EXPERIMENTS

It is well known that a piece of insulating material, such as polythene, perspex or PVC, when rubbed on a duster (also an insulator) acquires the property of attracting small objects (Fig. 15.1).

Fig. 15.1 Attraction of uncharged material to charged objects.

The nature of the "attracted" objects does not seem to matter, provided their mass is small, but only an insulating material can cause this attraction. The word "charged" is used to describe **what happens** to the polythene when it is rubbed. The results of this test on many materials suggest as a basic rule that:

- **Charged objects attract uncharged objects.**

The attraction will cause movement of the uncharged object if it has a small mass (and therefore a small weight).

Pairs of charged objects have two possible effects. A strip of charged polythene will

Fig. 15.2 Similar charges repel.

**repel** another strip of charged polythene (Fig. 15.2). However, a piece of charged cellulose acetate is **attracted** by a piece of charged polythene (Fig. 15.3).

Fig. 15.3 Unlike charges attract.

This led to the idea that **two** sorts of charges can be produced, the **types which repel** and the **types which attract**. For simplicity they are called **positive** ⊕ and **negative** ⊖.

- **Similar charges** ⊕ and ⊕ **repel** or ⊖ and ⊖ **repel**.
- **Opposite charges** ⊕ and ⊖ **attract** or ⊖ and ⊕ **attract**.

The model for an atom does not contain "charge" as one of its properties, so the model needs changing to include charges. Since charging happens to a piece of polythene when it is rubbed, then **originally** it must have the charges present in **equal** quantities. Atoms do not usually show charge-like properties **unless** energy is transferred to them in some way. A strip of polythene which has not been charged would have equal ⊕ and ⊖ charges (Fig. 15.4). This seemed to be true for all large-scale pieces of matter. If the polythene is rubbed, there is a transfer of energy and charges may be enabled to move. The **charges which move** are electrons, i.e. **negative charges**. A material which ends up with an **overall negative charge** has **received electrons**; a **positively charged** material has **lost electrons**.

Fig. 15.4 Most objects are electrically neutral.

Fig. 15.5 Charge movement.

A simple diagrammatic, and unrealistic, situation is given in Fig. 15.5. Originally X had equal numbers of $\oplus$ and $\ominus$ charges. After rubbing it gains two extra $\ominus$ charges, so that its *overall* charge is now **negative**. The "rubber", having lost negative charge, now also has an unbalanced situation, with its

*overall* charge being **positive**. Becoming positively charged means **losing electrons**. Charge can be "induced" in an uncharged object. A positively charged rod near an uncharged object attracts it because the mobile electrons redistribute in the uncharged material (Fig. 15.6).

Fig. 15.6 Charge redistribution.

**CURRENT AND CHARGE**

The unit of charge is the **coulomb** (C); 1 C is the charge associated with about $6.2 \times 10^{18}$ electrons.

Fig. 15.7 "Shuttling ball" experiment.

Demonstrations like that illustrated in Fig. 15.7 suggest that an electric current is simply a **flow of charge**. The ball in the diagram is made of polystyrene, but painted with a carbon-based paint (or aluminium paint) to make it conduct. The high-voltage supply connected across the metal plates charges them $\oplus$ and $\ominus$ respectively. If the ball is touched on to one plate it becomes charged and is repelled, moving across to the other where the process is repeated. The ball shuttles to and fro, carrying charges across the gap, and the **ammeter** (a sensitive light-beam meter) records a small current.

A flow of 1 C/s gives a meter reading of 1 A. Therefore

$$\text{Current} = \frac{\text{Charge}}{\text{Time}} \text{ or } I = \frac{Q}{t}$$

(See also direct currents section, Chapter 7.)

In the arrangement of Fig. 15.7 the current was a flow of both $\oplus$ and $\ominus$ charge, in opposite directions – both were contributing to the current and the meter reading was in one direction only. A similar effect occurs if a small flame, from a match or a candle, is placed in the gap between the plates (Fig. 15.8). The flame "splits", being attracted part to one plate and part to the other, and a small current is again recorded. This suggests that a flame contains charges of **both** kinds.

Fig. 15.8 "Flame splitting".

These charges originate in the hot gases of the flame and are called **ions** (Fig. 15.9).

Neutral atom    – ve ion

$+ \ominus = $
Electron

Neutral atom

Loses
electron

+ ve ion
and a free
electron

Fig. 15.9 Ionisation.

Make sure that you remember that:

■ **An atom which gains electrons is a negative ion.**
■ **An atom which loses electrons becomes a positive ion.**

The process, which requires energy, is called *ionisation*.

## 3 THERMIONIC EMISSION

❝❝ Not all syllabuses require knowledge of thermionic emission or the motion of electron streams. Check your own syllabus. ❞❞

Energy is required to cause electrons to be removed from atoms. One way of doing this is by using heat energy. Figure 15.10 shows a

Fig. 15.10 Thermionic emission.

suitable apparatus. A glass tube containing two plates, X and Y, is *evacuated* (i.e. a vacuum between X and Y). X has a small heater circuit behind it which gives energy to the atoms of the metal of plate X. An ammeter and voltmeter are also in the circuit. The following are typical results:

1. With X and Y made negative and positive as shown, no current flows.
2. If X is then heated, and there is a voltage between X and Y of a few hundred volts, a current will flow.
3. If X is heated, but it is made positive and Y is negative, there is again no current.

This suggests that heating X *releases negative particles* (*electrons*) which are attracted to Y, completing the circuit. The release of electrons from a metal by heating is called *thermionic emission*.

An electron "gun" is a useful way of producing a stream of electrons thermionically (Fig. 15.11). The heater and negative

Fig. 15.11 Electron gun.

plate are arranged as before. The positive plate is a cylinder with a hole in it. Electrons are accelerated to the positive plate. Many simply hit the plate and are absorbed by its atoms – but some pass out through the central gap. The greater the voltage between the plates, the more the energy of the electrons, and the greater their velocity. After leaving the area between the plates they travel with constant velocity since there is no longer a resultant force acting on them.

The whole arrangement is still in an evacuated tube since an electron colliding with a gas molecule would lose energy to the molecule.

## 4 ELECTRONS IN ELECTRIC AND MAGNETIC FIELDS

Modifications of the "electron gun" tube can be used to show some other properties of a stream of electrons. The deflection tube (Fig. 15.12) has a gun at one end and a screen coated with a fluorescent chemical inserted into it. This screen is supported by metal plates which can be charged, creating an electric field between the plates.

With no p.d. across the "deflector" plates, and the electron gun arrangement connected, a light is emitted from the screen in a straight line. Electrons hit the screen on emerging from the gun and then kinetic energy is

Fig. 15.12 Electron deflection tube.

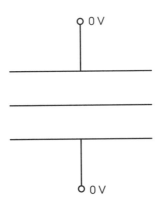

Fig. 15.13 Deflector plates with no potential difference.

Fig 15.15 Fine-beam tube arrangement.

converted to light emitted by the fluorescent material (Fig. 15.13). If the top plate is made positive and the lower plate negative the beam curves upwards. The **amount of curvature** depends on the **voltage** between the plates (Fig. 15.14).

(Fig. 15.15). The region where the electrons hit the screen can be placed in a strong magnetic field, using either permanent magnets or a pair of coils. With the field into the plane of the page, the deflection is downwards, and with the field out, the deflection reverses, to be upwards (Fig. 15.16).

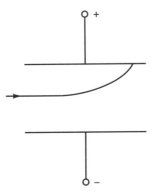

Fig. 15.14 Electrons deflected by an electric field.

Fig. 15.16 Magnetic field deflection.

This is like the effects seen in **electromagnetism**. If the charge flow (current) and field are at right angles, the direction of the force on the charges is at 90° to both field and charge flow.

Electron streams constitute a current, and can therefore be deflected by magnetic fields.

Reversing the polarity of the plates reverses the force on the electrons, and the direction of movement. Electrons can be deflected by electric fields. The force on the charges acts towards the positive plate. This reinforces the idea that electrons carry negative charge. A similar arrangement, with no p.d. between the plates, can be used to show the effect of a magnetic field

*Note*: Sometimes the apparatus is slightly different to that shown. The various electrodes are the same but the screen is made by coating the end of the tube with a phosphor. With no fields applied the electron beam will make a dot at the centre of the screen. Electric fields will move the dot up or down and magnetic fields will move the spot horizontally.

**5 > ATOMS, ELECTRONS AND IONS**

At this stage some statements about these particles may be helpful:

1. An atom is the **smallest** particle which is recognisable as having properties which are also those of larger groups of atoms. Atoms are electrically neutral.
2. Atoms must, within themselves, have **electrical charges** called ⊕ and ⊖ charges.
3. The **negative charges** are fairly mobile. They are called **electrons**.
4. To release electrons from atoms, **energy** is required.

5. A **stream of moving electrons** is the same as an **electric current**.
6. A stream of electrons is **deflected** by both **electric** and **magnetic fields** and can cause **fluorescence** of some chemical compounds.
7. An **ion** is an atom which has **either gained electrons (negative ion)** *or* **lost electrons (positive ion)**.

## 6 ▷ RADIOACTIVE MATERIAL

## (a) HANDLING RADIOACTIVE MATERIALS

Radioactive sources used in schools are usually very weak, but care must be used in handling them.

> 1. *Forceps* should always be used in moving a source; the source should *not* be touched with bare hands.
> 2. Sources should be held so that they point *away from* the body.
> 3. Sources should *not* be brought close to the eyes.
> 4. When using radioactive sources, an *authorised person* must be in attendance. Sources should be stored in a locked and labelled store.
> 5. On handling sources, you should *wash your hands before eating.*

❝❝ Even weak sealed sources may only be handled by students who are over 16 years old (DES regulation). ❞❞

## (b) DETECTING RADIOACTIVITY

All radioactive sources cause *ionisation,* and detection methods all rely in some way on detecting the ions which are produced. A simple demonstration uses a gold leaf electroscope. This can be charged positive or negative using an EHT (Extra High Tension) power supply (Fig. 15.17). The electroscope casing is connected to the earthed negative terminal of the EHT and the positive terminal is touched with a flying lead to the electroscope cap. This charges the electroscope positively and the gold leaf *rises* (positive charges repelling the leaf).

❝❝ EHT stands for "Extra High Tension" meaning a power supply capable of several kilojoules of energy per coulomb! ❞❞

Fig. 15.17 Charging an electroscope from EHT.

A flame, which contains ions of both types, brought near the cap causes the leaf to fall rapidly, discharging the electroscope – the negative charges in the flame neutralise the positive charge (Fig. 15.18). If a *radioactive source* is brought near the charged cap, a similar effect occurs, suggesting that the source causes *ionisation* of the air near the cap.

## IONISATION

All radioactive materials cause ionisation, and it is this property which enables detection of

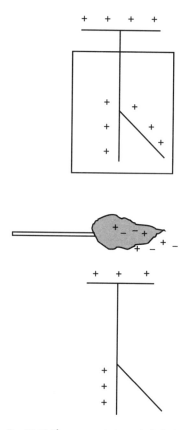

Fig. 15.18 Flames contain ions which discharge a charged electroscope.

radioactivity and helps our understanding of what happens in radioactive decay. The most versatile method of detecting radiation is the *Geiger-Müller tube* connected to some form of counting device. The whole arrangement is often called a *Geiger counter.* The "count" can be a sound pulse, or a digital electronic counter. The Geiger counter only operates when there is a p.d. of about 400 V across the tube. It is measuring *ionisation caused by radioactive sources.*

## MEASUREMENTS WITH A GEIGER COUNTER

Fig. 15.19 Geiger tube and counter.

The tube and counter are arranged as shown in Fig. 15.19. With no radioactive source near the tube, a small count will be registered, about 16–30 counts per minute. This is called the *background count.* The background count is caused by radiation from space and from naturally occurring sources in the earth. Experimental measurements with radioactive sources should take account of background figures, especially if the source is weak.

Measurements are taken as ***count rates,*** meaning the number of counts in a particular period of time, for example in 1 min. An average over several time intervals should be taken.

## (c) ABSORPTION OF RADIATION

Radioactive matgerials emit three recognised forms of radiation:

1. α (**alpha**)-particles;
2. β (**beta**)-particles;
3. γ (**gamma**)-waves (sometimes called γ-rays).

Fig, 15.20 Absorption of ionising radiation.

These behave differently when materials are placed between the source and the detector (Fig. 15.20).

- ■ α-particles are ***absorbed*** by thin paper or card, or even by travelling through 10–20 cm of air.
- ■ β-particles can ***penetrate*** card, but a thinsheet of aluminium foil will absorb them.
- ■ γ-waves show a ***reduced count rate*** on passing through several centimetres thickness of lead, but the count is still above the background count.

The α and β particles hit atoms and ***knock electrons off*** them causing ***ions*** to be formed. Each collision takes some energy and the particle is slowed until it eventually doesn't have enough energy to cause any more ionisation. α *particles are relatively large* (in atomic terms) and therefore hit a lot of atoms in short distance and go out in straight lines. Their range is short but the ionisation is concentrated. β *particles are much smaller* (they are high speed electrons) and therefore travel between some of the atoms without hitting them so that the range is greatly increased. As they slow down they will be deflected more by the collisions and their tracks can show random changes in direction. The ionisation caused will be much more spread out than that caused by α.

γ radiation is quite different as each γ is a short burst of electromagnetic waves called a ***photon.*** The waves are very short wavelength, high frequency waves and they are very penetrating and carry a lot of energy.

They will pass between most other particles but, when they do hit one, all the energy is used in the one ionisation releasing an electron with enough energy to behave rather like a β particle and cause more ionisation.

## (d) ELECTRIC AND MAGNETIC FIELD EFFECTS

If a source which emits all three types of radiation is arranged as shown in Fig. 15.21, and if at first there is no magnetic field present, the count rate can be recorded and corrected for background count. If the field is then applied, using either a strong permanent magnet or a

Fig. 15.21 Deflection of ionising radiation in a magnetic field.

strong electromagnet, and the position of the Geiger tube changed, it is found that the following effects occur:

1. β-particles are deflected in such a direction as to suggest that they carry negative charge.
2. α-particles are deflected by a much smaller amount, and in the opposite direction to β-particles.
3. γ-waves are not deflected at all.

The identification of α, β and γ could be achieved by noting the ***absorption properties*** in the three positions of the tube.

In a similar way, an ***electric field*** shows that:

- ■ β have the properties of negative charge;
- ■ α have the properties of positive charge;
- ■ γ show no charge properties.

Since α and β show ***different amounts of deflection,*** they must also have ***different masses.***

Further experiments show that:
- ■ α-particles are ***helium nuclei,*** consisting of two protons and two neutrons. They have two units of positive charge.
- ■ β-particles are the same as electrons. They have negative charge and 1/1800 the mass of a proton.
- ■ γ-waves are high-frequency eletromagnetic waves, like short-wavelength X-rays.

## (e) UNITS FOR MEASUREMENT

Radioactive sources have to be measured in terms of their activity rather than their mass.

A small mass of short half life could be much more dangerous than a larger mass with a very long half life that was emitting very little radiation. An activity of one decay per second is called a **bequerel** (Bq).

Sources used to be measured in curies (Ci) where

$$1 \text{ Ci} = 3.7 \times 10^{10} \text{ Bq}.$$

This is a very large unit and sources for schools were about 5 μCi. The same source would now be simply stated as 185 kBq.

The effect of the radiations on human tissue is different for the three types. Alpha radiation is about 20 times more dangerous to us than beta or gamma. The dose received by a person is measured in units called **sieverts** (Sv) which take into account the type of radiation and the organs affected.

A dose of 10 Sv can be fatal. A year's dose from background and routine X-rays or aircraft flights (where there is less atmosphere to protect you from cosmic radiation) will be about 0.003 Sv.

## 7 A MODEL FOR AN ATOM

The simple model of an atom as a neutral object has now acquired new properties. It can be **ionised,** so it must have both ⊕ and ⊖ charges. Atoms of different elements are chemically different, so the differences must be explained. Some atoms are radioactive and emit positive or negative particles or electromagnetic -waves.

Part of the solution to the problem came from the experiment conducted by **Geiger and Marsden,** under the supervision of **Rutherford.** The experiment is simple: the results are surprising.

A source of α-particles is arranged to direct an α-particle beam at a thin metal foil (gold, silver and platinum are typical). The particles pass through the foil and are detected on emerging from it. The whole apparatus is in a vacuum tube, to prevent energy loss through

gas ionisation. At the "straight through" position, $D_1$, most α-particles are detected (Fig. 15.22).

As the detector is swung through an angle, $D_2$, fewer and fewer are detected, but some can be detected as having moved through an angle of 90°. Most surprisingly, a few particles are detected at large angles, when the detector is in a position such as $D_3$. They seem to have bounced back from the foil.

α-particles from the source have large energy and positive charge. It is no surprise that most pass through the foil, losing little energy, but the few which deflect through large angles must have encountered a **large force** to stop them and to return them in their original direction. Rutherford, analysing the results, concluded the following:

1. If most α-particles can pass through atoms with no effect, then most of an atom must be **space.**
2. If a few α-particles are given large deflections, then within that space they must find a positive charge which is great enough to repel them.
3. Since few α-particles return, compared with the many which pass through the atom, the positive charge of the atom must occupy a very small volume.

He called the **positive centre** of the atom the **nucleus.**

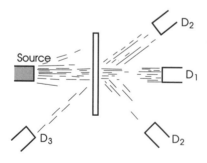

Fig. 15.22 The scattering of α-particles by thin foils.

## 8 ATOM STRUCTURE AND ELEMENTS

### (a) NUCLEUS

Rutherford was aware that his "nucleus" had no electrons in it – since the nucleus has positive charge. An atom must, then, be a nucleus ⊕ with electrons ⊖ occupying the space around the nucleus. Electrons have a very small mass, so most of an atom's mass consists of the nucleus.

The nucleus itself is made up of two further particles: **protons,** which have one unit of ⊕ charge and one unit of mass, and

**neutrons,** which have one unit of mass and no charge.

A neutral atom has the same number of **electrons ⊖ outside** the nucleus, as there are **protons ⊕ inside** it.

A simple, **but incorrect,** picture of the structure of an atom looks like a small solar system, with the nucleus at the centre and the electrons moving like planets. The more likely picture is a very **chaotic** one, but the solar system model is easier to understand (Fig. 15.23).

Fig. 15.23 Nuclear model of an atom.

## (b) CHEMIST'S TABLE OF MASS ORDER

The simplest atom of all is the *hydrogen atom.* It has a nucleus with one mass unit and one unit of positive charge (i.e. a proton). It must also have one electron to balance the charge of the proton (Fig. 15.24).

Fig. 15.24 A model for the hydrogen atom.

**Helium** is the next atom in the chemist's table of mass order. It has two electrons outside a nucleus which has two protons (positive charge) but it has four mass units. The mass of the nucleus must be made up then of two protons and two neutrons (Fig. 15.25).

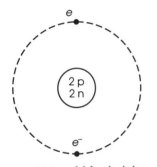

Fig. 15.25 A model for the helium atom.

All atoms are made up in the same way:

- The total mass is all in the nucleus which is made up of protons ⊕ and neutrons (no charge).
- The proton ⊕ charge is balanced by the electrons ⊖ charge.
- Electrons have very small mass, and can be discounted for their mass contribution.

**Uranium** and **thorium** are both naturally occurring radioactive materials. They have an excess of neutrons in their nuclei and this may be a clue to the reason for their radioactive nature.

## (c) SYMBOLS

Chemists use *symbols* to write down the names of atoms, H for hydrogen. O for oxygen, Cu for copper and so on. A physicist uses these to write out what a nucleus is like, and *adds numbers to the symbol* to say how much charge and how much *mass* is present:

- $^1_1H$ is a **hydrogen** nucleus;
- $^4_2He$ is a **helium** nucleus;
- $^{16}_8O$ is an **oxygen** nucleus.

The *top number* is called the *nucleon number.* It is the *total number of protons and neutrons in the nucleus* (i.e. the total particles making up the nuclear mass). The *lower number* is called the *proton number.* It is the *total positive charge in the nucleus* and is therefore the same as the total number of electrons in a neutral atom.

## (d) ISOTOPES

Sometimes atoms occur which are identical except for the number of neutrons in the nucleus. Such atoms are *isotopes.* They will belong to the same element because they have the same number of protons and they will have identical chemistry. One will be slightly more massive than the other. Some elements have several stable isotopes.

$^1_1H$ and $^2_1H$ are isotopes of hydrogen. $^2_1H$ is called Deuterium and is sometimes known as "heavy hydrogen".

$^{35}_{17}Cl$ and $^{37}_{17}Cl$ are isotopes of chlorine. There is about three times as much of the first isotope as the second in natural chlorine so that its average mass is 35.5. Sometimes an isotope has a nucleus with a number of neutrons that is not quite stable. It will then throw out a piece of the nucleus – it will be radioactive, and is called a radioisotope.

---

## 9 ▷ RADIOACTIVE DECAY

Nuclei do not emit radiation for ever. Eventually they become stable and behave like ordinary atoms with no excess of energy. The process is called *decay.* This can be investigated in a laboratory using a source which decays (becomes stable) quickly.

A sealed source called a **protactinium generator** can be used to demonstrate radioactive decay. When the generator is shaken and inverted the liquid in it chemically separates a small quantity of a radioactive material. Place a Geiger tube above and close to the source and record the count rate after each half minute. Plotting a graph of count rate against time produces the sort of graph shown in Fig. 15.26 (called an exponential curve) and enables the *half life* to be determined.

Fig. 15.26

Similar experiments can be carried out with appropraite sources and a Geiger counter. The results always show the same pattern, though the time-scale will be different for different sources.

1. The decay is *random.* You cannot exactly predict what the count will be at any time. (This is particularly noticeable in recording background counts.)
2. The overall pattern is one of *decreasing activity* (Fig. 15.27).

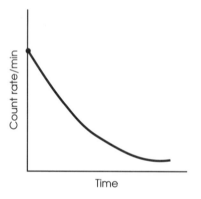

Fig. 15.27 Decay of count rate (activity) with time.

Apart from the decrease in count rate, it is found that the *decay* has the *same mathematical pattern* for *all* sources.

This is illustrated in Fig. 15.28. The time taken for the count rate to fall from 5000 counts per minute to 2500 counts per minute

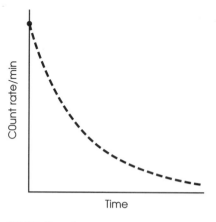

Fig. 15.28 Radiator decay.

(i.e. to reduce the activity by a half), is the *same* as the time to fall from 3000 counts per minute to 1500 counts per minute. In fact the time for a radioactive source to decay in activity from any value to half that value is the same for that particular source, and cannot be altered by external changes of temperature, pressure, etc. This time is called the *half-life* of the source, and it can vary from source to source from fractions of a second to millions of years.

---

**Half-life** can be defined in a number of ways:

1. The time for the activity of a source to be reduced by half its original value.
2. The time for a given number of radio-active nuclei in a source to be reduced by half.
3. The time for a given mass of active material to be reduced by half. So if 68 g of radioactive material is originally present, and it has a half-life of 12 h then after 12 h there will be 34 g still active; after 24 h, 17 g is still active; after 36 h, 8.5 g is still active . . .

---

## NUCLEAR CHANGES AND RADIOACTIVE DECAY

While a nucleis is emitting radiation it is removing particles or changing its energy by emitting $\gamma$-waves. Each $\alpha$-particle emitted consists of a helium nucleus $^{4}_{2}He$, which means two protons and two neutrons. Each $\beta$-particle means emitting an electron. If a nucleus emits particles it becomes a different chemical element, since each element has its own pattern of protons, neutrons and electrons. *$\alpha$-particle decay* is shown by a particular uranium nucleus, $^{238}_{92}U$. This has 92 protons and 146 neutrons in its nucleus. Removal of an $\alpha$-particle means removing 2 neutrons and 2 protons. This changes the nucleus to a new material, thorium. The following equation shows the effect:

$$^{238}_{92}U \xrightarrow{\ \alpha\ } {}^{234}_{90}Th + {}^{4}_{2}He$$

($\gamma$-waves are also emitted. These do *not* change the type of nucleus, but help stabilise its energy.)

▶ In *general* if a nucleus of an element X is $^{A}_{Z}X$ where A = nucleon number and Z = proton number, then $\alpha$-particle decay gives a new material Y where

$$^{A}_{Z}X \xrightarrow{\ \alpha\ } {}^{A-4}_{Z-2}Y + {}^{4}_{2}He$$

*$\beta$-particle decay* is a little harder to understand, since $\beta$-particles are the same as electrons, and the nucleus does *not* contain electrons. However, the neutron in the

nucleus is itself unstable and can at times behave like a proton–electron combination:

$$_0^1n \rightarrow _1^1p + _{-1}^0e \text{ emitted as } \beta\text{-particle}$$

If a $\beta$-particle is emitted then the **mass of the nucleus is not changed** but the **proton number** (number of positive charges) **is increased by one**, and **again the nucleus**

**is changed**. A typical $\beta$-particle decay is shown by strontium:

$$_{38}^{90}Sr \xrightarrow{\beta} _{39}^{90}Y + _{-1}^0e$$

(again energy is also emitted in the form of $\gamma$-waves).

The general equation is

$$_Z^AX \xrightarrow{\beta} _{Z+1}^AY + _{-1}^0e$$

# EXTENSION MATERIALS

## 1 > CLOUD CHAMBERS

Fig. 15.29 Cloud chamber.

This is another method by which the effects of a radioactive source can be noted. It again relies on ionisation but the effects are **visible.** The principle is simple. A mixture of air and water vapour is cooled to the point where the water molecules are about to condense. The presence of charged particles, like ions, enables **condensation** to take place, and a trail of condensing liquid droplets forms along the path of any such ions.

The saturated vapour is contained in a "cloud chamber" (Fig. 15.29) and is cooled by using solid carbon dioxide. A radioactive source inserted in the chamber emits particles ($\alpha$ or $\beta$) or ionising $\gamma$-waves. Water droplets condense around the ions leaving **visible**

**tracks**, illuminated by a light source. The tracks differ, depending on how heavily the original radiation caused ionisation of the air. Typical tracks are shown in Fig. 15.30.

- $\alpha$-tracks are straight and easily seen, because $\alpha$-particles cause a lot of ionisation. They are about the same length, showing that each $\alpha$ has about the same energy.
- $\beta$-tracks are less clear since they cause less ionisation. They show straight tracks for high kinetic energy particles, but a slower-travelling $\beta$-particle is easily deflected by electrons of the atoms in the chamber and gives rise to sudden direction changes.
- $\gamma$-waves leave no direct tracks, but are able to eject electrons from atoms and these low-energy electrons leave faint patterns.

In the particular case of $\alpha$-sources, the tracks occasionally show an additional interesting piece of behaviour. The tracks caused by ionisation are typically thick and straight and can be seen to be **randomly** produced. Very infrequently, tracks show a **fork** (Fig.

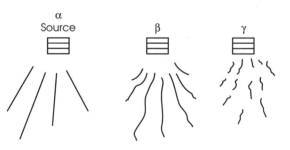

Fig. 15.30 Particle tracks in a cloud chamber.

15.31), resulting from the approach of a positively charged ∝-particle to a nucleus. The α and the nucleus **repel** each other and the angle of the fork depends on the relative masses of the α-particle and nucleus. In the particular case where the cloud chamber is filled with helium gas, the fork is a right angle. This follows since α-particles and helium nuclei are identical, and since collision between identical masses gives rise to this particular behaviour.

Fig. 15.31 The rare occurrence of a nuclear collision.

## 2 MEDICAL APPLICATIONS

All radioactive sources cause ionisation; background radiation accounts for about 78 per cent of the total radiation dose received each year by an average person in the UK. Apart from this there is a further likely dosage from medical applications like X-rays which also cause ionisation, and a very small (0.4%) amount from the fall-out of nuclear waste disposal or weapons testing. The body can clearly withstand a limited exposure to ionising radiation. Stronger doses cause ionisation of body cells, which can be changed or destroyed in the process. All exposure to radiation **can** cause damage in this way. Large doses can produce cancers and genetic change producing hereditary defects in the children of people exposed to radiation.

On the positive side, carefully controlled radiation doses can be used to kill cancer cells, and there is widespread use of γ-radiation to kill bacteria, as in the sterilisation of medical instruments where heat would damage the material (e.g. plastic replacement joints).

Radio-isotopes can also be given internally to patients for diagnostic tests, typically to produce images of parts of the body, like the lungs or kidneys, which are transparent to X-rays. The source is usually a γ-wave emitter which causes little ionisation inside the body, but which will affect a photographic plate giving an image of the organ to be examined.

## 3 INDUSTRIAL USES

A radioactive substance added to a liquid or gas in a pipeline in an industrial plant can be used to measure flow rate and to detect leakage. γ-radiation can pass out of pipes so that a Geiger counter or other detector will reveal the rate of flow of the fluid, or the position of any leaks in a building complex or in an underground system of pipes.

Control of the thickness of metal sheets, or of paint layers, can be achieved by sending radiation through the material on a production line. A radiation detector measures the intensity of (usually) β-radiation; **variations** in intensity can be fed back to the machinery to cause standardisation of sheet thickness.

## 4 FISSION AND NUCLEAR REACTORS

When the nucleus of some large atoms is hit by a neutron the neutron is absorbed for a very short time and then the new nucleus splits into two parts together with some more neutrons. This is called **fission**. The energy needed to hold together the new smaller nuclei is less than the original large nucleus and the surplus **binding energy** is released as heat. If the masses of all the parts before and after the fission are checked very carefully, it is found that there is a small loss of mass which has been converted into energy and obeys Einstein's $E = mc^2$ equation (where E = energy, m = mass and c = the velocity of light). Only certain nuclei will produce this effect and the best known ones are the nuclides $^{235}U$ and $^{239}Pu$.

e.g. Fission of uranium-235.

$$^{235}_{92}U + ^{1}_{0}n \rightarrow ^{236}_{92}U \rightarrow \begin{array}{c} 2 \text{ or } 3 \text{ neutrons} \\ + \\ 2 \text{ nuclei} \\ + \\ \text{ENERGY} \end{array}$$

It is then possible for some of the new neutrons to go on and hit other nuclei and cause them to fission. If this process continues it is called a **chain reaction**. If the mass of the fuel is very small the neutrons leave it without hitting another nucleus and

**Fig. 15.32**

the reaction stops. If the mass is big enough, one neutron (on average) will hit another nucleus and cause it to fission so that the chain reaction carries on. This mass, where the chain reaction is just maintained, is called the *critical mass*. If the mass is bigger than the critical mass, then more than one neutron hits another nucleus and the chain reaction starts to grow. Since the atoms are very close together this will happen very rapidly and in a very short time millions of atoms are splitting at the same time releasing huge amounts of energy in a nuclear explosion. This is the basis of atomic weapons.

In a *nuclear reactor* the chain reaction is controlled by removing some of the neutrons. The energy appears as heat which is steadily removed from the reactor core and used to boil water to make steam. The steam is then used in the same way as in other types of power station (i.e. it drives turbines which in turn drive generators to produce the electricity). The main parts of the reactor are shown in Fig. 15.32.

The main parts of the reactor have the following purposes:

- *fuel pins:* The fuel pins or rods are made from stainless steel and contain the *uranium* or *plutonium* fuel. They are lowered into the centre of the reactor (the reactor core) and can be taken out again when the fuel in them is used up ("spent"). The rods will then contain the *"fission products"* which include the new nuclei produced when the fuel atoms split. These new isotopes will include many dangerously radioactive ones and the spent fuel needs careful treatment. The rods are first put into a large pool of water and left there until the short half-

life nuclides have decayed. Water is used because it is quite good at absorbing the neutrons that are being produced. The rods are then stripped open by remote control in a sealed workshop and the remaining chemicals dissolved in acid so that they can be chemically separated. The long half-life isotopes that are still dangerous are then stored until they can be safely disposed of. One way of doing this is to seal the radioactive material in glass or ceramic bricks so that it cannot leak away and then bury the bricks in caves in a stable rock.

- *Moderator:* The neutrons that are produced in the fission have too much kinetic energy for them to be easily absorbed and produce another fission. The moderator, which is usually made of graphite or water, slows down the neutrons so that they are more likely to be captured by a $^{235}U$ nucleus. A reactor that operates using these slower neutrons is a *thermal reactor.*

- *Control rods:* The chain reaction has to be controlled so that the reaction is just "critical"; i.e., it is just keeping itself going. The control rods are made from cadmium or boron steel which are good at absorbing neutrons. If the reaction goes too fast the rods are lowered further into the reactor so that they absorb neutrons and the reaction is slowed down. The reactor will have a lot of this type of rod so that they can all be put into the core and shut the reactor down quickly in any sort of emergency.

- *Coolant:* The purpose of the reactor is to produce heat and this heat must be steadily removed from the core as it is produced by the chain reaction. The heat is removed by sending a coolant through the core and then sending the coolant through a heat exchanger. The coolant may be carbon dioxide or water (under pressure so that it does not boil) and it is circulated in a closed circuit so that radioactivity is not transferred to the outside.

The materials of the reactor will absorb neutrons and become radioactive. (Materials can deliberately be made radioactive in this way – isotopes for medical use, tracers, genetic research, etc.) The reactor must be *shielded* to prevent radiation leaving and should be contained in a *pressure vessel* that can withstand accidents and prevent the loss of radioactive material. The coolant circuit should be completely closed for the same reason. The proportion of fissionable material in the core of a reactor is not large

enough to cause an explosion after an accident but it can produce enough heat to cause a *"melt-down"*. The pressure vessel containing the core should be able to withstand this for a while but, because of the huge quantities of energy available, there would be serious consequences. (Chernobyl.) Modern reactors are designed to be shut down very quickly in the case of accidents such as a loss of coolant.

A properly managed reactor can produce a lot of electricity with little or no pollution to the air or surrounding countryside. It does not require very large quantities of chemical fuel and does not produce large waste tips or spoil heaps. The waste products are the main problem in that they have long half-lives and present long term problems in safe storage or disposal. Dismantling the power station at the end of its life may be very difficult and expensive.

# EXAMINATION QUESTIONS

## QUESTION 1

The name of one type of particle found in the nucleus of an atom is

A  An ion
B  An electron
C  A molecule
D  A proton
E  An isotope
(NISEAC)

## QUESTION 2

When a polythene rod is rubbed with a duster, the rod becomes negatively charged. This charge is caused by the transfer of

A    Electrons from the duster to the rod
B    Atoms from the duster to the rod
C    Protons from the duster to the rod
D    Electrons from the rod to the duster
(SEG)

## QUESTION 3

Fig. 15.33

In Fig. 15.33 a positively charged plastic rod is brought close to a metal rod XY on an

insulated stand. How are the charges redistributed in the rod?

A    Negative charges at both ends of the rod
B    Positive charges at both ends of the rod
C    Negative charges at end X and positive charges at end Y
D    Positive charges at end X and negative charges at end Y  (ULEAC)

## QUESTION 4

A mercury atom contains 80 protons, 80 electrons and 120 neutrons. How many particles are there in its nucleus?

A  80
B  120
C  200
D  280          (ULEAC)

## QUESTION 5

Which of the following statements about nuclear fission is true?

A    Atoms gain electrons to form ions.
B    Several atoms combine to form a molecule.
C    A nucleus splits into smaller nuclei.
D    The materials used must be in a strong magnetic field.
E    The atom loses all its electrons.

## QUESTION 6

The half-life of radioactive carbon is 5600 years. What will be the time after which the activity has reduced to one-quarter?

A  1400 years      D  11 200 years
B  2800 years      E  22 400 years
C  8400 years         (NICCEA)

## QUESTION 7

Which statement about the half-life of a radioactive substance is true?

A   It always remains the same.
B   It increases with pressure.
C   It is affected by chemical reactions.
D   It becomes less as time goes on.
E   It varies with the temperature of the substance.

## QUESTION 8

A nucleus contains 12 protons and 15 neutrons. Which one of the following gives the proton number and nucleon number?

|   | Proton number | Nucleon number |
|---|---|---|
| A | 12 | 15 |
| B | 12 | 27 |
| C | 12 | 12 |
| D | 15 | 27 |
| E | 27 | 12 |

## QUESTION 9

Which one of the following best describes beta particles emitted by a radioactive substance?

A  Atoms      D  electromag-
B  Electrons          netic energy
C  Ions      E  Neutrons

## QUESTION 10

| Count rate per second | 55 | 35 | 15 | 5 | 6 | 5 |
|---|---|---|---|---|---|---|
| Thickness of aluminium (mm) | 0 | 2 | 4 | 6 | 8 | 10 |

The table shows how the count rate varied as the thickness of an aluminium absorber was increased between a beta source and a detector. The count rate does not fall to zero because

A   The thickness of aluminium is not great enough.
B   Aluminium cannot absorb beta radiation completely.
C   There is background radiation of about 5 counts per second.
D   The beta particles are deflected by the aluminium.
E   The energy of the beta particles is too great.     (NICCEA)

**STRUCTURED QUESTIONS**

## QUESTION 11

(a)  State the nature of each of the following radiations (1 line for each):
    (i)   Gamma radiation;
    (ii)  Ultraviolet radiation;
    (iii) Beta radiation;
    (iv) Infra-red radiation;
    (v)  Alpha radiation.
(b)  Which, if any, of the radiations listed in (a)
    (i)   does not travel at the same speed in a vacuum as visible light   (1 line);
    (ii)  are not emitted from the nucleus of an atom.   (1 line)
(c)  When radiation passes through matter, it may cause ionisation.
    (i)   Explain briefly what is meant by ionisation.   (1 line)
    (ii)  Which of the radiations listed in (a) will produce the greatest amount of ionisation per centimetre of path length?   (1 line)
(d)  An isotope of uranium $^{235}_{92}U$ decays with the emission of alpha radiation to give an isotope of thorium (Th).

(i)   Name the particles which make up the nucleus of $^{235}_{92}U$ stating clearly how many there are of each in the nucleus.   (2 lines)
(ii)  State the atomic number and mass number of the isotope of thorium which is formed.
Atomic number
        (Proton number) . . . . . . . .
Mass number
        (Nucleon number) . . . . . . . .
(iii) The isotope of thorium which is formed has a half-life of 25 hours. What is meant by the half-life of a radioactive element?   (2 lines)
(iv) If 0.64 mg of the thorium is isolated and placed in a lead container, after how long will the mass of thorium have dropped to 0.04 mg?
(e)  Is $^{238}_{92}X$, where X represents the symbol of the element, an isotope of uranium? Give a reason for your answer.   (2 lines)
                            (NICCEA)

Fig. 15.34

## QUESTION 12

In a factory which makes baking foil changes in the thickness of the foil are detected using a radioactive source and a detector (Fig. 15.34). The source emits $\beta$-particles.

(a) Explain how changes in the thickness of the foil covering are detected. (3 lines)

(b) Explain why neither alpha nor gamma sources would be suitable for this application. (3 lines) (NEAB)

Fig. 15.35

## QUESTION 13

(a) Figure 15.35 represents a diffusion cloud chamber. The top half is transparent, so that light may be shone in, and particle tracks may be seen from the top. Alpha particles emitted from the radioactive source form ions.

Fig. 15.36

(i) What are ions?

(ii) To achieve the correct conditions the cloud chamber base must be cooled. How is this done?

(iii) The tracks are formed by alcohol condensing along the paths followed by the alpha particles. On what does the alcohol vapour condense? (2 lines)

(iv) Looking down on the cloud chamber, the alpha particle tracks appear as in Fig. 15.36. The tracks are about equal in length. What does this suggest about the energies of the $\alpha$-particles? (4 lines)

(v) Imagine that an alpha particle from the source were to collide with a stationary particle of equal mass within the cloud chamber. Give a labelled sketch to show what the cloud chamber track would look like.

(b) The count rate near a radioactive source was measured over a period of time using a Geiger counter. After subtracting the "background" radiation count rate the following graph was plotted (Fig. 15.37).

(i) Describe how you would measure the background radiation count rate. (3 lines)

(ii) Use the graph to find the half-life of the radioactive source. (1 line)

(c) (i) What type of charge is carried by $\alpha$-particles? (1 line)

(ii) What type of charge is carried by $\beta$-particles? (1 line)

(iii) Which is more easily absorbed. $\alpha$-particles or $\beta$-particles? (1 line)

(iv) How would you distinguish between $\alpha$-particles and $\beta$-particles? Describe tests you would carry out to identify each source. (4 lines) (ULEAC)

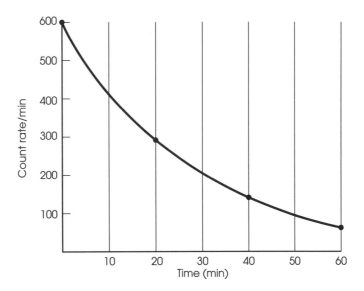

Fig. 15.37

# ANSWERS TO EXAMINATION QUESTIONS

**MULTIPLE CHOICE QUESTIONS**

| Question | 1 | 2 | 3 | 4 | 5 | 6 | 7 | 8 | 9 | 10 |
|----------|---|---|---|---|---|---|---|---|---|----|
| Answer | D | A | C | C | C | D | A | B | B | C |

**STRUCTURED QUESTIONS**

## ANSWER 11

(a) (i) Gamma radiation is short-wavelength, high-frequency, electro-magnetic radiation.

   (ii) Ultraviolet radiation is electromagnetic radiation with a wavelength longer than gamma but smaller than visible light (see Ch. 9).

   (iii) Beta radiation consists of a stream of fast-moving electrons.

   (iv) Infra-red radiation is electromagnetic radiation with a longer wavelength than visible light (see Ch. 9).

   (v) Alpha radiation is a stream of high-energy helium nuclei.

(b) (i) Alpha and beta radiation.

   (ii) Ultraviolet and infra-red radiation.

(c) (i) Ionisation is the process by which a neutral atom loses electrons to become a positive ion or gains electrons to become a negative ion.

   (ii) Alpha radiation causes the heaviest ionisation.

(d) (i) 92 protons, 143 neutrons.

   (ii) Atomic number 90; mass number 231.

   (iii) Half-life is the time for the original number of radioactive nuclei to be reduced by half.

   (iv) 100 hours.

(e) Yes. Isotopes are chemically identical (same proton number) but have different numbers of neutrons. Proton number of uranium given in the question is 92.

## ANSWER 12

(a) The beta source emits beta particles most of which can penetrate the baking foil. Beta particles are not very penetrating and any change in thickness of the foil will result in a greater or smaller number arriving at the detector.

(b) Alpha particles would be totally absorbed by the foil and the air between the source and the top surface of the covering. Gamma waves would hardly be absorbed at all, so small variations in thickness would not be registered by the detector.

## ANSWER 13

(a) (i) Ions are the result of atoms either losing electrons or gaining electrons. If they lose electrons they become positive ions and if they gain electrons they become negative ions.

   (ii) The cloud chamber is cooled by using solid carbon dioxide (dry ice) in the base.

(iii) The alcohol condenses around the ions formed by the passage of the alpha particles through the vapour in the chamber.

(iv) Track length shows the extent of the ion path, so this suggests that α-particles have roughly equal energies.

(v) See Fig. 15.38.

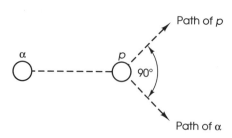

**Fig. 15.38**

(b) (i) Turn the Geiger counter voltage to its operating value. Record the count over several minutes. Take a mean value of counts per minute.

(ii) Half-life is 20 min.

(c) (i) Positive charge.

(ii) Negative charge.

(iii) α-particles.

(iv) Either absorption (α easily absorbed by paper, β absorbed by alumium) or by magnetic deflection.

# STUDENT'S ANSWER WITH THE EXAMINER'S COMMENTS

## STUDENT ANSWER TO QUESTION 13

a) i) Ions are electrically charged particles, formed by loss or gain of electrons

**Good. Clear.**

ii) This is achieved by using frozen $CO_2$ or dry ice which emits cool vapour when heated above its freezing point

**It cools the air so water and alcohol vapour condenses.**

iii) The alcohol vapour condenses on the perspex lid

**No. It condenses around the ions formed in the air in the box.**

iv) The equal track lengths suggest that the energies of $\alpha$ particles are about equal.

**Yes, Good.**

v)

**Not clear. Both particle tracks must be shown. There is a 90° angle between tracks.**

b)(i) The background count would be measured with a Geiger counter several times so that an average can be found over a set time scale.

**Vague. This needs more detail.**

(ii) The half life of this source is 20 minutes

c) i) Alpha particles have negative charge.
ii) Beta particles have negative charge. ✓
iii) Alpha particles are more easily absorbed than beta particles. ✓
iv) Alpha particles and beta particles can be distinguished by placing a piece of paper or card between the source and the geiger counter. If there is little reduction in count the source is beta.

**Silly error.**

**Could add a little more detail.**

# MORE EXAMINER'S COMMENTS
# CENTRAL/HIGHER LEVEL

(a) Information on the average amount of radiation received by a person in a year is shown in the table.

| source | amount/arbitrary units |
|---|---|
| natural background | 125.0 |
| medical sources | 55.2 |
| occupational hazards | 1.7 |
| other radiation | 2.0 |

(i) Give one cause of natural background radiation.

............Cosmic Radiation...........................

...........................................................(1 mark)

(ii) Explain why the dose of X-rays you receive should be measured.

*So that you don't receive too much radiation from it., as too much radiation (too bigger dosage of it) can lead to skin cancer or other cancers.*

**66** 2 marks – stress the idea of a cumulative dose **99**

..........................................................(3)

(b) The diagram represents the structure of a helium nucleus.

*outer Shell*

*nucleus*

**key:**
⬤ = proton
◯ = neutron
X — *electrons*

(i) Add information to the diagram so that it represents a helium atom. (2)

(ii) Use the information in the diagram to help you explain the difference between mass number and atomic number.

**66** Mass number is the number of protons and *neutrons* in the nucleus **99**

**66** 1 mark **99**

*The mass number is the number of Photons and electrons added together in an atom., the atomic number is the number of protons in an atom...*

..........................................................(2)

# REVIEW SHEET

■ A hot wire can emit _____ . This is called _____ .

■ The two types of particle that are found in the nucleus are _____ and _____ .

■ In a neutral atom the number of electrons will be the same as the number of _____ .

■ Two atoms are isotopes of the same element. They will have the same number of _____ but a different number of _____ .

■ The half-life of a radioisotope is the time taken for _____ .

■ There are three types of radioactivity. Name them in order of their penetrating power: _____ .

■ Which of the three types of radioactivity is not a particle? _____ .

■ Name three sources of background radiation.

  1. _____ .      2. _____ .

  3. _____ .

■ The number of protons in the nucleus is called the _____ or the _____ .

■ The type of radioactivity deflected easily by a magnetic field is _____ .

■ For each of the following parts of a nuclear reactor state what the part is for and name a suitable material.

| Part | Function | Material |
|---|---|---|
| Fuel pin | | |
| Coolant | | |
| Moderator | | |
| Control rod | | |

■ Complete the following table

| | Mass | Charge |
|---|---|---|
| proton | | |
| neutron | | |
| electron | | |
| $\alpha$ particle | | |
| $\beta$ particle | | |
| $\gamma$ photon | | |

■ An isotope has a half-life of 10 mins. If you had 0.08 g of it, how much would be left after half an hour? _____ .

■ Name two uses for $\beta$ sources.

  _____ _____ .

■ Name a medical use for $\gamma$ radiation. _____ .

■ $\alpha$ particles consist of _____ so they are the same as the nucleus of a _____ atom.

■ Briefly explain what is meant by a *chain reaction*.

_____

_____

_____ .

■ $^{226}_{88}$Ra is an isotope of radium which emits α particles.

What is its nucleon number? _____ .

What is its proton number? _____ .

How many neutrons are there in its nucleus? _____ .

■ Write an equation for the α emission if the new atom is an isotope of radon (Rn)

■ Ions are formed when atoms _____ .

■ Two charges that are _____ will repel each other.

■ State a method of disposing of long half-life nuclear waste. _____

_____ .

■ A worker wears a badge to detect exposure to radiation. It contains a piece of photographic film which is half covered by aluminium foil. Which types of radiation can each half of the film detect?

Foil covered half _____ . Other half _____ .

■ Name the following units:

Dose of radiation _____ . Activity of a source _____ .

## GETTING STARTED

The earlier electronics section dealt with some of the individual *components* which are found in a simple electronics circuit. The use of *integrated circuits* means that many such components can be connected in a single miniature "chip" which can do the job of many larger-scale pieces of equipment. The technology of this branch of physics is moving fast, and it is more useful to analyse the behaviour of a circuit in terms of the way the output and input voltages are related, rather than by looking in detail at what goes on inside the circuit. This means treating each electronics block as a building brick, which can link with others to give a useful result; the method of analysis is called a "systems" approach, and is the way in which a professional engineer would be likely to solve problems.

Voltage signals applied to a system are described as *analogue* or *digital*. An **analogue** system has an input and output voltage which may have any value. **Digital** systems respond only to one of two signals, high or low, which are described commonly as logic level 1 or logic level 0. We will deal with digital systems first.

There has been some confusion over standard symbols for logic gates. Some boards simply draw a square box and write the name of the gate in it whilst others use "standard" symbols. The only one likely to cause any confusion is that for the AND gate (and therefore for the NAND gate).

AND gate symbols

NAND gate symbols

Fig. 16.1

The symbols on the right are the more commonly accepted ones. Check with your teacher to see which you should use.

# ESSENTIAL PRINCIPLES

Digital systems only show two states, ON and OFF. These two states are described as *logic 1* and *logic 0*. A simple way of illustrating the idea would be to use ordinary switches, as shown in Fig. 16.2.

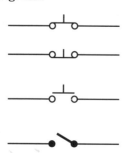

Fig. 16.2 Closed and open switches.

One way of showing how some circuits behave is by using a *truth table*. This summarises what is possible for a circuit. The circuit in Fig. 16.3(a) can only have its switch ON or OFF and the lamp is also either ON or OFF. Representing ON = 1 and OFF = 0 gives the table in Fig. 16.3(b).

| Switch | Lamp |
|--------|------|
| 0 | 0 |
| 1 | 1 |

Fig. 16.3(b)

A more complicated example is shown in the circuit of Fig. 16.4(a). Switches are labelled S and lamps labelled L (truth table, Fig. 16.4(b)).

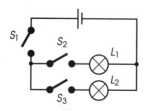

Fig. 16.4(a) Parallel ON/OFF logic.

| Switch | | | Lamp | |
|--------|--------|--------|--------|--------|
| $S_1$ | $S_2$ | $S_3$ | $L_1$ | $L_2$ |
| 0 | 0 | 0 | 0 | 0 |
| 1 | 0 | 0 | 0 | 0 |
| 1 | 1 | 0 | 1 | 0 |
| 1 | 0 | 1 | 0 | 1 |
| 1 | 1 | 1 | 1 | 1 |

Fig 16.4(b)

Many systems are complicated. To simplify the circuit diagram, the supply is often removed, and a "line" is drawn to represent the positive (+) side of the circuit. Another line represents the (–) side, which is usually written as 0 V. The circuit of Fig. 16.3(a) would then be represented as in Fig. 16.5.

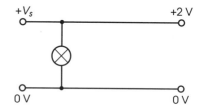

Fig. 16.5 Representing a logic circuit.

The switch can also be left ON, suggesting that it is possible to make all possible connections.

Another system, with its corresponding truth table, helps to illustrate this point (Figs. 16.6(a) and (b)).

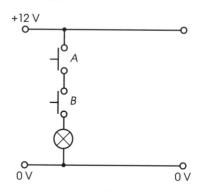

Fig. 16.6(a) Series logic with such switches.

| Switch | | Lamp |
|--------|--------|--------|
| A | B | |
| 0 | 0 | 0 |
| 1 | 0 | 0 |
| 0 | 1 | 0 |
| 1 | 1 | 1 |

Fig. 16.6(b)

These circuits are quite easy to work out, with more practice being given in the examination questions at the end of the chapter.

Fig. 16.3(a) ON/OFF logic.

**2 > LOGIC GATES**

An electronic "gate" is a circuit which will only allow an output signal under particular input situations. The word "gate" is used because the circuitry can effectively only be either open (logic 1) or shut (logic 0), and different combinations are needed to achieve opening and shutting.

Each gate is a piece of electronic circuitry and it is described by the way in which its output will become logic **high = 1** when its input is changed.

## AND-GATE

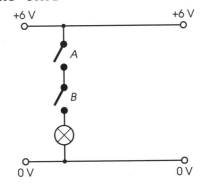

Fig. 16.7

A gate description called AND simply means that the output will go high if **both** of two inputs are also high. In simple switch terms this could be a circuit of the type shown in Fig. 16.7, where the lamp only lights if both A **and** B are on. Any version of an AND-gate can be shown as in the circuit of Fig. 16.8(a). If the out terminal is connected to a lamp or a voltmeter between the out terminal and 0 V, it will give the truth table (Fig. 16.8(b)) as A and B inputs are moved between input high = 1 and low = 0.

Fig. 16.8(a) AND-gate.

| Input | | Output |
|---|---|---|
| A | B | |
| 0 | 0 | 0 |
| 1 | 0 | 0 |
| 0 | 1 | 0 |
| 1 | 1 | 1 |

Fig. 16.8(b)

Any system giving this output is called AND. The output is high if both one input AND the other is at logic high.

All of the circuits will always need a positive and negative supply connection. This is left off the diagrams to make them simpler but it is really there to give the "complete circuits" that you read about in chapter 7.

## OR-GATE

OR-gates work differently. The output goes high if either one **or** the other or both inputs go high. The symbol is shown in Fig. 16.9(a), with the corresponding truth table (Fig. 16.9(b)).

Fig. 16.9(a) OR-gate.

| Input | | Output |
|---|---|---|
| A | B | Z |
| 0 | 0 | 0 |
| 1 | 0 | 1 |
| 0 | 1 | 1 |
| 1 | 1 | 1 |

Fig. 16.9(b)

## NOT-GATE

A NOT-gate is also called an inverter. A high = 1 input causes a low = 0 output, and vice versa. The symbol is given in Fig. 16.10(a), and here the truth table (Fig. 16.10(b)) simply says that the output is the inverse of the input.

Fig. 16.10(a) Inverter.

| Input | Output |
|---|---|
| 0 | 1 |
| 1 | 0 |

Fig. 16.10(b)

## NAND-GATE

The NOT-gate can reverse the behaviour of another gate. So AND followed by NOT gives NOT-AND, written as NAND (Fig. 16.11(a)). The truth table (Fig. 16.11(b)) is the inverse of that for AND.

Fig. 16.11(a) AND + inverter.

| Input | | Output |
|---|---|---|
| A | B | |
| 0 | 0 | 1 |
| 1 | 0 | 1 |
| 0 | 1 | 1 |
| 1 | 1 | 0 |

Fig. 16.11(b)

Fig. 16.12 NAND-gate.

The NAND-gate function is represented by Fig. 16.12. The circle following the gate implies a negative gate "instruction".

## NOR-GATE

In a similar way, NOR means NOT-OR (Fig. 16.13(a)) and the truth table (Fig. 16.13(b)) is the inverse of OR.

Fig. 16.13(a) NOR-gate.

| Input | | Output |
|---|---|---|
| A | B | |
| 0 | 0 | 1 |
| 1 | 0 | 0 |
| 0 | 1 | 0 |
| 1 | 1 | 0 |

Fig. 16.13(b)

If the two inputs of NAND are connected together, the gate behaves as an inverter (NOT). The same is true if the two inputs of a NOR are connected together (Fig. 16.14).

In all logic gate circuits you should make sure that all the inputs are connected to either high or low. If you leave inputs not connected some gates will not behave properly.

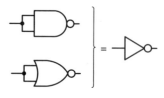

Fig. 16.14 Single input NOR or single input NAND inverts.

**3** **COMBINING LOGIC GATES**

Once the function of a logic gate is known, it can be combined with others to give a required output behaviour. Some examples are given below.

### EXAMPLE 1

Fig. 16.15(a)

Figure 16.15(a) represents a two-input system. Construct its truth table and suggest a use for it.

The system is made up of two NOT-gates (inverters) followed by NOR. The outputs at C and D are therefore the inverse of the inputs at A and B. Output E will be high when *neither* one, *nor* the other, *nor* both its inputs is high. This gives us the truth table in Fig. 16.15(b). The combination can therefore be used as an AND-gate, passing a signal only when both inputs go to logic 1.

| Inputs | | Outputs | | |
|---|---|---|---|---|
| A | B | C | D | E |
| 0 | 0 | 1 | 1 | 0 |
| 1 | 0 | 0 | 1 | 0 |
| 0 | 1 | 1 | 0 | 0 |
| 1 | 1 | 0 | 0 | 1 |

Fig. 16.15(b)

### EXAMPLE 2

Complete the truth table for the system shown in Fig. 16.16(a).

Fig. 16.16(a)

This is a NOT-gate leading to one input of a NAND-gate. The other NAND input may go either to logic 1 or logic 0 (Fig. 16.16(b)).

| Inputs | | Outputs | |
|---|---|---|---|
| A | B | C | D |
| 0 | 0 | 1 | 1 |
| 0 | 1 | 1 | 0 |
| 1 | 0 | 0 | 1 |
| 1 | 1 | 0 | 1 |

Fig. 16.16(b)

## 4 > PRACTICAL USE OF LOGIC GATES

The input to a logic gate is a voltage applied between a gate terminal and the 0 V line of the system. Inputs are typically close to 0 V (certainly below 0.7 V) or close to 5 V, giving the two states logic 0 and logic 1.

+5 V                    +5 V

A

B                      Z

Gate

V                      V

0 V                    0 V

Fig. 16.17

Figure 16.17 shows that both input and output voltages are read between a terminal and the 0 V line. A lead from terminal B could connect the gate to the 5 V line or the 0 V line.

Often the voltage is caused by a current through a resistive component, such as a thermistor or LDR, in a similar way to the earlier electronics applications. An example is shown in Fig. 16.18, where the input is applied to a NOT-gate. The output will be high if the input is near 0 V; this will happen if resistor R has a low voltage across it compared with the thermistor.

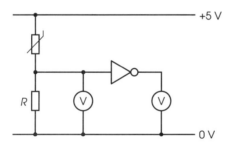

+5 V

R         V          V

0 V

**66** Voltages are proportional to resistance values. **99**

Fig. 16.18

If the minimum required voltage is 0.7 V then the values of the resistances must be in the ratio

$$\frac{R_{\text{thermistor}}}{R} = \frac{4.3}{0.7}$$

since there is a total of 5 V across the two of them.

Usually a light emitting diode (LED) is used as an output indicator in place of a voltmeter. The voltage required to operate it is about 2 V and the current through it should not exceed about 10 mA. In practice a series resistor is also connected into the circuit to prevent an overlarge current flowing in the LED (Fig. 16.19).

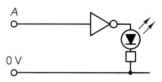

A

0 V

Fig. 16.19

Since the output of a gate is typically 5 V, the resistor must have a voltage of 3 V across it, so its values will be about

$$\frac{3}{10 \times 10^{-3}} = 300 \ \Omega$$

The maximum current output of a gate is only a few milliamps. A LED can be driven directly but a more powerful device, such as a headlamp bulb or motor, would need indirect switching. The gate output could be fed to a transistor which could in turn switch a *relay*.

## 5 > INFORMATION AND BINARY NUMBERS

Gates are used extensively in information and data processing. Much of this information is numerical and can be handled by the use of *binary* arithmetic.

We are used to counting in a scale of 10 using 1 2 3 4 5 6 7 8 9 0. Digital system outputs can only use the *two* states of logic high = 1 and logic low = 0. However, the two symbols are enough to encode numerical information. If only 1 and 0 are available, then numbers become

| Scale of 10 | Binary |  |
|---|---|---|
| 0 | 0 | |
| 1 | 1 | |
| 2 | 10 | |
| 3 | 11 | |
| 4 | 100 | |
| 5 | 101 | |
| 6 | 110 | |
| 7 | 111 | |
| 8 | 1000 | etc. |

There is an advantage in doing this as compared to transmitting information with a voltage of precise value to represent a number. Namely that when a voltage is transmitted between parts of a system, its value can be modified by electronic disturbances called "noise" which are picked up from signals in the environment. As a result the voltage value will not remain totally the same. This is illustrated in Fig. 16.20.

In a similar way music is not faithfully reproduced on older records because of variations in the electrical signal to the sound centre.

However, if the signal representing a number is transmitted digitally, using a "bus" of wires, the signal fluctuations are small and the output is still accepted as logic 0 or logic 1.

Sending the number 5 would need three wires carrying a 0 or 1 value. Digitally 5 = 101.

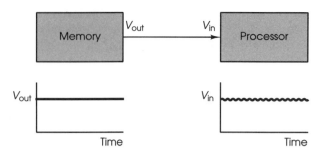

**Fig. 16.20**

The fluctuations still take place but the number is still recognisable (Fig. 16.21).

 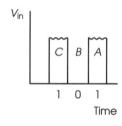

**Fig. 16.21**

If a four-bus wire is carrying a binary number, its value can be read by connecting an LED to each wire. For a logic 1 voltage the LED will glow, for logic 0 the LED remains OFF.

In Fig. 16.22 the system is carrying the number 1010 = TEN.

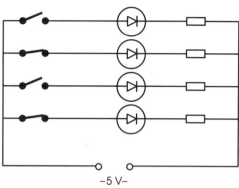

**Fig. 16.22**

A seven-segment display consists of seven separate LEDs arranged in a single unit to "decode" a binary number into a decimal number. The diodes are arranged as in Fig. 16.23. To make number 3, the diodes which are lit would be A, B, G, C, D.

**Fig. 16.23 Seven-segment display.**

Seven-segment displays are driven by special integrated circuits known as "decoder-drivers". These have an input in binary form, and automatically illuminate to correct combination of LEDs to give the decimal equivalent.

## 6 BISTABLE MULTIVIBRATOR SYSTEM

This may be constructed in a number of ways. The important thing is that whatever happens to the input, the output has only one of two stable states. These are achieved by *feedback*. A connection between output and input *reinforces* information.

In Fig. 16.24 if input A is high and input B is not connected, then indicator A is off and the B input is at logic 0.

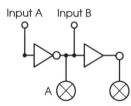

**Fig. 16.24**

Similarly if input A is not connected and B is at logic 1, the output of B is at logic 0 and of A is at logic 1.

Now if the output of B is fed back to the input of A a *bistable system* is obtained (Fig. 16.25). Input A goes high, input B is not yet connected, output A goes low, output B goes high and reinforces the high input to A. The original connection to A can be removed and the message is retained. The system has a *memory*.

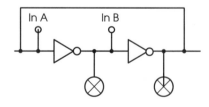

**Fig. 16.25 Bistable system**

The same sequence is obtained using two linked NOR-gates (Fig. 16.26). NOR gives a logic 1 output if neither one NOR another NOR both inputs is high (i.e. only when *both* are at logic 0).

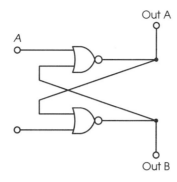

Fig. 16.26 Bistable system.

Here, if A input is at logic 1, A output is logic 0 and the feedback to the other NOR gate is logic 0. If input B is also at logic 0 then output B will be at logic 1 and will stay like that (because it is fed back to NOR gate A). The only way to change the system is to let input A go to logic 0 and then make input B go to logic 1. This will "reset" the circuit so that output A is logic 1 and output B is logic 0. If you make A logic 1 for a short time the circuit can be "set" again. This *latch* is used in section 2 of the "Extension materials".

**7 > ANALOGUE AND DIGITAL SIGNALS**

An analogue signal can vary smoothly and continuously. Most natural changes are like this; e.g. temperature, time, the brightness of the light from the Sun.

A digital signal changes in small steps and cannot have values that fall between the steps. Most computers accept signals of this type because the size of each step is easily represented by a number. The digital signal will be accurate enough if you keep the steps small.

Watches can be analogue (with motor driven hands that rotate smoothly through all the times) or digital (so that they go up in small steps of either a second or a minute). Natural analogue measurements can be turned into digital ones by an analogue to digital converter (ADC) in a computer.

# EXTENSION MATERIALS

The circuits discussed in this section use other components with logic gates in order to achieve a useful end product. The LED indicators normally used to show output voltages require little current, and to control more powerful apparatus, relays are often needed.

**1 > A MOTOR-CONTROL SYSTEM**

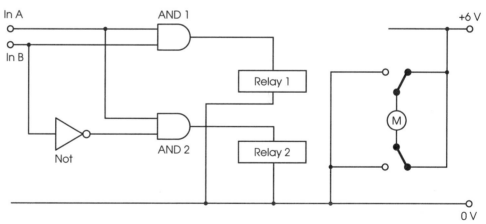

Fig. 16.27

If input A and B (Fig. 16.27) are at logic 1, AND-gate 1 is open but 2 is closed. Relay 1 drives the motor circuit switch and the motor rotates in a particular direction.

If B is now made logic 0, AND-gate 1 closes, 2 opens. Relay 2 now switches and the motor rotates in the opposite direction.

**2 ▷ A BISTABLE LATCH**

The circuit in Fig 16.31 will work as a *latch* so that once the buzzer is triggered it will stay on until *reset* by switch S. It is the same bistable as shown in Fig. 16.26 but uses only one of the outputs. If the LDR is in darkness its input to the upper NOR gate is low. The other input, the feedback from the buzzer, is also low so the output of the upper NOR gate is high. This logic 1 is fed back into an input of the lower NOR gate so that the buzzer is held off. If a light shines onto the LDR its resistance falls, the input to the upper NOR gate goes high, and the output of the gate goes low. Both inputs to the lower NOR gate are now low so the buzzer is switched on. The circuit is latched in this state by the feedback from the buzzer to the upper NOR gate so that the buzzer continues to sound even though the LDR is no longer illuminated.

If the LDR is no longer illuminated the circuit can be reset by switching S up and then back down again. The high input to the lower NOR gate will have put the buzzer back to off and the circuit is back in its original state.

The whole circuit can be obtained in a "chip" called a RS flip-flop. (The RS stands for Reset Set. In some syllabuses it is called a SR flip-flop) (Fig 16.28).

When both inputs are low the output Q stays in its previous state. Pulsing (sending high for short time) the S (set) input sends Q

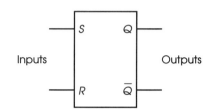

Fig. 16.28

low and $\bar{Q}$ high. Pulsing the R (reset) input reverses this. If both inputs go high at the same time the result is unpredictable.

When this is used as a latch the circuit is often drawn as a labelled box (Fig 16.29).

Fig. 16.29

This can be the basis of a burglar alarm where the reset is usually a key (or number pad) controlled switch. The sensor could be inside a cupboard where it is normally dark. Exchanging the LDR and its resistor would give a sensor that was switched on by a short period of darkness. Simple switches in door frames or under carpets could also connect the upper NOR gate to a high input and trigger the system (Fig 16.30).

Fig. 16.30

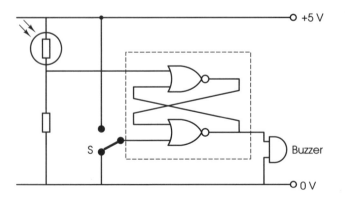

Fig. 16.31

## 3 ANALOGUE SYSTEMS – THE OP-AMP, BASIC CONNECTIONS

The systems dealt with before have only two states (logic 1 and logic 0). The OP-AMP (operational amplifier) is an *analogue* system. It can *follow changes as time goes on* and this represents them directly, not just as high and low.

The amplifier has five connections and is represented in Fig. 16.32. The connections to the supply are labelled $+V_s$ and $-V_s$. The supply is connected differently from most systems.

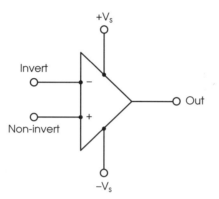

Fig. 16.32 Operational amplifier.

It is usual to describe a circuit as having a ⊕ and ⊖ line (+5 V and 0 V in an electronics system).

Here the connections are such as to give the variation of voltage in both a positive and a negative direction. This is done by dictating the 0 V of potential, by earthing a terminal (Fig. 16.33).

Fig. 16.33 OP-AMP supply connections.

A *potentiometer* connected between $+V_s$ and $-V_s$ will give an input between the maximum positive and negative values: typically +15 V to –15 V and +5 V to – 5 V. But to do this there must always be one voltmeter terminal which is connected to the reference value of 0 V (Fig. 16.34).

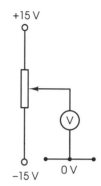

Fig. 16.34 Potentiometer control of OP-AMP supply.

The connections required to power an OP-AMP are not often shown in circuit diagrams. The behaviour of the OP-AMP depends on the way in which the remaining connections are made. The output value is, as in gate circuits, taken as the voltage between the output terminal and the 0 V line (Fig. 16.35). The other two connections are called the *inverting input* (denoted ⊖) and the *non-inverting input* (denoted ⊕). These, and a feedback connection, dictate how the system behaves.

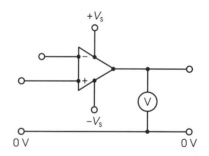

Fig. 16.35 OP-AMP connections.

## 4 BEHAVIOUR OF THE OP-AMP INVERTING INPUT

If a voltage is applied between the inverting input and the 0 V rail, and the non-inverting input is connected also to 0 V, the output is very large. The amplifier gives the same large output regardless of the input. A more controlled system is obtained if a further feedback resistor is connected, as in Fig. 16.36. If $R_f = R_i$ the output voltage is the same as the input, but its direction is reversed:

$$V_{in} = -V_{out}$$

When $R_f$ is greater than $R_i$, the output

Fig. 16.36 OP-AMP with feedback.

voltage is greater in value than the input, and again its direction is reversed. Now

$$V_{out} = -\frac{R_f}{R_i} V_{in}$$

and the device amplifies. Careful measurements of the behaviour can be made by varying $V_{in}$ slowly with a potentiometer (Fig. 16.37). Suppose that $R_f = 10$ k$\Omega$ and $R_i = 1$ k$\Omega$. Then $V_{out} = -10\ V_{in}$.

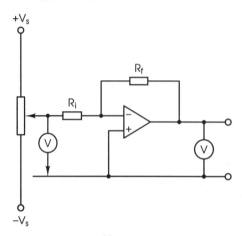

Fig. 16.37 Inverting amplifier.

A graph showing how $V_{in}$ and $V_{out}$ behave may look like that of Fig. 16.38. It is seen that amplification is limited. The voltage of the supply in this case was + 5 V to 0 V to –15 V, and this is the maximum output.

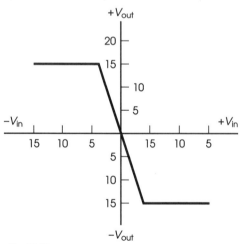

Fig. 16.38

The **range of amplification depends on the supply voltage**. When this value is reached, no further amplification is possible. The amplifier has reached **saturation**. The amplification factor within this limitation is $-R_f/R_i$.

An alternating voltage may also be amplified. Setting the value $R_f/R_i = 5$ and applying 1 V AC to the input resistor gives the following results which may be seen on a dual beam oscilloscope. If the two beams have the same voltage sensitivity setting, amplification of the signal is clear. If the time bases are connected to a common earth, the inverting of the output can be seen (Fig. 16.39).

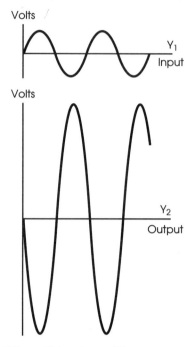

Fig. 16.39 a.c. with inverting amplifier.

However, the amplifier is still limited by the supply. If a larger input is applied, say 4 V a.c. with the same (5) amplification factor, the signal "clips" at 15 V leading to a distorted output (Fig. 16.40). In the extreme this can be used to provide a square-wave output.

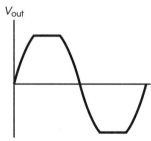

Fig. 16.40 Output with distortion due to "cut-off".

Within the limitation set by the supply, the voltage gain with a.c. is fairly constant regardless of the frequency of the signal. However, it does tend to fall off with high frequencies, i.e. those above about $10^4$ Hz.

The non-inverting input may also be used with connections as in Fig. 16.41. The output is now in the same direction as the input, but the gain is now given by

$$V_{out} = V_{in}\left(1 + \frac{R_2}{R_1}\right)$$

which is smaller than in the inverting amplifier case.

Fig. 16.41 OP-AMP with non-invert-ing input.

## 5 THE VOLTAGE COMPARATOR

The op-amp can also be used as a voltage comparator.

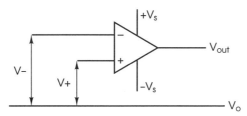

**Fig. 16.42**

The gain of the amplifier without the feedback resistors is **very** large. If two voltages are connected to the inverting and non-inverting inputs the amplifier will saturate and its output will go to either $+V_s$ or $-V_s$.

If $V+ > V-$ then the output becomes $+V_s$.

If $V+ < V-$ then the output becomes $-V_s$.

This can be used in circuits such as that of Fig. 16.43.

When the LDR is in the light it will have a low resistance and a low voltage across it so that the non-inverting input is higher than that set by the variable resistor $R$. The output is therefore high $(+V_s)$. When the LDR is in the dark the non-inverting input goes lower than that at the inverting input and the final output is low $(-V_s)$. The level of light at which the op-amp switches can be set by the variable resistor $R$. This effect can be useful when the next stage is a digital circuit such as a logic gate as the output is always high or low and not slowly changing.

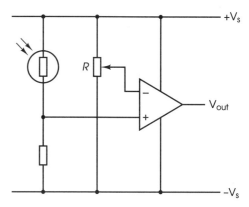

**Fig. 16.43**

# EXAMINATION QUESTIONS

## MULTIPLE CHOICE QUESTIONS

### QUESTION 1

Which one in Fig. 16.44 is the circuit symbol for a NAND gate? (NISEAC)

**Fig. 16.44**

### QUESTION 2

**Fig. 16.45**

On testing a logic gate with the conditions shown in Fig. 16.45, a student found the output Z to be a logic level "1". The gate could be

A   A NOR gate or an AND gate
B   An AND gate or an OR gate
C   An OR gate or a NOR gate
D   A NAND gate or an OR gate
E   An AND gate or a NAND gate

(NICCEA)

### QUESTION 3

Which one of the following conducts electricity in one direction only?

A   Diode         C  Lamp
B   Fuse          D  Thermistor

### QUESTION 4

Figure 16.46(a) shows an incomplete truth table for an AND gate which has inputs X and Y and output Z. Which of the following in Fig. 16.46(b) is the correct version of the last column of the truth table? (ULEAC)

| X | Y | Z |
|---|---|---|
| 0 | 0 | |
| 0 | 1 | |
| 1 | 0 | |
| 1 | 1 | |

Fig. 16.46(a)

| A | B | C | D |
|---|---|---|---|
| Z | Z | Z | Z |
| 0 | 0 | 0 | 1 |
| 0 | 0 | 1 | 0 |
| 0 | 0 | 1 | 0 |
| 0 | 1 | 1 | 1 |

Fig. 16.46(b)

## QUESTION 5

In Fig. 16.47, box Y contains a component. When connected as shown the lamp lights more brightly than normal. If the cell is reversed the lamp does not light at all. Which is component Y most likely to be?

A    A cell
B    A resistor of large resistance
C    A coil of copper wire
D    A diode rectifier
E    A capacitor

Fig. 16.47

**STRUCTURED QUESTIONS**

## QUESTION 6

In the circuit in Fig. 16.48, the relay coil is energised and can close switch S if the **output** of the NOT gate is high. When a bright light is shone on the light-dependent resistor the input to the NOT gate falls.

(i)   Why does this happen?   (2 lines)
(ii)  What happens to the rest of the circuit because of this?   (2 lines)
(iii) Suggest a practical application for the circuit shown above.   (3 lines)

Fig. 16.48

## QUESTION 7

(a) The circuit in Fig. 16.49(a) contains two switches A and B which can either be open or closed. Figure 16.49(b) is a truth table for the circuit. It shows what will

Fig. 16.49(a)

happen to the lamp when the switches are in different positions.
   (i)   Complete the truth table for the circuit.
   (ii)  State in words the condition for the lamp to be lit.   (1 line)

| Switch A | Switch B | Lamp ON or OFF |
|---|---|---|
| Open | Open | |
| Closed | Open | |
| Open | Closed | |
| Closed | Closed | |

Fig. 16.49(b)

(b) The truth table (Fig. 16.50) refers to a certain two-input logic gate.
   (i)   What logic gate is indicated by this table?
   (ii)  Draw a symbol representing this logic gate.

| Input | | Output |
|---|---|---|
| A | B | |
| 0 | 0 | 0 |
| 0 | 1 | 1 |
| 1 | 0 | 1 |
| 1 | 1 | 1 |

Fig. 16.50

| A | B | P |
|---|---|---|
| 0 | 0 | |
| 0 | 1 | |
| 1 | 0 | |
| 1 | 1 | |

Fig. 16.52(c)

(c) A circuit is to be designed so that a bell will ring if a push switch is operated, but only if there is also an input from a light (or heat) sensor or both. These requirements can be summarised in the table (Fig. 16.51).
   (i) Complete the table.
   (ii) This result can be achieved by using two 2-input logic gates between the switch and sensors and the bell. Show how this can be done completing the lines below.

Push switch _____
Light sensor _____    to bell.
Heat sensor _____

(NISEAC)

| Push switch | Light sensor | Heat sensor | Output |
|---|---|---|---|
| 0 | 0 | 0 | 0 |
| 0 | | | 0 |
| 0 | | | 0 |
| 0 | | | 0 |
| 1 | 0 | 0 | 0 |
| 1 | | | |
| 1 | | | |
| 1 | | | |

Fig. 16.51

(b) The circuit symbol for a two-input NAND (NOT AND) gate is shown in Fig. 16.53(a). Also given is the truth table for a two-input NAND gate (Fig. 16.53(b)). In the design of logic systems, a NAND gate is a basic "building block" as in the circuit shown in Fig. 16.54(a).

Fig. 16.53(a)

| A | B | P |
|---|---|---|
| 0 | 0 | 1 |
| 0 | 1 | 1 |
| 1 | 0 | 1 |
| 1 | 1 | 0 |

Fig. 16.53(b)

Fig. 16.54(a)

## QUESTION 8

(a) A NOT gate can be added to the output of a two-input OR logic gate to produce a two-input NOR (NOT OR) logic gate. The completed truth tables for a NOT and an OR gate are given in Fig. 16.52(a) and (b). A and B are inputs. P is the output. Complete the truth table for a two-input NOR gate (Fig. 16.52(c)).

**NOT**

| A | P |
|---|---|
| 0 | 1 |
| 1 | 0 |

Fig. 16.52(a)

(i) Complete the truth table for this circuit (Fig. 16.54(b)).
(ii) What arithmetic function does this circuit perform?

(c) The output of a logic circuit can be displayed using an LED and associated series resistor as shown in Fig. 16.55.
(i) When the LED is lit, what is the logic state at A?

**OR**

| A | B | P |
|---|---|---|
| 0 | 0 | 0 |
| 0 | 1 | 1 |
| 1 | 0 | 1 |
| 1 | 1 | 1 |

Fig. 16.52(b)

| A | B | X | Y | Z | P | Q |
|---|---|---|---|---|---|---|
| 0 | 0 | 1 | | | | |
| 0 | 1 | 1 | | | | |
| 1 | 0 | 1 | | | | |
| 1 | 1 | 0 | | | | |

Fig. 16.54(b)

**Fig. 16.55**

(ii) The LED has a potential difference of 2 V across it and a current of 10 mA flowing through it when it is lit. What is the potential difference across resistor $R$ when the LED is lit?

(iii) Calculate the resistance of $R$.

(iv) Why is resistor $R$ needed?

(d) In a factory a particular piece of machinery has an alarm button to warn the operator of a fault. The system has a

blue lamp (alight when the machine is operating normally), a red warning lamp and a buzzer. There is a fault detection system and an "operator acknowledge" button. If a fault is detected the blue lamp goes out, the red lamp comes on and a buzzer sounds. When the operator acknowledges the fault, by pressing the button, the buzzer stops but the red light stays on. Complete the output columns of the truth table (Fig. 16.56) to show what states are wanted.                    (NEAB)

| Input | | Output | | |
|---|---|---|---|---|
| Fault | Operator acknowledge | Red | Buzzer | Blue |
| 0 | 0 | | | |
| 0 | 1 | | | |
| 1 | 0 | | | |
| 1 | 1 | | | |

**Fig. 16.56**

# ANSWERS TO EXAMINATION QUESTIONS

| Question | 1 | 2 | 3 | 4 | 5 |
|---|---|---|---|---|---|
| Answer | E | B | A | B | A |

## ANSWER 6

(i) The resistance of the LDR falls when the light is shone on it. The voltage across it also drops.

(ii) The NOT input falls, so its output becomes high, energising the relay coil and switching the bell circuit.

(iii) The system could act as a warning against excessive light levels or to control lighting conditions.

## ANSWER 7

(a) (i) See Fig. 16.57.

| Switch A | Switch B | Lamp |
|---|---|---|
| Open | Open | Off |
| Closed | Open | On |
| Open | Closed | On |
| Closed | Closed | On |

**Fig. 16.57**

(ii) The lamp is ON if either A or B or both are closed (an OR gate).

(b) (i) The table represents an OR gate.

(ii) See Fig. 16.58.

**Fig. 16.58**

(c) (i) See Fig. 16.59(a).

(ii) See Fig. 16.59(b). The system needs to link the heat and light sensors with an OR gate. The output combines with the push through an AND gate.

**Fig. 16.59(a)**

| Push switch | Light sensor | Heat sensor | Output |
|:---:|:---:|:---:|:---:|
| 0 | 0 | 0 | 0 |
| 0 | 1 | 0 | 0 |
| 0 | 0 | 1 | 0 |
| 0 | 1 | 1 | 0 |
| 1 | 0 | 0 | 0 |
| 1 | 1 | 0 | 1 |
| 1 | 0 | 1 | 1 |
| 1 | 1 | 1 | 1 |

Fig. 16.59(b)

### ANSWER 8

(a) See Fig. 16.60.
(b) (i)  See Fig. 16.61.
    (ii) Addition.

| A | B | P |
|:---:|:---:|:---:|
| 0 | 0 | 1 |
| 0 | 1 | 0 |
| 1 | 0 | 0 |
| 1 | 1 | 0 |

Fig. 16.60

| A | B | X | Y | Z | P | Q |
|:---:|:---:|:---:|:---:|:---:|:---:|:---:|
| 0 | 0 | 1 | 1 | 1 | 0 | 0 |
| 0 | 1 | 1 | 1 | 0 | 0 | 1 |
| 1 | 0 | 1 | 0 | 1 | 0 | 1 |
| 1 | 1 | 0 | 1 | 1 | 1 | 0 |

Fig. 16.61

(c) (i)   Logic state of A is level 0.
    (ii)  p.d. across $R = (5 - 2) = 3$ V.
    (iii)

$$R = \frac{V}{I} = \frac{3}{10 \times 10^{-3}} = 300 \ \Omega$$

    (iv)  $R$ protects the LED from high currents.
(d) See Fig. 16.62.

| Input | | Output | | |
|:---:|:---:|:---:|:---:|:---:|
| Fault | Operator acknowledge | Red | Buzzer | Blue |
| 0 | 0 | 0 | 0 | 1 |
| 0 | 1 | 0 | 0 | 1 |
| 1 | 0 | 1 | 1 | 0 |
| 1 | 1 | 1 | 0 | 0 |

Fig. 16.62

# TUTOR'S QUESTION AND ANSWER

**QUESTION**  This question is about a freezer alarm. Figure 16.63 shows a freezer alarm system which uses an operational amplifier.

Fig. 16.63

(a) The two inputs of the operational amplifier are called inverting and non-inverting.
    (i)  State which of the inputs is connected to the 0 V line.

    (ii) What is meant by the term inverting input of the operational amplifier?
(b) When the freezer warms up above its working temperature of –20 °C a red LED comes ON to give a warning.
    (i)  Explain why a resistor is placed in series with the LED at the output of the operational amplifier.
    (ii) When lit, the LED has a forward voltage drop at 2 V at a current of 10 mA. Calculate the value of the output resistor A.
(c) It is required to add a second, green LED to the output of the system, such that it will go OFF when the red LED comes ON.
    (i)  Complete Fig. 16.63 showing the correction position of the green LED.
    (ii) What advantage is there in adding the green LED to the system?
(d) Explain carefully the action of the operational amplifier when the temperature of the freezer increases.                (MEG)

**ANSWER**

(a) (i) Non-inverting.

(ii) The output is in the opposite direction to the input. An increasing input gives a decreasing output and vice versa.

(b) (i) The resistor limits the current through the LED to avoid damage.

(ii) Voltage across $R = 15 - 2 = 13$ V. Therefore

$$R = \frac{13}{10 \times 10^{-3}} = 1300 \ \Omega$$

(c) (i) See Fig. 16.64.

(ii) It shows if the temperature of freezing is correct, or if the green LED goes OFF and the red LED does not come ON, the battery supplying the system is low.

(d) The voltage across the thermistor decreases so the voltage across $V_R$ increases. The voltage across $V_R$ is greater than 0 V, so since the input is inverting the output voltage goes below 0 V and the red LED lights.

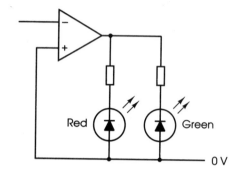

**Fig. 16.64**

# STUDENT'S ANSWER WITH THE EXAMINER'S COMMENTS

## STUDENT ANSWER TO QUESTION 8

a) 2-input NOR

| A | B | P |
|---|---|---|
| 0 | 0 | 1 |
| 0 | 1 | 0 |
| 1 | 0 | 0 |
| 1 | 1 | 0 |

**"Correct."**

b) i)

| A | B | X | Y | Z | P | Q |
|---|---|---|---|---|---|---|
| 0 | 0 | 1 | 1 | 1 | 0 | 0 |
| 0 | 1 | 1 | 1 | 0 | 0 | 1 |
| 1 | 0 | 1 | 0 | 1 | 0 | 1 |
| 1 | 1 | 0 | 1 | 1 | 1 | 0 |

**"Correct."**

**"A very good answer."**

ii) This is a 'half adder' circuit. It adds A and B to give an output P and a 'carry' Q. With only 2 one-bit inputs PQ (ie. 00, 01, 10, 11) = A + B where + means arithmetic add not logical OR.

**"This is a correct interpretation, but logic OR is equally valid in the context of the question."**

c) i) When L.E.D. is lit A is at '0'

ii) Assuming power rails of 0V and 5V and that the inverter can supply 10mA at 5V PD across R = (5-2) = 3V.

**"Good explanatory note."**

(Since P.D. across R and L.E.D together = 5V)

(iii) $R_R = \dfrac{V}{I}$ (ohms law) $= \dfrac{3}{10 \times 10^{-3}} = 300 \ \Omega$

(iv) Resistor R is needed to limit the current flowing in the LED, to prevent damage.

d)

| FAULT | OP AC | RED | BUZZER | BLUE |
|-------|-------|-----|--------|------|
| 0 | 0 | 0 | 0 | 1 |
| 0 | 1 | 0 | 0 | 1 |
| 1 | 0 | 1 | 1 | 0 |
| 1 | 1 | 1 | 0 | 1 |

**"An excellent answer. This standard would gain a grade A."**

RED = FAULT         BLUE = OPP. ACTION + FAULT
BUZZ = ~~FAULT~~ OPP. ACTION

# MORE EXAMINERS COMMENTS CENTRAL/HIGHER LEVEL

(a) The diagram below shows one way of protecting a valuable vase in a museum. The idea is that an alarm bell rings if a burglar lifts up the vase.

Vase on = 1 (high)
Vase off = 0 (low)
X
Bell
Push switch

(i) Write down the name of the logic gate which is used as X. (1 mark)

> ❝ also called a NOT gate ❞

.................... Inverter ....................................

(ii) Explain how this logic gate will cause the intended effect. (2 marks)

..... When vase is lifted switch turns off ............
..... inverter then turns the bell on .................
.................................................................

(iii) Suggest another output transducer which could be used instead of the alarm bell.

> ❝ Could be a siren or flashing light ❞

........................ buzzer ........................... (1 mark)

(b) In order to improve the security system, another sensor is added which detects a light being switched on at night. The improved circuit is shown below.

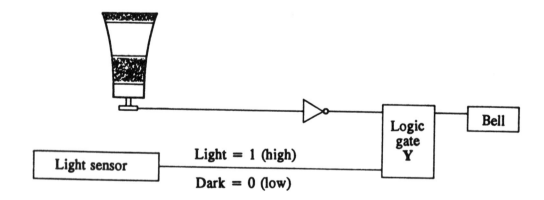

Light sensor
Light = 1 (high)
Dark = 0 (low)
Logic gate Y
Bell

(i) Write down the name of the logic gate Y. (1 mark)

> ❝ Should be OR so that either sensor sets off the alarm ❞

........................ AND ...........................................

(ii) Besides the two sensors already used, suggest one other sensor which could be used to detect the presence of a burglar. (1 mark)

> ❝ Could be a magnetic switch in the door ❞

............ Pressure mat switch ...........................

# REVIEW SHEET

■ Draw the symbols for each of the following logic gates:

NOT                    AND                    OR

NOR                    NAND

■ Complete each of the following truth tables:

**NOT**

| Input | Output |
|-------|--------|
| 1     |        |
| 0     |        |

**AND**

| Input | | Output |
|---|---|--------|
| 0 | 0 |        |
| 0 | 1 |        |
| 1 | 0 |        |
| 1 | 1 |        |

**OR**

| Input | | Output |
|---|---|--------|
| 0 | 0 |        |
| 0 | 1 |        |
| 1 | 0 |        |
| 1 | 1 |        |

**NAND**

| Input | | Output |
|---|---|--------|
| 0 | 0 |        |
| 0 | 1 |        |
| 1 | 0 |        |
| 1 | 1 |        |

**NOR**

| Input | | Output |
|---|---|--------|
| 0 | 0 |        |
| 0 | 1 |        |
| 1 | 0 |        |
| 1 | 1 |        |

■ How can a NAND gate be connected so that it behaves as a NOT gate?

_____

■ Write the following numbers in binary:

ten _____          seven _____          five _____

■ When there is feedback in a circuit the _____ is connected to the

_____.

■ The two inputs of an op-amp are called the _____ and the

_____.

■ When the output voltage of an op-amp reaches the supply voltage it has reached _____. This will cause the output to be _____ as the waveform is cut off (clipped).

■ Draw a circuit diagram to show how two NOT gates can be connected to make a simple latch circuit.

■ Why is it more reliable to transmit digital data than analogue data?_____
_____
_____

# EARTH, SPACE AND WEATHER

## GETTING STARTED

This chapter is about the planet that we live on and its place in the universe. We will look at how the Earth and the other planets were created, and what they are made from. We will look at why we divide our time into night and day and the reason for the seasons. In many countries earthquakes are important events and we will study their cause and try to understand why the Earth's surface has the structure that it does. Finally we will have a look at the complicated system in the atmosphere that we call weather.

■ In this chapter you should remember that a billion = 1000 million and that distances in astronomy are measured in light years. One *light year* is the distance travelled by light in a year (at 300 000 km per second).

# ESSENTIAL PRINCIPLES

## 1 ▷ THE ORDER OF THINGS

We live on a *planet*, the Earth, that is a satellite of a star that we call the *Sun*.

Our **Sun** is an ordinary star. It is about 1 392 000 km across and the temperature at its centre is about 13 million °C. At this temperature electrons are separated from their atoms and form a *plasma*. (A plasma is not solid, liquid or gas and is really a fourth state of matter with its own special properties.) The sun is mostly made of hydrogen and at such a temperature the hydrogen nuclei hit each other hard enough to join together in a fusion reaction. This releases heat energy and fuels the Sun. The Sun then radiates energy at $4 \times 10^{26}$ W.

The *universe* is made up of lots of *galaxies*, about a hundred billion of them. Each galaxy is a collection of a huge number of stars. Some of the galaxies are close to each other and such a group is called a *cluster*. Each galaxy will contain dust and clouds of gas as well as stars. It is possible that lots of stars have planets round them but even the nearest stars in our galaxy are too far away for us to be sure. (The brightest, Sirius, is about 8.6 light years away. The nearest, apart from the Sun, is Proxima Centauri about 4.2 light years away).

Our star, the Sun, belongs to a galaxy called the *Milky Way*. We are on the edge of the galaxy and you can see it at night looking like a bright band of stars across the sky. It looks like this because we are looking at it edge on. If you could see it from a distance it would look like a giant flat spiral with several arms. Many other galaxies have this shape but some are just elliptical (oval). The Milky Way contains about 100 billion stars and is about 100 thousand light years across. Its spiral shape spins round once in 250 million years.

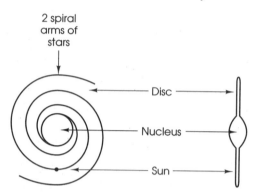

**Fig. 17.1**

It is part of a small cluster called the *"Local Group"*. The other big galaxy in the Local Group is called M31 but is better known as the Andromeda galaxy. The numbers involved in this sort of science are extremely large and show us to inhabit a rather small planet orbiting an ordinary star that is one of a huge number of similar stars arranged in galaxies.

## 2 ▷ THE SOLAR SYSTEM

**Fig. 17.2**

The nine planets that orbit the Sun form our *solar system*. As the distance from the Sun increases the radiation that reaches each planet from the Sun becomes much less and the planets become colder. The temperatures range from the day side of Mercury at about 450 °C to Neptune at −228 °C with the Earth at a comfortable (for us) 17 °C. Of our near neighbours, Venus has a thick atmosphere with a lot of $CO_2$ that creates a strong greenhouse effect and raises its surface temperature to about 475 °C. Mars has a number of Earthlike features such as mountains, polar icecaps and volcanoes but is colder and its thin atmosphere has a pressure only about 1/100 of that on Earth. When Viking 1 landed on Mars in 1976 the temperature at midday was only –31 °C

The planets are of two types. The **rocky** (terrestrial) planets are the four closest to the Sun and are small and dense with a rocky surface. They mostly have cores of iron and nickel surrounded by rock. The **icy** planets further out are large low density worlds with a thick atmosphere. They seem to be mostly made of hydrogen and helium turned liquid by the huge pressure with a rocky core of some sort at the centre. Most simple chemicals such as water or ammonia or our atmos-

pheric gases would be liquid or solid on such a world. Pluto does not fit either type very well. It is small, like the rocky planets, but is so far from the Sun that it is very cold and has a low density like the icy planets.

Many of the planets are large enough to have captured passing objects which now orbit them as moons. Most moons are small but four of those round Jupiter are as big, or bigger than, our moon.

In the table mass, diameter and gravity are related to that of Earth which is taken as 1. Density is relative density (i.e. number of times the density of water). Average distance to Sun is in millions of km.

**Mass, diameter and gravity are relative to earth (=1). Density is relative to water (=1).**

|  | Mercury | Venus | Earth | Mars | Jupiter | Saturn | Uranus | Neptune | Pluto |
|---|---|---|---|---|---|---|---|---|---|
| Mass | 0.06 | 0.81 | 1 | 0.11 | 318 | 95 | 14.5 | 17.2 | 0.1 |
| Diameter | 0.38 | 0.95 | 1 | 0.53 | 11 | 9 | 4 | 4 | 0.2 |
| Gravity | 0.38 | 0.9 | 1 | 0.38 | 2.6 | 1.2 | 0.9 | 1.2 | 0.1 |
| Density | 5.4 | 5.2 | 5.5 | 3.9 | 1.3 | 0.69 | 1.2 | 1.7 | 1.8 |
| Rocky/icy | rocky | rocky | rocky | rocky | icy | icy | icy | icy | icy |
| Moons | 0 | 0 | 1 | 2 | 16 | 17 | 10 | 8 | 1 |
| Orbit time | 88d | 225d | 1y | 1.9y | 11.9y | 29.5y | 84y | 165y | 248y |
| Average dist. to Sun (mn km) | 58 | 108 | 150 | 228 | 778 | 1,427 | 2,870 | 4,500 | 5,900 |

## 3 > AN EXPANDING UNIVERSE

When materials are at high temperatures they radiate light. The exact spectrum that is produced depends on the type of atoms that are present. If we look at the spectrum from a low density gas such as that in a sodium lamp it will be made up of exact lines in a pattern that is special to the sodium atoms that they come from. When atoms are more closely packed they give out a more continuous spectrum like the spectrum from a bulb and the hotter the atoms are the shorter the wavelength of the light will become. (You can see this when you slowly increase the current through a bulb. At first it glows dull red, then more orange and eventually the shorter green and blue waves are emitted as well so that the mixture of waves appears white.) Stars will emit this sort of continuous spectrum of light. As the light leaves the star it passes through more of the atoms that make the star and these will **absorb** their own special pattern of light waves so that the continuous spectrum that comes to us is crossed by dark lines. The lines are called Fraunhoffer lines after their discoverer. The pattern of these lines tells us what the stars are made from. We know that most of the Sun is hydrogen with about 25% helium and only about 2% heavier elements.

When astronomers looked at the lines in the spectrums of stars they found that the patterns were as they expected but they were

moved more towards the red, longer wave, end of the spectrum than they should be. This effect is called **red shift**. It is caused by the star that you are looking at moving away from you as it gives out the light. This spreads out the waves more so that they have a longer wavelength and are moved towards the red end of the spectrum. The faster the star moves away from you the bigger the red shift of its spectrum. (This an example of the **Doppler effect**.) Astronomers were surprised to find that **all** the other galaxies were moving away from us and that more distant ones were moving away faster. The explanation seems to be that the entire universe is getting bigger and bigger as the galaxies spread out. We live in an **expanding universe**. Astronomers think that the force of gravity is attracting all the material back towards the centre and that this is slowing down the expansion so that it will eventually stop and the universe might begin to collapse back again.

### Activity

One problem is that you cannot tell where the centre of the universe is. Wherever you are it will still appear that all the stars are moving away from you.

In Fig. 17.3(a) you are near to the Sun S and looking at stars A and B. These move

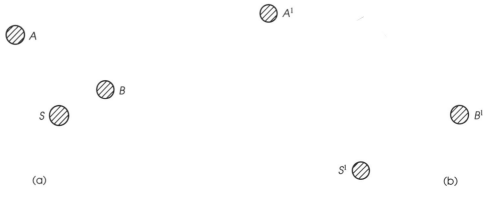

Fig. 17.3

away from you until they look like Fig. 17.3(b). Make a tracing of Fig. 17.3(b) using thin paper. You don't think that you have moved so put the tracing on top of Fig. 17.3(a) with S' on top of S to show stars A and B leaving you along straight lines. If an alien living near star B has also been star-gazing it will think B has not moved. Slide the tracing across until B¹ is on top of B and you will see that he also thinks that all the stars are moving away from him! The fact is that all the stars are separating as the universe gets bigger and we are not in the centre.

Any two masses will attract each other with the force that we say is caused by *gravity*. The force gets bigger as the masses get bigger and rapidly gets smaller as the distance between them increases. The force is only significant when one of the masses is very large – as it would be for a planet or a star.

A large object such as a planet or a star will make a force on any object in the space around it. This is called a gravitational field. The strength of the field at a particular place is the force that is exerted on a 1 kg mass at that place. The field strength is given the symbol $g$ and will also be the same as the acceleration of a mass released at that place. The weight of an object near to a star or planet is given by

$$\text{weight} = \text{mass} \times g$$

At the surface of the Earth $g = 10$ N/kg, so a man of mass 70 kg will weigh 700 N.

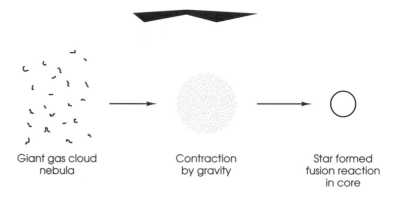

Fig. 17.4

The space between stars is filled with a very thinly scattered gas. Most of this is hydrogen gas with a few other atoms and occasional specks of dust. In some places in the sky we can see giant clouds of this gas and dust and we call such a cloud in space a *nebula*. Dark nebulas block our views of the stars beyond them and contain dust about the same size as the dust in cigarette smoke.

In some cases a giant cloud of gas will be pulled together by gravity and start to collapse towards its centre.

As more material is drawn in and the centre becomes more dense the arriving atoms are attracted more and are travelling faster and therefore have more energy. The energy increases the temperature of the material and a *star* begins to grow. When the temperature is great enough some of the atoms are travelling so fast inside the star that their nuclei are forced together and they form a new larger atom. This is called a *fusion reaction* and releases energy to power the star. Eventually the outward pressure of the fast-moving particles inside the star is balanced by the inward force of gravity and the star becomes stable, emitting radiation and powered by the fusion reaction in its core. Really big clouds of gas can form clusters of stars.

As the star is being formed some of the gas and dust can form a spinning disc that surrounds the star. Some of the material in the disc round our Sun condensed together and formed lumps that could then attract other material and slowly grow into the planets which still spin round in the plane where the disc of gas used to be. Close to the Sun it would be hotter and at first only those materials that had higher melting points would be able to condense out of the gas and form the basis of the *rocky planets*. Farther away from the Sun it was cooler and other materials with lower melting points could condense to form the *icy planets*. The planets are trapped in their orbits by gravity which provides the centripetal force that is needed (see chapter 5.) The Earth appears to be about 4600 million years old so our solar system probably began about 5 billion years ago.

## 6 > CREATION

### (i) Old ideas

There have been many theories to explain how the universe started and most ancient civilisations and religions had their own to explain the facts as they were known. Many included a flat surface for the Earth with the sky somehow held above it and stars moving on the surface of the sky. Most had a god that created the system at some time in the distant past. Since, to men at the time, the Earth was clearly the largest and most important object it was placed at the centre of most models of the universe. After discovering that the Earth was round, western civilisation believed that the Earth was at the centre and that the other planets rotated round it. A sun-centred (helio-centric) theory was strongly resisted.

### (ii) The "Big Bang"

We now accept the idea of a solar system and our place in a galaxy and the universe as we have already described it. Scientists now try to explain how it all began. The universe is still expanding, all the galaxies moving apart so they may have all come from one central place. Tracing the movements back would suggest that all the material in the universe might have been in one place about 15 billion years ago. Then there was a gigantic explosion called the *"big bang"* that threw all the matter outwards. As it moved outwards gravity would have pulled some of it together to form the stars and galaxies.

### (iii) The steady state theory

Another theory was that matter was always being created in the space between galaxies as they moved apart. This would then form new galaxies so that the universe remained in a "steady state" overall. This was a commonly accepted idea in the 1950s and 1960s but then microwave radiation was discovered that appears to have originated in the big bang and the big bang theory became more widely accepted. In the 1990s the data collected by special satellites such as COBE has confirmed this radiation is real and even that it is not quite evenly distributed where the first galaxies began to form not long after the big bang.

### (iv) A repeating universe

The big bang theory does not explain how all the matter came to be in one place to begin with. There are a number of possibilities but one is that gravity will eventually cause the universe to collapse back inwards to its original place and size in a "big crunch" and the whole cycle will begin again with another big bang.

This cycle could then keep on repeating.

## 7 > THE LIFE CYCLE OF A STAR

Stars don't remain the same for ever. A star like the Sun is called a *main sequence* star and is stable as we found in section 5.

A star the size of the Sun will eventually start to run out of nuclear fuel (hydrogen) for fusion and grow a lot bigger. It will also be cooler at its surface and become a *red giant*. The red giant may be hundreds of times bigger than the Sun, overcoming some of the inner planets, and last for millions of years.

Our Sun is expected to last for about 10 billion years as a "normal" star and then another billion as a giant. We are about halfway through the "normal" stage. Inside the giant, near its core, the helium formed by the fusion process will be fused to make

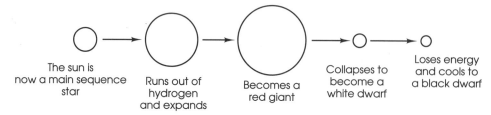

The sun is now a main sequence star → Runs out of hydrogen and expands → Becomes a red giant → Collapses to become a white dwarf → Loses energy and cools to a black dwarf

Fig. 17.5

larger nuclei. As it eventually dies the giant will send some of its matter out into the galaxy as glowing gas and what is left will contract smaller and smaller until it becomes a *white dwarf*. This will be very dense (more than a ton per teaspoonful) and gives out a lot of radiation. This will again last for millions of years but is continuously losing energy and eventually cools and becomes a cold and dark *black dwarf* (sometimes called a dark body).

A star bigger than the Sun will probably make an even more dense core that will explode and be seen from other stars as a *supernova* as the light and dust is thrown outwards. A smaller piece of the centre will probably be left behind and become a *neutron star*, small but almost unbelievably heavy – about the weight of a mountain per teaspoonful and perhaps only a few tens of km across.

Stars that are even bigger can end in another different way. They are so big that gravity keeps on pulling the matter together until the star, perhaps 20 times the size of the Sun, has become about the size of a city. It is so dense that the force of gravity has become enormous and nothing, not even light, can escape. It has become a *black hole*.

When stars explode or throw out part of their matter into space it is eventually captured in a gas cloud and becomes a part of a new star or planet. We think that a lot of the heavier, more complicated elements were made by fusion reactions inside stars and then thrown out as a sort of dust into space. Planets like ours contain material that was formed in other suns billions of years ago, thrown out into space and eventually collected together near our Sun. There is some evidence that a lot of it came from a supernova that exploded just before our Sun evolved. We think that our Sun is therefore made from the remains of others – it is a second or third generation star. Without the bits left from earlier stars we wouldn't exist because there wouldn't be any of the larger atoms such as oxygen, iron, etc.

## 8 DAYS AND SEASONS

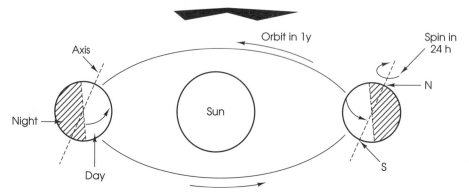

Fig. 17.6

The Earth rotates on an axis through the N and S poles once every 24 hours. Only the side of the Earth facing the Sun is lit by it and in daylight whilst that part of the Earth facing away from the Sun has night. At the same time the Earth is moving in its orbit round the Sun, which takes one year.

The N–S axis that the Earth is rotating round is tilted by about 23° so that the radiation from the Sun is not evenly spread over its surface. At one time in its orbit the N pole is tilted away from the Sun and the S pole towards it (the right hand side of Fig. 17.6). The result is that the northern half of the Earth is getting less heat and the southern half is getting more. The northern hemisphere is in winter and the southern hemisphere is in summer. At places tilted towards the Sun the period of daylight is longer than the night and the Sun rises higher in the sky. The pole tilted towards the Sun will get 24 hours of daylight in the middle of its summer. At the same time the pole tilted away from the Sun remains in darkness for the whole day. Six months later, on the opposite side of the orbit, the reverse will be true as the northern hemisphere gets more energy and is in summer (the left hand side of Fig. 17.6).

## 9 INSIDE THE EARTH

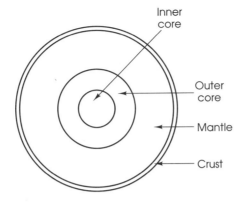

Fig. 17.7

The Earth is almost spherical and about 12 800 km in diameter. It is made up of a number of layers as seen in Fig. 17.7. The outer layer is the **crust** and it is quite thin varying from about 70km under the continents to about 10 km under the oceans. The **continental crust** is mostly granite and floats on top of the more dense **oceanic crust** which is mostly basalt.

The **mantle** is a dense layer of rock and metal oxides between the crust and the core. It is not melted but is "plastic" which means that it can flow. (The bitumen used to make roads is this sort of a plastic – it seems solid but can be squashed by a big truck and slowly flows downhill, especially when it is warm.) As you go towards the centre the temperature increases and the **outer core** is hot enough to be made from molten iron and nickel. The outer core is about 2200 km thick. Currents moving round in this liquid outer core are believed to produce the Earth's magnetic field rather like a giant electromagnet. Farther in the pressure becomes so great that the metals cannot remain melted and there is a solid **inner core** that is about 2600 km in diameter. These facts are known because of the way that earthquakes travel through the earth.

Fig. 17.8

## 10 EARTHQUAKES AND WAVES

The place where an earthquake occurs in the rocks of the Earth's crust is called the **focus**. The place directly above this on the surface of the Earth is called the **epicentre**. The waves generated by an earthquake will travel through the Earth and be detected at other places by a **seismometer**. An earthquake will send out three types of wave:

- **P waves** (Pressure waves) are longitudinal waves and therefore travel as a series of compressions in the same way as a sound wave. These waves can move through both solids and liquids and can therefore travel through both the mantle and the core to reach the opposite side of the Earth. The changing density of the mantle may cause the path of the P waves to bend (as they are steadily **refracted,** see chapter 6).
- **S waves** (Shear or Shake waves) are transverse waves and they can travel through the solid of the mantle but not the liquid of the outer core. Some of the S waves may be **reflected** from the surface of the liquid core and a shadow is left at the other side of the Earth that the S waves cannot reach. This proves that the core does exist and helps scientists to work out its size.
- **L waves** (Long waves) are the waves that travel round the crust on the surface. They will arrive last but do the most damage.

The strength of earthquakes is measured on two scales:

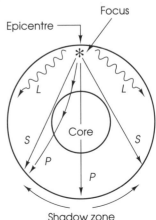

Fig. 17.9

- The **Richter scale** measures the energy of the earthquake and going from one point to the next (e.g. from 5 to 6) is an increase of ten times (so from 5 to 7 is 100 times!). This is useful for large powerful earthquakes.
- The **Mercalli scale** is more help when describing earth tremors or smaller earthquakes and describes the effects that would be noticed. Some of the levels are as follows:

  2  Hardly felt. Noticed by people in bed.
  4  Hanging objects swing. Doors and windows rattle.
  6  People frightened, run outdoors. Felt by all. Some damage.
  8  Cracks open in ground. Some buildings collapse.
  10 Landslides. Most buildings damaged badly.
  12 Large areas of ground moved up and down. Total damage.

If you collect evidence from witnesses and then use the Mercalli scale to mark the strength of the earthquake on a map, it can be seen that equal levels can be joined forming circles with the epicentre at the middle. The effects get weaker as the circles get wider.

Information about earthquakes is called **seismic**; e.g. seismic waves are measured by a **seismometer** in which a pen plots the waves on a chart as they arrive. This would then be examined by a seismologist.

## 11 TECTONIC PLATES

Earthquake zones ——— Plate movement

**Fig. 17.10**

Plotting where earthquakes occur in the Earth's crust shows that they are not randomly spread but are in a pattern as shown in Fig. 17.10.

Some of the continents also seem to have shapes that fit together. If you trace a map and then cut out the three shapes of Africa, South America and North America you can see that they fit together quite well. If the older rocks from the edges of these shapes are compared they are also a good geological match. This leads us to believe that the surface of the planet is made up of a set of large **plates** which are slowly moving about on the planet surface. Further evidence is found by studying the evolution of plants and animals on the separated continents. These show us when the continents were joined (common evolution) and when they separated (after this the evolution was different on each continent

– e.g. marsupials in Australia have only a few close relatives in South America). Movements of the plates cause the major earthquakes. The movement may be caused by convection currents in the mantle that the plates rest on.

- The plates can be sliding sideways past each other. This may happen in sudden "jerks" when the energy has built up enough to force the plates along. This happens along vertical **transform faults** in the crust like the one in California called the San Andreas fault. Satellite pictures show how features like river beds can be suddenly re-routed by the surface movement.
- The plates can move apart from each other at **constructive plate boundaries**. This leaves a gap and **magma** (melted rock) comes up from below,

Fig. 17.11

(a) Plates moving apart

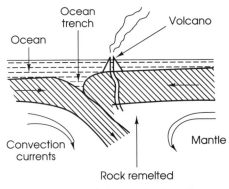

(b) Oceanic plates moving together

Fig. 17.12

solidifies and forms new crust. The earthquakes are not as strong as in the other cases. The new rock is basalt and forms an *oceanic ridge*. This happens in the "mid-Atlantic ridge" where Africa and South America are moving apart. In the Atlantic this movement is about 2 cm per year and about 9 cm per year in the Pacific. If plates move apart under continents instead of the ocean then a *rift valley* is formed on the surface. As Africa moved away from Arabia a rift valley was formed which is now filled by the Red Sea.

■ The plates can slide towards each other at *destructive plate boundaries*. The thinner but denser ocean plate gets pushed under the continental plate where it eventually melts. This is called *subduction*. The continental plates are forced upwards and there will be a lot of violent earthquakes and volcanoes. This happens along the western coast of South America and in Japan. If two continental plates collide, the rocks from the ocean that was between the two continents gets squashed together and pushed upwards to form *fold mountains*. This produced the Himalayas where the Indian plate and the Eurasian plate are moving towards each other. The rock that is pushed downwards may gain so much energy that it is remelted and finds its way back to the surface to form volcanoes.

## 12 > PHASES OF THE MOON

We only see the moon by the sunlight that is reflected from it. Since only the half of the moon that is facing the sun get light from it, we see different phases of the moon as it orbits round the Earth.

When the moon is between us and the Sun (1 in the diagram) the illuminated side is away from us and we have a dark "*new*" moon. By position 2 we can see some of the side of the moon facing the Sun as a bright *crescent*. By 3 we can see half of the moon and it is a quarter of the way round its orbit. The bright part that we can see increases through the *gibbous* stage (4), where more than half of the moon can be seen, to the *full* moon (5) where we can see all of the side that is facing the Sun. For this half of the orbit where the lit area that we can see is increasing, the moon is *waxing*. The reverse then happens in the other half of the orbit and the moon is said to be *waning*. The whole orbit takes 28 days. Since the moon also rotates once on its own axis in the same time, it always has the same side facing the Earth.

Fig. 17.13

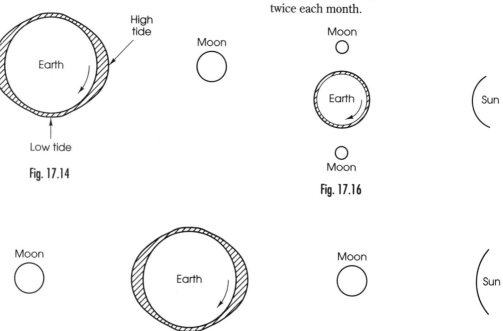

## 13> TIDES

On the side of the Earth nearest to the moon the water in the seas will be attracted to the moon by gravitational attraction and will bulge out slightly. On the other side of the Earth, opposite to the moon, there is another bulge of approximately the same size where the moon has least attraction. As the Earth rotates once per day, any place where you observe the sea level will pass through each of these bulges and the water level will rise (**high tide**) and fall (**low tide**) about twice each day. (Fig. 17.14)

Even though it is a lot farther away the Sun also has an effect on the tides. When the Earth, the moon and the Sun are all in a straight line the Sun increases the effect and the tides are bigger than usual and are called *spring tides*. (Fig 17.15)

When the Sun is at right angles to the Earth and moon it will cancel the effect of the moon a little and smaller tides are produced. These are called *neap tides*. (Fig 17.16)

Spring and neap tides will occur about twice each month.

Fig. 17.14

Fig. 17.16

Fig. 17.15

## 14> ATMOSPHERE

An atmosphere will be created round a planet from the gases that condense as it is made and from volcanic gases released by the hot rocks afterwards. If the planet is small or hot the molecules of gas will be going fast enough to escape into space and the atmosphere is lost (e.g. mercury). A large cold planet will attract the molecules in its atmosphere a lot and they will move more slowly at the lower temperature so they cannot escape. The Earth is massive enough and its atmosphere is cool enough for it to keep all but the very lightest gases from escaping. The atmosphere of the Earth was probably first made of carbon dioxide, water vapour, methane and ammonia.

The carbon dioxide would be reduced and the oxygen increased as plants developed.

More carbon dioxide became trapped in coal, oil and gas deposits and in sedimentary rocks that are carbonates (limestones and chalks).

The methane and ammonia reacted with the new oxygen until they were eliminated.

Nitrogen was put into the air by bacteria. Some of the oxygen became ozone in the upper atmosphere and this protected the plants and animals, speeding up the process of creating our present atmosphere.

Our atmosphere is now made up of:

- nitrogen about 78%
- oxygen about 20%
- carbon dioxide about 0.03%
- inert gases less than 1%
- water vapour varies a lot from nil to about 5%
- dust and other particles.

The atmosphere has been very similar to this for the last 200 million years. The average pressure exerted at sea level by the atmosphere in Britain is 101 300 Pa. This pressure will fall rapidly as you go upwards so that it is halved when you are about 6000 m above sea level. (See chapter 11 for more about Pa and about barometers to measure pressure.)

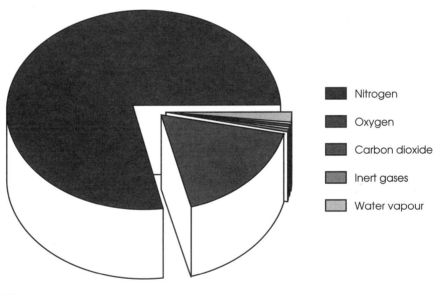

Nitrogen

Oxygen

Carbon dioxide

Inert gases

Water vapour

**Fig. 17.17**

## 15> WEATHER

As the Earth spins on its axis it causes some of its atmosphere to swirl into eddies rather than being uniform. These areas can have pressure above or below the average. Energy from water vapour condensing in colder air and from convection currents can increase these effects and they move through the atmosphere changing our weather. So that we can see the pattern of the pressure changes we join all places on our map that have equal air pressure by lines called *isobars*. A pressure of 100 000 Pa (the same as 10 N/cm²) is called 1 *bar* and the isobars usually have their pressure marked in *millibars*. Winds will be stronger where the isobars are closer together.

Regions of high pressure are called *anticyclones*. The wind will spiral outwards in a clockwise direction (in the Northern hemisphere), the air being replaced by air from much higher in the atmosphere falling into the centre of the system. The winds are usually light and the anticyclone is slow moving. The weather produced is usually bright and clear with little cloud. This can be warm in summer but the lack of cloud gives low temperatures, especially at night, in winter. The weather close to a high pressure tends to be calm and settled.

Regions of low pressure are called *depressions* (or cyclones). The weather close to a depression is usually wetter and unsettled.

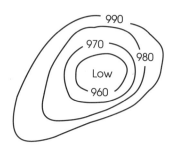

(a) Anticyclone    (b) Depression or cyclone

**Fig. 17.18**

The wind will spiral inwards in an anticlockwise direction (in the Northern hemisphere) and can be much stronger than that from a high pressure. If you stand with the wind on your back the centre of the depression will be on your left. Depressions will move quite rapidly and cause the weather to change often in Britain as they move, usually from west to east. A depression will usually have weather fronts linked to it. As more air spirals into it the depression will eventually fill and disappear.

Air can have different properties depending on where it has been. Air from over the ocean – *maritime* air – will be saturated with water. Air from over land masses – *continental* air will be dry. Air from the tropics will be warm but that from the polar, Arctic areas will be cold. In the British Isles the main airstreams are as shown in Fig. 17.19. There is also an *arctic maritime* air mass which comes down from the north. The dominant air stream is from the south-west. This usually prevents very long periods of extreme cold weather but the depressions moving across us usually keep our weather changeable.

**Fig. 17.19**

When cold and warm air masses meet they form a *front*. Depressions often develop a warm front and a cold front. In a *warm front* the warm moist air rises over the cold dry air and it is shown on a map as a line with semicircles. In a *cold front* the cold dry air is pushing under the warm moist air and it is shown on the map as a line with triangles on it. Between the two fronts there will be a wedge of warmer moist air and the weather will change as the two fronts pass over. A map showing all of this information and the wind speeds and directions is called a *synoptic chart*. An example of this for a depression is shown in Fig. 17.20.

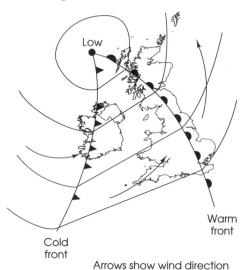

Arrows show wind direction

**Fig. 17.20**

The two fronts and the clouds that usually go with them are shown in Fig. 17.22. There will be a change of wind direction and air temperature as each front passes. The depression will move approximately in the direction of the isobars between the fronts (WNW in Fig. 17.20). Sometimes the cold front will catch up with the warm front pushing it upwards. This is called an occluded front and is shown as a line marked with alternate triangles and semicircles. (Fig 17.21)

All of these things cause the weather and help us to try and predict it. Satellite pictures now show us the weather systems and we can

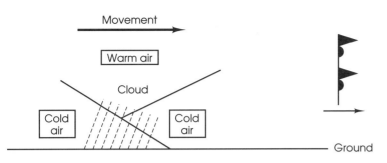

Fig. 17.21

Fig. 17.22 shows what will happen when the fronts from a depression pass.

■ At A high cirrus cloud is seen. The weather is fine but the pressure starts to fall.

■ At B the pressure is still falling, the cloud thickens and it starts to rain.

■ At C the pressure steadies, the air temperature rises and the wind turns more westerly. The warm front passes.

■ At D it is dull with low cloud and some drizzle.

■ At E there will be heavy rain, the pressure starts to rise and the wind turns more northwesterly. The cold front has passed and the temperature will fall again. Clouds gradually become more scattered and the wind dies away.

track their movement. In Britain a radar system also tracks the rainfall. To describe the weather you would need to take measurements of temperature, atmospheric pressure, mm of rainfall, amount of cloud cover, wind direction and speed at regular intervals together with the hours of sunshine each day.

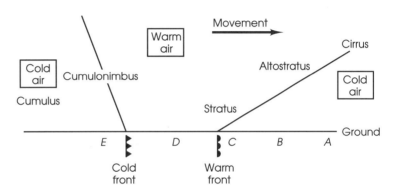

Fig. 17.22

# 16 CLOUDS AND FOG

Water can be held in the air as *vapour*. The amount that can be held by the air depends on temperature. If the air holds as much water as possible it is *saturated*. If air is cooled it will eventually become saturated and if cooled further some of the water has to *condense* as small droplets. This may happen on summer nights causing *dew*.

In autumn the ground is often wet and the air becomes saturated. If the night sky has

little cloud the ground will cool quickly by radiating heat and the air near the ground will become colder. The water vapour will condense in lots of droplets forming *fog*. In industrial areas with dust in the air the water condenses on the dust particles forming smog.

In a similar way air that is pushed upwards will become colder and the water will start to condense forming *clouds* of small droplets. If the cloud is cooled more these drops grow in size until the drops become too heavy to stay in the air and fall as rain. This can happen on the western side of our hills as the westerly wind from over the Atlantic is pushed upwards. Clouds at different heights look different and have different names. The names can help you remember their features:

cumulus    fluffy or lumpy
stratus     flat layers
cirrus      high and made of ice crystals
nimbo-      giving rain
alto-       medium height

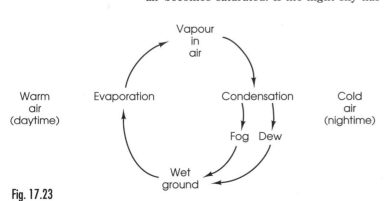

Fig. 17.23

| Name | Height/km | Description |
|------|-----------|-------------|
| cirrus | high 6–12 | delicate, wispy. Called "mares tails" |
| cirrocumulus | high 6–10 | small lumps of cloud in lines |
| altostratus | medium 4–5 | high flat layers |
| stratus | low 0.5–2 | continuous thick low cloud |
| cumulus | low 1.0–2 | separated heaps of cloud with flat base |
| cumulonimbus | low 1.0–6 | high big cumulus, heavy rain, thunder. |

## 17〉 ROCKS

There are three types of rock depending on how they were formed.

■ *Igneous rock* is rock that has been formed by the cooling of molten rock (magma) that has been forced up from under the crust. It will then turn solid as a mass of crystals. If you examine a piece of *granite* you will be able to see three different sorts of crystal, all fitting perfectly together with no spaces between them. The black, shiny pieces are mica, the white crystal is quartz and the larger white or pink crystals are feldspar. The crystals are packed in randomly, the ones with the highest melting points separating out first and the others filling the spaces in between. If the rock cools quickly the crystals will be smaller. (A drop of melted salol put on a warm slide forms larger crystals than a drop put onto a cold slide from a fridge.) Lava will often have cooled very quickly and the crystals will be too small to see. The lava may seem very light because volcanic gases that were bubbling through it when it left the volcano are trapped inside it.

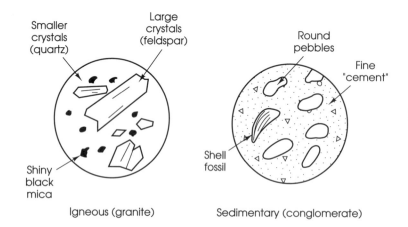

Igneous (granite)      Sedimentary (conglomerate)

Fig. 17.24

■ *Sedimentary rock* will have been formed from smaller particles of rock that have settled to the bottom of water. As water flows down rivers it carries small pieces of rock that have been broken away from the higher ground (see weath-ering). These pieces will wear away the river bed producing more pieces and the grinding of the pieces against each other makes them rounded in the same way as pebbles on a beach. The faster the water flows the larger the pieces of rock it can carry. A big river in flood from a storm or melting snow can move large boulders.

When the river reaches a lake or the sea the water slows down and the particles sink to the bottom forming layers. The tiny particles form layers of mud. Bigger ones, sand and pebbles can be mixed with the mud or put in separate layers. As the layers build up the water is squeezed out and the weight slowly cements the pieces together making a solid rock. *Sandstones* and *limestones* are sedimentary rocks. Sedimentary rocks, especially limestone, may contain *fossils*. The most common are sea shells that have fallen to the bottom and become trapped in the sediment. Remember that younger sedimentary rocks will be on top of older ones. The type of fossil preserved in the rock may help to identify rocks of the same age as the rock will usually contain fossils of the particular plants and animals from the time when the sediment was laid down.

The rocks will not always appear in flat horizontal layers as they were first formed. Movements in the Earth's crust since may cause the rock to be tilted, folded or even turned upside down.

■ *Metamorphic rocks* are rocks that have been changed by heat and pressure. They may have been pushed deep underground, crushed by mountain folding or they may have been close to hot magma that has pushed up close to the surface. Examples are *marble,* which was originally limestone, and *slate,* which was originally mudstone.

*Minerals* are the crystal materials from which rocks are made. Each different mineral is a single chemical compound. The exact proportions of minerals in a particular type of rock will vary in different specimens. Some minerals may be metal ores that are worth mining for the metal or chemicals with other uses, e.g. galena is a lead ore found in veins in the rock in Derbyshire that was mined for its lead content. Fluorspar is quarried for use in the iron and chemical industries.

*Weathering* breaks rocks into smaller pieces. *Erosion* carries away the pieces. There are a number of processes that all help to weather and erode rocks and which eventually wear away even the biggest mountains.

*Rain* can dissolve some minerals and wash away smaller pieces.

*Ice* has a bigger volume than the water that it is formed from. When water freezes in cracks in the rock the forces can be big enough to split pieces off.

*Glaciers* grind rocks away as they slowly move downwards. Glaciers can transport much larger pieces than rivers.

*Wind* will carry away small pieces and can rapidly erode soft rock if the wind has grit in it (a sort of natural sand-blasting process).

Hot *sunshine* will raise the temperature of the surface of a rock so that it expands more than the rock underneath and the outer layer is split off.

Tree *roots* and plant roots grow down into cracks, gradually pushing them apart.

*Acid rain* and other atmospheric pollution may react with the rock and greatly speed up the weathering process. This is seen clearly in industrial areas where gravestones of marble will be much more eroded than those in cleaner air or those, like granite, that resist acids.

*Soil* is made from small pieces of rock mixed with the dead remains of plants and animals (called *humus*). The type of rock, the amount of humus, and the depth of the soil will alter how fertile it is.

# EXTENSION MATERIALS

## 1 STAR GAZING

Looking at the sky at night with a telescope or binoculars will enable you to see many stars and some nebula as well as getting a clear view of the moon. (Checking that you understand and can follow the phases of the moon is easy if you observe it regularly.) Some of the stars appear in recognisable patterns even though they may actually be great distances apart. These patterns are called *constellations* and can be useful in identifying which particular part of the sky you are observing.

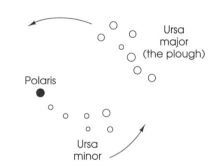

Fig. 17.25

The exact view of the stars that you get depends on where we are along the Earth's orbit (time of year) and how the Earth has rotated on its axis (time of day). You can find out what you can expect to see, or identify particular stars, by using a planisphere. Only the pole star (Polaris) will appear to be stationary because it is along the line of the Earth's axis. As the Earth rotates the other stars seem to go in an arc around the pole star as can be seen on photographs with a long time exposure.

You may see *shooting stars* which are properly called *meteors*. They are really small bits of rock in space that hit the atmosphere and burn up, producing the bright streak that we see. If a small bit survives to reach the surface of the Earth it is called a *meteorite*.

The *planets* will move across our sky as they travel in their orbit round the Sun. You would need tables of dates and times to know when to see them best. Don't confuse them with the more rapid passage of a satellite across the sky which is much more easy and common to see on a clear night. Venus is closer to the Sun and can only be seen clearly at dusk or dawn.

*Comets* also orbit the Sun in long elliptical orbits that sometimes swing close enough to the Sun for them to be seen for a few weeks before moving away again. The head of the comet is probably mostly carbon dioxide and ice and a few tens of km across. The tail is gas and dust released from the comet by the heat of the Sun. The tail always faces away from the Sun.

## 2 FOSSILS

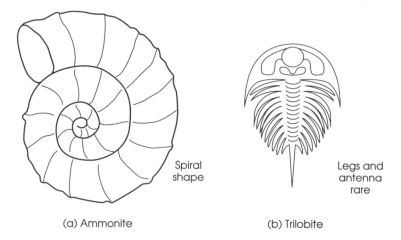

Spiral shape

Legs and antenna rare

(a) Ammonite

(b) Trilobite

Fig. 17.26

Fossils are the remains of plants and animals that have been preserved in the rock. Common ones are *sea shells* and *corals* in limestone and *ferns* and *club mosses* in coal and shale. *Ammonites* are spiral shells that once contained an animal rather like the nautilus with its head and tentacles out of the opening. They can be cut in half to show chambers inside the shell where the animal produced larger chambers as it grew bigger.

*Trilobites* were rather like large water-dwelling woodlice with lots of legs and an armoured three piece shell. They are sometimes found curled up, presumably for defence, and the tracks of their feet have been found in soft sedimentary rock from the ocean bottom. Fossils give us a lot of evidence for our modern theories about rocks. For example sea shells are common in the limestones high in the Alps giving more evidence of the mountain folding and uplifting process.

## 3 THE ROCK CYCLE

The three types of rock do not stay in the same form forever. They are steadily cycled through the different forms as summarised in the diagram. Some parts of the cycle may take millions of years to complete.

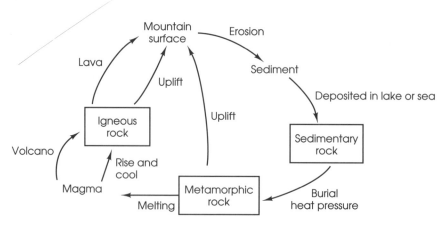

Fig. 17.27

## 4 NEWTON'S LAW OF GRAVITATION

The gravitational force between any two objects of mass $m_1$ and $m_2$ that are a distance $d$ apart is given by

$$F = \frac{Gm_1m_2}{d^2}$$

where $G$ is the universal constant of gravitation and has a value of $6.67 \times 10^{-11}$ Nm$^2$/kg$^2$. Note that the force depends inversely on the square of the distance between the masses which is why it seems to reduce so quickly. If you ever use this equation you can measure $d$ between the centres of mass – for many common shapes such as spheres for planets this is at the centre of each mass. This is the attractive force that usually provides the centripetal force needed to keep a satellite (or planet or moon) in its orbit.

## 5 THE UPPER ATMOSPHERE

The air thins rapidly as you go upwards. 50% of it is below 6 km and 99% of it below 40 km. Various levels of the atmosphere have special properties and names.

- **Troposphere** Up to about 12 km. Contains all Earth's climate and weather. Temperature falls by about 6 °C for each 1000 m.
- **Stratosphere** From 12 km to about 46 km. Temperature rises again because of a layer of ozone that absorbs incoming ultraviolet radiation.
- **Mesosphere** From 46 km to about 80 km. Temperature falls rapidly to about

–90 °C. No water, dust or ozone.

- **Thermosphere** Above 80 km. Virtually no atmosphere at all above 100 km. Small amount of atomic oxygen at high temperature.
- **Exosphere** Above 600 km. Merges with interplanetary medium. About equal proportions of hydrogen and helium up to 2400 km and then mainly hydrogen.
- **Ionosphere** Charged particles between about 65 and 800 km. The particles form layers that can reflect radio waves and cause the **auroras** (northern lights, southern lights).

## 6 ECLIPSES

A **lunar eclipse** will occur when the moon orbits into the shadow of the Earth. Remember that the moon, like all other objects in space except stars, is only seen by reflected light. This is NOT the same effect as that which causes the phases of the moon.

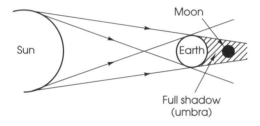

Fig. 17.28

A **solar eclipse** will occur when the moon orbits between the Sun and the Earth so that a shadow is cast onto the Earth's surface. Scientists will try to observe the Sun in a total eclipse so that its bright disc is covered and solar flares can be seen more clearly.

The shadow of the moon will cross the Earth's surface as the moon moves in its orbit. At a place in the path of the middle of the shadow the area of the Sun that appears to be covered increases (partial eclipse) until it is all covered (total eclipse) and then decreases again. Only a narrow strip of the Earth's surface will get a total eclipse but a wider area on each side will see a partial eclipse.

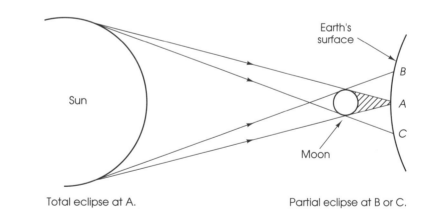

Total eclipse at A.　　　　Partial eclipse at B or C.

Fig. 17.29

## 7 POWERING THE SUN – FUSION

We know the mass of the Sun and the rate at which it radiates energy. If it produced the energy by burning its mass in some sort of a combustion reaction it would have used up all its fuel in a few thousand years. Since this is not true the reaction must be of a different type. We believe the reaction to be a **fusion reaction** in which hydrogen nuclei collide and join to form helium nuclei which can then

fuse with other nuclei to produce larger nuclei. Each fusion releases some energy because the energy needed to bind together the particles in the larger nucleus is slightly less than the sum of the separate energies. The reaction will only happen at the high temperatures and pressures at the centre of a star because the particles are both positive in charge and will strongly repel when pushed closer together. The masses needed to produce energy by this reaction are relatively small compared with combustion. The heavier isotopes of hydrogen used in the reaction are called deuterium and tritium.

$$^1_1H + ^1_1H \rightarrow ^2_1H + e^+ + v$$

$$^1_1H + ^2_1H \rightarrow ^3_2He + \gamma$$

$$^3_2He + ^3_2He \rightarrow ^4_2He + ^1_1H + ^1_1H$$

Overall this is the same as

$$4\,^1_1H \rightarrow ^4_2He + energy$$

The new particles $e^+$ and $v$ are called a positron (like an electron but positively charged) and a neutrino.

---

## 8 INSIDE THE EARTH AGAIN

Some courses look at the structure of the Earth in more detail and use the following terms:

- **Lithosphere** [10–50 km]   The layer containing the tectonic plates. Made from continental crust, oceanic crust and mantle rock, all solid.
- **Asthenosphere** [50–250 km]   The layer containing the convection currents that move the plates. Viscous liquid mantle rock.
- **Mesosphere** [250–2900 km]   Solid mantle rock.
- **Outer core** [2900–5200 km]   Liquid mixture of nickel and iron.
- **Inner core** [5200–6371 km]   Solid mixture of nickel and iron.

# EXAMINATION QUESTIONS

## MULTIPLE CHOICE QUESTIONS

### QUESTION 1

A year is

   A   the time for the Earth to rotate on its axis.
   B   the time for the Earth to orbit the Sun.
   C   caused by the tilt of the Earth's axis.
   D   the time between annular eclipses.

### QUESTION 2

At a spring tide the moon is

   A   full.
   B   gibbous.
   C   at its first quarter.
   D   a crescent.

### QUESTION 3

A star much larger than the Sun will eventually become

   A   a black hole.
   B   a supernova.
   C   a red giant.
   D   a white dwarf.

### QUESTION 4

In a total lunar eclipse

   A   the moon is on the opposite side of the Sun to the Earth.
   B   the Sun is on the opposite side of the Earth to the moon.
   C   the Sun and the moon are on the same side of the Earth.
   D   the Earth is in the moon's shadow.

### QUESTION 5

Metamorphic rocks

   A   come from volcanoes.
   B   always contain large crystals.
   C   have been reformed under heat and pressure.
   D   are formed from solids that settle out of water.

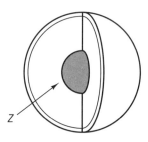

Fig. 17.30

### QUESTION 6

The part of the Earth lettered Z is called the

   A   crust.

B    outer core.

C    inner core.

D    mantle.

## QUESTION 7

Our galaxy is

A    at the centre of the universe.

B    a spiral nebula.

C    the local group.

D    the Milky Way.

## QUESTION 8

At a warm front

A    warm air is riding over cold air.

B    cold air is pushing under warm air.

C    the pressure suddenly falls.

D    the clouds will be very high.

## QUESTION 9

Low flat clouds producing a lot of rain are

A    cirrus.

B    altostratus.

C    stratus.

D    cumulus.

## QUESTION 10

In an earthquake

A    only the P waves can reach the opposite side of the Earth through its centre.

B    L waves go into the Earth and reflect from the core.

C    S waves are the slowest of the waves produced.

D    it is the P waves that do the most surface damage.

## QUESTION 11

Isobars join places with the same

A    temperature.

B    humidity.

C    pressure.

D    height.

## QUESTION 12

Which of the following lists some planets in order of their distance from the Sun?

A    Earth, Saturn, Pluto.

B    Mercury, Mars, Earth.

C    Earth, Venus, Jupiter.

D    Mars, Venus, Saturn.

---

**STRUCTURED QUESTIONS**

## QUESTION 13

(a)  The average surface temperature on the Earth is about 10 °C. Suggest a value for the average surface temperature of the planet Mercury.

(b)  Explain why the surface temperature of a planet depends on its position in the Solar System.

(c)  Explain how each of the following affects the surface temperature of the Earth.
(i)   The Sun.
(ii)  The Earth's atmosphere.
(iii) The rotation of the Earth.

(d)  There is evidence that planets other than the Earth have turbulent atmospheres.
(i)   Name ONE planet which we know to have an atmosphere.
(ii)  What evidence is there to suggest that this planet has an atmosphere?

(e)  The moon has no atmosphere. How has this affected the surface features of the moon?

(ULEAC)

## QUESTION 14

The diagram (Fig 17.31) shows the different air streams (air masses) that can affect the British weather. Use the diagram to help you answer the questions that follow it.

(a)  In the summer of 1989, there were long periods of hot, dry weather. People noticed that their cars were often covered with a fine dry, red dust.
(i)   Which *one* of the five airstreams dominated the weather during the summer of 1989?
(ii)  Mark on the map with an X where the dust is likely to have come from.
(iii) How did the red dust get to Britain?

(b)  The weather in the south-west of Britain is usually warm and humid (damp).
(i)   Which *two* airstreams are most likely to bring damp weather to Britain?
Give a reason for your answer.

**Fig. 17.31**

  (ii) Which *one* of the airstreams gives the south-west of Britain its usual weather conditions? Give a reason for your answer.

(c) Which *one* of the air streams would cause the weather conditions described below?

  *Very dry, cool in summer, very cold in winter.*

           (SEG)

## QUESTION 15

In an earthquake the sudden movement of the rocks produces 3 types of seismic waves known as P, S and L waves.

  The diagram below illustrates how these waves travel away from the epicentre of the earthquake.

(a) Explain in detail how the movement of the P and S waves through the Earth provides evidence to support the layered structure of the Earth shown in the diagram.

(b) Why do the L waves provide no evidence to support the layered structure of the Earth?

(c) What evidence is there to support the idea that the liquid in the outer core is moving?

           (SEG)

**Fig. 17.32**

# OUTLINE ANSWERS

**1 ▷ MULTIPLE CHOICE QUESTIONS**

| Question | 1 | 2 | 3 | 4 | 5 | 6 | 7 | 8 | 9 | 10 | 11 | 12 |
|----------|---|---|---|---|---|---|---|---|---|----|----|----|
| Answer | B | A | A | B | C | D | D | A | C | A | C | A |

**2 ▷ STRUCTURED QUESTIONS**

## ANSWER 13

This is an intermediate/higher level question.

(a) The temperature must be greater than 10 °C. (The actual figure is in the table earlier in this chapter.   1 mark

(b) A planet that is closer to the Sun will receive a greater amount of energy per square metre on its surface.   4 marks

(c) (i) The Sun radiates energy which is received by the Earth.
(ii) The Earth's atmosphere traps the energy. Some heat is retained in the water vapour and heat radiated back out by the Earth is absorbed or reflected back by the cloud layer (greenhouse effect).
(iii) The rotation of the Earth ensures that the energy received is spread more evenly over the whole surface.   2 marks each part

(d) (i) Venus or Mars, etc.   1 mark
(ii) Evidence depends on the planet chosen, e.g. Venus has dense clouds that stop us seeing the surface and we can see storms in these clouds.   2 marks

(e) The surface is more cratered because meteorites are not burned up before hitting the surface.
The surface is not eroded away by winds and rain.
The temperature difference between night and day is greater than if there was an atmosphere and climate.   1 mark each.

## ANSWER 14

This is a foundation/intermediate level question.

(a) (i) Tropical continental.   1 mark
(ii) X at North Africa/southern Europe.   1 mark
(iii) Picked up and carried by the air mass.

(b) (i) Polar maritime, tropical maritime.   1 mark
The air masses spend a lot of time passing over the sea so that they pick up moisture.   1 mark
(ii) Tropical maritime.   1 mark
The air is both wet and warm   1 mark

(c) Polar continental   1 mark

## ANSWER 15

This is a higher tier question.

(a) The following facts would each be given 1 mark as they are stated in your answer. A second mark is given for what is inferred.

Waves refract as they travel inwards (1) suggesting a change in rock density (1).
S waves cannot pass through a liquid (1) and cannot pass through the centre of the Earth which must be liquid (1).

The shadow zone (1) and the reflection of some P waves shows that there must be a solid core (1).

(b) The L waves provide no evidence because they only travel in the Earth's crust.   1 mark

(c) The Earth has a magnetic field which is explained by the movement of the liquid outer core.   1 mark      (SEG)

# STUDENT'S ANSWER WITH THE EXAMINER'S COMMENTS

## STUDENT ANSWER ON AN EXAMINATION QUESTION

❝ Direction should be more SE. ❞

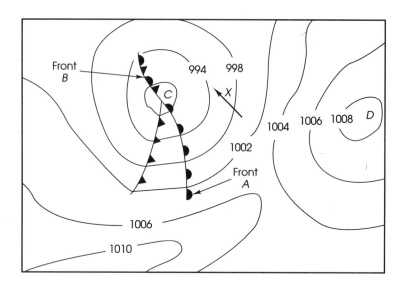

❝ Good answers at first. ❞

a) What is a *front*?

The line where two air masses meet.

b) What sort of front is front A? __Warm__

c) What sort of front is front B? __Occluded__

❝ Easy mark missed C is low. ❞

d) What sort of pressure centre is C? ⟶ _____

e) Mark on the diagram the wind direction at X.

f) If it is summer what do you think the weather will be like at D? _____

❝ Also light winds and clear sky. ❞ ⟶

Hot and Sunny

g) Explain why fog might be formed above wet ground on a clear night in winter.

When it gets cold the water in the air condenses and forms fog because cold air can't hold as much water as warm air. It will be cold because the skies are clear.

❝ Good answer but order a bit muddled. Water evaporates into air in warmer daytime. ❞

# REVIEW SHEET

■ The nearest star to earth is the _____. The next nearest is _____.

■ The name of our galaxy is _____.

■ Our galaxy is part of a cluster called the _____.

■ What will the next two stages be in the life of the Sun?

1. _____.          2. _____.

■ Name the planets in the solar system starting nearest to the Sun.


■ Which planet is

a)  largest? _____.

b)  smallest? _____.

c)  hottest? _____.

d)  coldest? _____.

e)  the one with most moons? _____.

■ What is the name of the theory for the creation of the universe that most scientists believe in? _____ _____.

■ A cloud of dust and gas in space that could form stars is called a _____.

■ The reaction that powers a star is a _____.

■ The three types of rock are

1. _____          2. _____          3. _____

■ The outer layer of the Earth is called the _____.

■ In the northern hemisphere the star that does not appear to move is _____.

■ The moon orbits the Earth in _____ days.

■ There will be higher tides called _____ _____ when the _____ is also in line with the moon and the Earth.

■ Granite that contains large crystals will have been cooled _____.

■ Name an example of a plant fossil and an animal fossil.

Plant fossil _____.          Animal fossil _____.

■ Winds in the northern hemisphere will rotate _____ -wise into a depression.

■ High wispy clouds are called _____.

■ Low flat rain clouds are called _____.

- The three types of earthquake wave are _____.

- The type of earthquake wave that only travels in the crust is _____.

- A _____ tide is lower than a normal tide. At such a tide the phase of the moon will be _____.

- Name five ways in which rocks can be broken down or eroded.

  1. _____.    2. _____.    3. _____.

  4. _____.    5. _____.

- Between Africa and South America at the mid-Atlantic _____ the plates are moving _____.

- The Earth orbits the _____ in 1 _____ . Its axis is tilted at about _____ ° so that more heat reaches the northern hemisphere in _____ but less in the _____ hemisphere at the same time so it is in winter. The Earth spins on its axis once each _____ which gives us one period of dark and one of light each _____.

- The layer of the Earth that is liquid is the _____ and it is made from _____.

- A man who has a mass of 75 kg will weigh _____ on Earth and _____ on the moon where the gravitational field strength is about one sixth of that at the Earth's surface.

- The highest layer of the atmosphere merges with "space" and is called the

  _____.

- In a fusion reaction _____ nuclei join to make a _____ nucleus and release energy.

- The biggest stars will eventually become _____.

- Mountains like the Alps are produced by _____ when the crust is pushed together between two _____ that are moving towards each other.

- A rift valley occurs when _____.

- Make a list of some of the evidence for tectonic plates.

  _____

  _____

  _____

  _____

  _____

# APPENDIX 1: EQUATIONS

The equations in this list are all put into alphabetical order so that you can find the one that you need more quickly. Some of the equations may be given to you in the examination but there are some equations that you most learn. These equations that will not be provided for you are marked with a star (✪) in the following list:

✪ Acceleration $= \dfrac{\text{change in velocity}}{\text{time taken}}$ $\qquad a = \dfrac{v-u}{t}$

Boyle's Law :
  Pressure × volume = constant $\qquad P_1V_1 = P_2V_2$

Charge stored = capacitance × p.d. $\qquad Q = CV$

✪ Charge transferred = current × time $\qquad Q = It$

Charles' Law :
  $\dfrac{\text{Volume}}{\text{Temperature}} = \text{constant}$ $\qquad \dfrac{V_1}{T_1} = \dfrac{V_2}{T_2}$

Density $= \dfrac{\text{mass}}{\text{volume}}$ $\qquad D = \dfrac{m}{v}$

Energy = mass × specific heat capacity × change in temperature $\quad W = msT$

Energy changed = p.d. × current × time $\qquad W = VIt$

Energy changed = current$^2$ × resistance × time $\qquad W = I^2Rt$

Efficiency $= \dfrac{\text{energy output}}{\text{energy input}} = \dfrac{\text{work output}}{\text{work input}}$

Efficiency $= \dfrac{\text{MA}}{\text{VR}} \times 100\%$

Expansion = linear expansivity × original length × rise in temperature.

✪ Force = mass × acceleration $\qquad F = ma$

General Gas Equation :
  $\dfrac{\text{Pressure} \times \text{volume}}{\text{Temperature}} = \text{constant}$ $\qquad \dfrac{P_1V_1}{T_1} = \dfrac{P_2V_2}{T_2}$

Gravitational PE = weight × height $\qquad PE = mgh$

Heat loss per sec (power loss) = U - value × area × temperature difference

Heat of fusion = mass × specific latent heat of vapourisation

Heat of vapourisation = mass × specific latent heat of vapourisation

Kinetic Energy $= \frac{1}{2} \times$ mass × velocity$^2$ $\qquad KE = \dfrac{m \times v^2}{2}$

Mechanical advantage $= \dfrac{\text{load}}{\text{effort}}$

Moment = force × perpendicular distance to pivot

Momentum = mass × velocity

$$\text{Potential difference} = \frac{\text{work done}}{\text{charge moved}}$$

Potential divider equation :
$$V_{\text{out}} = \frac{V_{\text{in}} \times R_1}{(R_1 + R_2)}$$

$$\text{Power} = \frac{\text{energy changed}}{\text{time taken}} = \frac{\text{work done}}{\text{time taken}} =$$
$$P = \frac{W}{t}$$

❂ Power = p.d. × current
$$P = VI$$

Power = current$^2$ × resistence
$$P = I^2 R$$

❂ Pressure = $\dfrac{\text{normal force}}{\text{area}}$
$$P = \frac{F}{A}$$

Pressure of a liquid = depth × density × g
$$P = h\rho g$$

Pressure law :
$$\text{Pressure} = \frac{\text{constant}}{\text{temperature}}$$
$$\frac{P_1}{T_1} = \frac{P_2}{T_2}$$

Ohm's Law :
❂ Resistance = $\dfrac{\text{potential difference}}{\text{current}}$
$$R = \frac{V}{I}$$

Resistors in series :
$$R_{\text{TOTAL}} = R_1 + R_2 + ...$$

Resistors in parallel :
$$\frac{1}{R_{\text{TOTAL}}} = \frac{1}{R_1} + \frac{1}{R_2} + ...$$

❂ Speed = $\dfrac{\text{distance moved}}{\text{time taken}}$
$$V = \frac{S}{t}$$

❂ Transformer equation :
$$\frac{V_{\text{out}}}{V_{\text{in}}} = \frac{N_{\text{secondary}}}{N_{\text{primary}}}$$

Velocity = $\dfrac{\text{change in displacement}}{\text{time taken}}$
$$V = \frac{S}{t}$$

Velocity ratio = $\dfrac{\text{distance moved by effort}}{\text{distance moved by load}}$

Voltage gain = $\dfrac{\text{voltage output}}{\text{voltage input}}$
$$A = \frac{V_{\text{out}}}{V_{\text{in}}}$$

❂ Wave velocity = frequency × wavelength
$$v = f\lambda$$

❂ Work done = force × distance moved in direction of force
$$W = Fs$$

Weight = mass × gravitational field strength
$$\text{Weight} = mg$$

# APPENDIX 2: CIRCUIT SYMBOLS

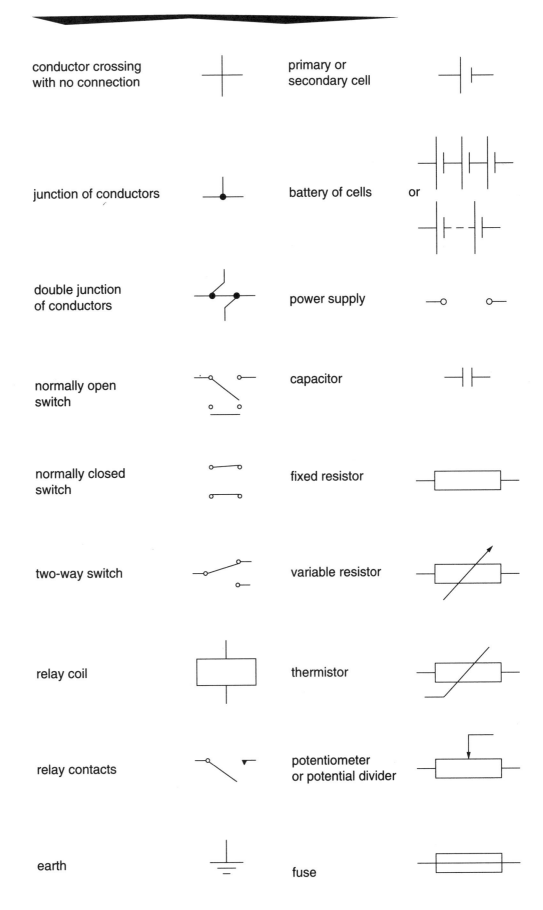

| | |
|---|---|
| conductor crossing with no connection | primary or secondary cell |
| junction of conductors | battery of cells or |
| double junction of conductors | power supply |
| normally open switch | capacitor |
| normally closed switch | fixed resistor |
| two-way switch | variable resistor |
| relay coil | thermistor |
| relay contacts | potentiometer or potential divider |
| earth | fuse |

| | | | |
|---|---|---|---|
| ammeter | —(A)— | transformer with magnetic core | |
| voltmeter | —(V)— | microphone | |
| signal lamp | —(⊗)— | loudspeaker | |
| filament lamp | —(⊖)— | electric bell | |
| motor | —(M)— | buzzer | |
| generator | —(G)— | AND gate | |
| diode | —▷⊢— | OR gate | |
| | | NAND gate | |
| light emitting diode (LED) | —▷⊢↗↗ | NOR gate | |
| light dependent resistor (LDR) | —▭— ↘ | NOT gate | |

# INDEX

# Longman - for all your study guide needs

Addison Wesley Longman publishes a wide range of curriculum-related books to help you with your studies. If you have enjoyed using this book and have found it useful, you can now order others directly from us - simply follow the ordering instructions below.

Don't forget to tell your fellow students about *Longman Study Guides* - they might find them useful too!

## HOW TO ORDER

A full list of titles is given overleaf. Decide which title(s) you require and then order in one of the following ways:

**by post**

Fill in the quantity alongside the title(s) you require, select your method of payment, complete your name and address details and return your completed order form and payment to:

*Addison Wesley Longman Ltd*
*PO BOX 88*
*Harlow*
*Essex CM19 5SR*

**by phone**

Call our Customer Information Centre on 01279 623923 to place your order, quoting mail number: HESG1

**by fax**

complete the order form overleaf and fill in your name and address details and method of payment, and fax it to us on 01279 414130.

**by e-mail**

E-mail your order to us on awlhe.orders@awl.co.uk listing title(s) and quantity required and providing full name and address details as requested here. Please quote mail number: HESG1. Please do not send credit card details by e-mail.

---

**Mail no: HESG1**

Your Name _____

Your Address _____

_____

Postcode _____ Telephone _____

**Method of payment**

☐ I enclose a cheque or a P/O for £ _____ made payable to Addison Wesley Longman Ltd
☐ Please charge my Visa/Access/AMEX/Diners Club card

Number _____ Expiry Date _____

Signature _____ Date _____

*(please ensure that the address given above is the same as for your credit card)*

*Prices and other details are correct at time of going to press but may change without notice. All orders are subject to status.*

☐ *Please tick this box if you would like a complete listing of York Notes Literature Guides (suitable for GCSE and A-level English students)*

LONGMAN

Addison Wesley Longman

## LONGMAN HOMEWORK HANDBOOKS (KEY STAGE 3)

*£7.99 each unless otherwise stated*

QTY *(0582)*

| | | |
|---|---|---|
| 1 | _____ 29330 8 | English (KS3) |
| 2 | _____ 29331 6 | French (KS3) |
| 3 | _____ 30423 7 | French pack*(KS3) (£12.99) |
| 4 | _____ 30425 3 | French cassette (KS3) (£6.00) |
| 5 | _____ 29329 4 | German (KS3) |
| 6 | _____ 30427 X | German pack*(KS3) (£12.99) |
| 7 | _____ 30428 8 | German cassette (KS3) (£6.00) |
| 8 | _____ 29328 6 | Mathematics (KS3) |
| 9 | _____ 29327 8 | Science (KS3) |

## LONGMAN GCSE STUDY GUIDES

*£9.99 each unless otherwise stated*

| | | |
|---|---|---|
| 10 | _____ 30481 4 | Biology |
| 11 | _____ 31538 7 | Business Studies |
| 12 | _____ 30482 2 | Chemistry |
| 13 | _____ 31539 5 | Economics |
| 14 | _____ 30484 9 | English |
| 15 | _____ 30483 0 | English Literature |
| 16 | _____ 30485 7 | French |
| 17 | _____ 03839 1 | French pack* (£14.99) |
| 18 | _____ 03836 7 | French cassette (£6.00) |
| 19 | _____ 30486 5 | Geography |
| 20 | _____ 30487 3 | German |
| 21 | _____ 03837 5 | German pack* (£14.99) |
| 22 | _____ 03838 3 | German cassette (£6.00) |
| 23 | _____ 30495 4 | Higher Level Mathematics |
| 24 | _____ 30494 6 | Information Technology (£10.99) |
| 25 | _____ 30496 2 | Mathematics |
| 26 | _____ 30497 0 | Music |
| 27 | _____ 31540 9 | Physics |
| 28 | _____ 28700 6 | Psychology |
| 29 | _____ 31542 5 | Religious Studies |
| 30 | _____ 30498 9 | Science (£10.99) |
| 31 | _____ 22651 1 | Sociology |
| 32 | _____ 22652 X | Spanish |
| 33 | _____ 24509 5 | Spanish pack* (£14.99) |
| 34 | _____ 24511 7 | Spanish cassette (£6.00) |
| 35 | _____ 23771 8 | Technology |
| 36 | _____ 30545 4 | World History |

## LONGMAN GCSE EXAM PRACTICE KITS

| | | |
|---|---|---|
| 37 | _____ 30381 8 | Biology £4.99) |
| 38 | _____ 30383 4 | Business Studies (£4.99) |
| 39 | _____ 31191 8 | English (£4.99) |
| 40 | _____ 30384 2 | Geography (£4.99) |
| 41 | _____ 30385 0 | Mathematics (£4.99) |
| 42 | _____ 30379 6 | Physics (£4.99) |
| 43 | _____ 30380 X | Science (£5.99) |

## LONGMAN GCSE REFERENCE GUIDES *£6.99 each*

| | | |
|---|---|---|
| 45 | _____ 05790 6 | Chemistry |
| 46 | _____ 05072 3 | English |
| 47 | _____ 05077 4 | French |
| 48 | _____ 05074 X | Mathematics |
| 50 | _____ 05076 6 | Science |

## GCSE SURVIVAL GUIDE *£2.95*

| | |
|---|---|
| 51 | _____ 05078 2 |

_____ **YORK NOTES LITERATURE GUIDES** *(see overleaf)*

## LONGMAN A-LEVEL STUDY GUIDES

*£9.99 each unless otherwise stated*

| | | |
|---|---|---|
| 52 | _____ 22569 8 | Accounting (£10.99) |
| 53 | _____ 31545 X | Biology |
| 54 | _____ 31652 9 | Business Studies |
| 55 | _____ 31546 8 | Chemistry |
| 56 | _____ 05782 5 | Computer Science |
| 57 | _____ 27688 8 | Economics (£10.99) |
| 58 | _____ 31656 1 | English |
| 59 | _____ 05784 1 | French |
| 60 | _____ 24495 1 | French pack* (£14.99) |
| 61 | _____ 24497 8 | French cassette (£6.00) |
| 62 | _____ 05173 8 | Geography |
| 63 | _____ 31654 5 | German |
| 64 | _____ 24498 6 | German pack* (£14.99) |
| 65 | _____ 24508 7 | German cassette (£6.00) |
| 66 | _____ 28702 2 | Government and Politics (£10.99) |
| 67 | _____ 31549 2 | Law (£10.99) |
| 68 | _____ 31550 6 | Mathematics (£10.99) |
| 69 | _____ 31551 4 | Modern History |
| 70 | _____ 27690 X | Physics |
| 71 | _____ 31655 3 | Psychology |
| 72 | _____ 27691 8 | Sociology |

## LONGMAN A-LEVEL EXAM PRACTICE KITS *£6.99 each*

| | | |
|---|---|---|
| 73 | _____ 30386 9 | Biology |
| 74 | _____ 30387 7 | Business Studies |
| 75 | _____ 30388 5 | Chemistry |
| 76 | _____ 30389 3 | Mathematics |
| 77 | _____ 30390 7 | Psychology |
| 78 | _____ 30382 6 | Sociology |

## LONGMAN A-LEVEL REFERENCE GUIDES *£6.99 each*

| | | |
|---|---|---|
| 80 | _____ 06390 6 | Chemistry |
| 81 | _____ 06396 5 | English |
| 82 | _____ 06398 1 | Mathematics |
| 83 | _____ 06392 2 | Physics (£7.99) |

## LONGMAN PARENT'S AND STUDENTS' GUIDES

*£2.99 each*

| | | |
|---|---|---|
| 86 | _____ 29971 3 | Longman Parent's Guide to Pre-school Choices and Nursery Education |
| 87 | _____ 29975 6 | Longman Parent's Guide to Key Stage 1 of the National Curriculum |
| 88 | _____ 29974 8 | Longman Parent's Guide to Key Stage 2 of the National Curriculum |
| 89 | _____ 29973 X | Longman Parent's Guide to Key Stage 3 of the National Curriculum |
| 90 | _____ 29972 1 | Longman Parent's Guide to GCSE and Key Stage 4 of the National Curriculum |
| 91 | _____ 29978 0 | Longman A-level Survival Guide |
| 92 | _____ 29969 1 | Longman Students' Guide to Vocational Education |
| 93 to | _____ 29970 5 | Longman Students' Guide to Returning Learning |
| 94 | _____ 29976 4 | Longman Students' Guide to Higher Education |

*\* pack = book and cassette*